THE CAMBRIDGE COMPANION TO
REFORMATION THEOLOGY

The European Reformation of the sixteenth century was one of the most formative periods in the history of Christian thought and remains one of the most fascinating events in Western history. *The Cambridge Companion to Reformation Theology* provides a comprehensive guide to the theology and theologians of the period. Each of the eighteen chapters is written by a leading authority in the field and provides an up-to-date account and analysis of the thought associated with a particular figure or movement. There are chapters focusing on lesser reformers such as Martin Bucer, and on the Catholic and Radical Reformations, as well as the major Protestant reformers. A detailed bibliography and comprehensive index allows comparison of the treatment of specific themes by different figures. This authoritative and accessible guide will appeal to students of history and literature as well as specialist theologians.

DAVID BAGCHI is Lecturer in the History of Christian Thought, Department of Theology, University of Hull. He is the author of *Luther's Earliest Opponents* (1991).

DAVID C. STEINMETZ is the Amos Ragan Kearns Professor of the History of Christianity, Divinity School, Duke University. His major publications include *Misericordia Dei: The Theology of Johannes von Staupitz in its Late Medieval Setting* (1968); *Reformers in the Wings* (1981); *Staupitz and Luther* (1980); *Luther in Context* (1986); *Memory and Mission* (1988); and *The Bible in the Sixteenth Century* (1990).

CAMBRIDGE COMPANIONS TO RELIGION

A series of companions to major topics and key figures in theology and religious studies. Each volume contains specially commissioned chapters by international scholars which provide an accessible and stimulating introduction to the subject for new readers and non-specialists.

Other titles in the series

THE CAMBRIDGE COMPANION TO CHRISTIAN DOCTRINE
edited by Colin Gunton (1997)
ISBN 0 521 47118 4 hardback   ISBN 0 521 47695 8 paperback

THE CAMBRIDGE COMPANION TO BIBLICAL INTERPRETATION
edited by John Barton (1998)
ISBN 0 521 48144 9 hardback   ISBN 0 521 48593 2 paperback

THE CAMBRIDGE COMPANION TO DIETRICH BONHOEFFER
edited by John de Gruchy (1999)
ISBN 0 521 58258 x hardback   ISBN 0 521 58751 6 paperback

THE CAMBRIDGE COMPANION TO LIBERATION THEOLOGY
edited by Chris Rowland (1999)
ISBN 0 521 46144 8 hardback   ISBN 0 521 46707 1 paperback

THE CAMBRIDGE COMPANION TO KARL BARTH
edited by John Webster (2000)
ISBN 0 521 58476 0 hardback   ISBN 0 521 58560 0 paperback

THE CAMBRIDGE COMPANION TO CHRISTIAN ETHICS
edited by Robin Gill (2001)
ISBN 0 521 77070 x hardback   ISBN 0 521 77918 9 paperback

THE CAMBRIDGE COMPANION TO JESUS
edited by Markus Bockmuehl (2001)
ISBN 0 521 79261 4 hardback   ISBN 0 521 79678 4 paperback

THE CAMBRIDGE COMPANION TO FEMINIST THEOLOGY
edited by Susan Frank Parsons (2002)
ISBN 0 521 66327 x hardback   ISBN 0 521 66380 6 paperback

THE CAMBRIDGE COMPANION TO MARTIN LUTHER
edited by Donald K. McKim (2003)
ISBN 0 521 81648 3 hardback   ISBN 0 521 01673 8 paperback

THE CAMBRIDGE COMPANION TO HANS URS VON BALTHASAR
edited by Edward T. Oakes, S. J. and David Moss (2004)
ISBN 0 521 81467 7 hardback   ISBN 0 521 89147 7 paperback

THE CAMBRIDGE COMPANION TO ST PAUL
edited by James D. G. Dunn (2003)
ISBN 0 521 78155 8 hardback   ISBN 0 521 78694 0 paperback

THE CAMBRIDGE COMPANION TO MEDIEVAL JEWISH PHILOSOPHY
edited by Daniel H. Frank and Oliver Leaman (2003)
ISBN 0 521 65207 3 hardback   ISBN 0 521 65574 9 paperback

THE CAMBRIDGE COMPANION TO POSTMODERN THEOLOGY
edited by Kevin J. Vanhoozer (2003)
ISBN 0 521 79062 x hardback   ISBN 0 521 79395 5 paperback

THE CAMBRIDGE COMPANION TO JOHN CALVIN
edited by Donald K. McKim (2004)
ISBN 0 521 81647 5 hardback   ISBN 0 521 01672 x paperback

Forthcoming
THE CAMBRIDGE COMPANION TO THE GOSPELS
edited by Stephen C. Barton

THE CAMBRIDGE COMPANION TO ISLAMIC THEOLOGY
edited by Tim Winter

THE CAMBRIDGE COMPANION TO

REFORMATION THEOLOGY

edited by David Bagchi and David C. Steinmetz

PUBLISHED BY THE PRESS SYNDICATE OF THE UNIVERSITY OF CAMBRIDGE
The Pitt Building, Trumpington Street, Cambridge, United Kingdom

CAMBRIDGE UNIVERSITY PRESS
The Edinburgh Building, Cambridge, CB2 2RU, UK
40 West 20th Street, New York, NY 10011–4211, USA
477 Williamstown Road, Port Melbourne, VIC 3207, Australia
Ruiz de Alarcón 13, 28014 Madrid, Spain
Dock House, The Waterfront, Cape Town 8001, South Africa

http://www.cambridge.org

First published 2004

Printed in the United Kingdom at the University Press, Cambridge

Typeface Severin 10/13 pt.   *System* LATEX 2ε   [TB]

A catalogue record for this book is available from the British Library

Library of Congress Cataloguing in Publication data
The Cambridge companion to Reformation theology / edited by David Bagchi and
David C. Steinmetz.
    p.   cm. – (Cambridge companions to religion)
Includes bibliographical references and index.
ISBN 0 521 77224 9 – ISBN 0 521 77662 7 (pbk.)
1. Reformation.   2. Theology, doctrinal – 16th century.   I. Bagchi, David V. N., 1959–
II. Steinmetz, David Curtis.   III. Series.
BR305.3.C36   2004
230′.09′031 – dc22   2004045829

ISBN 0 521 77224 9 hardback
ISBN 0 521 77662 7 paperback

Contents

Humanist
Methods

Notes on contributors

David Bagchi is Lecturer in the History of Christian Thought at the University of Hull, UK. His writings include *Luther's Earliest Opponents: Catholic Controversialists 1518–25*.

Peter Newman Brooks is Fellow emeritus in Ecclesiastical History, Robinson College, Cambridge, UK. His writings include *Thomas Cranmer's Doctrine of the eucharist* and *Cranmer in Context*.

Thomas A. Fudge is Lecturer in History at the University of Canterbury, Christchurch, New Zealand. His writings include *The Magnificent Ride: The First Reformation in Hussite Bohemia*.

Ian Hazlett is Reader in Ecclesiastical History at the University of Glasgow, UK. His work includes the editing of volume 5 of Bucer's Latin works, in addition to contributions to *Bucer und seine Zeit, Martin Bucer and Sixteenth-Century Europe*, and *Martin Bucer: Reforming Church and Community*.

Scott Hendrix is James Hastings Nichols Distinguished Professor of Reformation History and Doctrine, Princeton Theological Seminary, USA. His writings include *Ecclesia in via: Ecclesiological Development in Medieval Psalms Exegesis and the Dictata super Psalterium (1513–15) of Martin Luther, Luther and the Papacy*, and *Tradition and Authority in the Reformation*.

Denis R. Janz is Provost Distinguished Professor of the History of Christianity, Loyola University, New Orleans, USA. His writings include *Luther and Late Medieval Thomism* and *Luther and Thomas Aquinas*.

Robert Kolb is Mission Professor of Systematic Theology and Director of the Institute for Mission Studies at Concordia Theological Seminary, Missouri, USA. His recent works include *Luther's Heirs Define his Legacy: Studies on Lutheran Confessionalization* and (edited with Timothy Wengert), *The Book of Concord: The Confessions of the Evangelical Lutheran Church*.

Sachiko Kusukawa is Fellow in the History and Philosophy of Science at Trinity College, Cambridge, UK. Her writings include *The Transformation of Natural Philosophy: The Case of Philip Melanchthon* and (ed.) *Melanchthon: Orations on Philosophy and Education*.

Richard A. Muller is P. J. Zondervan Professor of Historical Theology, Calvin Theological Seminary, Mississippi, USA. His writings include *Christ and the*

Decree: Christology and Predestination in Reformed Theology from Calvin to Perkins and *The Unaccommodated Calvin. Studies in the Foundation of a Theological Tradition.*

Werner O. Packull was formerly Professor of History at Conrad Grebel College, University of Waterloo, Ontario, Canada. His writings include *Hutterite Beginnings. Communitarian Experiments during the Reformation.*

Erika Rummel is Professor of History at Wilfrid Laurier University, Waterloo, Ontario, Canada. Her writings include *Erasmus as Translator of the Classics*, (ed.) *Erasmus's Annotations on the New Testament*, (ed.) *Erasmus on Women*, *The Humanist–Scholastic Debate in the Renaissance and the Reformation*, and *The Confessionalization of Humanism in Reformation Germany.*

Wendy Scase is Geoffrey Shepherd Professor of Medieval English Literature at the University of Birmingham, UK. Her writings include *Piers Plowman and the New Anticlericalism* and *Reginald Pecock.*

David C. Steinmetz is Amos Ragan Kearns Professor of the History of Christianity at Duke University Divinity School, North Carolina, USA. His writings include *Calvin in Context, The Bible in the Sixteenth Century*, and studies of Contarini and Pole.

W. Peter Stephens is Professor emeritus of Church History at the University of Aberdeen, UK. His writings include *The Theology of Huldrych Zwingli* and *Zwingli: An Introduction to his Thought.*

Carl R. Trueman is Associate Professor of Church History and Historical Theology at Westminster Theological Seminary, Philadelphia, USA. His writings include *Luther's Legacy: Salvation and the English Reformers, 1525–1556.*

David F. Wright is Professor emeritus of Patristic and Reformed Christianity at the University of Edinburgh, UK. His works include articles on Knox and on the fathers in the Scottish Reformation and (ed.) *The Dictionary of Scottish Church History and Theology.*

Introduction: the scope of
Reformation theology

DAVID BAGCHI AND DAVID C. STEINMETZ

Even in an age suspicious of grand narratives, the European Reformation has somehow maintained its status as 'a decisive event' in the history of the West. It remains a lively and fascinating subject of study: something of the vitality and variety of fairly current scholarship on the subject – to say nothing of its sheer bulk – can be gauged by English readers from the four volumes of the recent *Oxford Encyclopedia of the Reformation*. All students of the early modern period, from social and economic historians to historians of art to students of literature, have sooner rather than later to engage with the impact on their field of the Reformation, and especially of its religious ideas. But how does one get to grips with what might strike the beginner as the least concrete aspect of the Reformation? This *Companion*, with contributions from the leading authorities in the area, is designed to be not only a stimulating collection of essays for theologians but also an accessible and reliable introduction to Reformation theology for non-specialists.

Until recently, it would have seemed eccentric to publish a companion to the theology of the Reformation. Towards the end of the twentieth century, theology came to be seen by many as marginal to Reformation studies. This was in part a reaction to the 'great man' approach to the past. In the same way that history in general was no longer primarily about what kings and queens did or what parliaments enacted, so the motivating force of religious history was not to be found in the writings of the ecclesiastical elite. Attention turned instead to the 'simple folk'. They were discovered to be not mere recipients of elite preaching and teaching, but active agents who took from the preachers what related to their own experience – the more egalitarian and iconoclastic part of the reformers' gospel – and developed it in ways the mainstream reformers would never have countenanced. It was the social historian, not the historical theologian, who seemed better equipped to answer the real question about the Reformation, 'What impact did it have on ordinary people?'

Several factors have led to the rehabilitation of theology as an essential tool for the student of the Reformation. First, there has been the widespread (but not universal) acceptance of the 'confessionalization' thesis. This presupposes that the systems inspired by the 'great men' of theology, and implemented by the 'great men' of state, actually did have a decisive impact on the lives of ordinary individuals in the sixteenth century and beyond. Secondly, there has been the rise of cultural history, which takes an interdisciplinary approach and weaves theological factors, quite unapologetically, into the wider web of intellectual and social forces. Thirdly, the interest in popular religion, which initially seemed to disenfranchise the student of elite religion, has served rather to demonstrate the impossibility of separating 'popular' and 'elite' cultures in any meaningful way: Luther himself would have acknowledged no distinction between the 'superstitious' and 'higher order' elements of his theology, while the highly educated Melanchthon shared an interest in astrology with many semi-literates of his day. At the other end of the expected educational scale, we find among the worldly goods of Tyrolean miners not just books but complex books of theology.

The result of these factors is that the theology of the Reformation has once again taken its place centre-stage. It cannot claim to be the queen of Reformation sciences – the field is now too diverse and too extensive for any one discipline to claim pre-eminence in it – but it is certainly a handmaid to all. However, the nature of Reformation theology is now different, or at least the approach taken to it is different in important respects, from its previous incarnations. First, it is *pluralist*. 'Reformation theology' is no longer synonymous with 'early Protestant theology' but includes in its scope the theologies of all sides, Protestant, Catholic, and Radical, as well as of those who do not fit neatly into these categories. This is not to deny that scholars, particularly Germans, still attempt to distil the essence of *reformatorisch* (by which they mean mainstream Protestant) thought; but the similarities and parallels between the different confessions are now given their due weight, alongside the very clear differences. Modern Reformation theology is therefore pluralist; but is it also ecumenical? The term is unsatisfactory in several ways, partly because it presupposes Christian belief on the part of present-day scholars of Reformation theology, partly because a strong tendency among ecumenically minded Christians is to minimize the importance of the Reformation and of confessional differences. The latter tend to regard the Reformation as an embarrassing relative who insists on producing snapshots of oneself as an infant, just when one is trying one's best to be grown up. It could even be said that, while in the 1970s and 1980s the severest critics of a theological approach to the Reformation were often social historians with no personal Christian sympathies, its greatest enemies today can be found among Christian ecumenists.

Secondly, it is *chronologically fluid*. 'Reformation' as the description of an era is no longer limited to the sixteenth century but takes in the 'long' sixteenth century, from around 1400 to around 1650. This is, in part, a recognition of the tendency over the last four decades to see the Reformation as an organic unity with the later Middle Ages rather than as a break with them. (Put like that, the point seems obvious enough. But the previous emphasis on discontinuity too conveniently served the interests both of Protestant scholars who wanted to depict the Reformation as an act of God and as a condemnation of what had gone before, and of Roman Catholic scholars who wanted to exculpate the late medieval church from responsibility for spawning the reformers.) As Denis Janz notes in his essay, it is an insight that has transformed the study of the Reformation, and of Reformation theology, entirely. It is an insight that is, however, being challenged by a renascent progressive ('Whig') approach. The confessionalization thesis proposed by continental historians emphasizes the importance of theology in the Reformation period only as a means of state-building, concentrating on its forward-looking aspects. In a similar way, most modern accounts of the English Reformation emphasize the discontinuity of Protestantism with the late medieval tradition. Both approaches see the Reformation as a reaction to, rather than a continuation of, earlier tendencies. But the scope of Reformation theology has also been extended forwards in time, and this is a recognition that not even the immediate outworking of the Reformation as a historical or theological event was complete by the Religious Peace of Augsburg (1555), the traditional end-point of investigations. In particular, the full impact of Calvinism was not felt in German lands until the Thirty Years War.

Thirdly, it is *contextual*. Reformation theology today differs from its predecessors is that it is no longer solely the preserve of historical theologians. As the contributors to this volume demonstrate, Reformation theology is as likely nowadays to be the concern of the historian and the literature specialist as of theologians. Although academic guilds do not normally welcome the introduction of free-market principles, in this case it is quite proper. All theology is done in a context. The theologians of the Reformation era were perhaps more conscious of their context than most. The theologizing in which they were involved was not pure or abstract (it never is), but applied. They were not for the most part concerned with revisiting the fundamental doctrines of the Trinity and the incarnation, which were not significantly at issue during the period. They were, however, concerned with practical questions that would have exercised many in late medieval Europe: What must

I do to be saved? Where they disagree, do I follow the Bible or the church? How can I be a good Christian and a good subject, citizen, merchant, soldier, husband, or wife?

A point which can never be made too often is that the theologians of the Reformation were not ivory-tower academics. Their principal tasks were in most cases pastoral, and we derive their theologies from utterances from the pulpit, from spiritual advice given in letters, from rushed polemical outbursts, in the midst of persecution. Even the leisurely disquisitions that they have left turn out on further inspection to be occasional pieces in disguise, or else works that need to be supplemented by their other writings. It is from polemic that we get the offensive sense of the word 'theologian': one who is concerned with abtruse theorizing of no practical value to the ordinary Christian. Whether anyone has ever fitted this description is doubtful; but certainly the theologians of the Reformation period did not.

This *Companion* follows a roughly chronological, rather than thematic, structure: the chapters are devoted to movements and individuals, not doctrines. There are three reasons for this. First, it allows the different theologies to be set more coherently within their historical context without excessive repetition. Secondly, most scholars in the field tend to specialize in particular movements or individuals rather than in synchronic studies of doctrines, and this approach allowed contributors to play to their strengths. Thirdly, most university and college courses on Reformation thought take the approach adopted here, so it allows the volume to be an actual 'companion' throughout a term's or semester's work. But although the essays are not ordered thematically, the index should prove helpful to those readers who wish to compare for themselves different treatments of the same theological topics.

1 Late medieval theology

DENIS R. JANZ

If there is one thing that can be called a genuine breakthrough in the last half-century of Reformation studies, it would be the 'discovery' that the Reformation had a background. The reformers, all of whom were theologians, and a good number of whom had formal academic training in the discipline, emerged out of a theological landscape that profoundly shaped their horizons. Some elements from this late medieval theological bequest they rejected; some they appropriated; and still others they sublated by taking something old and fashioning from it something new. In other words, their ideas did not spring to life *ex nihilo*, or descend from above, or emerge full-blown from an 'objective' study of the Bible alone. They worked in the intellectual context of late medieval theology, and consequently, without some grasp of this context, there can be no adequate understanding of their theology. By today, this realization has had an impact on every area of Reformation studies.

One of the most prominent features of this landscape was its pluralism. The major theme of sermons preached at the papal court on the eve of the Reformation was that 'Peace now reigns in Christian doctrine'. The research of the last half-century has made it increasingly apparent that nothing was further from the truth. The achievement of a *pax theologica,* proclaimed for whatever reason by these hand-picked sacred orators, was a chimera. The reality was that theological faculties at virtually all universities in Europe, from the venerable older institutions of Paris and Oxford to the newer German ones, were deeply divided into factions or 'schools' that differed not only on specifics but often also on fundamental approaches to the discipline.

This meant that theology, as it was practised in universities, was more often than not enveloped in an atmosphere of debate, contention, and rivalry. Deep disagreements were often exacerbated by the narrow loyalties of religious orders to particular masters. Arguments between the schools could at times degenerate into sheer rancour and name-calling. Thus a Thomist, for instance, buttressed his argumentation by adding that his opponent was a 'huge, boorish dog, an infernal worm, a delirious wasp, and a dung-eating pig'. Theological discussion did not often descend to this level of acrimony, but the point is that disagreements were deep and debates were heated. This essay attempts to sketch the major contours of this land-scape. In doing so it takes its cue from Martin Luther and other reformers who regularly named the 'scholastic sects' as 'Thomists, Albertists, Scotists, Occamists', and so on. Who were they, and what did they represent?

THOMISM

A good number of late medieval theologians took as their task the defence, interpretation, and development of the thought of Thomas Aquinas OP (d. 1274). To begin with, though, the shadow of heterodoxy had hovered over the teaching of Thomas. By 1323, the date of his canonization, these questions had effectively been laid to rest. But even then, for the remainder of the fourteenth century, the fortunes of the Thomist school were dismal. Among the various theological schools represented at Paris, for instance, the Thomists seem to have had the least capable adherents. Furthermore, in 1387, the low point was reached: the Thomists were expelled *en masse* from the citadel of academia, the University of Paris, for their denial of the immaculate conception. Only in 1403, when concessions were made, were the Thomists allowed to return. And this development signalled a reversal in their fortunes.

For the first time, major thinkers now began to take up the development and defence of Thomas' teaching, so much so that scholars today feel jus-tified in speaking of a fifteenth-century 'renaissance' of Thomism. Capable individuals such as Antonius of Florence OP (d. 1459), John of Ragusa OP (d. 1443), John Tinctoris OP (d. 1469), John Werd OP (d. 1469), and Henry of Gorkum (d. 1431) joined the cause. By mid-century, prominent theological faculties offered courses of study 'in the way of St Thomas'. Moreover, the school's centre of gravity was now shifting from Paris to the new German universities, most especially Cologne. Thomism had clearly been reborn as a prominent school in the intellectual world of the fifteenth century.

This rebirth was led above all by John Capreolus OP (d. 1444), by far the most imposing representative of the late medieval Thomist school. Known as the *'Princeps Thomistarum'* ('prince of the Thomists'), Capreolus offered a comprehensive and cogent defence of Thomas against rival schools which had attacked almost every facet of his theology. He also established reasoned norms and principles for the historical-critical interpretation of Thomas' texts, thereby eliminating substantial confusion over what Thomas had really held. The renewed interest in the theology of Thomas which Capreolus' work inspired meant that by the eve of the Reformation, almost all theological faculties including Erfurt and Wittenberg, had professors lecturing *in via sancti Thomae*.

What positions, then, were the hallmarks of Thomism? No doctrine can be cited as the single, infallible litmus test, unless it be simply the intention of a thinker to resolve all questions *ad mentem sancti Thomae* (according to the mind of St Thomas). Nevertheless, one can name several tendencies and emphases that were typical of this school, theological signposts that were regarded as 'Thomist' on the eve of the Reformation.

First, Thomists posited a fundamental harmony between faith and reason. What is known by faith comes ultimately from God by way of revelation. Likewise, what is known by reason comes ultimately from God, since the structure of the mind was established by God. The two can therefore, in principle, never contradict each other. Furthermore, reason can demonstrate some of the prolegomena to faith (such as the existence of God), but not the saving truths of revelation.

Secondly, there is a parallel continuity between nature and grace. Both have their origins in God, and grace builds on rather than subverts or destroys human nature. Thus the concept of merit is affirmed, but on the understanding that grace is always the principle of merit with respect to eternal life. Some Thomists emphasized this last point more than others, thereby distancing themselves further from the Pelagian error (the view that the human will is the decisive factor in salvation).

Besides these, the following positions can be regarded as Thomist. First, the final end and ultimate happiness of the human person consists in the intellectual vision of God. Secondly, God would not have become incarnate had Adam not sinned. Thirdly, The doctrine of Mary's immaculate conception compromises the universality of Christ's redemptive act, and therefore it is rejected. Fourthly, especially after the Council of Constance (1414–17), Thomist ecclesiology tended in an increasingly papalistic direction. Most Thomists embraced most of these views most of the time, and thus they can be regarded as indicators (not litmus tests) of late medieval Thomism.

ALBERTISM

An alternative within the *via antiqua*, albeit a minor one, was to build one's theology on the foundation laid by Albert the Great OP (d. 1280). Albert had been Thomas' teacher in Cologne and had outlived his student, producing a vast corpus of works in theology, philosophy, and the natural sciences. This body of writing, while uncommonly rich, nevertheless set forth views which were ambiguous if not downright inconsistent. Thus, for instance, while Albert's thought was in many respects Aristotelian, it was also at times heavily coloured by Neoplatonic tendencies (inherited above all from Proclus and Pseudo-Dionysius).

Already in the fourteenth century, Albert had a scattered following, especially, it seems, at Paris. Early in the next century, these few disciples coalesced into a 'school' at Paris under the leadership of Johannes de Nova Domo (fifteenth century). Besides holding to certain philosophical views that were at odds with the Thomists, this school's thought can be characterized as follows. First, the style of thought is thoroughly hierarchical, with all beings graduated according to their perfections. Secondly, a doctrine of 'cosmic sympathy' is common: the life of God somehow permeates the whole universe. Thirdly, the deductive method is favoured, but is not used exclusively. And finally, there is a certain propensity for somewhat obscure imagery that hampers clarity of expression.

In 1410 a young Flemish student, Heymeric de Campo (or Heymeric van de Velde) (d. 1460), began to study under Johannes de Nova Domo in Paris. In 1422 Heymeric moved to Cologne, where he joined other Albertists, eventually becoming the most prominent among them. Here the simmering antagonism between Albertists and Thomists broke into the open in 1425. For the remainder of the century, German Albertism was defined by its opposition to Thomism. And its centre was Cologne, where lectures *secundum modum Albertistarum* were a regular part of the curriculum. Thomists continued to dominate at Cologne, but Albertists constituted the most significant alternative.

In lesser ways Albertism's influence also eventually made inroads at other universities: Louvain, Cracow, Heidelberg, Ingolstadt, Tübingen, Basel, Prague, Copenhagen, Uppsala, Padua, and others. A few important thinkers were heavily indebted to the Albertist approach: Wessel Gansfort (d. 1489) and Nicholas of Cusa (d. 1464) are examples. Perhaps most importantly, Albertist perspectives penetrated deeply into the tradition of German Dominican mysticism, from Meister Eckhart OP (d. 1327) to Henry Suso OP (d. 1366), Johann Tauler OP (d. 1361), and the *German Theology*. Thus, while late medieval Albertism could not begin to challenge the dominant position of other schools, it was not without its own sphere of influence.

SCOTISM

If any religious order dominated the intellectual landscape in the centuries preceding the Reformation, it was certainly the Franciscans. And yet theologians of the Franciscan order were split in their loyalties. Most thirteenth-century Franciscans initially followed the lead of Bonaventure OFM (d. 1247). Very quickly, though, his influence was largely supplanted by the work of Johannes Duns Scotus OFM (d. 1308). Soon thereafter, many

Franciscans found themselves drawn to the theology of William of Occam OFM (d. 1349). Thus Franciscan theologians in the late Middle Ages were divided between Scotists and Occamists.

Of the two, the greater number of Franciscans explicitly identified themselves with the school of Occam. But the number of self-proclaimed Scotists was not negligible. And when Franciscan theologians were not explicit about their loyalties, it is extremely difficult to differentiate them into Scotists or Occamists. This is because many 'Scotist' ideas, emphases, and positions were absorbed wholesale by Occam and his followers.

If we identify Scotism with those who explicitly defined themselves in this way, the school was quite limited and its representatives could hardly be designated as major thinkers. Franciscus de Mayronis OFM (d. 1325), Antonius Andreas OFM (d. 1320), William of Alnwick OFM (d. 1333), John of Bassolis (d. 1347), and Francesco Licheto (d. 1520) were hardly household names, even within the household of late medieval theology. If we identify Scotism with a complex of theological ideas which found its origins (more or less) in Scotus, however, then we have to recognize that these ideas had enormous currency among thinkers who did not call themselves 'Scotists', foremost among them the Occamists. Seen in this light, Scotism was one of the most important intellectual currents on the eve of the Reformation.

The Scotist thought complex is most often associated with 'voluntarism', the doctrine of the primacy of will in God and in the human person (as opposed to Thomist 'intellectualism'). Accordingly, the emphasis in Scotism falls on the object of the will, namely the good (as opposed to the object of the intellect, the true), and on the proper act of the will, namely loving (as opposed to the proper act of the intellect, knowing). This starting point meant that for Scotists, theology was a practical, not a speculative discipline: the ultimate end for which humans were created was not the intellectual vision of God but rather loving God.

Because God is defined as will, and because his will is absolutely free, he initially had an infinite number of possibilities open to him. He could have created worlds radically at odds with the existing one, and he could have established a way to salvation for humans entirely different from the one in effect. This perspective on God's absolute power (referred to as the *potentia Dei absoluta*) takes the force out of any metaphysical arguments from causality. The world did not have to be the way it in fact is, nor did the order of salvation. Both are radically contingent. As one interpreter puts it, 'God is no longer tied to creation by "deterministic" causation, but related to it by volition.'

Yet all talk about the *potentia Dei absoluta* remains speculative, and all thought on alternative possible worlds is hypothetical. Theology deals with the actual world God has in fact chosen to create and with the order of salvation he actually willed to establish. This existing order is that of God's ordained power (referred to as *potentia Dei ordinata*). While it is metaphysically contingent, it is nevertheless utterly reliable, since God has committed himself to it unalterably. It was on this voluntarist foundation, whether radical or moderate, that Scotists constructed their alternative to Thomism.

Other typically Scotist doctrines and emphases can be listed briefly. First, in Christology, Scotists held that the Son, as a manifestation of God's love, would have become incarnate even if Adam had not sinned. The distinction of the two natures in Christ, rather than their unity, was emphasized, as was the real humanity of Christ. The doctrine of the immaculate conception was defended on the grounds that Mary's redemption was most fittingly accomplished by preserving her from original sin. Secondly, in the area of soteriology, Scotists stressed what they called the *acceptatio divina*: no human can truly merit eternal life, but God in his mercy decided to accept and reward works which, by the standard of strict justice, would be unworthy of such reward. These are called 'merits', but only in an extended sense, *merita de congruo* (congruent merits) as opposed to *merita de condigno* (condign merits). Thus, for instance, attrition (sorrow for sins based on fear) rather than contrition (sorrow for sins based on love) was held to be a sufficient disposition for a valid reception of the sacrament of penance. God has decided to accept this, even though, strictly speaking, it falls short. Thus the *acceptatio divina* functions as a safeguard against the Pelagian heresy. The typical Scotist understanding of predestination also undercuts Pelagian tendencies: election is *ante praevisa merita* (prior to foreseen merit), while reprobation is *post praevisa demerita* (subsequent to foreseen demerit).

While these positions can be designated as 'Scotist', it must be emphasized that Scotists were not unanimous on all points. And their voice, as a school, was relatively weak. This does not mean, however, that their views were unimportant. Indeed, these teachings had enormous currency on the late medieval theological scene. But this was not owing to the prominence of individual self-designated Scotists. Rather it was due to the fact that many of their positions were adopted wholesale by the next school to be described here, the one towards which especially Franciscans increasingly gravitated, namely Occamism.

OCCAMISM

The vexed question of the name of this school cannot detain us here. 'Occamism' is preferred here only because it is somewhat less problematic than 'nominalism' or '*via moderna*'. But none of these terms is fully adequate, and herein is a reminder that such categorizing of late medieval theology is to some extent artificial.

William of Occam (d. 1349) was an English Franciscan who was schooled in the thought of Duns Scotus and who then in important ways charted his own course. His followers clearly dominated the theological scene down to the time of the Reformation. Among the most important of these were Robert Holcot OP (d. 1349), Adam Wodeham OFM (d. 1358), Pierre d'Ailly (d. 1420), Jean Gerson (d. 1429), and Gabriel Biel (d. 1495). The last half-century of scholarship has shown that the thought of these and many other Occamists was highly complex, not unanimous on all points, and not in every case veering away from what was understood to be Catholic orthodoxy. The following general picture can be sketched.

First, it is essential to recognize that Occamism inherited large parts of the Scotist theological programme. Among these could be mentioned its voluntarism, its distinction between the *potentia Dei absoluta* and the *potentia Dei ordinata*, its stress on the *acceptatio divina*, and generally its anti-speculative, affective thrust. At the same time Occamism embodied a critique of Scotism for failing to carry its anti-speculative impulse through to its logical conclusion. Occamists now tried to do this, and the result was that for them, the range of Christian truths that was open to purely rational investigation shrank. More and more of these truths fell under the rubric of 'faith', and theology came increasingly to be understood as reflection on revealed truths.

A further characteristic feature of Occamism was its nominalism. This is the view that particulars (e.g. a human being) are the most real, while universals (e.g. humankind) are essentially empty terms. Nominalism, which is the opposite of medieval 'realism', could take moderate or extreme forms. It used to be a commonplace of medieval scholarship to hold that this philosophical position led logically and more or less inevitably to unorthodox theological positions. In the light of more recent studies, this can no longer be sustained: there are simply too many examples to the contrary.

One of the most contentious issues among twentieth-century scholars has been over the typical Occamist theology of nature and grace. What was the decisive factor in the salvation of the human person? Was it the grace of God, as Augustine had insisted a thousand years earlier? Or was it human action, as Pelagius, his opponent, had argued? A millennium of debate had made this one of the most complicated theological conundrums by the eve of the Reformation. Modern scholarship has taken great pains to sort this out, and by today we can speak of a consensus: Occamism did indeed exhibit a Pelagian tendency. Some explanation is necessary.

It was a generally held axiom among the scholastics that *facienti quod in se est, Deus non denegat gratiam* (God does not deny grace to one who does what is in his or her power). The infusion of grace that follows makes human merit possible, and this in turn is rewarded with eternal life. But most thirteenth-century scholastics, at least, protected themselves from the charge of 'Pelagianism' with three safeguards. First, a prevenient gift of grace is required for humans to 'do what is in them'. Secondly, the 'merit' they thereby achieve is *meritum de congruo* (congruent merit) rather than *meritum de condigno* (condign merit): by a strict standard of justice it is not worthy of its reward, but God in his generosity has determined to accept it (*acceptatio divina*) and reward it nevertheless. And thirdly, it was ultimately God's predestining, done *ante praevisa merita* (prior to his foreknowledge of merit), which determined who would receive this initial grace. Clearly, on this understanding, the decisive factor in human salvation was the grace of God.

The Occamist school, and notably its most prominent representatives such as Gabriel Biel, distanced itself from this general view by abandoning two of these safeguards against Pelagianism. First, unlike the Thomists, they held that no prior gift of grace was required for humans to 'do what is in them' and thereby dispose and prepare themselves for the first grace. Thus purely natural moral acts that were meritorious *de congruo* constituted the *initium fidei* (the beginning of the salvific process). Secondly, unlike the Thomists and the Scotists, they held that God's decision in the matter of predestination was made *post praevisa merita* (subsequent to God's fore-knowledge of human merits). The concept of congruent merit was retained but relativized, since it was held that even condign merit was not truly worthy but rested upon the divine acceptation. With the abandonment of these safeguards, it is possible to see the natural human act as the decisive factor in human salvation. Here, then, is Occamism's Pelagian tendency.

A final noteworthy feature of Occamism was its ecclesiology. This must be seen in the context of the institutional crises that shook the church, from the Avignon papacy (1305–77) to the end of the Western Schism (1378–1415). Here various trends within Occamism must be distinguished. For some, the distinction between God's absolute and ordained power seemed to relativize the mediatorial role of the church and its sacraments. These were, after all, contingent: the church mediated God's grace not because of its intrinsic nature but because of God's free decision. In itself, they held, it was a strictly historical institution. Such thinking could point in the direction of an anti-papal ecclesiology.

More commonly, though, Occamists, even if they saw the church as a strictly historical institution, emphasized God's eternal and unalterable commitment to grant his grace through it. Their ecclesiology was not antipapal, but at most antipapalist: the church must have a pope, but the essence of the church is not to be identified with the papacy. Thus Gabriel Biel could defend papal authority without contradicting Occam's view that the laity belong to the essence of the church. And the 'Fathers of the Council of Constance', Pierre d'Ailly and Jean Gerson, sought the middle ground between a papalist and a democratized understanding of the church. Despite differences, then, it is fair to say that Occamists stood for a 'laicizing ecclesiology'.

AUGUSTINIANISM

Augustine's ideas, elaborated in his massive authorship, were part of the common inheritance of medieval scholasticism. Traces of his influence can be found everywhere, and in this sense all theologians were 'Augustinian'. But a new theological current emerged in the mid-fourteenth century that more properly deserves this label. It marked a return to a far more careful reading of Augustine than had generally been the case, it accorded the highest authority to him, and it allowed Augustine's late anti-Pelagian writings to dominate its theological agenda.

The stance which this school was to take was anticipated by Thomas Bradwardine (d. 1349), who launched a scathing attack on the 'modern Pelagians'. Far more influential, however, and consequently the one who must be seen as the founder of this school, was Gregory of Rimini OSA (d. 1358). With a unique expertise in the writing of Augustine, Gregory undertook a comprehensive refutation of the Pelagian tendencies that, as he saw it, dominated the theological landscape. In this he was followed by a substantial number of important theologians, such as Hugolin of Orvieto (d. 1373), Jacob Perez of Valencia (d. 1490), and Johannes von Staupitz (d. 1524).

Generally speaking, this school reaffirmed the absolute priority of grace in human salvation. Humans cannot by their natural powers alone prepare or dispose themselves for grace: a prevenient gift of grace is required. And when they 'do what is in them', this is not meritorious even *de congruo*. Those who receive the first grace do so because God has decided to give it to them by his absolute decree of predestination *ante praevisa merita*. Though this school retained a role for free will in the order of salvation, the decisive factor from start to finish was the grace of God.

The varied theological currents of the late Middle Ages described here were troubling to some at the time. They saw this pluralism as a symptom of decline – a chaotic jumble of contending opinions that posed a danger for the church. They called on authorities to rein it in, to impose order. But others saw it as a vibrant, healthy intellectual climate in which alternative points of view could be tested in relatively open academic debate. The proponents of order eventually got their way, but not until the period that has come to be called the Counter-Reformation. In the meantime, the different schools continued to vie for supremacy. And into this scene stepped the Protestant reformers.

2 Lollardy

WENDY SCASE

THE PROBLEM OF LOLLARDY

Lollard is a problematic label. A loan from the continent, where it denoted someone of dubious orthodoxy, the word *lollardus* was used in England from the late fourteenth century to denigrate certain theologians and preachers as heretics. (The word was linked to *lolia* – weeds – evoking the parable of the tares among the clean grain, Matthew 13:24–30.) The term continued to be applied as a series of episcopal investigations detected *lollardi* in various dioceses throughout the fifteenth century. Despite the label, there are many problems concerning the origins, coherence, and impact of Lollardy. Because of these problems, it is not possible simply to describe 'Lollard theology'.

From the earliest trials and councils in the process against Lollard heresy, the thought of the Oxford theologian John Wycliffe (d. 1384) was identified as its ideological source. A debt to Wycliffe was recognized, too, in some Lollard texts. Among modern historians of Lollardy, however, the nature and extent of that debt are the subject of debate. Until relatively recently, historians saw Lollard heresy as a debased version of John Wycliffe's teachings that was intellectually incoherent and extremely diverse. This view was largely based on study of hostile sources: the chronicles and refutations of opponents, and the records of ecclesiastical councils and trials, for example.

Study of the writings associated with the heresy has led to some new perspectives. Much of the recent scholarly interest has focused on the identification, editing, and analysis of vernacular Lollard writings. As a result it is now believed that most if not all of the English writings attributed to Wycliffe were not in fact written by him. The earlier views of Lollardy as an intellectually incoherent heresy motivated by social and economic grievance have been both revised and challenged. Some scholars now see Lollardy as a movement founded on and dedicated to the spread of Wycliffe's thought. For such scholars Lollardy is synonymous with 'Wycliffism'. At the other extreme, Lollardy is now seen, not as a movement at all, but as a projection of the anxieties of the church or of the monarchy. In this view the label 'Lollard' imposes the semblance of unity and coherence on a diverse range of beliefs and practices, real and imagined, that were perceived to threaten the authorities. From the first point of view 'Lollard theology' would be the belief system of those detected as heretics; from the second point of view it would be a series of propositions devised by the ecclesiastical authorities as part of their efforts to legitimate their own authority, or to contain and discourage dissent and subversion. It has increasingly been recognized that the whole question is complicated by the enduring influence of early modern Protestant writers such as John Foxe, in whose works Wycliffe and Lollardy are represented as venerable forebears of the sixteenth-century reformers.

One way forward (which will be adopted in this chapter) is to see Lollardy as the product of a complex interplay of forces, its shape and definition emerging from a dialectic between the expression and containment of reformist desires. Once the authorities defined certain beliefs as heretical, new possibilities were opened up for self-understanding and definition. Those who entertained some of those beliefs, or engaged in certain new kinds of associated textual and cultural production, developed their own counter view of what it meant to be a Lollard. As this dynamic played out, the use of English for Bible study and theological discussion came to be seen as a central characteristic of Lollardy and its legitimacy a major focus of debate.

THE DEFINITION OF LOLLARD BELIEF

The eucharist came to be central to the definition of Lollardy. By 1380 at the latest, in his Oxford lectures, and in his *De Eucharistia, De Apostasia* and other writings, Wycliffe opposed the doctrine of transubstantiation. The usual teaching was that, once the body of Christ was made present at the words of consecration (the real presence), the substance of the bread and wine disappeared and only their accidents – their colour, shape and taste – remained. Various explanations were put forward. Thomas Aquinas proposed that the accidents persisted after transubstantiation had occurred because substance was replaced by quantity, while Duns Scotus said that the accidents remained on account of a miracle. On the basis of philosophical and scriptural arguments, Wycliffe challenged the idea that accidents could exist without substance. He argued, for example, that, if true, this would mean that the material world might not exist at all, and he cited biblical and patristic writers to show that the notion had no basis in scripture. He reconciled the doctrine of the real presence with his argument about the impossibility of transubstantiation by arguing that the host was both sign

and presence of the body of Christ. The host co-existed with the body of
Christ, becoming Christ's body *sacramentaliter* (sacramentally).

Eucharistic doctrine came to be *codified* only at the Council of Constance, after Wycliffe's death, as a reaction to his teaching. Further glimpses
of the process by which Lollardy gradually became defined are provided by
a vernacular text that lists sixteen accusations against those the bishops
'call Lollards' (ed. Hudson, 1978; quotations below in my translation). Like
many Lollard writings, this text defines the Lollard position by imagining
dialogue with opponents, representing as well as intervening in the process
of dialectical interaction between the ecclesiastical authorities and those
accused of heresy. The Lollard position is articulated as a set of recommendations for replying to the bishops' accusations. Wycliffe's analysis provides
the language for defining the heresy, and for replying. The very first point
of contention is that 'the bread or the host on the altar, consecrated by the
priest, is really [*verrely* is the Middle English word] God's body, but in nature
[*kynde*] it is the same bread that it was before'. The author's recommended
reply echoes Wycliffe: on the authority of Jerome, Augustine, and Hilary,
'the sacrament on the altar is really [*verrely*] Christ's body sacramentally
and spiritually'.

Wycliffe's writings clearly influenced the development of thinking
about the eucharist, but they were not the only source. This is illustrated by
the longest single surviving Lollard text on the eucharist, the *Tractatus de
oblacione iugis sacrificii* ('Tractate on the offering of perpetual sacrifice'),
composed 1413–14. This academic text, probably the work of an Oxford-
trained writer, is probably aware of Wycliffe's thought. An important source
of the writer's authority is scriptural and patristic quotation. The writer
argues, for example, that scripture gives no authority for the terminology
of transubstantiation: *accident, subject, substance* and *transubstantiation*
belong to Antichrist's language, and he is probably aware of Wycliffe's
review of explanations for transubstantiation. This text, however, is not
entirely dependent on Wycliffe's survey.

Second in the list of bishops' accusations against Lollards is a point
about the sacrament of penance: 'oral confession is not needful to health
of the soul; sorrow of heart alone destroys every sin'. The reply is that confession *is* needful – but to Christ, not to a priest. Here the Lollard writer
engages in a long-standing debate. The Lateran Council of 1215 had imposed
annual confession to a priest as an obligation on all Christians. The interpretation and implementation of the decree raised issues of priestly power
and the nature of the church. By the time that Wycliffe and other late
fourteenth-century writers addressed the topic, the decree had been the subject of vigorous discussion and much ecclesiastical legislation. In particular,

competition between the orders of friars and the parish clergy had provoked debate about the source and nature of sacerdotal power. Wycliffe argued that only God could know if the penitent was truly contrite and forgive sin. It followed that oral confession to a priest was unnecessary, and that a priest could not claim to absolve sinners. Other arguments against oral confession and priestly absolution were based on scripture. The Lollard *Tractatus de confessione et penitencia* ('Tractate on confession and penitence'), for example, points out that there are no references to confession in the Bible and no evidence of it in the early church.

Debate about the friars' powers fed into discussion of the legitimacy of the religious orders. The friars claimed to be imitating the life of Christ and the apostles by renouncing wealth and living on alms. This claim was opposed by the secular clergy, and by the monastic orders who lived by communal property and manual labour. Lollardy came to be associated with questioning the principle of living by a religious rule. If 'God's law' – scripture – was sufficient, the rules by which members of orders lived were either unnecessary or without authority. Applying the standards of scripture to both possessioners and mendicants, Wycliffe and other writers castigated the religious orders as 'private religions' that departed from the example of Christ and the apostles and had no grounding in God's law.

Cults of saints and related devotional practices, especially the use of images in worship, and pilgrimages to saints' shrines, were also vigorously debated. Certain opinions on these subjects were quickly identified as characteristic of Lollard beliefs and were often investigated at Lollard trials. Images were criticized by Lollard writers as a failure to adhere to the first commandment, causing errors of faith and attracting idolatry (worship of the creature instead of the Creator). Offerings made to images would be better given to the poor; relics and miracles at shrines might be faked; images and pilgrimage were not attested in scripture. Lollard belief on this issue ranged from objections to the worship (but not the use) of images by the church, to iconoclasm (the earliest cases – according to chroniclers – occurring in the 1380s).

Lollard ideas about images and pilgrimages drew on the vocabulary and analysis in Wycliffe's writings, and probably also on those of other earlier writers. Images were not one of Wycliffe's major concerns. The relatively greater emphasis on the issue of images in Lollard writings has been explained as a reflection of Lollardy's popular dimension – Lollard belief about images was practical rather than theological. There is, however, another possible explanation. The issue of images was linked with what emerged, after Wycliffe's death, as a defining characteristic of Lollardy, namely, an emphasis on access to the word of God by means of the vernacular. Arguably, the developing discourse of heresy and orthodoxy organized itself around the issue of images because images were traditionally regarded as fulfilling the function of books for the unlettered. Accordingly, images became a focus for discussion of issues of access to scripture. In arguments that came to be seen as typically Lollard, images debarred access to scripture. Costly images deflected people from gospel truths, teaching instead desire for material wealth. Even when their devotional value was allowed, images were regarded as a poor substitute for true preaching of the word of God. 'Books for the unlettered' were no substitute for the Bible.

THEOLOGY AND THE VERNACULAR

Wycliffe's contemporaries believed that the centrepiece of his thought was the authority of scripture: this earned him the by-name *Doctor Evangelicus*. Wycliffe's *De Veritate Sacræ Scripturæ* argues that the Bible is the unerring authority against which all truth claims must be measured. For Wycliffe, the authority of scripture provided the basis for critique of eucharistic theology, the ecclesiastical hierarchy, the organization of the church, and the claims to authority of the clergy and the religious orders. The correct interpretation of scripture is not the preserve of clergy and theologians; anyone with humility of heart (even a layperson or a female) might have access to the wisdom of scripture.

If, for Wycliffe, the Bible was the measure of all truth claims, and its truths accessible to laypeople as well as clergy, Lollardy came to be seen as this belief in action. A number of projects used the vernacular to expand access to the word of God beyond the circle of clergy trained to read Latin. At least two distinct English translations of the Bible were made between 1382 and 1395. Wycliffe's ideals doubtless inspired this enterprise, but it is very unlikely that Wycliffe himself had a hand in the work of translation. In addition, English aids to Bible study were produced, such as biblical commentaries and concordances. Preaching was also very important. It became a core Lollard belief that preaching the Word of God was the primary duty of the clergy. Sets of sermons survive in both Latin and English; these are characterized by their strict adherence to biblical exegesis and their avoidance of story material from non-biblical sources.

Lollard theory and practice in this respect are an important strand in a broader movement. There was a spectrum of differing beliefs concerning the vernacular. The associated textual practice has recently been called 'vernacular theology' by Nicholas Watson and others. The definition of Lollardy was achieved by means of a polarization of views concerning theology in English. Theological discussion and scripture in the vernacular gradually became associated with heresy by the church. In 1409 Archbishop Thomas Arundel issued constitutions prohibiting possession of copies of the Wycliffite translation of the Bible and preaching in English on theological matters such as the sacraments. Some of those identified as Lollards could recite long portions of the gospels by rote. Others were found to own and read gospel books and other writings. Polarization also emerged through debate about the value of biblical translation into English. The Lollard argument echoed Wycliffe's view: God spoke to anyone, whether learned or not, who had his Spirit; the language in which he was heard was immaterial. But language was not *quite* immaterial. Translation came to be seen as providing a practical means of giving the less educated the means to read (or hear) what the Bible said (or did not say) on contentious issues. Use of the vernacular acquired an implicit polemical message: those who reserved such material to Latin were self-interestedly concealing God's law – gospel truths – from laypeople. Lollardy thus became defined as the reversal of the church's valuation of Latin over English as a medium for theological discourse.

HISTORICAL IMPORTANCE: REVOLUTION, REFORMATION, AND BEYOND

Wycliffe's ideas and Lollardy cannot be understood in isolation from the immense political and religious upheavals of late medieval and early modern England. Wycliffe's theology underpinned royal power, undermining the power of the church and the papacy as unscriptural. Wycliffe envisaged what Michael Wilks called a 'top-down' revolution sponsored by the king and by nobles such as his patron, John of Gaunt. Anticlericalism was also expressed, however, by participants in the Peasants' Revolt of 1381, and the teachings of Wycliffe and some of his followers were represented by members of the religious orders – no doubt for political reasons – as having inspired the revolt. A variation on this configuration of popular rebellion, anticlericalism, and support for royal power occurred in the mid-fifteenth century, when the Crown prosecuted the prominent opponent of Lollardy, Bishop Reginald Pecock, harnessing anticlerical feeling in an attempt to revive its power and credibility following the rebellion of 1450.

The contribution of Lollardy to the Reformation is still under-investigated, and the question of continuity between pre- and post-Reformation dissent remains undecided. Wycliffe and Lollardy have often been regarded as forerunners of the Reformation. It is now recognized however, that this view goes back to the Reformation itself: it is a product of the Protestant narrative of religious history. The continued (or renewed) importance of Lollard writings during the early Reformation period is attested by the printing of a number of Lollard texts. John Colet, dean of St Paul's, was suspended from preaching in 1513 – he was suspect partly because he had translated the Lord's Prayer into English. Foxe gives examples of heretics accused of knowing the *Paternoster* in English, and saw scripture-reading in English as one of the four principal points on which Lollards had opposed the papacy. These are some examples of how, when scripture in the vernacular was a Reformation issue, a link with Lollardy was perceived. Just as links between Lollardy and earlier reformism remain to be elucidated, however, so the precise impact on the Reformation of fears about Lollardy, and in particular about Lollard Bible-reading in English, is still not fully understood. But what does emerge clearly is that the *idea* that cause-and-effect connections were to be made between Lollardy, revolt, and reformism was from the beginning part of the discourse and dialectic that produced and defined Lollardy.

If it was not a movement with a coherent system of belief, but rather the product of a complex interplay of forces, still Lollardy has an important place in cultural and religious history for its significance in bringing theology into the English language. The discussion of theological matters in the vernacular that came to be seen as characteristically Lollard made an important contribution to the development of an English theological vocabulary that included (despite Lollard denigration of such words as unscriptural) terms such as *subject*, *substance*, and *accident*. Ultimately, inasmuch as Lollard theology was theology enabled by English, it helped to make the writing of this chapter, and this book, possible.

Note
For sources on which this chapter is based see the 'Lollardy' section in the Select Bibliography.

3 Hussite theology and the law of God

THOMAS A. FUDGE

APPLIED REFORMATION

Fifteenth-century Europe viewed Jan Huss and the Hussites as heretics while the latter perceived themselves as reformers. Conflict was inevitable. Huss was burned at the stake in 1415 and crusades were dispatched to suppress his recalcitrant followers. Despite these adversities, Hussitism aimed at reforming church and society. This reform programme codified its goals in the 'Four Articles of Prague', promulgated in 1420: free preaching of the Word of God, communion in both kinds for all believers, elimination of ecclesiastical secular power, and the punishment of serious sins. Free preaching existed virtually everywhere in Hussite Bohemia and utraquism – both bread and wine for all believers – began in 1414. Divesting ecclesiastical wealth became a consequence of the Hussite wars, and by the 1420s an office was established to deal with punishing sin. Across the broad expanse of Hussite theology, these 'Four Articles' functioned as a reform focus. Hussite reform can be fully understood only within an eschatological consciousness. This awareness can be detected principally within the radical dimensions of the Hussite movement.

In its earliest stages, the fifteenth-century reformation in Bohemia was neither doctrinal nor theological, but moral. This can be traced to a reforming tendency in the fourteenth century associated with Jan Milíč of Kroměříž, Matěj of Janov, and others. Huss stood in that tradition. Eventually, doctrinal reform and theology merged with moral renewal in an effort to reform the church 'in head and in members'. Reform advanced along several theological fronts, but three are especially important: sacraments, scripture, and soteriology. Before turning to these issues, it is important to note that the guiding principle for Hussite theology and reform lay in an idea called 'the law of God.'

The Hussite concept of the law of God was related to scripture, but it would be facile to make that relation exclusive or even dominant. The law of God was a composite concept, a cognitive construct embracing certain teachings of the Bible and theological motifs promoted by the church fathers. It encompassed the ideas of free preaching and utraquism.

22

Commensurate with the ethical mandates of the Sermon on the Mount, it possessed ecclesiastical, theological, political, and social implications. When radical Hussites abolished 'pagan and German laws' they were simultaneously advocating theocratic rule of the law of God based on these principles.

THE EUCHARIST

Reformation theology in Hussite Bohemia developed within the context of the law of God, emerging initially in sacramental piety, especially the eucharist. This tradition of reform was striking and significant. Commencing in the fourteenth century, frequent communion was introduced. This practice contravened normal expressions of piety and religious observation and contained social implications. In Prague, for example, men and women stood shoulder to shoulder, the rich with the poor, the righteous with reformed prostitutes, clerics with laypeople. Hierarchy was abolished, privilege set aside, everyone approached the sacrament of the altar on an identical level. Hussite detractors and defenders of the official church and traditional practices were quick to underscore the latent subversive elements in this new practice.

By the second decade of the fifteenth century, eucharistic interest mounted. Jakoubek of Stříbro, Huss's successor in the Bethlehem Chapel in Prague, inaugurated the practice of utraquism in 1414. This constituted a further innovation of official religious practice in later medieval Europe. Condemnation issued by the Council of Constance did nothing to avert the Hussites from their faith. By 1417, under the inspiration of Jakoubek and Priest Václav Koranda of Plzeň, Hussites began communicating all the baptized, including infants and small children. Synods in Prague ratified the practice, even providing instructions on the recommended method of administering the body and blood of Christ to infants.

There arose opposition from all sides; but, following a momentous Sunday morning in Prague, where Hussites led by priest Jan Želivský took over a Catholic parish church, stormed the town hall, defenestrated members of the town council and installed a new reforming, revolutionary government, the Hussites had passed the point of no return. Reformation in Bohemia gained institutionalization under the banner 'the law of God'. Hussite religious practice was openly possible. In terms of the *de facto* norm of eucharistic practice in Bohemia, there developed an alternative tradition to that of the Latin church. The chalice became the symbol of the Hussite movement and the Bohemian reformation. 'Warriors of God', fighting crusaders, went into battle under the sign of the chalice, were communicated by faithful priests each morning before engaging the enemy, and equated their holy war with defending the chalice.

Hussite theologians became increasingly preoccupied with the eucharist from doctrinal and theological perspectives. The second and third decades of the fifteenth century were filled with treatises on the sacrament; polemical literature arguing eucharistic theology; synods, assemblies and university debates devoted largely to articulating a reformed theology of eucharistic practice. Huss distinguished between spiritual and sacramental communion. Among the central issues of debate relating to the eucharist was the question of Christ's presence. The conservatives, such as Jan Příbram and Huss, retained the Lateran doctrine of transubstantiation. Radical Táborites eschewed that dogma, while extreme groups such as the Pikarts and Adamites appeared to devalue the sacrament entirely. Hussitism generally was suspected of harbouring Wycliffite remanentism (the doctrine that the substance of the bread and wine remain unchanged and continue to exist after the conservation), but this is applicable only to the radicals and superficially to reformers such as Jakoubek. Hostility lasted for decades. Hussite dissenters were executed on account of their 'unorthodox' views of the sacrament.

The Hussites were divided on many issues, but the right of laypeople to partake of the chalice was not among them. From the most conservative to the radicals at Tábor and Oreb, the law of God mandated the chalice for all baptized believers regardless of age, gender, social station, or religious standing. That point of theology and practice became non-negotiable, and Hussites were prepared to defend the law of God, with the sword if necessary, and lay down their lives in defence of that truth.

THE AUTHORITY OF SCRIPTURE

If the law of God functioned pivotally for the Hussite reformation, the question of authority gained prominence. Without a definite magisterium, or any clear means of enforcing one, following the break from the official church and exacerbated by the vagueness of the 'law of God' motif, especially during the uncertainty of the war years, there was a discernable paradigm shift away from scholastic authority embraced by the medieval church to a revised hierarchy of authority values. Scripture emerged as the court of appeal. Notwithstanding this, it would be erroneous to claim for them a *sola scriptura* posture. While radical biblicism emerged at Tábor, that position cannot be exported into the wider Hussite reformation. Even the Táborite interpretation and use of Wycliffe is somewhat suspect on this point. What is evident is that Huss, Jakoubek, and the mainstream did not

devolve from medieval authorities to a simplistic reliance upon scripture
as the sole authority, even though priests at Tábor developed alternative
approaches to judgement and authority. If 'naked scripture' proved sufficient for the radicals, it did not resonate with the Praguers. In general
they followed Huss in his conviction that canon law, patristic, and medieval
authorities were relevant and that authority resided in scripture, tradition,
and reason. Therefore, while scripture remained central, it was not exclusive, nor did the word of God have a textual limit. For Huss and mainstream
Hussites, scripture was never alone. When the Bible was juxtaposed to the
exclusive claims of popes or bishops, primacy was consistently given to the
former. By 1421 a national convocation decreed that every priest in the land
should own a copy of the Bible.

FAITH AND WORKS

One hundred years after the execution of Huss, Protestant reformers
championed the doctrine of *sola fide* (faith alone) as the soteriological
principle. That idea cannot be maintained successfully with respect to the
Hussites. Medieval scholastic theology advocated the notion *fides caritate
formata* (faith formed by love). On this point, Hussite theology stood closer
to Aquinas than to Luther. Faith was activated and facilitated by good works.
Hussite theologians taught the principle of faith for salvation, but also advocated the concept that one did good works for salvation by persevering in all
that the law of God required. Part of that obligation included faithful observance of the sacraments, for eucharistic piety constituted a means of salvation. Mainstream Hussites remained Augustinian in their basic approach
to salvation, acknowledging a theological predestination, despite holding to
a practical Pelagianism. Jan Huss was a medieval Catholic reformer rather
than a premature Protestant or a forerunner of movements and ideas yet to
come.

Salvation remained contingent upon the sovereignty of God and, while
the *viator* (traveller from this world to the next) persevered in faith, God
sustained the Christian. Huss adamantly insisted that one could not be righteous and a sinner at the same time. This constituted logical contradiction
and inconsistency with truth. The matter of justification cannot be said to
have been a burning issue for Hussites. Their focus centred on the law of
God, its meaning and practical applications. Much of the theological expression and writing within Hussite Bohemia was not theoretical. Rather, it
emerged from the context of applied reformation. The dominant soteriological principle for Hussitism remained *fides caritate formata* rather than
sola fide. For fifteenth-century Hussites, faith was formed by love. For many
sixteenth-century Protestants the dominant principle was faith alone.

REFORM AND THE LAW OF GOD

In practical terms, the Hussites raged against ecclesiastical and secular abuses, especially simony, social injustice, and immorality. The law of God was invoked to counter these offences, producing not insignificant results. Religious practice experienced renaissance with the introduction of renewed eucharistic observance. Apostolic rule controlled communities, while religion generally assumed broader dimensions, especially when the Hussites perceived themselves as God's chosen people, anointed for the eschatological moment to defeat Antichrist, Satan, and all unrighteousness. Liturgical practices were overthrown in radical centres such as Tábor, but moderates consistently adopted a more traditional form of liturgical reformation. The social implications of these ideas enacted in society created numerous significant changes, many of which can be traced theologically to the Hussite conviction of the meaning and application of the law of God. Táborite religion is most illuminating and instructive here. The chalice became the dominant symbol and practice. Secular law was abolished in deference to divine law. Egalitarianism stemmed from this social levelling represented by eucharistic reform, and this was temporarily translated into social relations. Communism – the abolition of slaves, debts and secular authority structures – became a hallmark of the new faith; even material possessions were surrendered in order fully to realize the law of God. A national assembly at the town of Čáslav effectively legalized the Four Articles for the Czech lands.

If the guiding theological principle for the Hussite reformers remained the law of God, then the idea of *revelatio* functioned as the impetus for application. This was the terse response given by Jakoubek when asked on what basis he introduced the lay chalice. Táborite religion fairly bristled with new revelations. The early context for Hussite reforming theology was the 'Jerusalem' experiment, associated with Milíč, wherein frequent communion began, and with Bethlehem Chapel, where vernacular preaching and the implementation of a multi-faceted reform sank roots in the heart of Europe. Theology in Bohemia, and reformation in the Czech context of the fifteenth century, attempted to liberate the law of God, which previously had been concealed behind locks and bolts, hidden from the people. Powerful enough to elicit an invitation to the Council of Basel in 1433 to represent their case, the Hussite delegation emphasized the Four Articles, and argued their essential necessity for reformation, while defending their intention to promote these ideas throughout Europe.

After 1437 Hussite reform underwent a time of transition. War ceased, reforms were recognized by the official church, and reformation in Bohemia began a new phase. Two streams of thought emerged. The *Jednota bratrská* (Unity of Brethren) continued in somewhat modified fashion the aims and theological ideas of the older radical brotherhoods. The conservative parties became known as Utraquists and, under the administration of leaders such as Jan Rokycana, the Hussite tradition passed into the sixteenth century, where it encountered the European reformations of Luther and Calvin, experiencing religious and theological syncretism.

In the light of achievements and advances secured during the initial Hussite period, it is impossible to identify the legacy of Jan Huss as premature reformation. The forerunner motif does not fit the reforms in fifteenth-century Bohemia at all well. Careful examination of Hussite theology reveals that the term 'Protestant' cannot be applied to the reformation in Bohemia without doing violence both to the Czech tradition and to the reformations of the sixteenth century. Hussite reformation theology created a new social and doctrinal form in which the Christian faith could be understood and practised anew in meaningful relation to the realities of the Czech world.

4 The theology of Erasmus

ERIKA RUMMEL

In Erasmus' time, Catholic critics circulated the tag, 'Erasmus laid the egg, and Luther hatched it.' The idea that Erasmus was a 'pre-reformer' and that his theology is best studied in the context of Luther's thought has been perpetuated by modern historians. Protestant theologians, of course, capitalized on the doctrinal differences between the two men rather than on their common ground. This approach prompted Ernst-Wilhelm Kohls to accuse them of using Erasmus as a 'dark foil against which their own hero could shine more brightly'. Alternatively, Erasmus' religious thought has been viewed in the context of Christian humanism, which seems to me a more productive way of examining his theology. In either case, however, Erasmus' lack of a systematic approach has raised serious questions for the would-be interpreter and has led some historians to deny him the title of theologian altogether. Any investigation of his theological concepts must therefore begin with the subject of Erasmus' own claim to the title and the testimony of his contemporaries on that point. Although Erasmus' professional status may be in doubt, it cannot be disputed that he engaged in activities that come within the purview of a theologian. He formulated a curriculum for theology students; he edited, translated, paraphrased, and expounded biblical and patristic texts; he commented on doctrinal questions; and he offered spiritual advice in devotional tracts. From these writings emerge the main points and general features of his religious thought. Indeed, some of these characteristics explain why we cannot expect to find in Erasmus' writings a systematic exposition of theology. Scepticism and the methodology of doubt, his principal heuristic tool, and a corresponding dislike for doctrinaire pronouncements prevented him from making assertions that are the underpinning of any theological system. The rhetorical style in which he expressed his thought presents another obstacle. Characteristic of humanist writers, it is not as precise or definitive as the conventional dialectical argumentation regarded in Erasmus' time as the quintessential mode of expression for theologians. Reflecting on Erasmus' approach to theology, John O'Malley rightly described it as 'principled rather than prescriptive'.

In content, Erasmian theology is characterized by a twin emphasis on inner piety and on the word as mediator between God and the believer. Emphasis on inner piety led Erasmus to develop his *philosophia Christi*, a term already used by the fathers to denote the living faith; emphasis on the word led him to bring his philological skills to bear on the scriptural text and to create for rhetoric the central place that dialectic was then occupying in the scholastic curriculum. My study of Erasmus' theology will begin with a discussion of his qualifications as a theologian and proceed, after an examination of his epistemology, to the two principal aspects of his theology: the centrality of the word and the spiritual nature of piety.

ERASMUS' QUALIFICATIONS AS A THEOLOGIAN

Erasmus, who was born in about 1466 as the illegitimate son of a priest, became an Augustinian canon regular in 1487 and was ordained priest in 1492. Soon afterwards, he entered the service of the bishop of Cambrai and in 1495 was sent to Paris 'to seek a doctorate in theology', as he told his friend Nicolaas Werner. Although he remained in Paris, with interruptions, for the next six years, he departed without taking a degree. His own inclinations and the rules of the University of Paris would indicate that his hopes for a doctorate were unrealistic in the first place. In an autobiographical sketch, Erasmus declared that he loathed the scholastic theology taught at Paris, and in letters from Paris he mocked the theologians as men 'whose brains are the most addled, tongues the most uncultured, wits the dullest, teachings the thorniest, characters the least attractive, lives the most hypocritical, talk the most slanderous, and hearts the blackest on earth'. In the *Praise of Folly*, published a decade later, he used similarly derogative terms to characterize the scholastics. But even if Erasmus had been drawn to academic theology, other considerations blocked his path. He had at the time neither the financial support to complete the long residency requirement of the university, nor the means of obtaining a dispensation from the illegitimate birth that barred him from graduation. As James Farge has shown, moreover, there is no evidence that Erasmus actually attended lectures in theology. On the contrary, we have his own word that by 1499 he had bidden 'goodbye to the title of theologian'. The works on which he was engaged during his years in Paris, when he was supporting himself by tutoring the sons of noblemen, were secular: pedagogical texts, a dialogue in defence of humanism, a collection of adages. When Erasmus finally did acquire a doctorate in theology from the University of Turin in 1506, it was bestowed on him *per saltum*, that is, without fulfilling the customary requirements. Not surprisingly, he rarely mentions his degree, which was greeted with disdain

by graduates who had fulfilled the rigorous requirements of the University
of Paris.

Evidence of serious engagement with theology comes only after Erasmus' first visit to England in 1499, where he made the acquaintance of
John Colet, and under his influence took up biblical studies. By the time
he published the first work whose content can be described as theological
(*The Handbook of the Christian Soldier*, 1503), he had begun to learn Greek
and to collate Bible manuscripts. In other words, he could be called a theologian in the broad sense in which the term was still used at the beginning
of the sixteenth century. Indeed, admirers hailed him as the father of a
'new' theology, or as a man who had brought back the pristine theology of
the early church. But there was now considerable debate at the universities over the qualifications that entitled a man to comment on theological
matters. Humanists, whose special expertise was in the area of philology,
had transferred their attention from classical to biblical texts and applied to
sacred writings the same critical methods that they had previously brought
to bear on secular works. Professional theologians vigorously objected to
what they saw as trespassing on their territory by amateurs. The Paris theologian Noël Beda contemptuously called them 'theologizing humanists'.
Not surprisingly, Erasmus' edition of the Greek and Latin New Testament
(1516) and the annotations justifying his editorial decisions involved him in
stormy controversies. A Dominican declared indignantly: 'What an imposter
Erasmus is! He writes paraphrases on the apostolic epistles, he writes annotations on the New Testament. He addresses responses to some theologians,
yet he is ignorant of all theology.' Representatives of the Spanish orders,
who examined Erasmus' works for heterodoxy in 1527, commented on the
'untheological' manner of his argumentation; and the faculty of theology at
Paris, which formally condemned passages in his writings as blasphemous
and heretical in 1531, concluded their verdict with a warning to all biblical
humanists usurping the title of theologian. They rebuked those 'who believe
that whatever is written in a splendid style is true and what is written in
a simple and plain style is false . . . and those who think that knowing
Greek and Hebrew amounts to perfect and consummate theology, although
those who know languages but are not otherwise trained in the discipline
of theology, must be regarded as philologists (*grammatici*) not theologians'.

Did Erasmus himself claim that he was a theologian? No clear self-
image emerges from his writings. His tendency to waffle on this point is
nowhere more in evidence than in the prefaces he added to his New Testament edition. In his preface to the *Reader* (1515), he attempted to divorce the
philological from the exegetical task, claiming that he was 'concerned solely
with the integrity of the text'. In the *Capita ad morosos* ('Points addressed to

critics'), added in 1519, he wrote: 'If anyone denies that I am a theologian: I have played the role of the grammarian ... If they exclaim that this service can only be provided by a theologian, I am the lowliest of theologians, and have taken on the lowliest function in theology.' He had answered an earlier challenge by Maarten van Dorp by modestly declining the title of theologian; in a letter to another critic, the Dominican Vincentius Theoderici, he was similarly coy. At the same time he proudly asserted that he was not ashamed of his training and would not exchange it for Theoderici's. He believed that the traditional scholastic curriculum did not produce competent theologians. The alternative he presented in his *Method of Theology* will concern us further below.

ERASMUS' METHODOLOGY: CHRISTIAN SCEPTICISM

Before we consider the content of Erasmus' theology, we need to examine its epistemological basis. Erasmus' definition of articles of faith may serve as a lead-in. He regarded as irrefutable 'that which the Catholic Church holds without controversy and by a large consensus, such as the doctrines expressly stated in holy scripture and in the apostles' creed, to which I am willing to add the decrees of councils properly constituted and following proper procedure'. Consensus and long-standing tradition clearly played an important role in Erasmus' eyes and became crucial in cases where scriptural evidence was unclear. The process Erasmus wished to follow in such cases is best exemplified by his polemic with Luther over free will. Erasmus initiated the controversy in 1524 with a work programmatically entitled *Diatribe* (in Latin, *Collatio*), that is, a 'comparison'. The title describes his method. To determine whether free will existed, Erasmus examined the evidence on both sides of the question, listing biblical and patristic passages that either affirmed or denied free will. Since this process did not lead to a clear-cut answer, Erasmus professed that he 'would gladly seek refuge in scepticism' and suspend judgement. This option, however, adopted by pagan philosophers, was not open to Christians. As an orthodox believer, Erasmus substituted for the missing rational solution the authoritative voice of the church, which had affirmed the existence of free will. In his reply, *On the Bondage of the Will*, Luther recognized the epistemological implications of Erasmus' argumentation, but ignored his carefully nuanced and qualified explanations. Taking up Erasmus' classical terms of reference, he declared himself a Stoic. What was needed in these times of crisis were Stoical assertions. He reproached Erasmus for 'wanting to compare everything, and affirm nothing'. Affirmation was the believer's quintessential mode of speech, he said,

'The Holy Spirit is no doubter.' In his reply to Luther, entitled *Hyperaspistes* ('The warrior's shield'), Erasmus again explained the brand of scepticism he was advocating. It meant refraining from facile definitions and from headstrong assertions and accepting instead 'as a probability what another accepts as certainty'. Probability was of course the Academic's solution to the epistemological dilemma. Erasmus modified, or rather Christianized, the classical method. The believer need not confine himself to rational solutions. He need not accept uncertainty or resort to probabilities in the search for the doctrinal truth, Erasmus said. 'I specifically exempt from uncertainty . . . what has been revealed in sacred scripture and has been handed down by the authority of the church.' Here Erasmus, the Christian sceptic, overcomes the limitations of a purely rational approach and converts probability into certainty by using church authority as a criterion. Once again he couples this authority with tradition and consensus. Articles of faith are based on scripture and 'the decrees of the church, especially those that were published at general councils and are confirmed by the consensus of the Christian people'.

The polemic with Luther is important, then, not only as a fundamental doctrinal discussion but also as a methodological showcase. Consensus and tradition emerge as essential decision-making tools for Erasmus the Christian sceptic, and came to shape his attitude toward the reformers. He was initially supportive of Luther, although he had, from the beginning, reservations about the reformer's confrontational style and his assertive mode of expression. After 1521, when it became clear that Luther's movement was schismatic, Erasmus withdrew his support. His turnabout was variously interpreted by contemporaries as a lack of moral fortitude or as a corollary of pacifism, but it can be more cogently explained by epistemological considerations. For the Christian sceptic, consensus was not only a sociopolitical desideratum; it was an essential criterion and the touchstone of true religion.

THE CENTRALITY OF THE WORD: ERASMUS' *THEOLOGIA RHETORICA*

In Erasmus' view, the word (and consequently language skills) were of crucial importance for an understanding of God. It is no coincidence that the clearest statements on this subject can be found in his prolegomena to the New Testament edition, that is, they are closely linked with the Word of God. Among the prefatory pieces, Erasmus placed the outline of a theology curriculum, entitled *Ratio seu Methodus . . . perveniendi ad veram theologiam* ('Method of attaining true theology'). He recommended starting

with the study of the three biblical languages because all mysteries of scripture were revealed through them. Elsewhere, too, he expressed the belief
that Theology, the acknowledged queen of all disciplines, would not disdain the services of her handmaid, Grammar, 'for though Grammar is of
less consequence in some men's eyes, no help is more indispensible than
hers'. It was utter madness for theologians to study the Bible without philological skills, he said. The study of grammar and rhetoric would enable the
aspiring theologian to interpret allegories and commonplaces. The study of
biblical languages in turn would lead him to the sources and allow him to
contemplate God's Word in its native glory, uncorrupted by careless scribes
and ignorant translators.

Because of the central role language arts played in Erasmus' theological
thought, both as hermeneutical and pastoral tools, Charles Trinkaus and
others have labelled his theology *theologia rhetorica*. The value Erasmus
put on rhetoric in particular can be seen from his description of the historical development of Christian theology. He distinguished three stages,
characterized respectively by simple faith, faith enhanced by rhetoric, and
faith overshadowed by dialectical reasoning. Clearly, he saw the second
stage, which describes the patristic age, as the apex, and the third stage,
which describes the scholastic approach, as a corruption rather than a further development of religious thought. Theology had become 'a form of
skill, not wisdom; a show-piece, not a means toward true religion', he said.
The discipline was in need of reform. In this process, 'a knowledge of the
tongues and liberal studies (as they call them) were of the first importance,
for it was neglect of them, it seemed, that brought us down to where we
are'.

Erasmus strongly objected to scholastic theology with its emphasis on
dialectical reasoning. In his eyes, a purely academic theology was useless
for providing guidance to Christians in their daily life. Rhetoric, by contrast,
fulfilled that mediating function which allowed God's injunctions to take
root in the human heart. The Word of God was inherently rhetorical in
the sense that it had persuasive and redemptive power; *theologia rhetorica*,
unlike scholastic theology, pointed the way to the Word and aroused 'a new
zeal for the true religion of the gospel'. This message remains constant in
Erasmus' writings. It informs the *Paraclesis* ('Invitation'), first published
with his New Testament edition in 1516, and constitutes the dominant
theme in his last original work, a manual of preaching entitled *Ecclesiastes*
('The preacher'). In the *Paraclesis* Erasmus devoutly wished for an eloquence
that would not only beguile the reader but enter his heart and transform
his very soul. In the *Ecclesiastes* Erasmus outlines the task of the preacher
in similar terms. He must be persuasive so that the congregation can hear

in his sermons the voice of God. Again he uses the images of rapture and transformation to indicate the power of the *theologia rhetorica*. The practical moral impact of the preacher and the theologian – that is, of sermon and exegesis – is of utmost importance to Erasmus. The parallels between the prolegomena to the New Testament and his manual of preaching show that in his opinion the task of the preacher and that of the exegete converged. It was therefore appropriate to focus attention on language and on the rhetorical power of scripture. Because the Word of God has the power to transform, Erasmus wanted the laity directly exposed to the text: 'Let the farmer sing a passage from the Bible at the plough, the weaver hum a passage to the movement of his shuttle, the traveller lighten the weariness of his journey with biblical stories!'

Erasmus began working on a critical edition of the New Testament in the early 1500s. He was confirmed in his approach by the discovery, in 1504, of a copy of Lorenzo Valla's *Annotations* on manuscript variants and on solecisms in the Vulgate translation. Erasmus published the fruit of his own researches in 1516 in the form of an edition that contained the Greek text of the New Testament and a revised Vulgate text on facing pages, followed by annotations explaining and justifying his editorial choices. This was the first Greek text made available to the public. He revised the edition four times during his lifetime (1519, 1522, 1527, 1535), making corrections to the text and adding substantially to his annotations. Their nature changed in consequence, from a primarily philological commentary to a rich collection of documentary material drawn from patristic and, to a lesser extent, medieval exegetes. Much of the added material reflects Erasmus' involvement in polemics with individual critics as well as the formal examination of his writings by the Spanish Inquisition and the faculty of theology at Paris.

In 1517 Erasmus began a series of *Paraphrases* on the New Testament, written in a homiletic style, and between 1515 and 1533 he wrote commentaries on eleven psalms. The *Paraphrases* were well received, especially in the Netherlands and in England. They became required reading in England by a decree of Edward VI, stipulating that each parish church should have a copy of the *Paraphrases*. Of Erasmus' psalm commentaries, two are of special significance because of the topical comments they contain: Psalm 28, published in 1530, subtitled *De Bello Turcico* ('On war against the Turks'), and Psalm 83, published in 1533, subtitled *De sarcienda ecclesiae concordia* ('On mending the peace of the church'). Ostensibly offering political advice on how to handle the Turkish threat and how to restore peace among the religious factions, a subject that came to dominate the imperial diets, the two psalm commentaries were in fact offering spiritual instruction. They made spiritual renewal a precondition of solving the pressing problems of the time. Here, as in the *Paraphrases*, Erasmus writes as a theologian within the meaning of *theologia rhetorica*, offering an authentic reading of sacred texts, that is, a reading which has the power to transform.

Erasmus' editions and translations of patristic writings are yet another example of works combining philology with theology. He collaborated with the Froben Press of Basel on the great editions of Jerome and Augustine. He also published works of Origen, Chrysostom, Irenaeus, Cyprian, Arnobius, Hilary, Ambrose, and others. Although the task involved was primarily philological, its significance for theology was obvious. The accessibility of printed texts was of crucial importance for biblical scholarship. Erasmus' close reading of the patristic texts found an immediate application in his own annotations on the New Testament. More importantly, his prefaces to the patristic editions and his glosses to the texts are replete with comments on the church in his own day. He frequently used the opportunity to reproach clerics for falling short of the patristic model and indirectly criticized modern theologians by pointedly praising the didactic gifts of the fathers, their learning, spiritual authority, and undoctrinaire conception of faith. He implied that these characteristics, so desirable in the theologian and so abundantly manifested by the fathers, were in short supply in his own time.

It was Erasmus' special merit to give a didactic turn to all of his scholarly enterprises. He regarded this combination as an essential feature of theology. As Cornelis Augustijn rightly noted, 'Erasmus was convinced that theology was a unity. In his time, that unity had been breached; the study of the Bible, systematic theology, and devotional reading had become separate from one another, and that in itself was wrong.' In the *Enchiridium Militis Christiani* ('Handbook of the Christian soldier') he gave a practical demonstration of what he considered a theologian's work.

ERASMUS' *PHILOSOPHIA CHRISTI*

The Handbook of the Christian Soldier is the principal source of what Erasmus calls 'the philosophy of Christ' or the 'celestial philosophy'. The work, written in 1501 on the request of a woman who wanted to improve her philandering husband, remained a sleeper until 1518, when it was republished with a substantial preface, putting the *philosophia Christi* in context. The new edition was an immediate success. Over the next five years it was reprinted more than thirty times and translated into four vernacular languages, and became one of Erasmus' most influential tracts. It contains important statements on the nature of piety, and offers, as he put it, 'a summary guide of living'. In the Pauline vein, Erasmus exposes the dualism between the material and spiritual world and encourages readers to cultivate their soul. He gives priority to prayer and devotion over external forms of worship. Pilgrimages, the veneration of saints, and the observance of rites are merely crutches to help the weaker brethren, he says. The goal of every mature Christian must be the internalization of the gospel message, 'to progress always from visible things . . . to invisible'. Faith must be realized in everyday actions and words rather than in ritualized and ceremonial observances confined to special occasions.

Christocentricity is a important feature of Erasmus' 'celestial philosophy'. Christ is the believer's model and guide to perfection. More specifically, he is the theologian's model: pastoral, persuasive, and transforming, paternal in his indulgence for the weak. Erasmus uses the metaphor of three concentric circles, with Christ at the centre surrounded by the clergy, the nobility, and the common people. It is the responsibility of clergy and princes to transmit the heavenly philosophy to the people. The hierarchy is not impermeable, however, for in the Christian body 'the foot may become an eye' and, conversely, the higher echelons are subject to degeneration. Baptism made all Christians equal; it was the only vow necessary for salvation. Erasmus' dictum *monachatus non est pietas* ('being a monk is not piety') became notorious in his day and was often quoted in this form by his critics to demonstrate his hostility to monastic orders. It is important, however, to note how the sentence continues: being a monk is not piety 'but a way of life that may be useful or not useful according to each man's physical make-up and disposition'. Piety was not the exclusive preserve of one class, but could be attained by anyone. The philosophy of Christ was malleable enough to accommodate all believers. Erasmus expressly connected the *Handbook* with the *Praise of Folly*, noting that he presented there in a witty manner the same ideas that he had presented in a serious vein in the *Handbook*. The common message was the rejection of materialism and of the topsy-turvy judgement of fools who place worldly before spiritual wealth.

The *Handbook* became a bestseller just as Luther rose to prominence, and soon Erasmus' words were translated into the reformer's idiom. Readers thought they discerned a resemblance between Erasmus' depreciation of works and the Lutheran principle of *sola fide*, between Erasmus' levelling of church hierarchies and the Lutheran slogan of a 'priesthood of all believers'. Other Erasmian works came under scrutiny as well, and were reinterpreted in the context of the Reformation. The similarities between his and Luther's thought were of course superficial. It is true that both men took aim at

corrupt practices – the commercialization of religion; the preoccupation
with external rites; the ignorance and worldliness of the clergy; the neglect
of the biblical text – but Erasmus was aiming at the correction of abuses
rather than at doctrinal innovation or institutional change. Unlike Luther,
he accepted papal primacy and the teaching authority of the church and did
not discount human tradition. The reforms proposed by Erasmus were in
the social rather than the doctrinal realm. His principal aim was to foster
piety and to deepen spirituality.

Erasmus protested against what he saw as a misreading of his intentions,
but by the late 1520s he was eyed with suspicion by both Catholics and
Protestants and regarded as a closet Lutheran, who concealed his sympathies
out of cowardice or conservatism. After his death in 1536, and in the wake of
the Council of Trent, the Catholic Church placed his writings on the *Index*.
Protestants remained ambivalent about his role in the Lutheran affair, but
continued to pay homage to his scholarship and to use his critical editions
and textbooks.

ERASMUS' IMAGE IN MODERN LITERATURE

Erasmus' image as a theologian changed with the historical circumstances. In his own time he was attacked by Catholic theologians as an
error-prone dilettante and by Protestants as an opportunist. Even those who
appreciated his religious thought tended to see him in terms of confessional
ideologies, either as a representative of Catholic reform or as Luther's inspiration. The Age of Enlightenment saw a revival of interest in Erasmus. He
came to be seen as a liberal and a rationalist, the Voltaire of the sixteenth century. This interpretation remained current through the nineteenth century,
but, as confessionalism revived, Erasmus was once again seen in the light of
denominational differences, and his tolerance was interpreted as weakness.
Doubts about his qualifications as a theologian continued. Durand de Laur,
for example, asserted that 'Erasme était né pour les lettres et non pour la
théologie'. In the twentieth century, Erasmian tolerance acquired new lustre
in the context of ecumenism, but some scholars still denied him the title of
theologian. Renaudet declared simply: 'Erasme n'était pas théologien.' On
the whole, however, the idea that Erasmus had a valuable message for theologians won the upper hand just as his reputation for what was regarded
as liberalism and rationalism in earlier centuries was fading. The rehabilitation of Erasmus as a serious theologian is most noticeable in Catholic
circles from the 1950s onward. Outlining this development, John O'Malley
identified him as a theologian belonging to the new epoch of church history

that began with Vatican II: 'Today it is worthwhile to reconsider the ideas of the man from Rotterdam. The name of Erasmus could become a symbol, indeed a warning for us to think and act as true Catholics.' It seems, then, that Erasmus has found acceptance on his own terms, as a man 'who fittingly explicates the scriptures, who speaks movingly of piety . . . and excites passion for heavenly things'.

5 Luther

SCOTT HENDRIX

INTRODUCTION

Martin Luther developed his theology in the course of a remarkable thirty-four-year career as professor of scripture at the University of Witten-berg and leader of the evangelical reform movement that became the Protes-tant Reformation. It is helpful to divide this career into three segments: (1) from 1512, when he began lecturing on the Bible, until 1522, when he returned to Wittenberg after appearing before the imperial diet at Worms and being declared an outlaw in Germany; (2) from 1522 until 1530, when Luther and his colleagues were busy shaping the new evangelical Chris-tianity that became Lutheran with the confession adopted by most German Protestants at Augsburg; (3) from 1530 until his death in 1546, when Luther devoted most of his time to university work and to the practical questions of Protestant politics and church life. The distinctive Reformation themes of Luther's theology were forged during the first period and then honed by the demands and disputes of the second and third periods. Interpreters are faced with the task of finding unity and coherence in a theology that contributed to such epochal change in church and society.

That task is exacerbated by the number and variety of Luther's writ-ings. Since no one work of Luther dominates his corpus in the way that the *Institutes* stand out among the works of John Calvin, the theology of Luther has to be reconstructed from a wealth of sources in the following categories. First, Luther's academic chair required that he lecture in Latin on many books of the Bible, beginning with the Psalms in 1512 and ending with Genesis in 1546. Many of these lectures were revised and published during his lifetime. Especially important for his theology are the lectures on Romans (1515–16), Psalms (1519–21), Galatians (1531), and the extended series of lectures on Genesis (1535–45).

Secondly, Luther wrote treatises on specific themes such as marriage, the sacraments, the bondage of the will, monastic vows, the church, civil authority, and Christian freedom. These themes were often suggested by

39

the events of the Reformation or by the attacks of his opponents, and some of them are highly polemical. Luther once remarked that the attacks of his opponents had made him 'a fairly good theologian', which he would not have become otherwise. Thirdly, Luther wrote edifying tracts in German for laity, including his large and small catechisms (1529), and works on prayer, the Ten Commandments, sacraments, confession, and good works. One can add to this group letters of consolation, hymns, and orders of worship. The distribution of these works through the new printing technology of the early sixteenth century made Luther the most widely read religious author up to that time. Fourthly, we have Luther's sermons, of which around 2,000 have been preserved. Their potential as a source of Luther's theology and how it was communicated has not yet been fully tapped. Fifthly, around 2,500 letters of Luther have been edited. They contain not only informative details about the people and events of Luther's day but also pithy discussions of theological issues.

Two approaches have dominated the presentation of Luther's theology. One approach is historical and traces the development of his thought, focusing primarily on the emergence of new Reformation insights during the earliest period. This focus on the early Luther marked the so-called Luther renaissance of the early twentieth century and remained prominent at mid-century in attempts to uncover the medieval roots of Luther's thought. A second approach is more topical, and it has always been a popular way of presenting Luther's thought, either one theme at a time or as a whole. The newer Finnish research on Luther, for example, has concentrated on the systematic connection of certain themes across the body of his writings. The most recent comprehensive treatment of Luther's thought combines both approaches, describing first the historical development of his theology and then placing it into systematic context.

Interpreters of Luther's thought are also challenged to identify the central theme of his theology. A popular candidate has been 'theology of the cross', since Luther once said that 'the cross alone is our theology'. But Luther also wrote in 1532 that the proper subject of theology is the human being guilty of sin and condemned, and God who is justifier and saviour. Other candidates for the centre of his theology are the hidden and revealed God, Christ, the Word of God, law and gospel, and justification. These themes are related to one another and describe different facets of the same purpose, which Luther stated bluntly in 1518: 'I teach that people should trust in nothing but Jesus Christ alone, not in prayers or merits or even in their own works.' That purpose, which describes both the centre and the goal of his thinking, runs like a silver thread throughout Luther's theology.

INFLUENCES

As a young theologian, Luther was subject to a number of influences, which can be identified in his writings. In 1521 Luther reflected as follows on his encounters with scholasticism and monasticism: 'But it was the Lord's will . . . that the wisdom of the schools and the sanctity of the monasteries should become known to me by my own actual experience . . . so that wicked people might not have a chance, when I became their adversary, to boast that I condemned something about which I knew nothing.' In spite of his attack on scholastic theology, the nominalist school in which he was trained taught Luther to appreciate the power of the word and the distinction between philosophy and theology. Likewise, even though Luther rejected the monastic life and its binding vows as a false claim to Christian perfection, his own years in the monastery gave him an intimate knowledge of scripture and inspired his conviction that all believers should take their Christian life with utmost seriousness.

The mystical traditions of the Middle Ages taught Luther the value of religious experience and suffering for theology and the Christian life. 'One does not become a theologian by understanding, reading, or speculating,' Luther told his students in late 1518 or early 1519, 'but rather by living, dying, and being damned.' At Wittenberg Luther was also part of a humanist reform movement, which replaced lectures on scholastic theology with courses on the Bible and the church fathers. By 1517, the same year as his ninety-five theses against indulgences, Luther was able to report:

> Our theology and St Augustine are progressing well, and with God's help rule at our university. Aristotle is gradually falling from his throne, and his final doom is only a matter of time. It is amazing how the lectures on the *Sentences* [of Peter Lombard] are disdained. Indeed no one can expect to have any students if he does not want to teach this theology, that is, lecture on the Bible or on St Augustine or another teacher of ecclesiastical eminence.

Luther's words indicate that next to the Bible the most important influence on his early theology was Augustine of Hippo (354–430), after whom his own order was named. In his lectures on Romans (1515–16) Luther cites Augustine's treatise *The Spirit and the Letter* in support of his interpretation of the righteousness of God in Romans 1:17, the same interpretation described by Luther in 1545 as a profound experience which scholars have labelled his 'Reformation discovery'. When Luther offered more public summaries of his views for debate in 1516 and 1517, he invoked the anti-Pelagian

Augustine in support of his theses. In 1518, Luther prepared theological theses for the Heidelberg Disputation 'so that it may become clear whether they have been deduced well or poorly from St Paul, the especially chosen vessel and instrument of Christ, and also from St Augustine, his most trustworthy interpreter'. Augustine served the young theologian primarily as a guide to scripture; Luther commented that he had even devoured Augustine before he came upon Paul. Scholars have failed to locate a distinct late medieval Augustinian school of thought that directly influenced Luther, but his mentor and superior in the Augustinian order, Johannes von Staupitz (1460/69–1524), certainly passed on some of the Augustinian heritage to his protégé while at the same time challenging his theology and providing pastoral guidance.

THE 'REFORMATION DISCOVERY'

The elements of what would become a new theology are found in Luther's 'Reformation discovery'. According to his own account, the discovery was a biblical and theological insight that solved a religious and exegetical problem. He could not understand how Paul could say that the righteousness of God was revealed in the gospel (Romans 1:16–17), when he had been taught to understand divine righteousness as the basis on which God punished unrighteous sinners. Despite his own irreproachable life as a monk, Luther says he hated this righteous God because God seemed to be adding the gospel with its threat of punishment to the burden of the law. After persistent study and meditation, however, he suddenly understood from the full text of Romans 1:17 that 'the person who through faith is righteous shall live', and that accordingly the righteousness of God revealed in the gospel was the passive righteousness through which God justifies us by faith. 'Here I felt that I was altogether born again and had entered paradise through open gates.' Luther then confirmed his insight by checking how scripture spoke of other divine attributes and by consulting *The Spirit and the Letter* where, unexpectedly, he found that Augustine, too, 'interpreted God's righteousness . . . as the righteousness with which God clothes us when he justifies us'.

Scholars have tended to isolate this discovery from the indulgence controversy in which Luther's account is nestled and to treat it as a personal problem of Luther the over-scrupulous monk. The discovery, however, should be seen as part of a larger context that generated Luther's new theology. While Luther was pondering the meaning of the righteousness of God in Romans 1, he was also attacking the late medieval way of salvation at two levels: at a theoretical and academic level, against the nominalist theologians; and, at a practical and popular level, against claims for indulgences put forward by the church hierarchy and its preachers. Typical of the first attack was the *Disputation against Scholastic Theology*, theses which Luther prepared for defence at the University in Wittenberg on 4 September 1517. Under the mantle of Augustine, Luther attacks the acquisition of a meritorious human righteousness from several angles. First, he discredits the nominalist position that one could meritoriously prepare for justifying grace by exercising one's natural powers, or, as the Latin phrase put it, to do what is in oneself (*facere quod in se est*), that is, without grace. Luther also attacks the notion that one can fulfil the law only in the grace of God because that would make grace more burdensome than the law itself. This statement is reminiscent of his complaint that the gospel was more burdensome than the law if it mediated a divine, punishing righteousness. Finally, Luther discards the Aristotelian notion that one becomes righteous by doing righteous deeds, and argues the reverse position, which agrees with his Reformation insight: having been made righteous, namely by God's own grace and passive righteousness, we do righteous deeds. The disputation shows that Luther is well on the way toward formulating a new view of justification when the indulgence controversy erupts two months later.

Issued on 31 October 1517 for another academic debate that never took place, Luther's ninety-five theses not only challenged the extravagant claims being made for indulgences, but also questioned the value of indulgences at all and the power of the pope to extend the efficacy of indulgences to souls in purgatory. The issue of papal jurisdiction raised a new point that led to conflict over authority in the church, but the debate over indulgences themselves bore on the meaning of God's righteousness and how it effected human salvation. If people believed they were saved by the acquisition of indulgences, then they would neglect the rest of the sacrament of penance, of which indulgences were officially a minor part. People did not need to be contrite for their sins, or to trust the absolution of the priest, or to perform the works of satisfaction that made up the temporal penalty for their sins. Luther pulled no punches: 'Those who believe that they can be certain of their salvation because they have indulgence letters will be eternally damned, together with their teachers' (thesis 32). The alternative for believers was to repent constantly for their sin, to consider the gospel as 'the true treasure of the church' (thesis 62), to give to the needy, and 'to be diligent in following Christ their head through penalties, death, and hell' (thesis 94).

The impact of the indulgence controversy forced Luther to clarify how the sacrament of penance functioned in accord with his Reformation insight into the passive righteousness of God. He worked out that clarification in the explanations to his ninety-five theses and in his encounter with Cardinal

Cajetan (Tommaso de Vio, 1469–1534) at Augsburg in 1518. In the explanation to his seventh thesis Luther wrote:

> People must be taught that if they really want to find peace for their consciences they should learn to place their confidence, not in the power of the pope, but in the word of Christ who gives the promise to the pope. For it is not because the pope grants it that you have anything, but you have it because you believe that you receive it. You have only as much as you believe according to the promise of Christ.

Faith was necessary if the sacrament was to bring peace of conscience as well as remission of sin. According to the 'Reformation discovery', that same faith solved both the theological dilemma of how one became righteous through the gospel and the religious dilemma of how Luther could find the certainty of God's favour that his blameless monastic life did not bring. The text also uses the concept of promise, which had played an important role in his first lecture course on the Psalms (1513–15) and would continue to be a central concept of his theology. In this case, the promise is the word of Christ to Peter in Matthew 16:19, upon which the power of the keys to forgive and retain sins, that is, the sacrament of penance, had been founded.

Cajetan's objection to this explanation seems to have crystallized the new theology of justification in Luther's mind. According to his memory, Cajetan and other opponents considered as 'new' and 'erroneous' the theology 'that no one can be justified except by faith' and he responds by appealing to Romans 1:17 as proof of the 'infallible truth that no person is righteous unless that person believes in God'. 'Therefore the justification and life of the righteous person are dependent upon faith.' 'Faith, however, is nothing else than believing what God promises and reveals, as in Romans 4[:3], "Abraham believed God, and it was reckoned to him as righteousness."' 'Therefore, the word and faith are both necessary, and without the word there can be no faith.'

Most scholars agree that Luther arrived at a new understanding of justification by the end of 1518, but they have disagreed about the dating, the location, and even the precise content of the 'Reformation discovery', taken as a single conversion experience in the way Luther described it. One disputed point concerns the issue of humility and its role in the process of justification. According to Ernst Bizer and Oswald Bayer, Luther arrived at a genuine Reformation theology when faith was no longer determined by humility but was reoriented toward God's Word as promise. In fact, Luther continued to insist on a certain kind of humility that was not aware of its own lowliness, and on contrition and repentance once the sinner was convicted and humbled by the law. Luther's new idea of justification was not just the correlation of promise and faith, but the richer cluster of insights sparked by the engagements and conflicts described above. The faith that received the passive righteousness of God was the same faith that grew out of genuine contrition for sin, clung to the promise of absolution for the sake of Christ, and issued in love for the needy instead of acquiring indulgences or performing other meritorious works. This discovery was not only the solution to the exegetical problem of Romans 1:16–17 and to his own religious dilemma. It was also the basis of a fundamental reorientation of Christian life and theology that turned into a reformation of Christianity.

EXPANSION (1517–1521)

From 1517 to 1521, as his conflict with the Roman hierarchy moved toward his excommunication and the imperial ban, Luther expanded his new insights in directions that would support such a reformation.

Theology of the cross

In 1518, Luther concentrated his attack on scholastic theology in a concept that some scholars have seen as the centre of his theology. The term *theologia crucis* was used by Luther only five times, four of them in the spring of 1518. The best-known text belongs to the set of theses prepared for the chapter of the Augustinians at Heidelberg in April of the same year. In thesis 21, Luther distinguishes between a theology of glory that 'calls evil good and good evil', and a theology of the cross that 'calls the thing what it actually is'. According to the preceding thesis, Luther means that a genuine theologian is one who can see God at work in suffering and in the cross, just as God was condemning sin and saving humanity through the suffering and death of Christ. In contrast to scholastic theology, as Luther read it, the way of salvation is not through human achievement and merit, but through the suffering of Christ and through the suffering of believers who are baptized into the death of Christ. For Luther, theology of the cross makes primarily this soteriological claim, although it is at the same time a statement about how God's wrath works redemptively against sin through suffering in what Luther, on the basis of Isaiah 28:21, calls God's strange or alien work. The distinction between the proper and the alien work of God remains an important element of Luther's theology.

The authority of scripture

As soon as Luther's criticism of indulgences provoked a reaction from the hierarchy, authority in the church became a prominent issue. Who decided what power indulgences had and who decided how the sacrament of penance actually led to forgiveness of sin and salvation? Cajetan raised both issues at his interview with Luther in 1518. In response, Luther appealed to the authority of scripture and declared on the basis of Galatians 1:8 that 'the pope was not above but under the Word of God'. From Rome, the pope's court theologian, Sylvester Prierias OP (1456–1523), upheld papal authority as supreme in the church, but Luther responded that scripture, church fathers, and canon law were also to be consulted on matters that had not yet been decided. At the debate with the Ingolstadt theologian Johann Maier von Eck (1486–1543) in Leipzig in 1519, Luther questioned the divine origin of the papal office ('divine right') based on the words of Christ to Peter in Matthew 16:18. Eck also forced him to state in principle the authority of scripture over church councils.

By the time Luther made his famous speech at Worms in 1521, he had elevated scripture above other authorities as supreme in the church. Luther never meant, however, to deprive church fathers of all their authority. Instead, scripture was supreme when other authorities disagreed. Nor did Luther intend to elevate private interpretation of scripture to a purely subjective criterion of truth. At Worms his stand was based on his duty as a teacher of the church to defend the consciences of all believers on the basis of that same scripture to which his own conscience had been made captive.

The priesthood of believers

In his *Address to the Christian Nobility* (1520), Luther maintained that the right to interpret scripture belonged to all believers on the basis of the spiritual priesthood shared by all Christians. Against the claim of the 'Romanists,' as he called the papal hierarchy and its clergy, that they alone constituted the spiritual estate, Luther interpreted several passages (1 Corinthians 12:12–13; 1 Peter 2:9; Revelation 5:9–10) to mean that all those who had become Christian through baptism, the gospel, and faith were priests and 'truly of the spiritual estate'. Consequently, argued Luther, all Christians 'have the power to test and judge what is right or wrong in matters of faith'. He took a verse that had usually been applied to the pope (1 Corinthians 2:15: 'A spiritual person judges all things and is judged by no one') and applied it to all Christians, since they were the spiritual people entitled to render judgement.

Their right to interpret scripture, however, did not support strictly private interpretation but was vested in the Christian community as a whole, which then charged some 'with the administration of the Word of God and the sacraments'. A pastoral office would interpret scripture on behalf of all spiritual Christians in the common priesthood. With this model, Luther disputed the claims of the Roman hierarchy on the basis of scripture while at the same time he tried to avoid the arbitrariness of private interpretation. His translation of the New Testament into German (the 'September Testament', 1522) initiated the process of making scripture more accessible to all believers and enabled them to exercise the power to which their common priesthood entitled them.

Church and sacraments

In June of 1520, Luther's work entitled *The Papacy in Rome* made explicit the ecclesiological implications of the priesthood of believers. The church was not defined by any particular hierarchy, not even the one based in Rome. Instead, true Christendom was a spiritual entity whose existence was marked by the signs of baptism, the Lord's supper, and the gospel. At first Luther had retained penance as a sacrament, but by the end of *The Babylonian Captivity of the Church* (1520), he had reduced the genuine sacraments to 'baptism and the bread' because they had visible signs (water, bread, and wine) attached to the promises that constituted them. Since the heart of penance was absolution, the declaration of forgiveness, Luther concluded that it was simply 'a way and a return to baptism', which Luther had redefined in terms of promise and faith, a lifelong covenant between God and the baptized believer. He also rejected the concept of the mass as a sacrifice and replaced it with that of a testament, the promise of one who was about to die. 'You have seen that the mass is nothing else than the divine promise or testament of Christ, sealed with the sacrament of his body and blood.' This redefinition of the sacraments had two effects. First, it placed baptism at the centre of the Christian life instead of penance and eucharist. Secondly, it provided the regular and visible means through which justifying faith was engendered and nurtured, that same faith that was not a work 'but the lord and life of all works'.

Important
Promise
＝ d
Sical

Good works

From the moment Luther and others began preaching justification by faith, they complained that people misinterpreted their message to mean that good works no longer needed to be done. The same charge was made against the new evangelical theology by its learned opponents. Luther responded by making two clarifications. To say that a person was saved by faith and not by works meant that works were not meritorious, but it did not mean they should not be done. A tree first had to be good before it could bear good fruit, but it did bear fruit. Faith, the 'lord and life of all works', would always bear fruit when it was present, because 'it is a living, busy, active, mighty thing, this faith. It is impossible for it not to be doing good works incessantly. It does not ask whether good works are to be done, but before the question is asked, it has already done them, and is constantly doing them.'

In 1520 Luther devoted an entire treatise to the second clarification. There are genuine good works and there are spurious works. The latter are those which are done without faith and without the command of God: for example, fasting, indulgences, almsgiving, endowments, pilgrimages, and other religious activities by which people sought to merit God's favour. Genuine good works, however, are those done in faith and in obedience to God's commandments. These may be religious in appearance, but they may also involve the activities of daily life that believers pursue in response to their callings. Consequently, Luther's treatise on good works becomes an exposition of the Ten Commandments in order to show people how Christian life should abound in good works once faith is present. Luther enunciates a principle repeated in his catechisms (1529) and elsewhere: to fulfil the first commandment by trusting God above all things is to obey all the commandments, because such faith can result only in the kind of activity that fulfils the others as well. In this way, Luther hoped, as he said, 'very much to teach the real good works which spring from faith'.

Christian freedom

The correlation of faith and love configures the Christian life described by Luther at the end of 1520 in *The Freedom of a Christian*. Through faith the Christian is the freest master of all, while through love the Christian is the most dutiful servant of all. Love flows from faith and freely helps the neighbour, so that 'each one should become as it were Christ to the other . . . and Christ may be the same in all, that is, that we may be truly Christian'. To help people become truly Christian according to this template and to help them appreciate 'the riches and the glory of the Christian life' was the unabashed goal of Luther's theology. In his estimation people did not know why they were Christian or bore the name Christian. 'Surely we are named after Christ, not because he is absent from us, but because he dwells in us, that is, because we believe in him and are Christs one to another and do to our neighbours as Christ does to us.' Luther's discovery of justification by faith aimed at the reform of Christian piety as well as the reform of theology. It cannot be divorced from the indulgence controversy in which it was born, because its goal was to renew Christian practice as well as faith.

Three of the writings from 1520 are often referred to as Luther's 'Reformation' treatises: *Address to the Christian Nobility*, *The Babylonian Captivity*, and *The Freedom of a Christian*. To be precise, *The Papacy in Rome* and *Good Works* should also be included in this category. They all demonstrate how Luther expanded his Reformation insights into a theological core that was

substantially completed by 1522 as a distinct evangelical Christianity began
to take shape.

REFINEMENTS (1522–1530)

The growth of the evangelical movement in the 1520s forced Luther to
refine his theology on several fronts, especially when disagreement arose
over the pace and the agenda of the Reformation.

Two kingdoms

Since church and state were so entwined in late medieval Christendom,
it quickly became important to define the relationship between the gospel
and civil authority. At Worms, Luther had disobeyed the imperial command
to recant, but he was being protected by his own prince, Elector Frederick
of Saxony. Meanwhile in the 'other' Saxony, Duke George was reminding
his subjects that it was forbidden to read Luther's pamphlets, including his
recent translation of the New Testament. How should Christians respond
in the light of the fact that Romans 13:1 required everyone to be subject
to the governing authority, while other passages, such as Matthew 5:38–41,
implied that Christians were not to use the temporal sword at all? Luther
resolved the dilemma by dividing humanity into two kingdoms under two
distinct governments. True believers in Christ live in the kingdom of God
and are governed by the gospel alone, while all others belong to the kingdom
of the world, where they are governed by the law. Real Christians, of whom
Luther says there are few, should not use civil law or power on behalf of
themselves but only for the sake of the neighbour, whom they are bound to
serve and protect.

This principle, formulated by Luther in his 1523 treatise, *On Secular
Authority*, implied that Christians should obey civil authority except when
government tried to obstruct their faith or access to the gospel. In that
case, believers should obey God rather than human authority (Acts 5:29).
The principle also meant that Christians could hold civil office and serve
as soldiers in a defensive war. As rulers, they should treat their subjects in
a Christian way. Luther never endorsed the use of violence by Christians
in rebellion against their own rulers, even for the sake of a more just and
nominally Christian society. For that reason he opposed the rebellion of the
peasants in 1525. In fact, Luther had to be persuaded that Protestant princes
could rightfully resist the emperor with force, should he move against them.
Few parts of his thought have been more controversial than this concept,
and it continues to be debated by interpreters. Luther's own concern was to
maintain a proper distinction between the kingdoms in order to protect both

Holy ordo S

the integrity of the Christian life and the dignity of daily vocations. He often grouped the vocations into the orders of church, family, and government; and in 1528, in opposition to the false and worldly orders of monasticism, he called them 'holy orders and true religious institutions'.

Sin and the bound will

REAL POWER

In his attack on scholastic theology, Luther argued that, before justification, sin was a real power that enslaved the intellect and the will, and that even after grace had come and the will had been liberated, real sin remained in the baptized to the extent that they could be called simultaneously righteous and sinful (*simul iustus et peccator*). 'After baptism and repentance all sins are forgiven, but sin remains present until death.'

Two theologians attacked Luther's position. The first, Jakob Latomus (1475–1544) in Louvain, defended the condemnation of Luther's teaching on this point in the papal bull that threatened Luther with excommunication (1520). The reformer responded with an important distinction between the righteousness and the grace of God. On the one hand, grace is a quality of God, not of the soul. It is the mercy of God that overcomes wrath by forgiving sin and making the sinner acceptable to God. On the other hand, the righteousness of God is the gift of faith that heals the believer by gradually purging the sin that has already been forgiven. 'Everything is forgiven through grace, but as yet not everything is healed through the gift.' For Luther, therefore, Christians are *simul iusti et peccatores*, but a process of healing is also under way:

> This life, therefore, is not godliness but the process of becoming godly, not health but getting well, not being but becoming, not rest but exercise. We are not now what we shall be, but we are on the way . . . This is not the goal but it is the right road. At present, everything does not gleam and sparkle, but everything is being cleansed.

The second opponent was the renowned humanist, Erasmus of Rotterdam (c. 1467–1536), who was persuaded to attack Luther on the issue of free choice. Luther's rebuttal in 1525 was a wide-ranging defence of the bondage of the will. Although for the most part Erasmus reproduced the nominalist argument that, prior to grace, the human will could choose in its own power to love God and obey the commandments, Luther analysed the capacity of the will both before and after grace. Before grace, the will remains completely enslaved to sin, and, although the Holy Spirit liberates the will from this bondage during justification, the will is still not free in the sense that it could choose God. Instead, the will has to be held in faith toward God by the constant support of the Spirit. To make his point, Luther used the illustration of a horse and rider. Like the horse, the will is always alive and active, but the rider has to set the direction. That rider is either God or Satan, holding the will toward God or driving the will away. Even after the will is liberated from bondage to sin, it still cannot choose God as if making a neutral decision. For that reason, the Holy Spirit regularly has to reinforce the will's orientation to God by renewing faith through the means of word and sacrament.

External means

In the early 1520s Luther was forced to articulate this component of his theology by former university colleague Andreas Bodenstein von Carlstadt (c. 1480–1541), who had initiated reform in Wittenberg before Luther returned in 1522 to displace him from the leadership. Carlstadt not only differed from Luther over the pace of reform, but under the influence of mysticism he also stressed the subjective side of the sacraments more than Luther could accept. Carlstadt emphasized the Lord's supper as an experience of remembrance, in which the communicant identifies with the death of Christ on the cross, where sin was actually forgiven, not in the sacrament itself. Luther reacted strongly because it seemed to make forgiveness dependent on the experience of the communicant and to undercut the peculiar function and benefit of the sacraments. In Luther's view, it was not the purpose of the sacrament to take the believer back to the cross, but to bring the cross and its forgiveness to the believer under visible signs to which faith could cling and through which it would be strengthened. Consequently, he gave priority to the sacraments as external means through which the Holy Spirit brought forgiveness: 'The inward experience follows and is effected by the outward. God has determined to give the inward to no one except through the outward.'

The real presence and infant baptism

This emphasis upon the sacraments as external means of forgiveness also influenced the stance he would take in the mid-1520s on the real presence of Christ in the supper and on infant baptism. A symbolic interpretation of the words of institution was adopted in 1524 by the reformer of Zurich, Huldrych Zwingli (1484–1531), who maintained that the bread represented the body of Christ and the cup his blood. If laity continued to think that bread and wine were real body and blood, feared Zwingli, then they would persist in the same superstitious abuse of the sacrament that he had observed prior to the Reformation. For Luther, however, the words of institution had to be taken literally, because they promised the presence of Christ and the forgiveness of sin in such a way that Christians could be certain of receiving both in the sacrament. According to Zwingli and his followers, the body or the human nature of Christ could not be in the sacrament, since after the ascension it was located in heaven. According to Luther, however, after the ascension the human nature was linked to the divine nature by a sharing of properties (*communicatio idiomatum*) in the one person of Christ, and therefore the human nature could be everywhere (*ubique*) the divine nature could be, especially in the supper. Luther was less interested in abstract Christology than in preserving the sacrament as the objective means of forgiveness and the locus of encounter between Christ and the Christian.

Luther also answered the challenge of the Anabaptists by emphasizing the objective side of baptism. When they rejected infant baptism and insisted that baptism be reserved for those who could make a profession of faith, Luther responded with several arguments. First, he suggested it was possible for children to have faith as a gift of the Holy Spirit. Secondly, he maintained that infant baptism must be valid and efficacious, given the number of people who had become Christian by that means through the centuries. Thirdly, although the promise of baptism needed to be received in faith, one should never be baptized on the basis of how much faith was present, but on the command of God. 'For faith does not exist for the sake of baptism, but baptism for the sake of faith.' If baptism depended on faith, then people could never be certain they were properly baptized. In that case, they might seek baptism over and over again because they were unsure they had adequate faith, just as, recalls Luther, he was uncertain that he had sufficiently confessed his sins, and sought one absolution after another. Baptism and the other external forms of the promise remained precious to Luther: 'Thus we can and should promise ourselves the things God has promised us with greater certainty, as if we held them in our hands. I have the kingdom of heaven, baptism, the Word, and the eucharist. These things pertain to me and are mine with greater certainty than this very life which I live.'

Law and gospel

Despite Luther's declaration that the ability to distinguish law from gospel made one a theologian, the relationship between the two was a controversial element of his theology. The controversy arose in the mid-1520s between two of his early co-workers and former students, Philipp Melanchthon (1497–1560) and Johann Agricola (c. 1492–1566). Melanchthon, who had come to Wittenberg as professor of Greek and quickly mastered Luther's emerging thought, argued that the law should be preached to effect contrition and repentance before the gospel brought forgiveness and comfort. Agricola, who had witnessed the indulgence con-troversy in Wittenberg and served as Luther's assistant before going to Eisleben as a pastor, maintained that repentance was the new heart given by the Holy Spirit through the gospel, not remorse caused by the law.

Melanchthon attacked Agricola's view in the so-called *Visitation Articles* (1527), which Luther also saw and approved. This document used Luke 24:47 to establish that repentance needed to be preached before the forgiveness of sins, the law before the gospel. It also urged that the Ten Commandments be taught in order to guide the doing of good works, the third element of the Christian life in addition to repentance and faith. Scholars debate whether or not Luther, like Melanchthon, taught this 'third use of the law', but Luther certainly advocated the preaching and teaching of the law while he insisted on distinguishing it clearly from the gospel. Luther maintained this position as he mediated the early 'antinomian' ('against the law') controversy in 1527, as he prepared his catechisms (1529), and once again in the late 1530s, when the controversy with Agricola erupted again. It surprised Luther, then, 'that anyone can claim that I reject the law or the Ten Commandments, since there is available, in more than one edition, my exposition of the Ten Commandments, which furthermore are daily preached and practised in our churches'.

ELABORATIONS (1530–1546)

After the Diet of Augsburg (1530), the context of Luther's theology changed again. Surrounded by colleagues in Wittenberg at the centre of an expanding Lutheran movement, Luther's later years were dominated by growing estrangement among the religious parties in spite of efforts to bring about their reconciliation. The outcome of the Reformation was never certain to Luther. The eschatological edge to his theology became sharper and his polemics shriller, but the basic components of his theology remained fixed. For this reason, perhaps, the theology of the later Luther has received less attention than the earlier development of its themes. After 1530, however, he did elaborate them in a variety of works including dispu-tation theses, the Schmalkaldic Articles, and in two major series of lectures, on Galatians (1531; published in 1535) and on Genesis (1535–45; edited and published after his death). The extent to which the latter were altered to reflect the theology of Melanchthon has been debated, but the current opinion favours their reliability as an indicator of Luther's later thought.

At the end of his *Confession concerning Christ's Supper* (1528), Luther supplied a summary of his thought as a confession of faith 'before God and all the world, point by point'. He begins by confessing his faith in the

Trinity, described by him in the Schmalkaldic Articles as 'the great articles of the divine majesty', which always lay at the basis of his theology and tied it to the orthodox, catholic tradition of early Christianity. Rather than speculating about the Trinity, however, Luther speaks more typically about the persons of the Godhead as the foundation of faith and life. On God the Creator, for example, instead of debating the details of the creation story, Luther says: 'I prefer that we reflect on the divine solicitude and benevolence toward us, because God provided such an attractive dwelling place for the future human being before the human being was created.' Interpreting Galatians 3:13 ('Christ redeemed us from the curse of the law, having become a curse for us'), Luther stresses the last two words: 'For [Paul] does not say that Christ became a curse on his own account, but that he became a curse for us.' This image is closely related to the joyful exchange between Christ and the Christian that Luther also used to describe how the death of Christ benefited the believer. Elements of classical atonement theories can be found in Luther, but he cannot be 'attached to any of those systems'.

The Holy Spirit plays a large role in Luther's theology because the controverted theological issues of Luther's day were mainly third-article issues. Although justifying faith is a human activity, it is not a good work, since it is a gift of the Holy Spirit, who also makes Christ present in the believer. The source of true holiness for Christians is the Holy Spirit, who 'sanctifies them [Acts 15:9], that is, renews heart, soul, body, work, and conduct, inscribing the commandments of God not on tables of stone, but in hearts of flesh [2 Corinthians 3:3]'. The church comprises holy, Christian people who 'believe in Christ . . . and have the Holy Spirit, who sanctifies them daily, not only through the forgiveness of sin acquired for them by Christ . . . but also through the abolition, the purging and the mortification of sins'. This holy people can be recognized by its possession of the holy Word of God, the sacraments, the ministry, prayer and praise of God, and 'the holy possession of the sacred cross'. These marks of the church vary slightly from place to place in Luther's works, but they stake out the same ecumenical ecclesiology which he described in 1520. The church is not tied to a specific hierarchy or geographical location; it becomes concrete and visible everywhere believers bearing those marks gather around word and sacrament to have their faith renewed by the Holy Spirit.

To have an ecumenical ecclesiology did not mean that Luther gave up his polemical rejection of Rome. In these later years, he was more convinced than ever that the devil had hardened the 'papists' into enemies of the gospel they continued to reject. Luther was not condemning the Roman church as a whole; through it he confessed that the evangelical movement had received the scriptures, the creeds, and the sacraments. It was mainly the papal office that had corrupted the faith and was unnecessary to the church.

Luther also numbered the non-Christians of his world, the Jews and the 'Turks' (Islam in the Ottoman empire) among the gospel's enemies. He was able to find good things in both religions, and early on he and other reformers hoped that the evangelical movement would convert the Jews to Christianity. When that failed to happen, Luther accused them of threatening the Christian faith by refusing to see the messianic passages of their scriptures fulfilled in Jesus. Although he recommended harsh measures against contemporary Jews in a very polemical treatise against them, he mainly attacked the rabbinic exegesis of scripture and Jewish religion. No continuous line can be drawn from Luther to the Holocaust, although the National Socialists exploited the anti-Jewish sentiments that Luther shared with the people of his day.

Despite the uncertainty surrounding the outcome of the Reformation, Luther's lectures on Genesis are filled with affirmations of resurrection, the continuity of the church, and life in the kingdom of God, which the believer already enjoys through promise and faith. 'Faith is nothing else than true life in God,' writes Luther. 'So great is the power of faith. It makes us live after we have died. And indeed in that very hour in which we begin to believe and to take hold of the word we also begin to live in eternal life; for the Word of the Lord remains for ever [1 Peter 1:25], and God, who speaks with us, is eternal and will be with us for ever.'

Luther does not deny the reality of death, and he prefers not to speculate about what happens, before the resurrection, to those who have died. But he does believe that the promises of God are so strong and will be fulfilled with such certainty that, instead of saying that in the midst of life believers are in death, he prefers to sing that in the midst of death they are in life. This faith in God's promises in the face of death 'is the theology we teach', says Luther, and the faith of patriarchs such as Jacob should inspire Christians to value those promises highly. When he was a monk, recalls Luther, it was by no means customary to speak of a promise. 'And I give thanks to God that I may live at this time, when this word promise resounds in my ears and in the ears of all the godly.'

CONCLUSION

The goal of Luther's theology was to teach how the triune God created and redeemed humanity for a life of trust in God's promises that would lead them out of sin and death into eternal life in the kingdom of God. This theological goal was part of a Reformation agenda to restore this teaching to the centre of Christian life and to reshape the church around this centre in communities of Christians who were sustained and sanctified by the Holy Spirit. For Luther, a Reformation theology was less the accumulation of a body of thought than a coherent message that helped to replant this biblically based Christianity in his culture through such communities of believers. He did not intend to create a new theology, any more than he intended to create a new church. Nevertheless, Luther's theology became the basis of a new Lutheran confession, and it also contributed through the centuries to other Christian theologies and to the ongoing renewal of Christian faith and life that lay at the heart of his own work.

6 Melanchthon

SACHIKO KUSUKAWA

Albrecht Dürer famously declared that even his expert hand could not flesh out the mind of Melanchthon. In many ways Melanchthon's thought has remained similarly elusive to modern scholars. The protégé of Johannes Reuchlin, whose precocious talents in the humanities much impressed Erasmus, seems by pedigree and training to embody the classicizing concerns and values of a humanist. Indeed, his influential educational reforms of schools and universities (for which he earned the title *Praeceptor Germaniae*, 'teacher of Germany') were firmly based on the study of the classical languages, rhetoric, and dialectic. As a colleague and ally of Luther, he also elucidated Reformation principles in the *Loci communes*, conducted church visitations and diplomatic missions, and composed the public declaration of Lutheran doctrine, the Augsburg Confession. Despite his mild and irenic demeanour, he openly supported capital punishment of heretics such as the Anabaptists and Michael Servetus. He could also be a fierce and devastating polemicist, leading Erasmus to exclaim that he was 'more Lutheran than Luther himself'. And yet, that was precisely what Melanchthon's erstwhile pupils and colleagues disputed in the last years of his life – for the 'gnesio-Lutherans' such as Nikolaus von Amsdorf and Matthias Flacius Illyricus, Melanchthon was no follower of Luther.

Traditionally, scholars have tended to locate Melanchthon's thought somewhere in between that of Erasmus and Luther, between 'humanism' and 'Reformation', wavering between the two poles at different times. More recent scholarship, notably of Scheible and Wengert, has questioned this paradigm, not least because of the oversimplification of treating Erasmus' thought as representative of humanism and equating Luther's thought with Reformation theology in general. 'Humanism' itself was never a single coherent movement with identifiable philosophical positions or ideology; nor can the 'Reformation' be considered a single movement with a fixed set of doctrinal positions and attitudes that remained unchanged throughout history. It would be further misleading to assume that 'humanism' and the 'Reformation' were mutually exclusive and contradictory categories. Melanchthon made significant contributions to both the promotion of classical learning and the elucidation of Reformation principles. Just as it would be anachronistic to judge Melanchthon's theology from the viewpoint of modern-day Lutheranism or Catholicism, so, it must be acknowledged, it is futile to measure it by the two artificial poles of 'humanism' and 'Reformation'.

The challenge, then, for Melanchthon scholarship is to reach an appreciation of his thought without resorting to artificial or anachronistic categories. We should beware of being too quick to condemn apparent inconsistencies or discrepancies in Melanchthon's thought as a whole by treating his works diachronically. His thought evolved in response to contemporary historical events, and was expressed in publications with specific audiences and opponents in mind. Rather than trying to establish any point in his career as the most authentic or representative of his theology, it seems that the character of Melanchthon the theologian may best be appreciated through tracing the process and continual shaping of his views in historical context. I have chosen to focus on Melanchthon's writings under four headings: the *Loci communes*, biblical commentaries, confessional and polemical writings, though it should be noted that these headings do not exhaust the range of writings in which he expressed his theological views.

THE *LOCI COMMUNES*

The *Loci communes* ('Commonplaces') grew out of his lectures on Romans. During the first few years of his appointment as professor of Greek at Wittenberg, Melanchthon intensively studied and taught the doctrines of St Paul. The fruits of his study appeared in 1520, as the *Declamatiuncula in Divi Pauli doctrinam* ('A short declamation on the doctrine of Paul the Divine'), *Theologica Institutio in Epistulam Pauli ad Romanos* ('Theological institute on Paul's letter to the Romans'), and *De studio doctrinae Paulinae* ('On the study of Pauline doctrine'). At the same time, student notes of his lectures on Romans were published without his knowledge as the *Rerum theologicarum capita seu loci* ('Heads or places of things theological'). In April 1521, he began working on a corrected version, which was finished in September and entitled *Loci communes rerum theologicarum* ('Commonplaces of theological matters') found through the scriptures. Erasmus had recommended in the *Ratio seu methodus compendio pervenienedi ad veram theologiam* ('Method of attaining true theology') that readers of the Bible gather their own theological *loci* as an aid to reading. Melanchthon similarly believed that the Bible should be read with the *loci* as guide, but he also believed that the main *loci* themselves arose out of the scriptures themselves, rather than through subjective selection.

The *Loci communes* was not conceived as a 'systematic exposition' of Lutheran principles – Melanchthon explicitly stated that not all theological topics were treated. In the 1521 edition, for instance, he shied away from explaining topics such as God, the Trinity, creation, and incarnation – these were theological topics that were better left to divine mystery rather than being subjected to minute philosophical scrutiny. In this first edition, Melanchthon's aim was twofold: to list what one ought to look for in the scriptures *and* to show that scholastic theology based on Aristotelian philosophy and distinctions was wrong. He emphasized the importance of law and gospel, sin and grace, *sola fide*, and the regeneration of a Christian life. He also argued that people should hold property in common and that public affairs should to be administered according to the gospel, views that were later abandoned or modified.

In the second edition of the *Loci*, published in 1535, Melanchthon extended his discussion to topics such as the two natures of Christ, creation, and the Trinity. The concept of Trinity, in particular, Melanchthon began to defend on biblical as well as on Nicaean grounds in view of Servetus' antitrinitarian doctrines. Melanchthon also reformulated some key concepts. For instance, he posited that there were three causes involved in conversion: the Word of God, the Holy Spirit and the (human) will. This human will is wholly inactive in meriting justification, but it nevertheless has to resist its own weakness. The believer must hear the message and not reject it. It is God who draws, but he draws him who is willing. In stressing the 'forensic' nature of justification, Melanchthon felt that this reformulation was necessary in order to counter determinism, which would leave humans oblivious to God's saving acts. Such determinism was being propounded by Zwingli, who put forward Stoic views on the autonomy of the will and on moral determinism.

The effort to counter the libertine implications of antinomian positions held within the evangelical camp (as Wengert showed in the case of Johann Agricola) and to oppose the Catholic legalism of works righteousness led to Melanchthon's further laying emphasis on the necessity of good works: this 'necessity' did not mean that good works necessarily caused or led to justification, but that the righteous would necessarily perform good works on account of being justified. In other words, works do not merit salvation, but works of the righteous are pleasing to God on account of their justification. This, of course, means that 'law' is necessary for the old as well as the newly reborn man.

Such reformulations, however, provoked protests from within the evangelical camp. As Kolb has shown, Amsdorf believed they were downright contradictory, if not confusing to those parishioners who had been

*helpful way to good
Christian living* [handwritten annotation]

taught to abandon the idea that good works were necessary for salvation. Melanchthon defended his position in a didactic context – the necessity of works for the justified was elaborated for the sake of teaching. This controversy flared up again when Melanchthon's student, Georg Major, reacting to parish-level antinomianism, argued that good works must accompany faith and were necessary for preserving the believer in a state of salvation (the Majoristic controversy).

The negotiations in the 1530s within the evangelical camp also led Melanchthon to expand significantly the section on the eucharist. The Lord's supper controversy was initially not his own battle – Melanchthon remained 'more a spectator than an actor' in the acrimonious pamphlet war between Luther and Zwingli on the topic since the mid-1520s. In 1529 he clearly identified himself with Luther's position on real presence against Zwingli and Oecolampadius. He composed the *Sententia veterum* ('Sentences of the Ancients') in Luther's defence, which in turn was heavily criticized by Oecolampadius in his *Dialogus*. Although the precise extent to which Oecolampadius' criticism affected Melanchthon is still unclear, Melanchthon's statements became more nuanced thereafter.

In the 1535 edition of the *Loci communes*, Melanchthon reiterated his earlier point that the sacraments were the signs of God's promise, and stated that the body and blood of Christ were truly and substantially (and not figuratively) given to those who ate and drank in the Lord's supper. Sacraments are signs, however, and therefore do not merit justification in or of themselves. It is the truly present Christ and the Holy Spirit that renders the promise efficacious. The increased role of the Spirit and the view of the sacrament in an ecclesial context may well have been a response to Oecolampadius' criticisms, as Quere suggested.

In 1543, another new edition of the *Loci communes* appeared. Again, Melanchthon declared that good works were necessary for eternal life, and he offered further elaboration on the uses of law, natural law, and ethics. He introduced the famous third use of law for the justified. Hence, the law coerces (God uses civil law to maintain order in this world), terrifies (God uses the law to reveal sin and terrify the conscience), and requires obedience (the righteous must obey the law even after justification). He also linked his distaste for predestination to his rejection of Stoic determinism in the choices of everyday existence.

The section on the eucharist received further elaboration. The principal function of the eucharist is to strengthen faith. Transforming the main purpose of the ceremony, as a sacrifice for the dead, was an abuse of the sacrament, just as using baptismal water for treating leprosy was. The other functions of the Lord's supper include thanksgiving, maintaining, and structuring the congregation, and confession of doctrine. For the primary purpose of the Lord's supper, Melanchthon argued that faith was necessary – the promise is offered to all, but its benefits may be received only by those who are worthy. According to 1 Corinthians 11:29, the eucharist will not benefit those who do not offer repentance or faith, or those who persist in vile deeds against their conscience. To reap the benefit of the Lord's supper, the communicants will have to resist evil deeds and be prepared to accept the gospel. As Melanchthon himself acknowledged, the Lord's supper had an analogy with faith. Just as the human will must resist temptation in order to be justified (though justification is not offered as a reward for that resistance), so the communicant must resist evil deeds to receive the Lord's supper (though the promise is not offered as a reward for that resistance). Melanchthon recommended frequent communion and set ministers the task of scrutinizing the faith of individual members of their congregation. For Melanchthon, the touchstone for a proper understanding of the meaning of the eucharist resided in its function as defined by the words of the institution – the body and blood of Christ were to be eaten and drunk. Parading, displaying, and worshipping the host were abuses.

The way in which Melanchthon presents his position on the Lord's supper reflects his growing concern not to deviate from the church or to introduce novelties into the church. He resisted participating in the debate over the precise manner in which the body and blood of Christ might be related to the elements of the Lord's supper. Melanchthon agreed with Luther that God's presence cannot be measured by physical things, like a wine in a tankard; but he preferred to call the real presence sacramental, and above all, voluntary: that is, the offer of the promise was entirely dependent on God's will. While Luther was continually emphasizing the Christocentric nature of justification and faith, which led him to claim the ubiquity of the risen Christ robustly, Melanchthon was more interested in who received the benefits of Christ and how they did so. He articulated his position in terms of its use as defined by the words of the institution. The implication was, then, that after their use in the ceremony, the elements of the eucharist ceased to be the true body and blood of Christ. A mouse eating the elements after the ceremony would therefore not receive the benefit. The effect of Christ's promise as confined to the act of the sacrament of the eucharist later became readily confused with Calvin's view of spiritual real presence.

Melanchthon's *Loci communes* was a powerful and successful means by which he sought to clarify and teach elements of doctrine. The different editions of the *Loci communes* exhibit differences of emphasis as well as of content, reflecting the contemporary debates with which he was engaged and to which he was responding. The *process* of the shaping of his theology is an important key to understanding why he wrote what he did, in the way that he did, at a particular time.

BIBLICAL COMMENTARIES

Nowhere is the inappropriateness of the humanism–Reformation dichotomy clearer than in Melanchthon's biblical commentaries. A corollary of *sola scriptura* and the priesthood of all believers was that the Bible could and should be read by all believers. Melanchthon insisted that the meaning of the scriptural text was inherently clear, since the Holy Spirit expressed itself in it most accurately and most simply. As Meerhoff has shown, this meaning could be established by using dialectics and rhetoric, since, for Melanchthon, a methodical analysis of a text by uncovering its logical coherence was tantamount to reconstructing the actual process of creating a text and thus to disclosing the author's intention. By analysing the text through classical, rhetorical principles, the reader could therefore grasp the intention of the author. St Paul, as supreme orator and teacher, wrote according to these rules: he used rhetorical tropes, examples, paradigms, similes, allegory, and logical argument. Thus, those who have learnt their rhetoric and dialectics have the means by which to read and grasp the true message of the Bible. This in turn meant that humanistic studies such as the classical languages, rhetoric, and dialectics became fundamental and essential to the evangelical cause.

Together with his annotations to biblical texts, Melanchthon's commentaries indicate a new hermeneutical practice firmly rooted in humanist rhetoric and dialectic, as Schneider and Meerhoff have argued. Melanchthon prepared the Latin text of the Bible for publication (and classroom use) with 'annotations', marginal notes explaining the rhetorical *dispositio* of the text. As Wengert's work on Melanchthon's biblical commentaries indicates, these 'annotations' by Melanchthon, and his commentaries on those texts, indicate clearly his approach through *loci*. Paul's letter to the Romans, for instance, belongs to the didactic genre of writing, intended to teach a single theological point – the *scopus* of the text is justification by faith alone. Many such topics run through the whole of scripture and are not necessarily confined to a particular passage. Cross-citation of other biblical passages is given, not in order to lend authority to a particular interpretation, but as a 'gathering' (*congeries*) of passages that speak to the same topic. The belief that a particular biblical passage belonged to a larger commonplace guided Melanchthon's hermeneutics; it allowed him to interpret difficult passages or to pass over sentences that were 'unimportant'.

It also guided his attitude towards other authorities such as the church fathers, medieval theologians, and contemporary commentators on philological and interpretive points. As noted by Fraenkel, Meijering and Keen, he judged their interpretations in the light of whether they illuminated the truth, rather than trying to work within the consensus of human tradition, as Erasmus had done. Melanchthon's commentaries were not based on a fundamentalist position on the biblical text, but were underpinned by his sense of history, in which a succession of scholars illuminated the truth of the gospel with varying degrees of success. Melanchthon's notion of history, in which the history of the church is subsumed under the history of (Lutheran) doctrine, is consistent with the dogmatic assumption he makes about the *loci communes*. The ultimate meaning of a biblical text resided in a set of (pre-selected) *loci*; Melanchthon never discusses how he had come to choose particular topics, but the selection of topics was decidedly Lutheran – law and gospel, righteousness, grace, sin, letter and spirit.

Although Melanchthon's biblical commentaries mainly arose out of his classroom teaching, they also reflect his concerns about contemporary events and disputes. For instance, he first elaborated on the concept of law and penitence in the 1527 *Scholia to Colossians*, as the Lutheran catechisms printed in great numbers between 1525 and 1527 displayed widely divergent definitions and uses of those terms. Melanchthon's concept of law was further sharpened in the 1528 *Scholia to Colossians*, as the debate with his erstwhile student and colleague, Johann Agricola, on the use of law intensified. This debate, studied fully by Wengert, eventually led Melanchthon to develop in the third edition of the *Scholia* (1534) the third use of law and to emphasize the necessity of good works. Furthermore, Rosin has shown that in his commentary on Ecclesiastes (*Enarratio brevis concionum libri Salomonis*), the beleaguered Melanchthon saw in the text the topics of vocation, divine control, and God's providence. Man must be faithful in his vocation, even if others around him do not heed his advice or example or things do not turn out as desired or planned. Humans do not control the outcome of their best-laid plans, and those who have to fulfil their vocation in an age of hostility and adversity must trust in God's providential plan. Melanchthon's further comment that true worship is true doctrine (not ceremonies or rituals) suggests a defiant stance against the complaint of the Gnesio-Lutherans that the externals of worship were not *adiaphora* (inessential to salvation).

CONFESSIONAL WRITINGS

The emperor called a diet at Augsburg for the spring of 1530 in order to overcome the religious differences in the empire with a view to forming a united front against the Turkish threat. On the advice of Chancellor Brück, the elector of Saxony decided to ask the Wittenberg theologians to compose a statement of faith in which the religious beliefs and practices of the land were justified on theological grounds. This statement drew on the theological articles drawn up earlier as requisite conditions on which Saxony was prepared to enter an evangelical league (the Schwabach Articles). Additional articles were formulated at the court in Torgau on the delegation's way to Augsburg. The *Unterricht der Vistatoren* and Luther's Confession were also consulted for this statement. Although Melanchthon became the chief composer, Luther was kept informed of the additions and revisions.

This statement, as Maurer showed, became the Augsburg Confession, a set of confessional articles and a set of theses justifying the articles as not contradicting the scriptures or the teaching of the church as a whole. Electoral Saxony, Hesse, Brandenburg-Ansbach, Nuremberg, Reutlingen, Anhalt-Zerbst, and Lüneberg subscribed to it. Strasbourg, Lindau, Constance, and Memmingen submitted their own Tetrapolitan Confession, and Zwingli his *Ratio fidei*, which indicated the extent of disagreement within the evangelical camp over the Lord's supper.

The German text of the Augsburg Confession was read out on 25 June 1530, and both the Latin and German texts were presented to the emperor. The Confession emphasized the concept of secular order as established by God, condemned Anabaptists as heretical, and set out the evangelical position on justification, free will, and good works. The sacrificial character of the mass, papal primacy, and the concept of purgatory were not directly attacked. The Confession was more a statement to demonstrate how current evangelical practices were not contrary to scripture than a crisp theological manifesto, and several modern scholars have noted its non-polemical or 'pussy-footing' style.

In reply, the Roman Catholic *Confutation* was publicly read on 2 August 1530, after which the emperor declared the evangelical position refuted, and demanded submission by the Protestants. A counter-reply, penned by Melanchthon, was ready by 22 September, but was rejected by the emperor, and the diet was adjourned. Melanchthon's defence of the Augsburg Confession was published as the *Apology* in May 1531, in which many of the articles are given sharper, clearer exposition. Significantly, the text on the eucharist was altered to state that the body and blood of Christ were offered (*exhibeantur*) to Christ with the elements, possibly as a result of reading Oecolampadius' criticisms. The *Apology* achieved an important legal status when it was adopted, alongside the Augsburg Confession, by the Schmalkaldic League in 1537.

The uncompromising reaction of Charles V at Augsburg led the Protestant princes to subscribe to the Augsburg Confession at Schmalkalden on 30 December 1530, and a Protestant league was formally formed in

February 1531. But serious differences remained with other evangelical territories in southern Germany, which needed to be overcome for the proper function of the league. Bucer and Melanchthon, in consultation with Luther, sought to overcome these differences, particularly on the Lord's supper.

Bucer and Melanchthon arrived at an agreed statement at Kassel (December 1534), which stated that the bread and wine are signs (*signa exhibitiva*), and that when these are offered and taken, the body of Christ is offered and taken at the same time. This was adopted in the Wittenberg Concord (1536), in which the southern Germans accepted that even the 'unworthy' receive the real presence of Christ. The Lutherans in turn accepted the substitution of the word 'with' for 'in' with regard to the elements: the body and blood are truly and substantially present, offered, and received, *with* the bread and wine. The Wittenberg Concord allowed the southern German evangelicals to join the Schmalkaldic League.

In 1540, the Augsburg Confession was republished. The preface remained unchanged, but several significant amendments and expositions (the *Variata*) were made to the text. In general, the *Variata* drew a sharper distinction from the Catholics as well as from the Anabaptists. Certain ecclesiastical customs were explained as *adiaphora*, indifferent to salvation. Melanchthon also underscored the duty of princes to care for the church, and appealed to the emperor to call a council. Most famously, the text on the manner of Christ's presence in the Lord's supper was altered from *vere adsint* (truly present) to *vere exhibeantur* (truly presented). The body of Christ was now 'with the bread', rather than 'in the bread'. These reformulations reflect the wordings of the *Apology* and the Wittenberg Concord. The belief that Christ was truly present also sufficed for Luther. Despite the fact that the *Variata* later came to be viewed with great suspicion (as crypto-Calvinism), this was the official document presented by the Schmalkaldic League on 30 November 1540 at the Colloquy of Worms.

Melanchthon further composed the *Confessio doctrinae Saxonicarum ecclesiarum* in 1552, a confessional document for use in the churches of Saxon lands, followed by the *Corpus doctrinae Christianae* (1560). He sought to ensure a proper implementation of doctrine as propagated in these confessional documents by publishing various instructions: *Unterricht der Visitatoren*, the *Church Orders* for Meckelenburg, Heidelberg, and Wittenberg, and the *Examen ordinandorum* ('Test of ordinands').

POLEMICAL WRITINGS

If we see Melanchthon at his clearest, diplomatic, or even most pusillanimous in his confessional compositions, we can see an altogether harsher side in his polemic tracts written explicitly in response to tracts attacking him or Luther, such as the *Adversus Thomam Placentinum* (1521) and the *Defensio contra Johannem Eckium* (1518). Melanchthon knew his philosophy and Bible well enough to launch learned attacks – he could be biting and devastating, but he was not above name-calling or sarcasm. He was also skilful in producing popular propaganda using sensational pictures of unnatural portents, as has been studied by Scribner. One example was the 'Bapsteesel', or pope-ass, a creature with the head of an ass and the body of a woman, purportedly found dead in the Tiber in 1496. Melanchthon interpreted it as an omen against the papacy.

Polemical skirmishes also took place in the form of correspondence or prefaces to Luther's works, especially over the *adiaphora*. After the defeat of the Schmalkaldic League by the imperial forces in 1547, a diet was held in Augsburg, where the emperor sought to establish religious peace. A provisional ordinance was drawn up until a general council could resolve disputed doctrinal issues. After much negotiation and political manoeuvring, an ordinance was formulated that was to be imposed on the Protestants alone, in which a return to Catholic practices and ceremonies were stipulated, except for the marriage of priests and communion in both kinds. Melanchthon opposed this 'Augsburg Interim' on the basis of its explanation of justification, of invocation of saints, and of the sacrificial nature of the mass. Faced with a real threat of further war with the imperial troops, Melanchthon sought to win concessions more tolerant of evangelical doctrine by remaining flexible with *adiaphora*, ceremonies or external worship that were 'indifferent' to personal salvation. With the new Elector Moritz's theologians, Melanchthon sought to work out an alternative ordinance, for which they won the agreement of Joachim II of Brandenburg in 1548. It was then presented to the Saxon estates (December 1548) in Leipzig (the 'Leipzig Interim'). It advised on which practices were *adiaphora* and sought not to appear seditious. At the Treaty of Passau (1552) and the Peace of Augsburg (1555), these interim ordinances were suspended, but, in the mean time, Melanchthon came under fire from those who believed that he was selling out too much to the Catholics. Those who believed that they followed Luther's genuine teachings more strictly, such as Flacius, argued that true worship of God involved external worship too – the rite carried doctrines – whereas Melanchthon believed that externals of worship could be separated from pure doctrine in times of persecution.

The extent to which Melanchthon's theology was excluded from orthodox Lutheranism belongs to another chapter, but what should not be forgotten is the enormous influence he exerted in overseeing educational reforms in Protestant German universities and schools. Even his future foes had learnt their lesson well. In Melanchthon's hands, *sola scriptura* became, not a licence for obscurantism, but an obligation upon theologians to be properly trained in classical languages, dialectics, rhetoric, and philosophy; and political leaders were required to maintain such an education. Even philosophy, once the *bête noire* because of its propping up of scholastic theology, now had a reformed role to play – reason no longer proved theological truths, but it could still help to confirm divine truths, such as the providential design of God in nature and in history, and to demonstrate from natural law the necessity of civil obedience.

Melanchthon could marshal to the aid of Luther's cause the Bible, classical dialectics, rhetoric, works of the church fathers, past and contemporary theologians, and at times even those of pagan philosophers, as the range of books available at the university library at Wittenberg testifies. Using such varied sources and authorities could imply subjective eclecticism – to choose what one wants – just like bees collecting juice from a great variety of flowers. As Meijering noted, Melanchthon answered this possible charge, however, by saying that bees by nature avoid what is poisonous to them. Similarly, with the help of God, he could avoid false opinions. For Melanchthon, the false opinions were, on the Catholic side, works righteousness, communion in one kind, and the primacy of the pope; and, on the Protestant side, the purely memorial understanding of the eucharist, Anabaptism, antinomianism, antitrinitarianism, and sedition. Melanchthon strove to define the saving message of the gospel in contradistinction to these positions, using a great variety of sources, strategies and authorities. Depending on the particular task in hand, and the poles between which he was operating, his writings could display changes of emphasis, shifts in inflection, and even substantial alterations. His definitional clarity allowed many, including modern scholars, to take him out of context and pass judgement.

To view Melanchthon as a blind or misguided follower of Luther would be to ignore the extent of learning and the clarity he brought to doctrine, and the substantial contribution he made towards the formation of a Lutheran theology. His was a time of tumultuous change and great experiment, through which Lutheran theology was taking shape. His contribution was essential to that process.

7 Confessional Lutheran theology

ROBERT KOLB

Martin Luther's followers first defined themselves as a church through the Augsburg Confession of 1530, which was composed by Luther's Wittenberg colleague Philipp Melanchthon to explain the introduction by certain princes and cities of the German empire of ecclesiastical reforms in accord with Luther's theology. This confession not only served as a legal document defining the teaching of the churches of these governments for the emperor Charles V but also quickly became a guide for public teaching for Luther's adherents. Melanchthon's defence of its contents in his *Apology* of 1531, the Schmalkaldic Articles of faith (composed by Luther in 1537 as an agenda for confession at the papal council called in 1536), Luther's Large and Small Catechisms, and the Formula of Concord of 1577 were brought together with the Augsburg Confession and the ancient creeds as the summary definition of the faith for Lutheran churches in the *Book of Concord* of 1580. Seldom cited in theological argumentation during the period, these documents nonetheless provided the legal and theological parameters within which Lutheran theologians expressed and explored their faith. These documents mark the path of Lutheran theological confessionalization.

SOURCES OF LUTHERAN THEOLOGY

Out of Luther's exegesis and experience, his struggles with personal and pastoral questions in the 1510s, emerged a paradigm shift in the formulation of the Christian tradition. His own study of scripture, coupled with his existential struggles over his relationship to God, led him to focus above all on definitions of the righteousness of God and of the human creature. Key to his insight into the justification of the sinner was his distinction between active righteousness (human performance of God's law in relationship to other human beings) and passive righteousness (the gift of identity as a child of God, given after the fall through the work of Christ and through trust in him).

Scholastically trained, Luther made rich use of the church fathers but recognized only scripture as authority for teaching and life. From his nominalist teachers Luther had learned to regard God's Word as the instrument through which he accomplishes his will. Luther thus defined God's Word, given in scripture, as the active, effective tool through which God transforms sinners into his children and restores them to his kingdom; this view of the Word, deposited authoritatively in scripture, as God's 'means of grace', permeated Luther's thought. In expounding the Bible he abandoned the 'allegorical' methods of medieval exegesis and sought the literal, historical meaning of the text, presupposing that all scripture points to Christ, prophetically or historically. Key to Luther's approach to biblical teaching is his application of the Word through the distinction of law and gospel. According to the Wittenbergers' definition of these terms, *law* is any demand God makes for human action or performance; *gospel* is God's deliverance from the condemnation of the law through Jesus Christ. This critical hermeneutical distinction determined all his interpretation of God's Word. Luther's understanding of God's calling people to the tasks of everyday life shaped his ethics, within a structure set in place by the distinction between the two kinds of righteousness; responsible action towards God's creatures does not merit God's grace, but is the product of God's gracious restoration of the sinner to righteousness in God's sight.

The subsequent generation of Luther's followers viewed him as God's special end-time prophet, or at least as the last of the doctors of the church. They strove to repeat his insights while adapting them to the issues of their own parishes and principalities. They did so within the framework of the patristic and medieval theological inheritance, which they continued to put to use. Other evangelical theologians, especially but not exclusively Luther's Wittenberg colleagues, also profoundly influenced the further development of Lutheran theology. Most important among them were Melanchthon and the south German reformer Johann Brenz, who contributed to Lutheran theological formulation through biblical commentaries and treatises, above all on the Lord's supper and Christology.

METHODOLOGICAL FACTORS

Melanchthon's method definitively shaped subsequent practice of Lutheran theology. His explication of scripture through *loci* – topics – reflected the general methodological approach to learning he bequeathed to all academic disciplines. His use of Aristotelian principles within his own rhetorical-dialectical system of analysis determined the manner of

argumentation among Wittenberg students and pointed the way to a
Lutheran return to the employment of metaphysics at the turn of the seventeenth century. His recourse to patristic citation led students to study
and cite the fathers, albeit according to a Lutheran analogy of faith. The
Wittenberg confidence in the 'living voice of the gospel', as God's tool for
effecting his saving will in a fallen world, led Lutherans to make public
confession of their faith, interpreting scripture positively and at the same
time defending their concept of the truth against opponents in Roman
Catholic, Reformed, and 'radical' camps. This polemic reflected the ancient
Christian practice of condemning error. Luther and his contemporaries had
learnt from the scholastic method how to conduct a sharp exchange of ideas.
Papal attempts to execute the Wittenberg heretic and eradicate his following
made theological retaliation a necessary habit, which was strengthened over
the course of the sixteenth century by feelings of betrayal within Lutheran
circles and by the commitment to propagate the truth against false teaching.

   Following Luther's abandonment of allegorical interpretation, his disciples pursued a biblical hermeneutic comprensively summarized in the *Key
to the Sacred scriptures* of Matthias Flacius Illyricus, Melanchthon's former
student and colleague, who led opposition to his thought after the Leipzig
Interim. He employed Melanchthon's rhetorical tools to find the historical
significance of the text through grammatical, contextual, and textual study.
Biblical texts, he presumed, point to Christ, either in prophecy or in fulfilment, and have to be interpreted through the application of law and gospel.
Flacius also organized the research and writing of the first Protestant church
history, the 'Magdeburg Centuries,' using the *loci* method, and he published
other historical works, particularly aimed at proving that Luther's teaching
corresponded to the ancient, catholic confession of the church.

   Lutheran pastors and professors conveyed their mentors' theology
to parishioners through such works as biblical commentaries and postils
(collections of sermons on the readings for the Sunday services), devotional
literature in several genres, and catechisms. Scholars' concentration on their
dogmatic and polemical texts has skewed the picture of the indigenization of
Wittenberg theology in the period, which also dealt with pastoral and ethical problems in daily life. Luther's fundamental concern for the pastoral
care of sinners struggling with their own failings and with the challenges
of daily life continued to shape such works.

THE SETTING OF THE DEFINING DISPUTES

   Much of sixteenth-century Lutheran theology was formulated in the
midst of controversy over the proper definition of Luther's thought, and

against other churches' interpretations of the Christian tradition. Before his death, debates had begun within Luther's inner circle over the precise meaning of his insights. One of the brightest and best of his early students, Johann Agricola, had not understood his mentor's distinction of law and gospel. Thus, he argued that God's plan for human performance, expressed in the law, had no role for the daily life of believers. Luther and Melanchthon sharply repudiated this idea in two public disputes with Agricola (1527–8, 1537–40) because it undermined the life of daily repentance. Melanchthon and a former colleague, later a pastor in Magdeburg and evangelical bishop of Naumburg-Zeitz, Nikolaus von Amsdorf, privately argued over the necessity of good works in salvation, freedom of the will, the definition of the presence of Christ's body and blood in the Lord's supper, the relationship between the church and secular government, and the relationship of Lutheran church life to medieval practice and polity (1535–45).

These tensions broke into open, often bitter controversy among Luther's and Melanchthon's heirs after Luther's death (1546) because of political circumstances generated by the emperor Charles V's attempt to suppress the Lutheran faith after his military victory over the evangelical princes in 1547. Charles imposed on evangelical territories a plan for reform, called the 'Augsburg Interim', that essentially returned them to the Roman obedience and to a version of medieval doctrine and practice shaped by an 'Erasmian' reform ideal. The victorious emperor awarded Wittenberg to Duke Moritz of Saxony, a Lutheran who had supported the emperor in the war against his fellow evangelical princes. Under severe pressure from the emperor to introduce this policy of return to Rome, which was countered by strong resistance from his estates, Moritz enlisted as counsellors in composing a compromise plan his new theologians in Wittenberg, led by Melanchthon. The result of their deliberations with secular counsellors and Roman Catholic theologians, the so-called 'Leipzig Interim', led to bitter reactions from former students who believed that their 'Preceptor' was betraying the faith with his compromises over practice, particularly in liturgical matters, and with ambiguous formulations of critical doctrinal positions.

Luther's and Melanchthon's followers divided into two contending parties, with different approaches to four aspects of church life: (1) formulation of doctrine, especially in regard to justification, anthropology, and the Lord's supper; (2) continuation or simplification of medieval liturgical practice and related usages; (3) relationship of church and state; and (4) the public profile of confessing the faith. Since the eighteenth century the more radical interpreters of Luther have been called 'Gnesio-Lutherans.' They repeated and sometimes sharpened the reformer's views of passive righteousness and God's grace as well as of human sinfulness; they introduced simplified liturgical rites and resisted every attempt to reconcile with Rome; they argued strongly for the integrity of the church independent of governmental regulation of teaching and practice (although they accepted governmental direction of the secular side of church life); and they boldly, often confrontationally, confessed their positions. The 'Philippists', by contrast, found more conservative (from a medieval perspective) doctrinal expressions on certain issues, were open to co-operation with Roman Catholic bishops if they would permit Lutheran preaching, and tended towards more traditional ecclesiastical usages (although Philippists reversed this attitude by the late 1560s); they were prepared to co-operate and compromise with governmental authorities, and sought public harmony as they pursued the practice of theology, even if the cost of harmony was the suppression of open discussion of issues. Both groups used Melanchthon's methods and accepted many Melanchthonian doctrinal accents.

These two were not the only groupings within sixteenth-century Lutheranism; Brenz's 'Schwabian' followers, for instance, formed another distinct circle; many pastors of the period adhered to no 'party.'

In criticizing the Leipzig Interim's liturgical usages and related ecclesiastical customs, Gnesio-Lutherans recognized the significance of the means by which the message is conveyed to parishioners. Philippists wished to compromise in regard to externals (*adiaphora*) as a means of avoiding persecution; Gnesio-Lutherans maintained that the impressions received by parishioners had to be taken more seriously than the intentions of the theologians; therefore, they concluded, these compromises betrayed Luther's gospel, for they were conveying to the common people the impression that the differences between Luther's theology and that of the papacy were not significant. Once the political threat of persecution receded, the preoccupation with the significance of liturgy and other means of conveying the biblical message abated as well. In Lutheran orthodoxy, the focus was on the content of the proclamation and not on its setting and method of delivery.

After a quarter-century of dispute, the Formula of Concord (1577) provided a majority of German Lutherans with a settlement of the disputed issues and a guide for further teaching. Its agenda was determined by Gnesio-Lutheran charges against Philippist positions regarding freedom of the will, good works, and Philippist charges against Gnesio-Lutheran positions on original sin, election, the use of the law in the Christian life, the Lord's supper, and Christology. The Formula arose out of the diplomatic efforts of Jakob Andreae of the University of Tübingen; its theology stems above all from Martin Chemnitz, whose devotion to Melanchthon had not separated him from Gnesio-Lutheran associates, whose views he largely shared. His finely tuned revision of Andreae's initial efforts at formulating concord affirmed the Tübingen professor's acceptance of the views of the main body of Gnesio-Lutherans, but sensitively wove together treatments of the doctrinal disputes that took seriously many Philippist concerns.

CENTRAL THEOLOGICAL TEACHINGS

Justification of sinners in God's sight

In the 1550s both Gnesio-Lutherans and Philippists honed their teaching about justification in response to Andreas Osiander's teaching that sinners become righteous in God's sight when faith brings the essential righteousness of Christ's divine nature to dwell in them. A prominent advocate of Luther's Reformation as preacher in Nuremberg, Osiander fled to Königsberg from the enforcement of the Augsburg Interim (1550). There, discussions with colleagues revealed that the Neoplatonic philosophical framework of his early training in kabbalistic studies had rendered it impossible for Osiander to grasp Luther's presupposition regarding the power of God's Word to re-create children of God out of sinners. He thus imposed upon other Lutherans the need to clarify several elements in Luther's theology. Osiander believed that a 'merely' forensic definition of justification would make God a liar: he would call sinners righteous when they were not. His critics, such as Chemnitz, affirmed that God's Word of absolution, based upon Christ's obedience to the Father in his incarnation, death, and resurrection, saves sinners. Through his Word of gospel God creates the reality of a new birth as children of God for sinners whom he has chosen to be his own. The gospel conveys the benefits of Christ's death and resurrection, which take sin away and restore the original relationship between God and human creature through trust. Trust – faith (*fiducia*) understood as dependence and reliance – is the natural human reaction to God's love. Sinners, unable to trust in God because they are 'turned in upon themselves' (Luther), are restored to their humanity when the Holy Spirit effects trust in the crucified and risen Christ through the 'means of grace', the various forms of God's Word (oral, written, and sacramental).

Others compared Osiander's view of justification with that of medieval scholastic theology, even though his Neoplatonic presuppositions differed greatly from scholasticism's Aristotelian framework. Both systems, however, defined human righteousness before God as something internal to the Christian. Lutherans continued Luther's critique of scholastic views of grace, which posited co-operation between the human will and the Holy Spirit and which understood grace in terms of a *habitus* as defined by Aristotelian psychology. Though not all his followers articulated his distinction between active and passive righteousness, they insisted, against Roman doctrine, that grace is simply God's loving favour and steadfast mercy, and that human righteousness before him, created by his grace, consists only in the trust that relies upon his promise of salvation in Christ and through his incarnation, death, and resurrection.

Bondage or freedom of the will and eternal election

From their earliest theological engagement, Luther and Melanchthon wrestled with theological anthropology, focusing on the relationship between the human will and God's grace. Reflecting his nominalist training, Luther viewed the creator God as the almighty Lord. Reflecting his experience of his own failure to fulfil God's expectations, Luther had a profound realization of the spiritual weakness of fallen human creatures. He insisted that the will is bound to sin and unable to please God because original sin permeates fallen human thinking, identifying this question, used by Erasmus to criticize the Wittenberger's theology (1524–5), as a key to understanding scripture. Luther's view of the bondage of the will had as its corollary a doctrine of single predestination. He believed that before the foundation of the world God had chosen those to whom he would give the gift of faith (Eph. 1:3–14). Luther rejected the implication, however, that God's unconditioned, gracious choosing of believers meant that he had predestined some to damnation; for Luther's distinction between law and gospel framed his view both of election to faith and salvation and of the bondage of the will in sin and unbelief. God's law revealed that human efforts could not please God, and that fallen human strivings always denied God his true place in human life because they tried to master life through means other than God's love and humans' trust in him. God's gospel revealed that no human performance could ever secure God's favour, that reconciliation with God and the justification of human life rests alone on God's unconditioned mercy.

Although Melanchthon had defended Luther's understanding of the bondage of the will during his dispute with Erasmus, other interests later altered his position. Roman Catholic accusations of 'Stocisim', his fear of a deterministic doctrine that would make God responsible for evil, and his concern for responsible human action (particularly after he had seen the dissolute state of peasant life in the visitation of 1527–8) caused him to explore the function of the will. As a humanist concerned about good communication, he analysed how to formulate the appeal of the gospel to move the hearer's will. His descriptions of the will's openness to God's grace aroused suspicion in some who adhered to Luther's insistence on the bondage of the will. The Leipzig Interim's language regarding the will's ability to open itself to receive grace occasioned sharp controversy within the Wittenberg camp after 1555.

In their defence of their position, Melanchthon's Philippist followers attacked Cyriakus Spangenberg's repetition of Luther's views on the bondage of the will and eternal election, within the framework of the distinction of law and gospel. They repudiated Spangenberg's teaching that God had elected certain individuals who would be converted, accepted in grace, and destined for eternal salvation, countering that the revealed Word teaches that God wants to have mercy on all. Spangenberg agreed, but also taught that the gospel rests on the assurance that no human contribution makes believers eligible for the gift of faith and that God had chosen them without condition before the foundation of the universe.

Chemnitz led the Concordists in encompassing concerns of both sides. The Formula of Concord acknowledged that the will functions psychologically but resists God until the Holy Spirit moves it to faith. The human contribution to conversion is therefore totally passive, as the Spirit uses the Word to turn the will to trust in Christ. The Formula distinguished God's foreknowledge from his eternal election, which determined who would come to faith in Christ; they can be certain of God's electing love through their reception of his promise of salvation in the means of grace.

Human sinfulness

Corresponding to Luther's understanding of grace, his concept of sin defined original sin as the failure to fear, love, and trust in God above all things. Sin is rooted in doubt and distrust of God and his Word. All acts of sin arise from this failure to base life upon God's presence, promise, and plan for his children. In defending Luther's view of the will, Flacius met the challenge of the Philippist Viktorin Strigel's definition of original sin as (in Aristotelian terms) an 'accident' by calling it the formal 'substance' or 'essence' of the fallen sinner. Flacius granted that the material 'substance' of the sinner remained human, with the structures and capabilities of humanity created by God, even if damaged by the fall into sin. But to be human meant, above all, Flacius believed, to love and trust God. When true knowledge of and trust in God were displaced by faith in some false source of life, sinners existed 'in the image of Satan', and were in their essence sin.

The Formula rejected Flacius' equation of the essence of the fallen human creature with sin itself, teaching instead that if Aristotelian language was to be used, sin should be seen as an 'accident' that has corrupted human nature and destroyed its relationship with God but is forgiven through Christ. Although that corruption diverts trust from God throughout human life, God's commitment to those chosen to be his own returns them to faith.

The law in the Christian life and the Christian callings

In defending the Leipzig Interim, Wittenberg professor Georg Major had espoused its proposition that 'good works are necessary for salvation'. His former colleague in Magdeburg, Nikolaus von Amsdorf, recalled that fifteen years earlier Magdeburg's Roman party had wanted to burn them for condemning this very assertion. He attacked Major for returning to papal doctrine, at the same time affirming that good works are a necessary part of Christian living. Amsdorf was certain that the laity would understand the proposition as claiming that good works earn salvation. Major intended instead to find a formula for compromise with the papal threat and to support moral living among the laity.

A synod in Eisenach (1556), called to deal with Major's view of good works, condemned his proposition but affirmed that 'good works are theoretically necessary for salvation in the doctrine of the law'. Some of Luther's close associates (Amsdorf, Anton Otho, Andreas Poach) rejected this proposition (though it was supported by some of Major's sharpest critics, including Flacius) because it posited a human righteousness before God based on human works rather than solely on his favour. They argued that this righteousness was passive, and that, even apart from sin, it could not be based on human works but is only a gift of God. In this context, Poach and Otho shared the view of Andreas Musculus, professor at Frankfurt on Oder, that the law had only two uses or functions: to regulate behaviour (the political use) and to accuse and crush sinners (the theological use), thus rejecting Melanchthon's third use, to instruct Christians in God's will. Poach, Otho, and Musculus believed that, 'in so far as they trust God', believers do good works spontaneously, 'from a free and merry spirit'. The law's accusation brings them to repentance, and they need no information on pious living from the law. This view reflects a fear that the third use of the law would bring believers to trust in their own works. The Formula affirmed this informative use of the law in believers' lives while making it clear that the law does not motivate pious living, which springs alone from faith in Christ.

In this period Luther's understanding of the relationship between the vertical and horizontal realms of human life (often falsely called his 'doctrine of the two kingdoms') was not clearly taught by many of his followers, but they did employ his understanding of God's calling to service and obedience in the callings of daily life in church, in the political realm and also the family and economic spheres of life.

The Lord's supper and Christology

Luther's last attack on the Zurich doctrine of the Lord's supper came in 1544, and was directed at Zwingli's successor, Heinrich Bullinger. A brief interlude in the controversial exchanges ensued; but in the Zurich Consensus of 1549 Bullinger won the agreement of John Calvin and his Genevan colleagues for a strong 'Zwinglian', 'symbolic' explanation of Christ's presence in the sacrament. A series of disputes erupted between Lutherans and followers of Calvin and Bullinger; in the late 1560s parallel debates developed among Melanchthon's students regarding Christ's presence in the supper and related Christological issues.

In 1552, Joachim Westphal, a pastor in Hamburg, attacked Calvin for his acceptance of the Zurich Consensus; Calvin replied, accusing Westphal and other Lutherans of teaching consubstantiation. Westphal repeated Luther's assertion that every Aristotelian attempt at explanation should be set aside to affirm the literal understanding of Christ's words of institution, 'This is my body; this is my blood.' In the early 1550s, the views of Albert Hardenberg, a follower of Martin Bucer and a pastor in Bremen, who emphasized God's gracious giving in the sacrament and avoided precise definition of Christ's presence in it, came under attack by another Bremen clergyman, Johann Timann. Both of them Dutch-born and Wittenberg-educated, they represented different interpretations of Melanchthon's and Luther's sacramental theology. Timann not only echoed Luther's insistence that Christ's words of institution must be understood literally, but also repeated his Christological argument that it is possible for Christ's body and blood to be present in bread and wine because of the ancient doctrine of the communication of attributes between Christ's divine and human nature (e.g. in his *Confession concerning Christ's Supper* of 1528). Hardenberg's position caused concern throughout neighbouring Lower Saxon Lutheran ministeria; in 1561 they rejected his position. Their own critique was supported by a work of Chemnitz, one of their number, in his *Recapitulation of the Correct Doctrine of the True Presence of the Lord's Body and Blood in the Supper.* That work marshalled copious biblical and patristic citations to affirm Luther's teaching on the Supper.

The accession of Frederick III to the electorate of the Palatinate (1559) brought the first Calvinist to a German princely throne. His dismissal of his ecclesiastical superintendent and theological professor in Heidelberg, Tilemann Hesshus, a dedicated disciple of Melanchthon, over the Lord's supper, opened another front in this debate. Melanchthon opposed Hesshus' confession that Christ's body and blood are truly present in the Supper and his insistence on using Luther's test phrases for the affirmation of that presence, 'oral partaking of Christ's body and blood' and 'the partaking of Christ's body and blood by the impious'.

In 1564, Friedrich's theologians met the theologians of the Lutheran Duke Christoph of Württemberg in a colloquy at Maulbronn. The Palatine delegation categorically rejected the Württemberg position, insisting that Christ's body and blood are not received orally or by unbelievers but that faith receives Christ spiritually. The colloquants also addressed the definition of 'God's right hand' and the 'locality' of Christ's human nature after the ascension. The Heidelberg theologians contended that the right hand is a place in a physical heaven where Christ's body must remain, and thus he cannot be present in the sacrament. The Lutherans argued that the biblical term designates Christ's possession of the divine characteristics of power and majesty. They also asserted that in the communication of the attributes between the two natures both natures enjoy those attributes in the unity of Christ's person even if they belong, strictly speaking, only to the divine nature. Württemberg spokesman Jakob Andreae argued that God can be present in three distinct ways: according to his Godhead, in grace, and in Christ. Christ can be present in three ways: according to his normal humanity, in his glorified body, and at the right hand of God. Without denying the distinctiveness of each of the two natures of Christ, Andreae insisted on their inseparability in the personal union. On this basis he taught a doctrine of the communication of attributes that posited that the divine nature shares its characteristics, including omnipresence, with the human nature.

Melanchthon had earlier expressed discomfort with the Christological argument for Luther's definition of the real presence. His colleagues in Wittenberg objected to the position of the Württemberg theologians and to Chemnitz's views as well. In his *On the Two Natures in Christ* Chemnitz sharpened Luther's doctrine of the communication of attributes by distinguishing three *genera* of this sharing of characteristics between the two natures. The first kind, the *genus idiomaticum,* was generally accepted by all contemporary theologians and stated that the characteristics peculiar to either of the natures were the characteristics of the entire person of Christ. The second kind, the *genus apotelesmaticum,* taught that in his redemptive actions each nature within Christ performed what is peculiar to itself, with the participation of the other. The third kind of sharing characteristics, *genus maiestaticum,* asserted that Christ's divine nature shares with his human nature all his divine characteristics for common possession, use, and designation within the one person of Christ. On the basis of the the third genus, Chemnitz affirmed that the human nature, and thus Christ's body and blood, could be present when and where God willed, including in the Lord's supper. He believed, not that this doctrine proved the presence of Christ's body and blood in the Lord's supper, but that it made the real presence possible.

Both fundamental arguments for Luther's understanding of Christ's presence in the sacrament – that the words of institution were to be interpreted literally and that his bodily presence is possible because of the communication of attributes between his two natures – rested on convictions learnt from nominalism. The Heidelberg theologians had grounded their rejection of his view on the philosophical principle that *finitum non est capax infiniti* (the finite cannot convey the infinite). Chemnitz and others followed Luther in arguing that God in his almighty power is bound by no such philosophical principles, that his Word is utterly reliable as he speaks it in scripture, and that he can and does use selected elements of the created order – his own human flesh, the sacramental elements, human language – to effect his plan of salvation.

The Formula of Concord effectively brought to an end most of the controversies that had plagued the Lutheran churches through the previous quarter of a century. A remnant of Flacius' followers repudiated its teaching on original sin, and some Philippists, along with the Calvinists of Germany, rejected its articles on the Lord's supper and Christology. Nonetheless, the Formula laid the groundwork and set the standard for the public teaching of 'Lutheran orthodoxy'. It remained the public faith of much of Germany, of Scandinavia, Finland, Estonia, and Latvia, and of frequently persecuted minority churches in several lands of central Europe throughout the early modern period.

8 The theology of Zwingli

W. PETER STEPHENS

Huldrych Zwingli was born in January 1484, just six weeks after Luther. His life and ministry developed differently from Luther's and some of the differences in context, education, and experience are factors in explaining the differences in their ministry and theology. Swiss patriotism influenced Zwingli as a boy, as Swiss humanism influenced him as a young man. His education in Vienna and Basel introduced him to scholasticism as well as to humanism, with the study of the writings of Peter Lombard, Thomas Aquinas, and Johannes Duns Scotus. The influence of the old way (*via antiqua*) contrasts with the influence on Luther of the modern way (*via moderna*). Zwingli was ordained in 1506 and served for a decade as priest in Glarus. His patriotism was expressed in his earliest surviving work, *The Ox*, an attack on Swiss mercenaries fighting for foreign powers. His experience of war as a chaplain deepened this opposition, especially the battle at Marignano (1515), in which thousands died fighting as mercenaries against the French. While at Glarus, Zwingli met Erasmus, who had a decisive impact on him. His crucial turning 'to Christ and to scripture' dates from this period. As a result, his reading shifted from the classics to the fathers, not least Augustine, and scripture.

After two years in Einsiedeln, a great centre of pilgrimage and Marian devotion, Zwingli was called to Zurich. His ministry there began on 1 January 1519 and lasted till his death in the battle of Kappel on 11 October 1531. In that period his influence went beyond Zurich to other cities in Switzerland and south Germany. His writings often reflect his engagement with supporters and opponents, especially conservatives and radicals in Zurich and Luther in Wittenberg. His early death meant that his theology was mediated in large part by others, especially Bullinger. Bullinger succeeded him in Zurich five years before Calvin went to Geneva in 1536, and was still there in 1575, eleven years after Calvin's death.

THE INFLUENCE OF LUTHER, ERASMUS, AND AUGUSTINE

The relationship of Zwingli with Luther and Erasmus is a major issue in Zwingli study – and scholars' views of this relationship often colour or reflect their interpretations of Zwingli's theology. Zwingli claimed that he became a reformer independently of Luther, when he turned to Christ and scripture, probably in 1516. Zwingli later invoked God as witness that he had learnt the gospel from John, Augustine's tractates on John, and Paul's epistles. He referred to Thomas Wyttenbach's disputation in Basel, probably in 1515, which showed indulgences to be a deceit, and also to the poem of Erasmus, from which he derived his faith that no one except Christ can mediate between God and us. As Zwingli regarded the fundamental difference between himself and his opponents as that between trusting in Christ and his atoning death, and trusting in the creature, he naturally regarded his discovery of that as a turning point.

This seems to be the decisive stage in his development, rather than the final one, for Zwingli's fully Reformation writings date from 1522. Yet he saw continuity between his understanding of the gospel in 1522 and what he held earlier in Zurich and Einsiedeln, a period in which most scholars see him as an Erasmian rather than as a reformer. Like Bucer, however, Zwingli saw continuity rather than discontinuity between Erasmus and Luther and recognized that God had raised up both of them.

Whatever one's views of the influence of Erasmus and Augustine on Zwingli's becoming a reformer, there is striking kinship between Zwingli and them. In common with Erasmus, Zwingli stressed the inwardness of religion and was critical of outward ceremonies. His way of interpreting the Bible shows Erasmus' influence, as does his emphasis on the gospels and the role of Christ as teacher and example. Like Erasmus, he understood the word 'sacrament' as 'oath', and in the eucharist accented John 6:63. The influence of Augustine on Zwingli's eucharistic theology is evident in his marginal notes on Augustine's tractates on John. It is present in the strong sense of the sovereignty of God, which characterizes the whole of Zwingli's theology, but especially the doctrine of predestination and the need to be taught by God.

THE BIBLE

The Bible was fundamental in Zwingli's ministry, as it was in his theology. In January 1519 he began to preach on St Matthew. He did not, however, preach on the passage for the day, as was the custom, but worked consecutively through the gospel, as some of the fathers had done. He then preached on Acts, 1 and 2 Timothy, Galatians, 1 and 2 Peter, and Hebrews, saying, 'This is the seed I have sown. Matthew, Luke, Peter, and Paul have watered it, and God has given it splendid increase.' Eventually he preached from most of the Bible, Old Testament as well as New. He was confident in the power of God's Word, which 'will as surely have its way as the Rhine, which you can stem for a while, but not stop'.

From June 1525 the preaching was supplemented by the 'prophecy' held daily except on Fridays and Sundays. The Hebrew and Greek text of the Old Testament was expounded in Latin before a final public exposition in German, the language of the people. For Zwingli, only by such a fundamental study of scripture could the church's preaching be free from error, both that of conservatives appealing to tradition and that of radicals appealing to the Spirit. The prophecy led to major biblical commentaries, and in 1531 to the Zurich Bible.

The Bible was at the centre, not only of preaching and the prophecy, but also of the disputations, which were to become a feature of the Zwinglian Reformation. Thus at the first disputation in January 1523 he pointed to the Bible, which had been brought into the assembly in Hebrew, Greek, and Latin, as the judge. He asserted that the sixty-seven articles that he was defending were based on the Bible. In this and in every subsequent debate he appealed to the authority of the Bible over against the authority of the church and its traditional teaching.

The authority of the Bible lay in its being God's Word, as opposed to man's word. Man's word included the teaching of the fathers, councils, and popes. There is no disharmony in scripture, as it derives from the Spirit, who is the Spirit of concord. Therefore, like Bucer, he argued for the agreement of apparently inconsistent passages. Moreover, unlike Luther, he did not have a canon within the canon. His appeal was to the whole of scripture. In his early writings there is frequently a contrast between the Old Testament and the New, but from 1525 he stressed their unity. This is related to his developing the view that the Bible has only one covenant, not two.

The reformers shifted the starting point of debate to scripture as alone authoritative, but controversy led them to develop various principles of interpretation. Against conservatives, whom he accused of using human reason to find scriptural support for their personal views, Zwingli stressed the necessity of the Spirit as the author in reading and interpreting scripture, for we must all be taught by God. He characteristically spoke of Spirit and Word, in contrast to Luther's Word and Spirit, for without the Spirit one cannot understand the Word. However, Zwingli challenged the appeal of some radicals to the Spirit, when there were clear passages of scripture against their position, as being an appeal to their own spirit rather than to the Holy Spirit, who is the author of scripture.

Zwingli's principles of interpretation show the influence of Augustine and Erasmus. They include the distinction of letter and spirit, which can be the Augustinian one between the letter and the Holy Spirit, or the more Erasmian one between the literal and the spiritual meaning.

In controversy, Zwingli appealed to faith and scripture, showing his indebtedness to Augustine and Erasmus. The appeal to faith is related to Augustine's use of Isaiah 7:9, 'If you do not believe, you will not understand.' For Zwingli, such faith was faith in Christ as the Son of God, who died for us. We know therefore that there is a trope if the literal interpretation of a passage conflicts with such faith. The principle of the glory of God is similar to that of faith. Where there are two contradictory passages of scripture, then the one that ascribes glory to God is to be accepted. The appeal to scripture shows Zwingli's indebtedness to Erasmus: for example, in comparing various passages of scripture, in understanding a passage in context, and in employing the various senses of scripture (natural, moral, mystical). For Zwingli, as for the other reformers, the natural sense was fundamental. Alongside the natural sense is the moral sense, for there is nothing in the Bible that does not teach, admonish, or console. The moral sense underlies the prayer at the beginning of the prophecy: 'Open and illuminate our minds, that we may understand your oracles in a pure and holy way and be transformed into that which we have rightly understood.'

Zwingli also saw the mystical sense as a biblical way of interpreting scripture (1 Corinthians 10:6, 11). The allegorical interpretation of the Old Testament is related to the New Testament and above all to Christ, who is the fulfilment of scripture. In the allegorical interpretation Zwingli was dependent on Origen, but he also criticized him for not treating a passage as historical. Zwingli was also more Christological in his interpretation than Origen. He frequently used typology, with Noah, Isaac, Joseph, and Moses serving as types of Christ.

The Old Testament was to be interpreted in the light of the New. Thus, in rejecting the Old Testament arguments of conservative opponents for the eucharist as a sacrifice, Zwingli held that one can find implicit in the Old only what is explicit in Christ. Against radicals who insisted on using only the New Testament, however, Zwingli defended his use of the Old on the basis that Christ and the apostles appealed to the Old Testament (John 5:39; Romans 15:4; 1 Corinthians 10:11).

Zwingli's insistence on the authority of scripture did not involve a simply negative attitude to the fathers, councils, or even the Schoolmen. They were used to support scriptural arguments and interpretations. This is particularly evident in the eucharistic controversy, when he made use especially of the fathers.

More striking is his use of pagan authors. This is particularly obvious in his *Commentary on True and False Religion* and *The Providence of God*. It is evidence of a humanist stamp on his theology. Zwingli sometimes uses non-Christian writers before arguing his case from the Bible. This may be simply a way of persuading those to whom non-Christian writers would be persuasive, but it also arises from his conviction, shared with fathers such as Jerome and Augustine, that 'all truth is from God'.

CHRIST

In 1515–16 Zwingli turned to Christ as well as to scripture. In 1523 he related his conviction that 'we need no mediator except Christ' to his reading of a poem of Erasmus's in which Jesus laments that we do not seek all that is good from him although he is the source of all good. He added the characteristic words, 'Why do we seek help in the creature?'

Faith is in Christ as God, and in him over against the creature, that is anything created, whether the sacraments or pilgrimages or works. To speak of Zwingli's theology as theocentric is not to detract from the centrality of Christ in his theology (though some take it that way), for Zwingli's emphasis is on Christ as God. On the title page of his works he regularly quoted the text, 'Come to me, all who labour and are heavy laden, and I will give you rest' (Matthew 11:28).

It is as Son of God that Christ saves us, by fulfilling the will of God. It is as man, however, that he can be the sacrifice that satisfies the righteousness of God. Salvation is related most frequently to Christ's death as satisfying the righteousness of God. Yet this Anselmian view is not the only interpretation of Christ's death. Like Irenaeus, Zwingli spoke of Christ's recapitulating all that happened in Adam, like Athanasius he spoke of Christ's becoming human so that we might become divine, and like Abelard he spoke of the love of God displayed in Christ. Christ's death is also presented as a victory over sin, death, and the devil. Nevertheless, the dominant stress is Anselmian.

Zwingli followed Augustine in seeing the death of Christ as effective for those who lived before Christ. Old Testament believers believed in the Christ who is to come, whereas New Testament ones believed in the Christ who has come. Zwingli also related the salvation of the Gentiles to Christ. He drew on biblical examples, such as Jethro and Cornelius. He argued from Malachi 1:11 that Gentiles before Christ sacrificed to the one true God. Their sacrifices were related to the one sacrifice of Christ. Following Augustine he argued that Gentiles who show by their works that the law is written on their hearts have faith. This, however, is not their achievement, 'For through Christ must come all who come to God.'

After Zwingli's death Luther was scandalized by a passage in Zwingli's *Exposition of the Faith*. It was a vision of heaven that included non-Christians such as Socrates. For Luther this meant that there was no need of Christ, or the sacraments, or scripture. Many have interpreted this vision as showing the influence of Renaissance thought on Zwingli, of which perhaps Erasmus' 'Holy Socrates, pray for us' is the best-known example. A careful study of Zwingli's writings, however, shows that he never relates salvation to human works or to free will, but to God. Salvation is rooted in God's election, Christ's death, which reaches as far as Adam's fall, and the freedom of the Spirit. There may be problems with his case, but it is argued biblically.

GOD

Whereas *The Exposition of the Articles* begins with statements about Christ, some works begin with God and with the knowledge of God. This could reflect a theological approach in which Christ is not the starting point, but it could also reflect the creed, which begins with belief in God rather than in Christ. Zwingli's discussion of the knowledge of God is scholastic. He made the traditional distinction between the knowledge of God's existence and the knowledge of his nature. He held that most people have been aware of God's existence, but he did not regard the knowledge of God as inherent in people. He argued from Romans 1:19 that such knowledge comes from God. Religion, also, is not natural to people, but dependent on God. In a reference to Adam, Zwingli said that religion 'took its rise when God called runaway man back to him'.

A sense of God's sovereignty is central to Zwingli's understanding and experience of God. It was influenced by non-Christian writers, such as Seneca, as well as by Christian writers such as Augustine, but also by Zwingli's personal experience, in particular of the plague in 1519. This probably confirmed his sense of God's sovereignty. It is expressed in his understanding of providence and predestination. In *The Providence of God* Zwingli sought to make a logically coherent case for the doctrine of providence, beginning from the nature of God as the highest good. He drew on Plato and Aristotle, Pliny, Plutarch, Pythagoras, and Seneca in a consciously philosophical approach to the subject. Some take this strongly philosophical approach as evidence that Zwingli's view was more philosophical than biblical, others that this work was a relapse into humanism. However, Zwingli's position was derived from scripture. He could write, 'The whole scripture of the Old Testament views everything as done by the providence of God.'

The conviction that salvation depends on God and not on our free will or works was expressed in the doctrine of providence, which maintains that God is the cause of all things. From 1526 – particularly in controversy with Anabaptists, who introduced the matter by their reference to Romans 9:11–13 – Zwingli began to argue in terms of predestination rather than of providence. He countered the Anabaptist appeal to faith as necessary for salvation by an appeal to election, which lies behind faith. Some are elect who have not yet come to believe. Faith is a sign of election in adults, but its absence in children is not a sign that they will be damned.

Zwingli's emphasis is on election rather than reprobation, even if the first implies the second. For him it is not that election flows from God's mercy and reprobation from his righteousness – rather, election comes from the goodness of God, which embraces his righteousness and his mercy. Like Calvin later, Zwingli rejected the view that God elects people when he foresees what they will be like. Election is rooted in God's will.

Zwingli discussed whether we can know if we or others are elect. Unlike some later Reformed and Puritan writers, he was not primarily concerned with this issue. He was concerned rather to attack the view that salvation depends on our faith and love, by asserting that salvation depends on God's election. We can, however, know from our works as well as from our faith that we are elect. On occasion Zwingli regarded faith and good works or their absence as evidence about the election of others. Yet elsewhere he recognized that we can be mistaken about others, for we can judge only by appearance. The stress on election can raise questions about the role of Christ, though Zwingli always insisted that election is in Christ, not apart from him.

THE SPIRIT

The emphasis on the centrality and sovereignty of God is evident also in the role of the Spirit and in Zwingli's insistence on his freedom. The Holy Spirit is nevertheless clearly related to Christ. The Spirit was sent by Christ at Pentecost in place of Christ. The text 'I will not leave you orphans' is paraphrased in the words: 'Then after the ascension I will be present with you in my Spirit.' Zwingli also spoke, however, of the Spirit as the creator Spirit who, because he created the whole universe and not just Palestine, is not limited to Palestine in his continuing work.

Zwingli refers to the Spirit as being at work in the writing of the law in the hearts of those who are not Christians, as in Romans 2. He followed Augustine in seeing the law of nature in terms of the Spirit. The work of the Spirit in non-Christians is related to Christ, however, as they were elected in Christ before the foundation of the world. Zwingli's insistence on the freedom of the Spirit is explicit when he writes of God's speaking 'also through sibyl prophetesses among the Gentiles, that we might recognize the liberty of his will and the authority of his election'.

The freedom of the Spirit is affirmed in the frequent use of 'The Spirit blows where he will' (John 3:8) and 'It is the Spirit who gives life, the flesh is of no avail' (John 6:63). He is not bound to Word and sacrament so that he must act through them or so that he cannot act apart from them. To assert the contrary is to make salvation dependent on human action. It is the Spirit not Word and sacrament, who gives faith. Word and sacrament are ineffective without the Spirit, but the Spirit is not ineffective without them. He does not need them, though they need him.

Zwingli's concern, however, is to affirm the Spirit rather than to deny the place of Word and sacrament, 'for we are to be taught outwardly by the Word of God and inwardly by the Spirit'. Ironically, the article on the outward Word drawn up by Luther at Marburg could have been written by Zwingli. It states that ordinarily the Spirit does not give faith to anyone without the Word and that the Spirit creates faith where and in whom he wills. Nevertheless, there is a difference between them, for Luther spoke of Word and Spirit, whereas Zwingli spoke of Spirit and Word, since for Zwingli the Word, even the words of Jesus and the apostles, is not effective without the Spirit.

Alongside the stress on the freedom of the Spirit, which reflects John and Augustine, and the insistence that only the Spirit can produce faith, there is in Zwingli's understanding a Platonist stress on the contrast between flesh and spirit. This is an element in the way he speaks of the Spirit, especially in his discussion of the sacraments and in his use of a text such as John 6:63. There is also a tension in Zwingli's anthropology between a Pauline and a Platonist view of flesh and spirit. Flesh is used both of the whole person as flesh and of what is outward, just as spirit can be used of the Holy Spirit and of what is inward. What is outward cannot affect what is inward, and therefore the sacraments, which are outward, cannot affect the mind or spirit, which are inward.

SACRAMENTS

Zwingli did not like the word 'sacrament'. It was not biblical. It was not German. It was, moreover, misunderstood, for when people hear the word 'sacrament', 'they think of something great and holy which by its own power can free the conscience from sin'. He repudiated this view in its conservative and Lutheran form. (The sovereignty of God meant that the

Spirit is not bound by the sacraments or limited to them, while Zwingli's Platonism meant that the outward could not affect the inward.) Following Augustine's definition of a sacrament as 'a sign of a sacred thing', he insisted that a sign cannot be what it signifies, otherwise it ceases to be a sign. He followed Erasmus in regarding a sacrament as an oath. At first he spoke of God's oath, but later – more subjectively – of our oath. From 1525, with a changed view of covenant, he called them signs of God's covenant of grace.

Zwingli always held that sacraments could not give faith, but initially he held that they could strengthen it. His early view that Christ gave us sacraments because 'our eyes want to see' was developed later to argue that sacraments strengthen faith by appealing to our senses.

BAPTISM

Zwingli's views on the sacraments were largely expressed in contro- versy – on baptism mostly with Anabaptists and on the eucharist mostly with conservatives and Lutherans. Before the refusal of some radicals to baptize their infants, and then, in 1525, the first rebaptisms, Zwingli wrote little on baptism. In what he wrote he emphasized faith rather than baptism and insisted that baptism is not necessary for the salvation of infants. His concern was that those baptized as infants should not be confirmed until they could confess their faith. He later rejected his earlier view that baptism could strengthen faith.

From December 1524, Zwingli used a range of arguments in support of infant baptism. He presented baptism as initiation 'both of those who have already believed and those who are going to believe' and argued that infant baptism replaced circumcision, which infants received before believing, and that forbidding the baptism of infants meant forbidding them to come to Christ (Matthew 19:13–14). He held that it is more likely than not that children were in the households baptized in 1 Corinthians 1 and Acts 16, and insisted that the New Testament, while not explicitly commanding infant baptism, does not forbid it.

In the course of controversy, Zwingli elaborated these arguments and developed new ones. He accused conservatives and Anabaptists of overem- phasizing outward baptism, for 'no outward element or action can purify the soul'. Baptism is a pledge. He held that baptism should be given to infants as, being the children of Christians, they are part of God's people.

In 1525 Zwingli moved from describing baptism as our pledge to God, to speaking of it as God's pledge to us. It is the sign of God's covenant of grace. It is his promise to us rather than ours to him. This understanding of pledge as God's rather than ours fits better than the earlier understanding, where pledge is a pledging of oneself in adult baptism and a pledging of one's children in infant baptism. Zwingli also began to argue that in the Bible there is only one covenant, not two. This enabled him to argue that, as children in the Old Testament received the sign of the covenant before having faith, so should our children.

The argument from election also began to be used, so that Zwingli could assert that elect infants are members of God's people though as yet they have no faith. He used election against the Anabaptist linking of baptism and faith, however, rather than as the basis of his case for infant baptism. Two propositions were fundamental to Zwingli's case: children belong to God and therefore should be baptized, and baptism replaces circumcision. Moreover, God is not less gracious now than he was before Christ. Zwingli rejected the view that unbaptized infants are damned. Salvation does not depend on baptism, or indeed on faith, but ultimately on election.

THE EUCHARIST

The term 'Zwinglian' is most often used of Zwingli's view of the eucharist. This is often misunderstood as his believing in the real absence, while others believed in the real presence. In reality, Zwingli insisted on Christ's presence, but according to his divine, not his human nature.

The reformers broadly agreed with Luther in criticizing the offering of the mass as a sacrifice for the living and the dead and communion in one kind. Zwingli appealed to the New Testament to support communion in both kinds and to assert the sufficiency and unrepeatability of Christ's sacrifice, of which the eucharist is a commemoration. It is notable that as early as 1523, long before the controversy with Luther, he preferred the term 'memorial' to Luther's term 'testament'.

Some scholars think that Zwingli changed to a symbolic view after his early writings, but a symbolic view is at least implicit in his writings in 1522–3. Their stress is on the body and blood of Christ as slain for us, not eaten, and, in expounding John 6, Zwingli placed the emphasis on faith ('eating is believing') and on the soul's being fed.

He expounded the symbolic view explicitly after reading Hoen's letter, which argued for interpreting 'is' in 'This is my body' as 'signifies'. Zwingli stated that Hoen helped him to see that the trope was in the word 'is'. (Oecolampadius saw it as in 'my body' and Carlstadt as in 'this'.) He later adduced the parallel with the Passover, stating that the disciples would understand 'This is my body' in the light of 'The lamb is the Passover.' By analogy with the Passover, Zwingli argued that the eucharist was given for commemoration and thanksgiving and not for bodily eating. Contrary to what Luther wrote of him, Zwingli did not argue that because 'is' means 'signifies' in some cases in the Bible, it must mean 'signify' in 'This is my body'. Rather, he gave reasons why it must mean 'signify'.

In the controversy with Luther he argued his case in terms of faith and scripture. The argument from faith contrasted two ways of salvation: the one by eating the body of Christ and the other by believing in him. The argument from scripture drew especially on St John's gospel. In his treatment of John 6, Zwingli followed Augustine in interpreting 'eating' as 'believing' and not as a reference to sacramental eating. The key text against bodily eating was 6:63: 'It is the Spirit who gives life, the flesh is of no avail.' We eat spiritually. John also provided examples of alloiosis (the sharing or interchange of properties). Zwingli used alloiosis to explain passages which appear to ascribe to one of Christ's natures what belongs to the other and to reconcile apparently conflicting passages, such as 'I am with you always', which refers to the divine nature, and 'You will not always have me', which refers to the human nature. Zwingli sharply distinguished the two natures. According to his divine nature, Christ is omnipresent, and so he is here and at the right hand of the Father. According to his human nature, he is not here, for after his resurrection he ascended into heaven. For Zwingli, Luther denied Christ's humanity by denying that Christ's body is in one place. He used many texts about the resurrection and ascension, as well as the clauses of the creed that speak of Christ's ascension, session, and coming in glory, to show that Christ will not be here bodily until he comes again.

The Marburg Colloquy produced an agreement on fourteen of the fifteen articles, and disagreement on the fifteenth, on the eucharist, was in only one point out of six – on the bodily presence. Nevertheless, that was sufficient for Luther to refuse fellowship with Zwingli, Bucer, and Oecolampadius. This division between Lutheran and Reformed was not overcome until the Leuenberg Concord in 1973.

In his later writings Zwingli expressed his views more positively, stressing the way the sacraments help to increase faith through their appeal to the senses and asserting in *The Exposition of the Faith* that Christ is 'truly in the supper' and that it is not the Lord's supper 'unless Christ is there'. Christ's body is present sacramentally and can be eaten sacramentally. There is, however, no change in Zwingli's fundamental position. For Zwingli, Christ is not bodily present, nor is he eaten bodily. If he were, that would put salvation at our disposal, not God's. To eat Christ bodily and so to receive salvation would deny God's election, the centrality of Christ's death, and the freedom of the Spirit in our salvation. It would contradict scripture, and the view that what is outward cannot affect what is inward.

Some scholars see Zwingli as essentially Erasmian, and the influence of Erasmus is undoubtedly to be seen in the central role of John 6:63, the stress on faith and commemoration, and the Platonist opposition between flesh and spirit. The influence of Augustine is at least equally important, however, as a comparison with his tractates on John 6 shows. It is evident in the stress on the sovereignty of God. Unlike Bucer and, later, Calvin, Zwingli did not link the sacraments positively to the sovereignty of God, for example in God's making the sacraments effective for the elect or in the Spirit's bringing Christ's death to our remembrance.

THE CHURCH

One characteristic of the sacraments is that they are seen as signs of membership of the church. They 'inform the whole church rather than yourself of your faith'. Zwingli's discussions of the church were first with the conservatives and then with the radicals. In his earliest writings he defined the church in terms of Christ as head over against the pope as head, consisting of those who live in the head, not those who are in communion with the pope. He rejected the view that the church is the episcopate. Later he referred to Christ as the true bishop, who was in fact freeing people from the bishops, as he had freed the people of Zurich from the bishop of Constance. Bishops, like others, are members of the church only as they have Christ as their head. Moreover, it is only as it is related to Christ and the Spirit that the church does not err. The Spirit, however, is not present automatically where the bishops are assembled, but only when the Word of God is master.

For Zwingli, the traditional marks of the church (one, holy, catholic) are all related to Christ. It was with conservatives that Zwingli argued about the catholicity of the church. He accepted two meanings of the word in the New Testament: the communion of all those who believe in Christ (catholic), and particular congregations (local). With these two meanings it is clear that the Roman church is a local church. The catholic or universal church is both scattered throughout the world and gathered together in one body by the Spirit. It does not come together visibly on earth, although it will do so at the end of the world. Like Augustine and Luther, Zwingli spoke of the church as visible to Christ, but invisible to us. It is discerned only by faith. The local church, as in Corinth, is a congregation, where Word and sacrament are present and where discipline is exercised.

Zwingli discussed the holiness of the church in debate first with conservatives and then with radicals. The church is not holy because of any inherent holiness; nor are its members holy by virtue of being priests or

religious. It is holy only in so far as it remains in Christ. Those who rely on him are without spot or wrinkle because he is without spot or wrinkle. Alongside this view of the church as holy is Zwingli's view of it as mixed, consisting of wheat and tares. He held this view from the beginning; it was not simply a response to the challenge of the Anabaptists; however, it was developed and more strongly emphasized in conflict with them. For them the church should admit only those who believe, and then should excommunicate those living unholy lives. Zwingli argued that in the Bible the church is a community of believers and unbelievers.

The unity of the church was also expounded in controversy initially with conservatives and then with radicals. The Anabaptists challenged the church's unity by excluding infants from baptism and also by separating themselves from the church. Zwingli used his understanding of the one covenant and one people of God in Old and New Testament to argue that infants belonged to the church just as they belonged to the people of God in the Old Testament. They should be baptized now, just as they were circumcised then. The later stress on election was used to show the unity of infants with their parents in the church. Zwingli defended the baptism of infants, who do not yet have faith, because election precedes faith. The church is therefore defined in terms of election, which can include children, as well as in terms of faith. The eucharist, like baptism, was related to the unity of the church, for it was instituted by Christ so that we might be united to him and to one another. For Zwingli, unity was also related to the Spirit, who, like Christ, does not separate people but draws them into unity.

The issue of excommunication focused in many ways the differences between the reformers and the conservatives and radicals in their understandings of the church. Against conservatives he argued that 'no private person may excommunicate, but only the church, that is, the community of those among whom the person excommunicated lives'. In 1525 he was to express the basic text (Matthew 18:15–18) vividly when he argued that Jesus said, 'Tell it to the church', not 'Tell it to the pope.' At this stage Zwingli stated that excommunication belongs to the whole church.

This position was compatible with the Anabaptist emphasis on excommunication as the responsibility of the local church. They believed in the total separation of the church from the magistrate. In the Schleitheim Confession the magistrate uses the sword, which has no place in the life of the church. The life of the church is safeguarded not by the sword but by excommunication, which belongs to the church. Unlike the radicals, however, Zwingli allowed a role in the life of the church for the city council, and this is clear as early as 1523.

In expounding article 40, on the power of the magistrate to take life, Zwingli quoted Matthew 18:15–18 and applied it to the magistrate. He accepted that the text's primary reference was to excommunication, but for the sake of the body of Christ the magistrate could take the life of those guilty of public offences – the council could remove members from the church for the good of the church. The way Zwingli involved the magistrate in the church's discipline led Oecolampadius to challenge Zwingli by pointing out that Jesus said, 'Tell it to the church', not 'Tell it to the magistrate.' In 1525, ministers excommunicated members for adultery, while the magistrates dealt with corporal punishment and property, but in 1526 it was the council alone that dealt with adultery.

Later, Zwingli gave a larger role to the magistrate in theory as well as in practice. In 1531 he saw the role of the magistrate in discipline as vital to the life of the church, particularly with flagrant sinners. He related this to the Old Testament's speaking of princes as shepherds. He could even say that 'without government a church is maimed and impotent'.

Zwingli, and later Bullinger, differed from others in the Reformed tradition, such as Bucer and Calvin, in the role they gave to government in excommunication. The others sought a greater independence from the magistrate.

GOVERNMENT AND SOCIETY

A major influence of Zwingli lies in the relation of church and society – not least in the Reformation in England. Some scholars hold that Zwingli began with a somewhat free-church view of the church when opposing conservatives, but that he moved to a different position when facing the challenge of Anabaptists. Some of Zwingli's statements and actions are compatible with this view, but far more are not.

From the beginning of his Zurich ministry Zwingli saw that the council had a vital role in the reformation of the church. This reflected in part the increasingly independent role the Zurich council already had in church affairs, and in part the recognition that, if bishops would not reform the church, then government would have to do so. The council's active role in Zurich is evident in the way it summoned the first disputation, and then at the end judged that Zwingli's preaching was scriptural and required that all other preaching be so too. It is notable, however, that Zwingli saw the assembly as 'a Christian assembly', not a civil gathering.

The council also summoned the second disputation, in which the division between Zwingli and the radicals emerged more sharply. He was willing, as they were not, to let the council determine when the mass and images were to be abolished. There is development, but also an underlying consistency in Zwingli's position through his years in Zurich. Circumstances probably strengthened his emphasis on the council's role, in particular Anabaptist disturbances in Zurich and conservative opposition and alliances in Zurich and elsewhere. Zwingli, moreover, became increasingly involved in city affairs, while the council became increasingly involved in church affairs. In the first disputation (1523), he held that one of the council's main tasks was to permit the preaching of the gospel. His letter to Strasbourg in December the following year implied that the council should remove preachers who were not preaching the gospel. It was concern for the preaching of the gospel that led him to make alliances and to seek to secure such preaching in the unreformed cantons.

The council did not, however, have the right to act independently. When Zwingli was challenged about allowing matters that belong to the whole church to be dealt with by the council, he argued that the council acted 'in the name of the church and not its own name'. He laid down four criteria for its acting: submission to the Word of God, the assent of the church, the need for peace, and the furtherance of the gospel. Writing to Blarer on 4 May 1528, he insisted that the magistrate's role was only in outward things. Interestingly, he appealed to Acts 15:6 in understanding 'elders' to mean councillors and senators, and not only those who preside over the Word.

Zwingli's view of church and society has sometimes been described as theocratic. That is appropriate if it means that the whole life of society is under the rule of God, and that both ministers and magistrates are to serve that rule. It is not appropriate, however, if taken to mean that society is subject to the ministers or the church subject to the magistrates. The role of the minister is vital in the community as he expounds and applies the Word of God to the whole life of society. Zwingli's most characteristic description of the minister is 'prophet'. In *The Shepherd* he described the prophetic character of the shepherd. The prophet challenges high and low alike, not only in religious matters but also in matters as diverse as greed, usury, war, the mercenary system, and monopolies. Zwingli's own preaching challenged people in every aspect of life. To the question 'What do finance and interest have to do with the gospel?' he answered, 'Much in every way.' To the question 'What do financial transactions, adultery, and drunkenness have to do with the minister?', his reply was that such a question is the same as that of the devils, when they said, 'Jesus, what have we to do with you?' Zwingli quoted the example of Elijah's challenging Ahab and Jezebel for the sake of only one person. Later he asserted that to refuse to attack greed, usury, war, the mercenary system, monopolies, and companies that harm the common good is to preach the gospel of Christ crucified without the cross.

Zwingli, like Luther and Augustine, related government to human sin. Like Luther he held that there would be no need of government if everyone were Christian. He used texts such as Romans 13 in expounding the origin and purpose of government. Government has a positive and a negative purpose: to protect the good and to punish the evil. To fulfil these purposes, government must make laws in conformity with God's Word. According to Romans 13, government is a servant of God. Everyone, including the pope, is bound to obey the authorities, whether they are good or evil. The duty to obey gives way to the duty to disobey, however, when the authorities act against God, whether in commanding what is contrary to his will or in seeking to control the preaching of the Word. Christians are to 'obey God rather than men'.

When rulers become tyrants, they are not to be obeyed. Article 42 stated, 'If, however, they are unfaithful and deal contrary to the rule of Christ, they may be deposed with God.' Zwingli interpreted this in terms of rulers supporting sinners and oppressing the innocent. He differed markedly from Luther in holding that tyrants should be removed. (The Reformed tradition developed this position.) He held that removal was not to be by murder or war or uprising, but by those who elected the ruler. He argued that though some rulers were not elected, there must at some point have been the consent of the people. Zwingli quoted Old Testament examples of God's punishing people with unjust rulers, but he also cited Moses to show that in his mercy God wishes to liberate us as he liberated Israel. This example was used initially of liberation from the pope, but later of liberation from temporal rulers. When discussing forms of government, Zwingli followed Aristotle in describing the three forms of government (monarchy, aristocracy, democracy) and their perversion (tyranny, oligarchy, mob rule). His preference for aristocracy, the rule of the best, may reflect both his experience of such a form of government in Zurich and the greater ease with which such a government can be removed, if it fails.

Zwingli's concern for society is a fundamental element in his theology. It is significant that where Luther saw God's wrath as directed to him as an individual, Zwingli saw it as directed to the people. He was later to refer to the way the preaching of the gospel transformed the life of the city. In 1522 he wrote, 'For Zurich more than any other of the Swiss cantons is in peace and quiet, and this all good citizens put down to the credit of the gospel.' 'I do not deny, nay, I assert, that the teachings of Christ contribute very greatly to the peace of the state, if they are set forth in their purity.' The final words of his major systematic work show his concern for society as well as for the individual: 'All that I have said, I have said to the glory of God, and for the benefit of the commonwealth of Christ and the good of the conscience.'

INTERPRETATIONS OF ZWINGLI

There have been widely different interpretations of Zwingli. He has been described as the liberal or rationalist among the reformers. He has also been presented as biblical, even Barthian, in his theology. Such diverse views derive in part from the interpreters' contexts: liberal scholars have often seen a liberal, not to say rationalist, Zwingli, and Barthian scholars a biblical, not to say Barthian, Zwingli. Mennonite scholars have often stressed change in Zwingli's understanding of church and state from his early years in Zurich, while some others have stressed development. In part, too, the diversity of interpretation results from the selection of his writings inter-preters make. For example, those who emphasize *The Providence of God* present a more philosophical view of Zwingli's theology, and those who use writings from 1524–5 give a more symbolic view of the sacraments than those using writings from 1530–1.

There are varying interpretations in several areas of Zwingli's theology, in particular in the influences that were important in shaping his theology, the relation of Word and Spirit, the sacraments (especially the eucharist), and the relations of church and society.

There is a general recognition that there were various influences, in particular Augustine, the Schoolmen, Erasmus, and perhaps Luther. While some regard Zwingli as essentially Erasmian in his theology – for example in the inwardness of religion – others lay an equal stress on Augustine – for example, on the sovereignty of God. There has been little detailed exam-ination of scholastic influence, though most stress Aquinas, Duns Scotus, and the old way (*via antiqua*), and elements that some used to attribute to Zwingli's humanism are now seen as deriving from scholasticism. Most scholars now do not see Zwingli as fundamentally dependent on Luther, though the extent of Luther's influence is still debated. The question of the most formative influences will be illuminated by further study of the marginal notes made by Zwingli in his books before 1522, but it will also be clarified by specialist studies both of specific doctrines and of his major works.

Some refer to Zwingli's theology as pneumatological, others as spiritu-alist. The term 'pneumatological' expresses the view that the Spirit is the Holy Spirit and that the Spirit is interpreted biblically, related to, rather than separated from, the Word. The term 'spiritualist' expresses the view that the Spirit is not closely linked with the Word. There is truth in both interpretations. Compared with the spiritualist views of radicals such as Sebastian Franck, where the Spirit is divorced from the Word, especially as incarnate in Christ and as expressed in scripture, Zwingli's theology is not spiritualist. The Spirit is the Holy Spirit given by Christ. He is the author of scripture, the one who inspired it and interprets it. It is, however, in the relation of the Spirit to Word and sacrament that there may be force in the use of the word 'spiritualist'. Here the differences from Luther and even from some in the Reformed tradition are clearer. As noted above, Zwingli insisted that without the Spirit the Word is not understood, and that the Spirit does not need the Word or the sacraments, but rather that it is the Word that needs the Spirit. This view is related to the Platonist opposition in his thinking between outward and inward, so that what is outward cannot affect what is inward. It is, however, also related to Zwingli's Augustinian stress on the sovereignty of God, which does not allow that word and sacraments can convey the Spirit, for this would put the gift of the Spirit in the power of those who preach the Word and celebrate the sacraments. Bucer and Calvin used the doctrine of election here to hold together the sovereignty of God and the effectiveness of Word and sacrament, so that Word and sacrament are effective where the person is elect. Zwingli allowed that the Spirit is present and active among the Gentiles outside the Bible, but this is not argued in a spiritualist way. It is carefully related to God's election and to the universal reach of Christ's salvation, and it is argued biblically both from the New Testament and from the Old Testament examples of Gentiles.

There is development in Zwingli's view of the sacraments, but also change as he repudiated in 1524 his earlier view that the sacraments can strengthen faith. There are therefore understandably different interpretations. They can depend on whether the emphasis is on the writings in 1524, in which the accent shifted from God to Christians as the subject of the sacraments, maintaining, for example, that we eat and drink 'so that we can testify to all that we are one body and one brotherhood'. They can depend on whether one sees Zwingli as essentially Erasmian, or whether one also emphasizes the influence of Augustine, for example, in his stress on the sovereignty of God. They can depend on whether one sees him in the light of Luther, who viewed him in terms of Carlstadt, and whether one presents him negatively in terms of what he denies rather than more positively in terms of what he affirms.

There are different interpretations of Zwingli's early eucharistic teaching and of how far his views are symbolic. Some, such as Köhler, have argued for several stages of development before he adopted the symbolic view. There is little evidence for this, however; his early writings could imply the symbolic interpretation, and certainly do not require a non-symbolic

one. There are changes of emphasis in the later Zwingli, especially in the
way the senses are used, which give a more positive presentation of the
sacrament.

There has been disagreement on Zwingli's role in Zurich and his understanding of church and state. Some stress discontinuity between Zwingli's
earlier and later views on church and state, regarding him as moving from a
more free-church position, which distinguished church and state, to a more
state-church position, which identified them.

ZWINGLI AND LUTHER

The later differences between Reformed and Lutheran theology reflect
in part the differences between Zwingli and Luther or different emphases
in their theology. Zwingli stressed the continuity between the Old and New
Testament, Luther rather the contrast between them, with an emphasis on
a canon within the canon of scripture. Luther spoke of law and gospel and
used that as a key in interpreting scripture, whereas Zwingli spoke of gospel
and law. Moreover, Zwingli employed the idea of the so-called third use of
the law, in which law does not only expose sin and curb evil, but also reveals
God's will for us so that we may lead our lives in accordance with his will.
Far from opposing the law to the gospel as Luther did, Zwingli could even
speak of the law as gospel, for from the standpoint of the believer it is
good news to know God's will. This positive view of the law is characteristic
of a theology that emphasizes living the new life of love and not just the
forgiveness of sin.

Justification by faith was central for Luther but not for Zwingli, in whose
works the emphasis is on making righteous rather than on declaring righteous. Both stressed faith, but for Zwingli it was faith in the Creator rather
than the creature, and therefore in Christ as Son of God as opposed to the
creature (that is, anything that is not God, not only works, as with Luther).
One of the differences between Luther and Zwingli that emerged in the
eucharistic controversy was Christological. Luther stressed the unity of the
two natures in the person of Christ, whereas Zwingli stressed the distinction of the natures. Some saw Zwingli as separating the natures (which he
denied) and called him a Nestorian, whereas Zwingli saw Luther as denying
Christ's humanity and called him a Marcionite. Providence and predestination feature in Luther's theology as well as in Zwingli's, but they have
a more influential and extensive role in Zwingli's theology, just as they do
in Reformed theology. The later distinction between the two kingdoms and
the kingdom of Christ in Lutheran and Reformed theology is partially seen
in Zwingli.

THE INFLUENCE OF ZWINGLI

Zwingli's influence was partly direct, through his ministry and writings, which made their impact far beyond Zurich. But it was also largely indirect – especially through his successor, Heinrich Bullinger. The theocentric character of Reformed theology, the sense of scripture as a whole, the emphasis on God's providence and election, the distinction between Christ's natures, the place and the freedom of the Spirit, the covenant, the new life, the vision of church and society under the rule of God with a role for the magistrate in the life of the church – all manifest a continuity between Zwingli and Bullinger.

Bullinger's theology was not identical to Zwingli's. Sometimes the differences are those of accent or emphasis, sometimes they reflect the development of the Reformation. Although Bullinger insisted on his loyalty to Zwingli in the doctrine of the sacraments, there were differences between them. This is evident in the confessions of the faith to which Bullinger agreed, not least in his immensely influential Second Helvetic Confession (1566). It has a stronger sense that God uses Word and sacraments, though with the qualification that they are effective only for the elect. There is a stronger emphasis on the role of the Spirit, and a clearer reference to being incorporated into Christ. Yet the confessions have characteristic Zwinglian elements: the sovereignty of God, the distinction of the two natures of Christ, the freedom of the Spirit.

The covenant is important in Zwingli and in Bullinger. Yet some would say that whereas Zwingli had a theology of the covenant, Bullinger had a covenant theology. Yet there is dispute as to how dominant the covenant is in his theology. Later developments of covenant theology owe more to Bullinger than to Zwingli.

Zwingli's practice also influenced practice elsewhere, especially in the role of government in the life of the church, in the opposition to images, and in the 'prophecy' (prophesying).

Zwingli's is the first expression of Reformed theology. Re-expressed and elaborated by Bullinger, it reached every part of Europe – through his letters, his writings (some translated into English, French, Dutch, and German), and through those who studied and stayed in Zurich.

9 Bucer

IAN HAZLETT

Martin Bucer (1491–1551) came from an artisan family in Alsace – then part of Germany – at Sélestat (Schlettstadt), south of Strasbourg. After a twenty-eight-year career, becoming a major reformer, he died exiled in England. Reared by his grandfather because of the migration of his parents, Bucer acquired a progressive schooling at the local prestigious humanist Latin school of Schlettstadt. Further education was guaranteed on entering the Dominican order there in 1507. Ordained at Mainz in 1516, he demitted his vows in 1521, becoming a secular priest. From 1517 till 1521 he had studied at Heidelberg University, also acting as tutor and lector in the local Dominican seminary. He had, in addition, developed an enthusiasm for Erasmian Christian humanism. Encountering Luther at the Disputation of Heidelberg in 1518, Bucer experienced a religious and theological sea-change. He perceived Luther as providing a cutting edge to what Erasmus advocated; both were lights of the gospel, showing the way from a depleted church, an atrophied theology, and a disorientated spirituality to the purer faith and love of original Christianity. Anxiety about the Cologne Dominican inquisitor, Hoogstraten, to whom he had been reported, helped Bucer to decide to flee the monastery in early 1521. Subsequently, his prospects were uncertain, though he networked with sympathizers with the humanist and evangelical causes, Erasmians and 'Martinians'. He was in the vicinity of the Diet of Worms when Luther was sentenced, obtaining his release there from the Dominicans at the time. Having secured the patronage of knights such as Sickingen and Hutten, during their religious and political agitation, Bucer was provided in 1522 with pastoral charges at Landstuhl, near Kaiserslautern, and then Wissembourg (Weissenburg) in northern Alsace. In these posts Bucer 'came out' as a Lutheran preacher of Christian freedom and haranguer against the Roman Antichrist. In Landstuhl, his marriage to an ex-nun, Elizabeth Silbereisen, made another Reformation statement. In Weissenburg, his eschatological preaching targeted church abuses, corruption, and exploitation of ordinary people. Disturbances occurred from which he distanced himself. In 1523, however, he was excommunicated. On the knights' defeat, Bucer fled to Strasbourg, his base for twenty-six years.

Bucer arrived encumbered with a new reality – a refugee, outlawed, unemployed, his wife pregnant. The city was affected by anticlerical, religious, social, and economic discontent. Its cathedral preacher, Matthäus Zell, and other clergy such as Capito and Hedio, were disseminating Lutheran and Erasmian ideas. The rulers of this republican imperial free city, one of Germany's largest metropolises, however, were pursuing a policy of circumspection. While Bucer occasionally deputized for Zell, and was assured of protection, he gained citizenship only in 1524, after three attempts, and after his election to St Aurelia's, a parish associated with the radical guild of market gardeners. The city council approved the appointment. He removed the saint's relics from the church. Bucer's rise to prominence in Strasbourg was not meteoric. In 1529, when the mass was abolished, he was appointed pastor of St Thomas' Church, a major city-centre parish. In 1531, he became president of the assembly of Strasbourg clergy. In 1533, he was moderator of the Strasbourg Synod. In 1540, he became superintendent of churches in the city and its environs. In 1541, he was nominated a prebendary in the chapter of St Thomas, and in 1544, its dean. Bucer had emerged as a quasi-bishop, his authority, however, deriving from his evangelical ministry, spiritual leadership, writings, force of intellect, and engagement in church and political affairs beyond Strasbourg – his good relationship with the Strasbourg leader and diplomat, Johannes Sturm, being crucial.

Bucer's mission regularly encountered controversy, facing challenges from Catholic resistance, the Peasants' Revolt in 1525, iconoclasm, Anabaptist and spiritualist manifestations, and a lukewarm reaction in the council to certain proposals. Relative openness to dialogue with dissidents ceded to traditional intolerance and advocacy of coercion, ecclesiastical and civil uniformity being paramount. His later attitude to Jews became equally intransigent and exclusivist. In the eucharistic controversy between Luther and Zwingli, Bucer tenaciously pursued mediation and concord, rewarded in 1536 with a reunited Protestantism, in Germany at least. The relative distinctiveness of the overall Strasbourg theology – not just an amalgam of Erasmian, Lutheran, and Zwinglian ideas – was reflected in the Tetrapolitan Confession submitted at the Diet of Augsburg. The aspiration was demonstrable individual and corporate ethical regeneration intrinsic to gratuitous justification by faith. Yet solidarity with Wittenberg, partly politic, was affirmed with Strasbourg's subscription to the Augsburg Confession in 1532. Further, while much in Strasbourg's Reformation followed Zurich, such as mandatory removal of images, Bucer – no Erastian – strove vainly for internal church autonomy. His utopian vision was a hallowed society led by the church and a devout government – for the common good and God's glory.

Committed to the Reformation beyond Germany, Bucer developed a pan-European mission perspective. French religious refugees stimulated an interest in France. He helped to disseminate Lutheran literature there, and his Latin commentaries on the synoptic gospels and Psalms were designated for a French (and Italian) readership. Contacts with English merchants apprised him of the cross-Channel scene. Later, his definitive commentaries on the gospels and Romans were dedicated to the English bishops Edward Fox and Thomas Cranmer respectively. He influenced the future by installing Calvin in a French church at Strasbourg (1538–41). Bucer also advised the Waldensians and the Bohemian Brethren. Within Germany, he was involved directly in the reformation of Augsburg, Ulm, Hesse, Wurttemberg, Cologne, and Bonn. In Switzerland, he participated in the Berne Disputation of 1528. Individuals with whom he felt close affinity were the Constance reformers (the Blarer brothers and their sister), Melanchthon (after a frosty start), and Oecolampadius. Yet his gratitude to Luther endured.

1536 was a plateau for Bucer. Radicals subdued and sacramental concord secured, he published his remarkable revised gospels commentary and the Romans commentary. These *tours de force* were more than expository commentaries; they were also compendia of theology and Reformation apologetics. Notwithstanding, the erudite Romans commentary also announced the theme that preoccupied Bucer thereafter: wider church and theological reconciliation, constituting his reputation as an 'ecumenist'. Since 1533 he had pondered the issue, stimulated by Erasmus' plea for entente and reunion. Understandably, Catholic rulers interested (temporarily) in amicable church reunion and reform, such as Francis I and Charles V, turned to reformers such as Bucer and Melanchthon, seen as moderates, to represent the Reformation case. A planned colloquy at Paris in 1535 was aborted but, from 1538 to 1541, negotiations took place at Hagenau, Worms, and Regensburg. Despite progress, the enterprise was torpedoed. Bucer's commitment was unrelenting until the Council of Trent, which he perceived as sealing church division. His idea of a gradualist and progressive reformation within traditional Catholic structures was also embodied in his blueprint, co-authored with Melanchthon, for the reformation in the Cologne archdiocese, but was vetoed by the emperor. Bucer's theological diplomacy, as during the eucharistic controversy, was often criticized as opportunistic, ambiguous, pliable, and insincere. He encouraged true believers who remained in the old church ('Nicodemites') not to secede, and accorded a primacy of honour to the papacy. Leading Lutherans were inimical to the subordinate authority he granted to the church fathers. Recent studies establish his integrity, correcting long-standing historiographical bias and myopia, and appreciating his ambivalence about rigidly formulaic solutions.

Following the Augsburg Interim, Bucer, now yesterday's man, was exiled to England in 1549. In his eventide, as Regius professor of divinity in Cambridge, he also advanced his concept of the regeneration of church and society within received, recycled structures, so that a reformed church would replicate the 'better' early church. This was the conservative vision of his last significant writing, *On the Kingdom of Christ,* a reform programme for England where, in general, he received overdue public recognition.

BUCER'S MINDSET: FORMATION AND TRANSFORMATION

When Bucer went public, his mental complexion and religious attitude – the latter focusing on love as efficacious faith, characteristically predicated by him as *pietas* – were conditioned by an extraordinary coalescence of humanist, Erasmian, Aristotelian, Thomist, Neoplatonist, Augustinian, Lutheran, and biblical influences. Added soon were Zwinglian, patristic, and Jewish medieval rabbinical components. This unique synthesis helps to explain the perceived enigmatic quality and subtlety of his thought, including its immunity to facile categorization. Scholars debate the balance of influences, especially that between the Erasmian, Augustinian Neoplatonist, Zwinglian, and Lutheran inputs. It used to be believed that, on aligning himself to Erasmus and Luther, Bucer renounced and erased his scholastic heritage. Latterly, the continuing Aristotelian and Thomist dimensions have been properly recognized, though their full evaluation remains to be done. Ultimately, renunciation was easier for Bucer than erasure, since by 1521 his intellect had been moulded.

How had such a complex colouration and religious attitude come about? The primary layer in Bucer's Schlettstadt education was more than formal Latin humanism, as its orientation was also firmly Christian, ecclesiastical, moral, and practical, though the school was not a church school. Church and society revitalized with the aid of classical antiquity and biblical truth had become the school's mission statement during the rectorate of Jerome Gebwiler, when Bucer was a pupil. Gebwiler had co-operated in Paris with Lefèvre d'Etaples, a principal Christian humanist. On transferring to the Dominicans, the teenage Bucer studied under their tutelage, which continued for a further fifteen years. The traditional scholastic curriculum was marked out – Aristotelian dialectics and metaphysics, Thomas Aquinas,

Lombard's *Sentences*, the Bible, and so on. Yet this did not deprive him of further exposure to extramural humanism until he encountered Erasmus. In fact, Dominican pedagogy absorbed Christian humanism, and, with a stress on Aristotle's *Nicomachean Ethics*, it was not averse to having Erasmus and the church fathers on its course bibliographies. At Heidelberg, where both philosophical realist and nominalist schools were represented, Bucer continued his Aristotelian and Thomist studies. Ironically, it was within the local Dominican seminary that he accelerated his enthusiasm for Erasmus – the philosophy of Christ, religion of the spirit, critique of external religiosity, Bible-centred piety, mystical overtones, ethical objectives, scepticism about scholastic theology, and recourse to the Christian antiquity. While, by 1518, Bucer sensed tensions between his scholasticism on the one hand and the 'new learning' and piety on the other, the latter's foundations were already embedded in him. It was not a late discovery. Increasing preference for it made him receptive to Luther, whose cause he espoused.

Scholars tend to maintain that, following the Luther experience at the Heidelberg Disputation, Bucer received the Augustinian's theology in an attenuated way due to a cognitive dissonance – Bucer saw Luther through Erasmian eyes. The issue is clouded if Luther is accorded an *a priori* normative status, so that anything other than full replication is due to misconception. It is incontestable that Bucer acclaimed Luther's pessimistic anthropology, so that innate human capacity and works righteousness as credit contributing to salvation, which is a work of God, are denied. This was the 'essential' or 'substance' (to allude to Bucer's typical way of thinking) that bound him permanently to Luther. He never deflected from this un-Erasmian belief, though he enthused about Erasmus' devaluation of religion of externals and his emphasis on moral amelioration. If Luther could imagine faith in Christ without works, Bucer could not, since, for him, faith and ethical uprightness – not of itself meritorious – were necessarily proximate. The difference can be illustrated respecting the law. If Luther saw it as bringing condemnation and as a bar to true righteousness, Bucer reckoned that that applied only when the law was seen as an external and unwelcome imposition. Genuine faith induces obedience to God's will and receptivity to the Spirit, who enables the law's internal appropriation.

This metamorphoses into the new law of regenerate living, of the Spirit, of the gospel, as the fruit of grace and faith. In early utterances, Bucer appealed to the Aristotelian notion of 'entelechy' – an active and effective energy (God's will and the Spirit) in the Christian. Thereby he reconciles Luther to his own Erasmian and Thomist thought structures.

At a subsequent disputation, however, Bucer repudiated Aquinas on Christian love. Agreeing with the notion that Christian love mirrored God's love for humanity, he disputed Thomas' inclusion of 'self-love' within Christian love, seeing that as egocentricity that the gospel impales. Arguably, Bucer misinterpreted Thomas here, since the latter was referring rather to the love of God in oneself. It appears, then, that Bucer not only adopted Luther for some alleged wrong reasons; he also rejected Thomas for other wrong reasons. Less evident in his reception of Luther are the law–gospel antithesis, faith in the crucified Christ, the theology of the cross, and so a Christological epicentre. Luther's Galatians commentary of 1520, high-lighting Christian freedom and disinterested love of neighbour, however, confirmed Bucer's adhesion to him.

On converting, Bucer read Augustine avidly. His early writings reflect prominent Augustinian Neoplatonist features – not unfamiliar, since there was some transmission via Erasmus and Thomas. Consequently, the concept of God is primarily moral and relational, compatible with biblical revela-tion. God is the Supreme Good, discoursing benevolently with humanity, generating faith and virtue by Word and Spirit, formally willing the salva-tion of all, implanting the law, and the source of good works. These tones marked Bucer's evolving theology, in which God's justice and wrath recede, as does the Lutheran law–gospel dichotomy that explains the double divine will; piety is enjoying and expressing God's goodness through service; no thing or creature exists for itself, but rather for the collective benefit; faith and good works are grounded in God, the first cause of all things, in a predestinarian sense; impious living entails exclusion from salvation, and damnation; accordingly, double predestination seems ineluctable, as God's 'internal' will is discriminate. Overall, this made Bucer sympathetic to the Zwinglian perspective on righteousness as moral and societal reformation.

PIVOTAL ELEMENTS IN BUCER'S RELIGIOUS STANCE

Bucer was, if imperialist, not an imperious theologian. In controversy, he normally displayed a propensity for dialogue, mediation, flexibility over non-essentials, apparent compromise, inclusiveness, and comparative toler-ance. This irenicism is manifest in the eucharistic controversy and reunion talks with the Catholics. He was slow to excoriate Anabaptists and spiritu-alists before finally burning his bridges with them, yet he pursued themes dear to them, such as holy living, church discipline, and discerning the oper-ation of the Spirit. This predisposition is less attributable to a chameleon character than to Bucer's acquired intellectual infrastructure.

His epistemology has caused unease among those wishing upon Bucer the exclusivist revelation theology of 'Jerusalem'. In his theory of knowledge,

Bucer inherits the realism of the *via antiqua* in the Thomist-Aristotelian tradition: the notion that, while truth is one and exists independently of human minds in God as the First Truth, qualities and features of it are perceivable. This is enabled by diffusive revelations, 'self-outpourings' or 'words of God', as Bucer in a Neoplatonist mode termed them, through the diverse operations of the Spirit. These are universal manifestations, albeit grasped fragmentarily, of the First Truth of God, the Supreme Good. Therefore everything true agrees with this truth, the foundation of unity, so that the quest for truth is the quest for unity. In Bucer, this is not syncretism, pluralism, or relativism; rather, it is the reconciliation of all partial truths with the one truth, since, to him, Christian truth embraces all truths. Certainty of access to the one truth is by faith in Christ and his special revelation. Through Christ there are convergence, resolution, and synthesis, although continuing human sin distorts the perception.

Bucer introduces this concept twice. Preface XI of his Romans commentary considers whether anything in classical philosophy is compatible with Paul. Some see his affirmative answer an 'aberration'. Yet it coincides with the patristic idea of the double preparation of humanity for the gospel, through Jewish religion and pagan wisdom. The 'gifts of God' imparted to the best philosophers, he holds, testify to the Spirit. Although he can refer to supremely virtuous pagans as being among the 'elect', he refrains from declaring them 'Christians before Christ', since, although 'instruments', they lacked the 'fruits of the Spirit', notably faith and regeneration. Division among the philosophers is no excuse for ignoring them, Bucer argues, since theologians are equally discordant. This paradigm determines his thrust towards Christian consensus, harmony, and peace. It also conditions his biblical hermeneutics and understanding of the church fathers: apparent antinomies are resolved if, illuminated by the Spirit, one seeks the 'reality' of one divine truth underlying the scriptural and patristic diversities. Not seeing beyond dissonance fuels division, sectarianism, obduracy, and lack of charity.

The second instance, which relates to the eucharistic controversy and concord policy, is in an unused draft of the Tetrapolitan Confession. There he makes some bold strokes. Right understanding being elusive, disputed formulations have a provisional status, as markers *en route* to the essential. Interim tolerance is therefore incumbent on theologians. Even Peter and Augustine erred. Hence those with faith and love can be fallible and ignorant, but their Christianity should not be impugned. This goes beyond a 'live and let live' attitude, for there must be joint bridge-building with a view to substantive agreement, not just mutual recognition of authentic piety. The same ideas undergird the preface to his commentary on the gospels (1530), dedicated to the Marburg academy. Bucer does not share Erasmian reserve and diffidence in this respect. He typically insisted that many disputes were essentially semantic, and so resolvable.

Two further concepts determined Bucer's optic. One derived from Erasmus' views on restoring church concord, namely *synkatabasis*, mutual accommodation and good will in commitment to a common goal. Bucer though is not content with Erasmian faith in more Christian behaviour, since he envisages fundamental theological agreement. Consequently, in both his 1533 tract *Preliminaries to a Church Council* and in the title of his Romans commentary he cites the notion of *epieikeia*. This conveys various notions surrounding 'equity': moral justice inadequately expressed in codified law, the spirit of good justice enabling magnanimous interpretation of law, and dispensing with prescriptive regulations in the interests of *ad hoc* utility. The concept, originating in Aristotelian jurisprudence, had been used by Aquinas and Lefèvre, and was revived by contemporary jurists, all sources familiar to Bucer. He associates it with Christian freedom and conscience, the distinction between internal and external, and the spirit and the letter. Provided that there is consensus on the truth of justification by faith, appeal to *epieikeia* enables revisionism and pluralism in externals, such as observances and polity, supposed barriers to reunion. Thereby God's goodness prevails, Christian conscience is not infringed, and Christian freedom is secured. Ideally, dogmatic consensus should be prior, but paradoxically, Bucer also envisaged subsequent doctrinal settlement. This is his theology of *adiaphora* and of inclusive evangelical optimism.

BUCER ON SELECT TOPICS

While Bucer's expansive theology is in his Latin biblical commentaries, summaries are found elsewhere; for example the Tetrapolitan Confession and its *Apology* (1531); the Strasbourg Catechisms (1534/37); the 16 Articles of the Strasbourg Synod (1533); *Instruction from Holy Scripture* (1534); part I of the *Defence against the 'Catholic Principle'* (1534); *Brief Summary of Christian doctrine* (1548). His ideas on concrete reformation are encapsulated in *Ground and Basis* (1524); *Preliminaries to a Church Council* (1533); *On the True Reconciliation of the Churches* (1542); *Cologne Reformation Ordinances* (1543); *On the Kingdom of Christ* (1557). Excepting David F. Wright's *Common Places*, there is a regrettable paucity of modern-language translations.

Scripture

For Bucer, scriptural primacy is self-evident, its unique authority consisting in salvation historiography revealing God's power, goodness, and will. Scripture clearly provides, then, the essential objective criterion for

Christian existence. The Bible is sacred, an oracle, its source and mediate author being the Word and Holy Spirit. Bucer's theology is accordingly profoundly scriptural in content and language, but hardly 'biblicist'.
His hermeneutics shun slavish literalism and textual verbalism, the only
valid interpretation being pneumatological, that is, assisted by the Spirit.
Otherwise the letter is dead to human reason (flesh). The principles of
sola scriptura and 'scripture its own interpreter' are subject to the Spirit's
operation in interpretation, individual or collective. Proper scriptural corroboration is admissible, but not proof-text use of scripture appealing to
the bald affirmation that 'scripture says so', Bucer maintains. Since the
Spirit is not self-contradictory, only his invocation can reconcile biblical
inconsistencies, such as the teaching of Paul and James on good works.
Bucer recognizes, however, that the Spirit, human mind, and text are rarely
conjoint, because of defective faith and love. This defect begets error, factions, schisms, anachronisms, and pseudo-evangelicals, so that interpretation needs renewal every generation for edification and the practical good.

The early church and patristic testimony

Bucer reflected humanist enthusiasm for Christian antiquity. It exemplified a superior church and a sounder theology in essentials, derived from
its proximity to apostolic Christianity. The special value of its corporate
judgement in the chain of historical continuity cannot be gainsaid. Polemical concerns play a role here, since, to justify Reformation realignments,
appeal to the fathers could provide corroboration. Modern studies address
this issue in Bucer: 'appropriation' of the fathers for the cause, and 'neu-
tralization' of them to prevent the Roman church claiming exclusive inheritance. Bucer's zeal for the fathers – as supporters, not neutrals – was such
that some see scriptural authority jeopardized by this 'double canon'. But all
he suggests is that, where there is no offence to scripture and conscience,
non-biblical customs and usages (except celibacy!) commanding patristic
consensus are commendable, such as honouring the saints and penance.
He accords no parallel canonical authority to the fathers, pursuing instead
what in them is compatible with scripture, to which they are subordinate,
as they knew. Not uncritical, he claimed that some erred on matters such
as celibacy, free will, predestination, and allegorical exegesis. Occasionally,
though, he strains the evidence of patristic unanimity on other doctrines.

Justification

For Bucer, justification is 'the chief article of divine wisdom'. While he
varies from Luther and Zwingli, any distinctiveness need not be exaggerated.
After all, justification was agreed on at the Marburg Colloquy, and was
not seen as divisive; all agreed that justification is a gratuitous divine gift,

grounded in God's grace and the work of Christ, private human merit being non-contributory. Any difference is at the level of analysis and formulation.

Bucer used the expression *sola fide*, but, for him, *sola* guaranteed faith's provenance in God's goodness, promises, election and adoption of believers as his children, Christ's merit, and their mediation by the Spirit. Salvation is by God alone through the merciful imputation and actual bestowal of faith. Moreover, true believers become 'co-workers of God', serving their neighbours in love. Accordingly, central to Bucer is the indivisibility of the vicarious attribution and imparting of the righteousness of faith, realized in 'right living'. Analogies were fire and heat, a tree and its fruit, a kernel and its shell. In short, he increasingly integrated faith and good works so that 'justification' comprises both; hence some misrepresent this as a reduction of faith to ethics. Paradoxically, others see his concept of faith as 'intellectualist', though his notion embraces trust, persuasion by the Spirit, knowledge, assent, and efficacious love. Bucer's concern was threefold. First, he rejects the scholastic notion of 'unformed faith', faith without love, dead faith, as an oxymoron; yet he admits 'weak faith'. Secondly, he dismisses evangelical antinomianism, whereby moral indifference might be legitimized by disjoined 'faith alone'. Thirdly, he shunned perfectionism, since sanctification is limited by the continuation of sin in believers. While justification activates a teleological process, and love is intrinsic and inherent, no ontological change is induced, because of abiding sinfulness. 'Effective righteousness' is more its potential, not completely actualized, since terrestrial love is defective.

Bucer also saw concord prospects in the formula of 'twofold justification', the justification of sinners through faith, and the justification of the justified by spontaneous good works (sanctification), not by virtue of human merits, but by God's recognition of his own enabling gifts. Bucer's mature thought on justification, strongly Augustinian, also made use of the Thomist category of faith formed by love.

Predestination

Bucer deals with predestination more confidently than other reformers before Calvin, chiefly in regard to Romans 9. Indifferent to speculation, he affirms predestination as a pastoral means of stabilizing faith's certitude of salvation and trust, not in one's own virtue, but in God's benevolence. Universal salvation is denied; rather, God has eternally selected some for salvation – the 'elect', called by the external Word but endowed by the Spirit with true faith – so that consequently others, the 'reprobate', the 'wicked', the 'ungodly', the 'obdurate' are (pre)destined to doom. There is no reference to hell in Bucer's treatment. This prior divine decision is grounded solely in God's sovereign freedom, and is not based on his foreknowledge of people's behaviour (a notion Bucer deplored in many of the fathers and scholastics), though the elect will normally display goodness. Damnation, then, flows not from divine wrath, but rather from the prerogative of God's choice. Bucer's Augustinian concept is not a 'double decree'. Predestination reflects rather than diminishes God's glory, as does the deliberate degradation of the obdurate and the Jews, which is seen as a testimony to God's goodness. To Bucer, the ecclesial 'elect' are invisible, though the church exists primarily for their benefit. The elect constitute the true church within the church(es), known only to God, though Bucer envisages discreet awareness of one's own election. By the grace of 'necessity, not coercion', they spontaneously exercise true free will, which is established, not abolished, by predestination.

Bucer's conception relates to a cosmological scheme of salvation initiated by God, operated by the Holy Spirit – variously described as the 'Spirit of God', 'of the Father', 'of Christ', and 'of Truth'. This 'order of salvation' includes predestination, vocation, justification, sanctification, and glorification, an order more logical than chronological. It has been criticized because the Christological dimension is subdued.

Ecclesiology

Accompanying his predestinarian perspective, Bucer increasingly thought more positively about ministry, external Word, and sacrament in the visible church, as 'means of grace' for true believers – if fanned by the Spirit. This middle view was adopted against spiritualists and the perception of Catholic notions of the inherently automatic efficacy of rites. To belong to the true church is to belong to Christ, her head. The priesthood of all believers is constituted not so much by baptism as by the Spirit's calling, which is simultaneous only in a qualified way. The impossibility of establishing a general sanctified community through autonomous presbyterial discipline, coercively enforced by the civil power, however, encouraged Bucer to stress unostentatious pedagogic worship, Christian education, rigorous pastoral care, confirmation, and parochial self-disciplining 'Christian fellowships' – a core church. Overall, he experienced disappointment. The civil community did not comply with the extent of Bucer's theocratic imperative. His concept of the 'Christian republic' or 'kingdom of Christ' was theologically satisfying but undeliverable. Based on a rather Thomist divine order of being, the two realms, spiritual and secular, were not 'separate' but 'distinct', and so potentially convergent. The degree of coercion and sanctions that this legitimized was in practice repudiated.

Bucer's critical accommodation to Catholic church structures, including episcopacy and the papacy (as having a primacy of honour only), cause some to wonder if he had a double ecclesiology – a principled Protestant one and a pragmatic ecumenical one. This does not do justice to his concern that the

provision of variable contingent conditions enabling God's will and Christian freedom to prevail is paramount. Hence he attributed interim status to
Reformation church forms and asserted the reformability of Catholic forms,
urging mutual acceptance pending future conciliar consensus. Criticism of
his commitment did not deter him; he confided to Philip of Hesse in 1543:
'It is all very well for those supping wine and beer in cosy bars to rubbish
those who slave away at these controversies and struggles. But if we do not
face these, our ministry would not be put to the true test.'

Sacraments

On baptism, Bucer became the big-hitting apologist for infant baptism
against Anabaptist believers' baptism. His predestinarianism had originally
encouraged him to undervalue the ceremony, envisaging a double baptism
of water and Spirit, one external, the other selectively internal, detached
from the ceremony. Infant baptism, then, was not paramount. In the Strasbourg baptism controversy of the 1530s, Bucer reacted conservatively, reinforced by the havoc caused by radicals in Munster, Westphalia. Following
Zwingli, he argued that, since children of Christians also benefit from God's
covenant promises, so baptism, like Old Testament circumcision, is a sign
and seal of this, and must be universal. Further, he resoldered external and
internal baptism in such away that the sacrament 'exhibits', that is, both
represents and (selectively) endows regeneration (or its potential), even in
ignorant recipients; it initiates rather a process of education culminating
in confirmation. Bucer then ends up with compulsory universal paedobaptism, doubtless influenced by the unitary covenanted community of Israel,
by the belief that Christ implicitly wished it, and by the inherited Theo-
dosian model of church as conterminous with society, constituted by the
Trinity. His church vision is double: externally general, internally particular,
comprising the elect.

On the eucharist, Bucer originally adopted Luther's rejection of transubstantiation as explaining the real presence. In the eucharistic controversy, he
allied himself with the Swiss, more because of his distinction between external visible signs (which are not objective channels of grace) and internal spiritual realities, than because of the influence of Zwingli's logical symbolism
and metaphysical dualism. Bucer's constant leitmotiv, conditioned by John
6:51ff., was that 'eating Christ's body' was the spiritual enjoyment of faith in
Christ, of which the sacrament was exemplary. His plea for mutual tolerance
was unheeded, until he made a breakthrough with Melanchthon in devising
a mediating theology that would be ultimately acceptable to Luther in the
Wittenberg Concord in 1536. Thereby Bucer acknowledged that Christ's true
body, which strengthens faith, is substantially and spiritually received in the
supper, and that unworthy Christians receive Christ's body sacramentally

to their discredit, while the Lutherans granted that unbelievers receive only bare sacramental signs. This eliminated the notion that reception of the sacraments was automically and inherently efficacious. Bucer's mature position holds that communion involves a parallelism and mystical convergence of two realities, heavenly and earthly, internal and external, uncreated and created, personal and impersonal, Christ and minister, soul and mouth, reality and symbol, invisible and visible, truth and sign, power and instrument – suggested originally by Luther's notion of 'sacramental union', which excluded Christ's *physical* presence. These distinct poles are inseparable, not fused or mixed, but co-inherent. This is the paradoxical, supernatural, but not miraculous means Christ uses to 'exhibit' himself to believers, nourishing their souls and bodies for resurrection. Self-abandoning participative communion with Christ's body also implies appropriating the benefits of his sacrifice, so that, consonant with patristic usage, the eucharist is legitimately called 'sacrifice', or with Aquinas, 'an image (re)presenting Christ's passion'.

CONCLUSION

Despite his ecclesiological and sacramental preoccupations, Bucer has been criticized for 'spiritualizing' tendencies and a thrust to perfectionism in the name of sanctification. This has been interpreted by some as the consequence of a paradoxical combination of sympathy with Anabaptist holiness piety and with Catholic notions of justification as gradual growth in 'merit' in a process of salvation. Whatever may be the case, the degree of perceived elusiveness about his final position on many controverted issues is attributable not simply to an alleged lack (or shunning) of systematic rigour. Rather, variable and provisional praxis fuelled by the self-determining freedom of the Spirit, and not a sectarian system hidebound by dogmatic precisionism, is what was always at the forefront of his flexible mind. This helps to explain the occasional use in his writings (unique among the Reformers) of the dialogue form – a device intended to encourage more access by the 'laity' to 'theology' or the understanding of Christian living. And while Bucer has also been criticized for diminishing the distinction between the Old and New Testaments, his deeper motive must be appreciated. This was that while the entire tradition of witness to revelation before Christ in the history of Israel and after Christ in the history of ecclesiastical Christianity contains deformation and falsity, it also contains truth and truths. To the degree that these derive from the Spirit, they therefore belong to all believers, past and present, the communion of saints.

10   The theology of John Calvin
DAVID C. STEINMETZ

John Calvin (1509–64) spent most of his adult life as a refugee from his native France. By far his longest exile was in Geneva, a city in which – in spite of his undoubted prominence – he seemed never to feel completely at home. Many of the figures who assisted Calvin in the reform of Geneva – energetic men such as Guillaume Farel and Pierre Viret – were forgotten by time, their books left largely unread after their deaths except by a handful of scholars. But Calvin's theological influence did not cease with his death in 1564. If anything, it grew stronger, especially in the English-speaking world. Thomas Norton's translation of Calvin's *Institutes* went through eleven editions by 1632. Calvin's catechism went through eighteen editions in English by 1628. Arthur Golding translated Calvin's sermons on Job, which went through five editions between 1574 and 1584. In America, the Calvinism of the low-church Anglicans of Virginia, the Congregationalists of Massachusetts, the Scotch-Irish Presbyterians of North Carolina, and the Baptists of Rhode Island was reinforced by the Dutch Calvinism of New Jersey and New York and by the German Calvinism of Pennsylvania. Even John Wesley, the founder of the Methodists, a notably anti-Calvinist movement on the American frontier, once confessed that his theology came within a 'hair's-breadth of Calvinism'.

Unlike Luther, Calvin was not a university-trained theologian. He had, of course, been sent by his father to the University of Paris in order to study for the priesthood. But the original plans for John's ordination were scuttled when his father, a notary for the bishop of Noyon in Picardy, quarrelled with the cathedral chapter. In the aftermath of the quarrel Calvin was sent instead to Orléans and later to Bourges to study law. By inclination Calvin preferred to be neither a lawyer nor a priest, though he did obey his father by earning a doctorate in civil law. In the preface to his commentary on the Psalms, written many years after the events, Calvin claimed that his chief ambition as a young man had been to lead a quiet life as a reclusive scholar, one who edited and interpreted classical texts. He might very well have lived such a quiet life, had he not experienced what he later described as a rapid, if somewhat reluctant, conversion to the Protestant movement. This unexpected conversion propelled him within a remarkably short time to prominence within Protestant circles of reform.

Though no one has dated with any degree of precision what Calvin calls his *conversio subita*, his sudden conversion to a new evangelical faith, it seems clear that it did not occur prior to 1529 or later than 1534. In 1534 Calvin wrote his first Protestant treatise, *Psychopannychia*, a polemical book that attacked the notion of some Anabaptists that the souls of the just sleep after death while awaiting the resurrection. He followed this treatise with the first edition of his *Institutes of the Christian Religion* in 1536 and the much more important second edition in 1539. In 1540 he published the first of his commentaries on the Bible, a lucid and detailed explanation of Paul's letter to the Romans. By the time of his death in 1564 Calvin had completed a large body of theological writings, including commentaries, sermons, catechetical literature, treatises, letters, and confessions, as well as several revised and expanded editions of the *Institutes* in Latin and French.

His most famous work was undoubtedly his *Institutes of the Christian Religion* (1536), a book which he revised and expanded four times in its Latin edition (1539, 1543, 1550, and 1559). The final edition of this important work, which Calvin himself regarded as a definitive statement of his teaching, was published in Latin in 1559 and in a French translation in 1560. Although almost no scholars still believe the claim, once made, that it is possible to master the theology of Calvin by reading nothing but his *Institutes*, the *Institutes* is nevertheless essential reading for any aspiring student of Calvin's thought.

An *institutio* is a handbook of the basic principles of a subject, concisely formulated and lucidly explained. It is intended to be an accessible introduction for beginners, who lack the background for more advanced and demanding works. In his letter to the reader at the beginning of the 1559 Latin *Institutes*, Calvin indicated that he thought he had written just such a work, an introductory manual of Christian faith and practice clearly and properly ordered by topic. He intended, as he put it, to provide for beginning students an accessible 'sum of religion in all its parts' that would enable them to read scripture correctly and to relate what they read to the Christian faith as a whole. In his 1560 French edition he indicated in much the same way that he believed he had provided a 'sum of Christian doctrine' that would show a 'way to benefit greatly from reading the Old as well as the New Testament'. In other words, Calvin wrote the *Institutes* with two purposes in mind: (1) to serve as a summary of basic Christian teaching and (2) to function as an introduction to the further reading of the Bible.

INTERPRETATION OF THE BIBLE

The vast bulk of Calvin's writings are expositions of the Bible in the form of commentaries or transcribed lectures and sermons. Many of the sermons have been lost (some through the carelessness of librarians), while still others remain to be edited. Nevertheless, between the commentaries and surviving sermons Calvin managed to interpret most of the Bible for his listeners and readers. Although Calvin wrote in Latin and French, English-speaking readers have long had easy access to his works through multiple translations of his exegetical and theological writings, beginning with the popular translations in Elizabethan England by Thomas Norton and Arthur Golding.

The first of Calvin's commentaries was his *Commentary on Romans*, published in Strasbourg in 1540. In the preface to this commentary dated 1539 Calvin compared his approach to scripture with the approach of three influential Protestant contemporaries, Martin Bucer from Strasbourg, Philipp Melanchthon from Wittenberg, and Heinrich Bullinger from Zurich. While Calvin praised all three for the quality of their biblical exegesis, he nevertheless criticized Bucer and Melanchthon for what he regarded as opposite but equally unfortunate failings. In Calvin's view, Melanchthon's exposition was too concise. Melanchthon was interested in discussing the main themes or *topoi* in each chapter of Romans but omitted a consideration of many of the details in the text. These details, left unexplained, puzzled less expert readers. Bucer, by contrast, was too prolix, and included in his commentary long, theological discussions of problems raised by St Paul. Such lengthy discussions deflected the attention of his readers away from the specific passages he was attempting to explain.

Calvin suggested an alternative approach to the exposition of scripture, a *via media* between Bucer and Melanchthon that he labelled 'lucid brevity'. Exposition should be as brief as the subject matter required, though never so brief as to omit detailed treatment of all the verses in a selected passage. At the same time Calvin promised to excise lengthy discussions of doctrinal topics from his commentaries and place them instead in the *Institutes*, where doctrinal issues could be discussed at length in relation to all other topics in the Christian faith. Calvin expected students who wished to make progress in their understanding of scripture to read both his individual commentaries on biblical books and his *Institutes of the Christian Religion* and to move from the commentaries to the *Institutes* as the subject matter of the biblical text dictated. Alexandre Ganoczy labelled this movement from Calvin's exposition of the biblical text to his *Institutes* and back again to the biblical text as Calvin's hermeneutical circle.

Christian biblical exegesis in the Middle Ages presupposed a standard commentary on the Latin Bible known as the 'ordinary gloss'. The gloss was a running exposition of the biblical text drawn largely, though not exclusively, from the writings of the early Christian fathers. Students of the Bible in medieval universities were not expected to learn Greek and Hebrew, but they were expected to master the glosses. They were aided in their exposition by a distinction explained in the *Postillae* of Nicholas of Lyra between the literal-historical and literal-prophetic senses of the Bible. The literal-historical sense was the narrative level of the text in its self-presentation; the literal-prophetic was the typological sense of scripture in which earlier events in the Old Testament foreshadowed later, more important events in the New. In addition, medieval exegetes made use of three spiritual senses: the allegorical or doctrinal, the tropological or moral, and the anagogical or eschatological.

Although he made considerable use of typology, Calvin was reluctant to appeal to spiritual senses of the text and did so very infrequently. He focused on an enriched literal sense, embracing both what the medieval theologians had called the literal-historical and literal-prophetic senses. The historical sense was for him the narrative or plain sense. He focused on the surface meaning of the text as the text presented itself to the reader. He did not have in mind a historical sense as sometimes defined by later historical critics, who search for the story behind the text, to which the text provides nothing more than tantalizing clues. Calvin was not a child of the Enlightenment. Nor did he rely on a previously glossed text. Calvin retained a hearty respect for the biblical interpretation of many of the early Christian fathers, whom he first came to know through reading canon law, though not so hearty that he refused to amend or contradict them.

Calvin followed humanists such as Desiderius Erasmus and Jacques Lefèvre d'Etaples, who insisted that biblical interpreters must master the biblical text in its original Greek and Hebrew rather than in Latin translation. The humanists made heavy use of the fathers, but preferred to do so in critical editions that they themselves had prepared. The ordinary gloss, which relied on brief snippets and summaries of patristic teaching in Latin translation, was spurned in favour of reading the entire works of the fathers in complete or nearly complete editions. Erasmus, for example, was particularly fond of Origen and Jerome, whereas Calvin favoured Augustine and Chrysostom.

The humanists were also interested in rhetoric and philology and suspicious of scholastic modes of argumentation, even when they agreed with the scholastics in their theological or philosophical conclusions. Although Calvin could be withering in his criticism of scholastics, especially those scholastics whom he called Sorbonnists, he nevertheless embraced a number of theological positions first taken by scholastics such as the Franciscan theologian, Johannes Duns Scotus. But particular agreement in substance did not mean general agreement in method. The starting point for the scholastics was the *Sentences* of Peter Lombard and the glossed Latin text of the Bible; the starting point for Calvin was the collected works of the fathers and the unglossed Hebrew and Greek original. The methodological heart of scholastic theological discourse was the question and disputation; the heart of Calvin's theological formulations was the locus or topic.

Calvin's exegesis was not an end in itself, but was directed toward the edification of his readers. The purpose of biblical study was to awaken and increase one's knowledge and love of God and thereby also love of one's neighbour. Frequently Calvin offered a layered exegesis, in which he moved from an interpretation of the details of the biblical text to an application of that text to the life of his readers and back again to the details of the text itself. He characteristically bridged the gap between past and present, between text and reader, by drawing analogies. Sometimes he bridged the gap by appealing to a dialectic between prophecy and fulfilment. What he did not do was ignore the gap or assume a merely antiquarian interest in the biblical writings on the part of his readers. For him human salvation was at stake in the pages of the Bible. Proper biblical interpretation could never be reduced to miscellaneous information about ancient Semites.

Important to Calvin was the close relationship between the Old and New Testaments. The two testaments were bound together by one covenant but separated by different administrations. Both Abraham and St Paul were justified by faith alone. But whereas Abraham's faith was sealed by circumcision, the rite appropriate to the Old Testament, St Paul's faith was sealed by baptism, the rite appropriate to the New. Anabaptists such as Pilgram Marpeck stressed the differences between the two testaments. For Marpeck the Old Testament was yesterday; the New Testament was today. The Old Testament allowed polygamy, the circumcision of infants, and the right to make war. The New Testament insisted on monogamy, the baptism of adults, and a life of non-violence. Whereas Marpeck saw only discontinuity and contrast between the testaments, Calvin saw continuity and the possibility of drawing useful analogies. As male infants were circumcised in order to be admitted to the community of Israel, argued Calvin, so male and female children should be baptized in order to be admitted to the community of the church. As it was in the Old Testament, so also it is by analogy in the New.

Often Calvin's exegesis of scripture was quite traditional and drawn from earlier commentators, either directly or as mediated by one or another of his contemporaries. In his interpretation of Romans 4, for example, Calvin compared Genesis 15:6, 'Abraham believed God and it was reckoned to him for righteousness', with Psalm 106:31, in which Phinehas, the son of the high priest Aaron, was reckoned righteous by the commission of a double homicide. Out of zeal for God's law Phineas murdered an Israelite man who had taken a Midianite mistress. As Abraham was justified by faith, so, according to Psalm 106, Phinehas was justified by his violent deed. How could such disparate and seemingly incompatible claims be reconciled? When Calvin attempted to harmonize these seemingly contradictory passages, he was continuing a discussion he had found in the previous exegetical literature.

Closer examination of the *Institutes* provides additional evidence that Calvin intended his commentaries and the *Institutes* to be read together. For example, Calvin commented on Genesis 15:6 and Psalm 106:31 not only in his expositions of Romans and Genesis, but also in the *Institutes*, where the verses were given a larger dogmatic context. In the third book of the *Institutes*, for example, Calvin used these texts to assist him in reconciling the apparent disagreement between Paul and James over righteousness by faith as exemplified by Abraham and righteousness by works as exemplified by Phinehas. Here as elsewhere the exegetical context and the dogmatic context belonged inseparably, for Calvin, to the proper understanding of a biblical passage. Unlike modern interpreters, who often hold to a strict separation between exegesis and dogma, Calvin refused to concede that either context, exegetical or theological, excluded the other. Only Calvin's passion for lucid brevity in his commentaries relegated longer dogmatic discussions to the *Institutes*. The separation between exegesis and dogma was methodological for him and not ideological.

THEOLOGICAL METHOD

John Dillenberger once remarked that Calvin was not a systematic theologian. By this remark he meant only to suggest that Calvin was not a systematic theologian in the modern sense of the term. Some historians, such as William Bouwsma, have pressed this claim further than Dillenberger intended by claiming that Calvin was not a systematic thinker at all. While the restricted claim is certainly true, the blanket assertion seems highly improbable. It all depends what one means by 'systematic'.

The *Institutes* is not, after all, a random collection of aphorisms. It is an orderly compilation of extended discussions of central themes and problems in the Christian faith, arising in large part out of biblical interpretation, and organized into four books corresponding roughly to the main articles of the Apostles' Creed. A topic that arises naturally out of some discrete

subject matter is known in the sixteenth century as a *locus* or common-place. Whereas medieval scholastics organized their theological discussions around a series of questions, Calvin followed the humanists in organizing his discussions around a series of topics. He could, therefore, like the human-istically inclined Melanchthon, have called his book the *Loci Communes* or *Book of Commonplaces*.

While Calvin did not adopt Melanchthon's title, he did imitate to some extent Melanchthon's method. Melanchthon was impressed by what he called the *methodus Pauli*, the method of St Paul. He used this phrase to designate the method followed by St Paul in his ordering of topics in the letter to the Romans. Whereas medieval Christian theology had discussed questions of election and predestination under the doctrine of providence, and therefore as a subdivision of the doctrine of God, Paul had not dis-cussed election until he had first discussed human sin and justification in Romans 1–8. Following Paul, Melanchthon adopted the same order of top-ics. Although in his earlier editions of the *Institutes* Calvin had followed the traditional order of theological topics, dealing with predestination as a sub-division of providence, he reverted in the 1559 edition to the *methodus Pauli* recommended by Melanchthon. He moved predestination out of its medieval locus in providence and placed it after justification, just as Melanchthon had done, thus explaining the apostolic faith by using what both regarded as an ancient apostolic method.

In spite of this break with medieval tradition, there were also some hints in Calvin's method of medieval antecedents. The most popular medieval theological textbook, the *Sentences* of Peter Lombard, was also ordered into four books: on God, creatures, Christ, and the sacraments, though Lombard's ordering of books depended as well on the Augustinian distinc-tion between 'things' and 'signs' and between the 'love of enjoyment' and the 'love of use'. Furthermore, like many of the medieval scholastics, Calvin called his *Institutes* a *summa*. In his French edition he described it as a 'sum of Christian doctrine' and in his Latin edition a 'sum of religion in all its parts'. By calling the *Institutes* a *summa* Calvin wanted to stress both its com-pleteness and its usefulness for teaching purposes. Just as Thomas Aquinas had written a *Summa Theologiae* to train beginning students in theology, so Calvin had written his own 'sum of Christian doctrine' to 'instruct and prepare candidates in sacred theology for the reading of the divine Word'.

THE KNOWLEDGE OF GOD

Calvin indicated that the first two books of the *Institutes* were devoted to the problem of the knowledge of God – the knowledge of God the Creator in Book I and of God the Redeemer in Book II. Calvin did not mean to imply by focusing on the word 'knowledge' that he was interested only in an intellectual apprehension of God. Knowledge of God was never, for Calvin, simply a matter of cognition in the narrow sense of the term, as though such knowledge were merely a matter of patterning the mind with the 'heavenly doctrine' revealed in scripture. But neither was knowledge of God reducible to an I–thou relationship in which cognitive content was downplayed in favour of personal encounter. Knowledge of God involved for Calvin love, trust, fear, obedience, and worship of God. It embraced mind and heart, affections and will, worship and devout work. It rested on the gospel of God's free grace towards sinners and included the duties of both tables of the law, duties toward God and toward one's neighbours. As knowledge of God expanded and deepened over time, so, too, did self-knowledge, which could never flourish without it. To claim to know God was therefore to claim a good deal more than to make the bare assertion that one knew some important, even essential, truths about God, however weighty and foundational such truths might necessarily be.

Calvin believed that Adam and Eve, whom Calvin and his contemporaries regarded without intellectual reservation as the first man and woman, knew God through his self-revelation in nature and history. God had left in every natural process and on every historical event evidence of his creative and providential care. The sun did not rise and set, flowers did not germinate and bloom, and animals did not migrate or hibernate without the will and action of the living God. Although God transcended the natural order and could not be contained within it, the world was nevertheless the theatre of his glory. The universe was a never-ending festival of divine self-revelation that stimulated the first human beings to the praise, thanksgiving, and love of God.

Unfortunately, the first human beings fell into sin, and their fall had catastrophic noetic consequences, not only for Adam and Eve themselves, but for all their descendants as well. God did not cease to reveal himself in nature and history as a result of human sin. The stars continued to move in their courses as before. Even in a fallen world not a sparrow fell to earth without the explicit will of God. Although creation was damaged by the fall, the damage was contained by divine providence and served to mute rather than to extinguish the perpetual self-revelation of God in his works. The heavens continued to show the glory of God, but fallen human beings were no longer receptive to what could be learnt from them.

Calvin first described the noetic damage caused by the fall as blindness, but modified his language when blindness seemed too strong a term to do justice to the human predicament. If human beings were completely blind, then perhaps they could be excused. How could they be fully culpable if they could not see? To be sure, human beings ought not to be blind and to that extent could be blamed for their own predicament. Still, the text of Paul's letter to the Romans seemed to suggest something more: namely, that fallen human beings were not completely blind but could at least see something. Calvin used three images to describe more exactly what he had in mind when he contemplated the human predicament: namely, the scattered sparks of a fire that had all but gone out, a sudden flash of lightning on a dark night, and the reduced vision of an old man who could read a book only with the aid of spectacles.

Just as scattered sparks can give neither adequate heat nor adequate light, so a sudden flash of lightning can provide no useful guidance to a traveller who has lost his way in the dark. In both cases the question for Calvin was not whether fallen human beings still have some natural knowledge of God – to which the answer for Calvin seemed to be yes – but whether such knowledge was at all useful – to which the answer for Calvin was clearly no. In other words, while Calvin accepted the possibility of a limited natural knowledge of God, he denied the possibility of a functional natural knowledge, one that could be used to construct a true and reliable natural theology.

The most powerful image Calvin employed to underscore the noetic damage caused by human sin was the image of an old man, who had been handed a book to read by a friend but who had forgotten to bring his spectacles with him. Without his glasses he could tell that he was holding a thick quarto volume with printed paragraphs but no illustrations. He might even be able to make a rough judgement about the quality of the binding and paper of his friend's book. What he could not do was read it. For that task he needed his spectacles. In the same way fallen human beings are unable to read the self-revelation of God in nature and history (the *opera Dei*) unless their vision is corrected by the self-revelation of God through the words of the prophets and apostles (the *oracula Dei*). To understand the self-revelation of God in creation, human beings need to make use of the spectacles of scripture.

When human beings attempt to find God in nature and history with uncorrected vision, they are unable to do so and instead construct idols in the place of God. They are driven to seek God in part because of what Calvin, following Cicero rather than St Paul, called a *sensus divinitatis*, an unshakable sense that there is a God who ought to be honoured and worshipped, and that the world is unintelligible unless there is a source beyond itself to account for its existence. This innate notion is a universal sense shared by all men and women of whatever place and time and not a conclusion reluctantly reached as the result of a series of logical proofs for God's existence. Human beings know by nature that there is a God. They do not need to have God's existence demonstrated to them. In this sense atheism is a profoundly unnatural condition.

Calvin did not think that human beings could again see God at work in nature and history merely by reading the Bible. Human reason needed to be redeemed and the human will restored to harmony with the will of God. Scripture played an essential role in this process, as did the work of the Holy Spirit, illuminating what was true and restoring what was damaged. Just as the human predicament was not narrowly defined by Calvin as a merely epistemological matter, so, too, the resolution of that predicament was not reduced by him to the bare cognition of certain truths. Knowledge of God had meant for unfallen human nature love, trust, fear, obedience, and worship of God. It meant exactly the same thing for redeemed human nature.

THE CHURCH AS MOTHER AND SCHOOL

The restoration of the knowledge and love of God did not take place, for Calvin, in a social and historical vacuum. Although Calvin believed firmly in the Augustinian doctrine of predestination, the notion that no one can participate in salvation who has not been chosen and called by God, he did not focus on the individual believer in isolation from the church. While it was true, as Calvin saw it, that every human act of faith had been pre-determined before all time by a sovereign God, the relationship between election and faith was not a simple one. The eternal decree was executed in time. It set in motion a long history in Israel and the church, centring in Christ but by no means limited to the events recounted in the four gospels. God's decision to awaken faith in a child was, for Calvin, an eternal decision mediated in time through the society of the church, in which the child was baptized, instructed, and loved. In short, God elected to save in and through the church. The church was included in the decree and provided the means of grace – scripture, baptism, eucharist, preaching, catechesis – without which faith would have been impossible. Calvin echoed the old dictum of Cyprian, *extra ecclesiam nulla salus* (outside the church there is no salvation). Election did not subvert the church for Calvin, but rather underscored its central importance.

Calvin was fond of another saying of Cyprian: that one could not have God for a father who did not have the church as a mother. The image of the church in whose womb the faithful are conceived, born, and nurtured was an ancient and powerful one. To this traditional image Calvin added a second when he called the church both mother and school. The notion that the church was a school underscored for Calvin the centrality of the teaching mission of the church and the theological responsibility of the whole people of God, lay as well as clergy.

Just as the knowledge of God is not a simple matter of cognition but also of trust, obedience, and love, so, too, not all the lessons the church as school teaches are matters of intellectual apprehension. The church moulds the character of its members, reshapes their disordered affections, disciplines their unruly wills, invites them to sacrifice, and even instructs them how to die. It is a social instrument through which the Holy Spirit forms a new creation. Had Calvin heard Wesley's dictum that there is no such thing as a solitary Christian, he would have embraced it as his own.

That is not to say that Calvin regarded the cognitive content of the church's theological task as insubstantial, even on the level of the local parish. All Christians were called to love God with their minds as well as their hearts and could not delegate their responsibility to trained professionals. Of course, not everyone had the same gifts or the same capacity to learn. But all Christians, whatever their gifts, were called to exercise an explicit faith in God informed by the 'heavenly doctrine' of scripture. No one could plead, as had so often been done in the old, unreformed church, that it was sufficient to have an implicit faith in the church's teaching authority. Implicit faith divorced from explicit knowledge was for Calvin no faith at all. It was indolence and ignorance masquerading as piety.

THE QUARREL WITH THE CATHOLIC CHURCH

Large portions of Calvin's teaching, even when judged by the strictest standards of medieval Catholic theology, remained traditionally orthodox. In many respects Calvin could be described after his conversion as a Catholic Christian in the Western Augustinian tradition. When Martin Luther claimed in the Schmalkaldic Articles that he had no quarrel with the Catholic Church over the doctrine of the Trinity or the two natures of Christ, he spoke for Calvin as well. Calvin regarded the Reformation as an unavoidable dispute between Catholics and evangelicals over a long agenda of contested issues, but it was not for him an argument about everything imaginable, as though Catholics and Protestants could agree on nothing. Calvin was committed to reforming the old faith, not to minting an altogether new one. Nevertheless, his disagreements with the Catholic Church were substantial. Four in particular should be mentioned here: disagreements over baptism, penance, eucharist, and priesthood.

Baptism

Calvin retained the sacrament of infant baptism but discarded its traditional theological justification. Traditional Catholic theology taught that infant baptism washed away the guilt and punishment (*culpa et poena*) of original sin. Anabaptists rejected infant baptism altogether and thought that baptism should be administered only to believers; that is, persons old enough to understand the proclamation of the gospel and to embrace it by faith for themselves. While Calvin agreed with the Anabaptists that justification was by faith and that infant baptism did not wash away the effects of original sin, he nevertheless thought that faith was a result of the gifts and calling of God and that it occurred within the nurturing embrace of the church, a church that was for Calvin both mother and school. Baptism was the covenant sign of the church as circumcision had been the covenant sign of ancient Israel. Through baptism children were entrusted to the nurturing care of the church, enrolled in the school of faith, and marked with the seal of God's covenant. Outside this church there was no salvation.

Like Thomas Aquinas and Duns Scotus, Calvin insisted on a doctrine of election that was wholly gratuitous, not based on foreseen merit or even on the foreseen good use of God's gifts. For Calvin, predestination explained as no other theory could how faith was possible in a fallen world that repeatedly demonstrated that it had no place or time for God. Election was the mystery that created faith. Faith was never the believer's gift to God but always God's gift to the believer. Faith was therefore less a constitutive cause of the church (against the Anabaptists) than a constitutive effect. God was creating the church out of a human race in revolt, one that in Calvin's view was not only not inclined to meet God halfway but even dug in its heels and resisted God's initiatives, however gently offered. Calvin agreed with the sentiment expressed in John Donne's later poem, 'Batter my heart, three-personed God!' The city of Mansoul could be captured only by laying siege to it. Infant baptism was the perfect sign and seal of a theology of grace that placed no confidence whatever in any natural human inclination to move toward God and relied instead on the implacable persistence of love, the unwavering intention of a God who would not be turned aside by human alienation and indifference.

Penance

In the late medieval church in which Calvin grew up, parishioners normally communed once a year at Easter. The church encouraged its members to commune more often than once a year, perhaps as many as four times, but the *de facto* norm remained once. The church taught that parishioners could not receive the benefits that were offered to them in communion unless they were in a state of grace. Since it was very likely that most parishioners had committed at least one mortal since in the long interval since their last communion, they were expected to confess their sins to a priest and receive absolution. Ideally, such confessions were detailed. The penitent listed every mortal sin and the circumstances of its commission. The priest assisted the penitent by asking questions and offering encouragement. Once satisfied that penitents had made a good confession, the priest absolved them and admitted them to communion.

The doctrine of justification by faith set aside for Calvin the penitential practice of the medieval church (although Calvin, like Luther, still recommended private confession to a pastor as a useful spiritual discipline). Sinners who trusted the good news of pardon for sins through the life, death, and resurrection of Jesus Christ had the righteousness of Christ imputed to them. To be regarded as just by God through faith in Christ did not mean that the process of being slowly transformed by grace had been sidetracked but only that it was not the basis of God's acceptance of sinners. Sinners were made just by faith, a work internalized by the Holy Spirit and transforming in itself. Justified sinners were then sanctified by the Holy Spirit in a long process that embraced the whole of one's life from the initial moment of faith to the final moments of one's death. For Calvin the phrase 'repentance and faith' was misleading, since faith does not follow true repentance but precedes it. The proper order in the school of faith was 'faith and repentance'. Only believers knew what sin really was. Repentance was therefore the daily activity of the godly.

The Eucharist

Since the Fourth Lateran Council in 1215 the Catholic Church had taught that the real presence of Christ in the eucharist could best be safeguarded by the use of the term 'transubstantiation'. The substance of a thing is what that thing really is. The accidents of a thing are its qualities. When philosophers speak of accidents they are asking how a thing appears to us, what impact it makes on our senses. The substance of a rose is what makes a rose a rose and not a turnip. The accidents of the rose are its appearance (lovely), its smell (fragrant), its weight (light) and its taste (not generally recommended).

The eucharistic elements of bread and wine are known by their accidents. The wine looks like wine, smells like wine, feels like wine, and tastes like wine. However, a miracle occurs in the celebration of the mass by a validly ordained priest, who shares in the priesthood of Christ. The consecrated wine continues to look, smell, feel, and taste like unconsecrated wine. Its accidents remain unchanged. But the substance of the consecrated wine has been transformed. It is no longer wine. It is the body and blood of Jesus

Christ. The transition in the mass from one substance to another without changing the accidents of the first substance is called 'transubstantiation'.

Furthermore, the Catholic Church taught that the Lord's supper was a sacrifice. Although Catholics acknowledged that the sacrifice of Christ on Calvary was a unique event that could not be repeated, they regarded the celebration of the mass as a re-presentation of Christ's sacrifice to God the Father for the forgiveness of the sins of the priest and his congregation. As such it was an unbloody offering to God of transubstantiated bread and wine in order to obtain from God a benefit for the church available in no other way. Christ was not re-sacrificed (clearly an unnecessary, even impossible, act) but his unique sacrifice was renewed for the life of the church in the present.

Luther and Zwingli rejected the notion that the eucharist was a sacrifice. In their view it was a benefit offered by God to the church, not a sacrifice offered by the church to God. Moreover, they were unified in their opposition to the doctrine of transubstantiation. While Luther was happy to affirm the real presence of Christ in the eucharist, he saw no reason to affirm the substantial transformation of the consecrated bread and wine. Christ was really present in the eucharist, but so, too, was the substance of the bread and wine. Zwingli, by contrast, was happy neither with the Catholic nor with Luther's view. For Zwingli the elements of bread and wine signified the body and blood of Christ. The real body and blood were present, not in the eucharist, but at the right hand of God the Father. The Lord's supper was therefore a sign rather than the reality itself.

Calvin wanted to affirm with Luther the real presence of Christ, but could not accept his doctrine of ubiquity. Luther taught that the risen Christ was no longer subject to the limitations of space and time and had taken on the divine attribute of omnipresence. The risen humanity could therefore be physically present in the bread and wine on a thousand altars at the same time. Calvin thought that such teaching undermined the reality of the humanity of Christ and gave him a 'monstrous body' unlike any other human body. Calvin agreed with Zwingli that the risen humanity of Jesus Christ was finite and was to be found, as the words of the creed suggested, 'seated at the right hand of God the Father'. The real presence of Christ that Calvin advocated was what he called a 'spiritual real presence'.

Calvin deployed four explanations to redefine the real presence of Christ. First of all, he asked what it meant to affirm that Christ was substantially present in the eucharist. The substance of Christ's humanity was not, in Calvin's view, bones and sinews and veins, but the power and effect of his crucified and risen humanity for human salvation. Christ is therefore substantially present wherever the power and effect of his life, death, and resurrection are present. The eucharist is an instrument through which Christ mediates such power to his church.

The second explanation of spiritual real presence relied on what one might describe as the ecstasy of faith. Calvin argued that worshippers were lifted by faith to contemplate the humanity of Christ seated at the right hand of God the Father. In this case, the finite humanity of Christ did not descend to earth but the believing community ascended by faith to heaven. Of course, the congregation did not literally rise. What Calvin described here was an inner event. But the access to Christ was real, even if the language was metaphorical.

The third explanation Calvin offered was trinitarian. The Holy Spirit is the Spirit of the Son as well as the Spirit of the Father. One of the principal functions of the Holy Spirit was to make Christ present to the church. Therefore Christ is present to the church in the eucharist through the power and activity of the Holy Spirit. Wherever the Spirit is, there also is the Son, since the *opera Dei ad extra sunt indivisa* (the works of God directed outside himself cannot be divided).

The fourth and most difficult explanation to understand is an explanation labelled by Calvin's Lutheran opponents as the *extra-Calvinisticum* (the Calvinist outside). The name comes from a phrase, 'also outside the flesh' (*etiam extra carnem*), which Calvin used in the *Institutes*. To understand this phrase one needs to put it in the context of the classical Christian doctrine of the incarnation. The story of the incarnation is the story of the assumption of human nature by the divine Logos, the second person of the Trinity. Because of the assumption of human nature by the second person of the Trinity, Jesus Christ has both a finite human nature and an infinite, divine one. Calvin argued that, although Jesus Christ was fully divine and fully human, his infinite, divine nature was not exhausted by the incarnation but remained active 'also outside the flesh' (*etiam extra carnem*). In other words, the second person of the Trinity continued to do all the things he had always done, even after his assumption of humanity in Jesus of Nazareth. He continued to hold the stars in their courses, maintain the life-cycles of animals and plants, and order the change of seasons. Though the humanity of Christ was finite and could be in only one place at a time, the divinity was not limited by space and time and could be wherever it willed to be. This notion meant for Calvin that Christ could be present in the eucharist by his divine nature.

When some Lutheran theologians objected that the divine nature of Christ did not die for human salvation and that Calvin's account placed Christ's humanity at the right hand of God rather than in the eucharist, Calvin responded with an argument for spiritual real presence based on the doctrine of the hypostatic union. He appealed to the common Christian teaching that the human and divine natures of Christ were substantially and permanently bound to each other in the incarnation. Wherever the divine nature was present, the human nature was also present by virtue of the indissoluble bond between them. Calvin therefore concluded that, if Christ were present in the eucharist by his divine nature, he was assuredly present by his human nature as well, even if his humanity was seated at the right hand of God the Father.

Priesthood

Calvin agreed with the general Protestant rejection of the hierarchical priesthood. Catholic theology taught that ordination conferred a power upon ordinands, which they shared with Christ and with all other priests, but which they did not share with the laity. Only a priest could preside at a valid eucharist or absolve the sins of a penitent. Furthermore, only a bishop could ordain additional priests and so perpetuate the structure of the hierarchical priesthood. Unordained laity could not preside at the eucharist, absolve from sin, or ordain new priests and deacons. Catholic theology drew a sharp line between priests and laity and affirmed that the orderly continuation of the hierarchical priesthood was essential to the life of the church.

Calvin agreed with Luther that the common priesthood of believers meant that all Christians had the right by virtue of their baptism to preach and preside at the sacraments. There was no difference in kind between ministers and laypersons, but only a difference of office and function in the church. Ordination set aside some Christians to perform certain duties in the interest of the orderly conduct of the church's ministry. Calvin substituted for the Catholic ministry of deacons, priests, and bishops, a fourfold ministry of pastors, teachers, elders, and deacons.

Pastors devoted all of their time to discharging the ministry of preaching, prayer, presiding at the sacraments, and governing the church. They were assisted in their work by elders, who shared with the pastor the oversight of the spiritual life of the local congregation, and by deacons, who oversaw its charitable activities. Although the deacons who set policy in Geneva were always men, the deacons who discharged that policy were sometimes women. Both elders and deacons were laity, who earned their living through secular employment. Teachers were charged with responsibility for the education of the young and their formation in the Christian faith. Calvin himself functioned as a pastor in Geneva, though he also spent part of his week lecturing to schoolboys.

Christian discipline was enforced in Geneva through the consistory. The consistory dealt with a wide range of issues from trivial offences such as making unwanted noise in church services to more serious matters such as domestic violence or adultery. The consistory had no authority to punish serious offenders, who were handed over to the secular authorities for appropriate punishment. But it did instruct, persuade, console, and admonish the lesser offenders, whose frequently noisy problems had come to the attention of the larger community.

The institutions of secular government in Geneva were not designed by Calvin, though he attempted to influence their functioning. Calvin, like Cicero, preferred a mixed constitution that was partly democratic and partly aristocratic, though he did not question the legitimacy of monarchy or worry unduly about civil constitutions. Although human beings were by nature social animals, the legitimacy of the state rested on the ordination of God on the one hand and the disorder caused by sin on the other. The sword of the magistrate was ordained by God and Christians owed obedience to the authorities set over them. God, after all, was reclaiming his fallen creation, not only through the church but also to some extent through the restoration of order by the state. Calvin rejected the contention of the Anabaptists that the office of magistrate was no role for a true Christian. Governing justly is an activity for which Christians are especially well suited and 'Christian magistrate' is no oxymoron.

When Calvin died in 1564 he instructed his friends to see to it that he was buried in an unmarked grave. It was partly an act of humility and partly an attempt to discourage an unwanted veneration of his grave. The memorial that he wanted was not an elegant inscription in marble or the reintroduction of a modified cult of the saints. The memorial he wanted was the memorial he already had, the living legacy of the men and women whose lives he had influenced, and the sermons, commentaries, treatises, catechetical literature, letters, confessions, and multiple editions of the *Institutes* he bequeathed to the church. Calvin never thought he was writing solely for his own place and time. In this conviction history has proved him correct.

11 John Calvin and later Calvinism: the identity of the Reformed tradition

RICHARD A. MULLER

•Synod of Dort, 1618

Between the middle of the sixteenth century and the beginning of the seventeenth, the Reformed theology of John Calvin and several of his predecessors and contemporaries developed into a significant international movement that has come to be known as 'Calvinism'. As is typically the case in history, the movement was named, not by its proponents, but by its detractors, who took the name of its most famous leader as the basis for a label. The movement itself was in fact fairly diverse – bounded by confessional norms but guided by the thought of a group of founders and formulators rather than by a single person, and developed on an international scale by numerous theologians and exegetes, none of whom took it as their central task to reproduce Calvin's theology in other times and places. Given this diversity in origin and in development, it is more accurate to speak of 'the Reformed churches' or of 'the Reformed tradition' than of 'Calvinism'.

ROOTS AND BRANCHES – PERSONS AND PLACES

The Reformed or Calvinist tradition is rooted in the Augustinian tradition of the Western church and, in the sixteenth and seventeenth centuries, found its antecedents not only in the works of Augustine himself but in the medieval Augustinian tradition. This is not to say that one must reify a 'new Augustinian school' of thought (*schola Augustiniana moderna*) as some scholars have tended to do, but rather that the Reformed tradition looked to the theology of grace as mediated and developed by a host of medieval thinkers – Aquinas and Scotus among them, as well as theologians of the Augustinian order such as Giles of Rome and Gregory of Rimini. The ways in which this tradition was transmitted to the earliest generation of the Reformed, notably reformers such as Huldrych Zwingli (1484–1531), Martin Bucer (1491–1551), Wolfgang Capito (1478–1541), John Oecolampadius (1482–1531), and Guillaume Farel (1489–1565), remain a matter for research and are certainly as diverse as the backgrounds of the thinkers themselves. Thus, Zwingli was a humanistically trained exegete who had little contact with either a monastic or a scholastic theological training. Bucer was a theologically trained Dominican who had studied at Heidelberg. Capito studied medicine, law, and theology at Freiburg and held strongly humanistic views concerning languages and method of study and exposition. Oecolampadius studied at Bologna and Heidelberg, first in jurisprudence and later in theology, and was well acquainted with the medieval tradition, both scholastic and mystical. Early on in his career he had lectured on Lombard's *Sentences*, but also was steeped in the classical and biblical languages. Farel came out of the humanistic and reformist circles of the University of Paris and the so-called 'circle of Meaux'.

Already in this earliest group of Reformed thinkers, there is a series of theological issues and conclusions that are identifiably Reformed and that provide a foundation for the tradition of doctrine that would be developed by successive generations of Reformed teachers and theologians. All of these writers held to the Reformation assumption of the priority of scripture over tradition as the sole, absolute norm for theology. This biblicism was governed not only by the careful interpretation of texts in the original languages of the Bible, but also by a conviction of the unity of the message of scripture in both testaments. This latter view related, in turn, to a doctrine, especially clear in the thought of Zwingli, of the unity of the covenant of God in both testaments, despite certain differences in the forms of its administration.

An example of this unity under two differing administrations can be found in the Reformed sacramental theology: baptism and the Lord's supper, although given only in the New Testament, parallel in meaning and replace in form the Old Testament sacraments of circumcision and the Passover. The strongly covenantal sense of baptism was shared by Bucer. So too are the early Reformed relatively in accord in their view of the sacraments: positively, they hold two sacraments, baptism and the Lord's supper and view both as signs of the covenant, borrowing the traditional definition, visible signs of invisible grace. In their teaching on the Lord's supper, these early Reformed were united in denying a bodily presence of Christ, although they differed – as would the later Reformed tradition – over the nature of the eucharistic presence, with some, such as Zwingli and Oecolampadius, holding for a memorialistic understanding of the sacrament. Corresponding to their views on the Lord's supper, these early Reformed thinkers affirmed the integrity of Christ's two natures, divinity and humanity, in the one person of Christ, and insisted that the risen Jesus could be bodily present only in heaven. In addition, this early Reformed theology held, uniformly, an understanding of salvation as occurring by grace alone,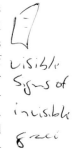

visible signs of invisible grace

to the point of affirming a doctrine of predestination, specifically of the gracious election of some members of the human race to eternal salvation.

No balanced comment on the trajectories leading from the early Reformed to the Reformed orthodox can leave aside the positive Lutheran influence, in some part from Martin Luther (1483–1546) himself, and in larger part from Philipp Melanchthon (1497–1560). Not only did Luther's theology influence early Reformed thinkers, such as Bucer, but Melanchthon's thought, both in its humanist methods and in its doctrinal content, had a profound impact on Reformed thinkers, particularly of the second generation, most notably Calvin. From Luther, both for the first and for the second generation of the Reformed, came the understanding of justification by grace through faith alone and the corresponding recognition that a Christian is at once justified and a sinner (*simul iustus et peccator*). In addition, the Reformed found in Luther's treatise on the *Bondage of the Will* a surer ally in the doctrine of God's predestination than mildly synergistic teachers of later confessional Lutheranism were able to discern. In Melanchthon, the Reformed found a Christological and eucharistic ally, who affirmed the integrity of the two natures in the union and who moved away from a bodily towards a more spiritual conception of Christ's presence in the Lord's supper. More importantly, they gained from Melanchthon a significant insight into the way in which doctrinal topics were to be elicited from scripture in the work of exegesis and then bound together in a suitable order for the creation of a teachable body of Christian doctrine, a set of 'Commonplaces' or *Loci communes*. The influence of Melanchthon's method is particularly evident in Calvin's *Institutes.*

In what can be called a second generation of Reformed theologians – second in the sense, at least, that its members matured later and provided the Reformed faith with a mid-century dogmatic and confessional codification – we count, among others, Calvin, Bullinger, Musculus, Vermigli, and Hyperius. It is certainly this group of writers that so placed its stamp on the thought of the church that we can speak of a Reformed tradition, and did so in such a varied way that we must call it 'Reformed' rather than 'Calvinist'. As, moreover, in the first generation of Reformed theologians, this second generation evidences considerable variety both in training and in intellectual development. This diversity is integral to the identity of the Reformed tradition.

John Calvin (1509–64) studied law and was trained in humanist methods at Paris, Orléans, and Bourges. What is perhaps most remarkable about Calvin as a theologian is that he was not theologically trained: some writers have attempted to claim that he studied theology at Paris under the Scotist thinker, John Major, but this cannot be documented and all of the evidence that can be gathered from Calvin's writings argues against it. Calvin's career as a Reformer and theologian, largely confined to Geneva, saw the production of one of the most influential theologies of the era, the *Institutes of the Christian Religion* (1536–59), and a host of commentaries, sermons, tracts, and treatises. Although the *Institutes* is the most significant single expression of Calvin's theology, it does not represent the entirety of his thought or even all of the topics he addressed. His thought, as it had an impact on his times, must be elicited from the larger body of his works, particularly the commentaries and sermons, which cover nearly the entire Bible.

Heinrich Bullinger (1504–75) studied first with the Brethren of the Common Life in Emmerich and then in Cologne, where he studied first scholastic theology and later the church fathers. He there became involved in church reform through the writings of Luther and Melanchthon. Before becoming overtly attached to the movement for church reform, Bullinger served as a teacher in Cistercian monasteries, first at Kappel and later at Zurich. As Zwingli's successor in Zurich, Bullinger wrote biblical commentaries and several larger works of theology, most notably the *Decades*, a series of formal sermons on all points of Christian doctrine, plus numerous tracts and treatises. Although not confined to these topics, Bullinger's influence on the Reformed tradition was strongly felt in his sacramental theology, which followed out the Zwinglian model, his teaching on covenant, and his eschatology. He was one of the first of the Reformed to write a separate treatise on covenant, and his commentary in the form of a hundred sermons on Revelation was perhaps the most influential work on the last things in his generation. Bullinger's influences extended far beyond Switzerland – notably to England and the Netherlands, where his works were widely diffused in translation.

Wolfgang Musculus (1497–1563) was a Benedictine monk who studied theology in the monastery near Lixheim. He was attracted to the Reform, most probably through reading tracts by Luther, and fled the monastery in 1518. He spent several years in Strasbourg, working as a preaching assistant to Matthäus Zell and studying theology and biblical languages under Bucer and Capito. After serving as a reformer in Augsburg, Musculus became the primary theological teacher of the academy in Bern. During his years at Augsburg and Bern, Musculus wrote a series of highly influential commentaries and a major theological system, the *Loci communes sacrae theologiae* ('Commonplaces of sacred theology') (1560). His commentaries were well received throughout Europe and the British Isles, and the *Loci communes* was translated into English.

Peter Martyr Vermigli (1500–62) was trained at the universities of Padua and Bologna and participated in reformist activity in Italy until 1542, when he fled to Strasbourg and became a member of the circle of leading Reformed theologians of his era. Vermigli later taught both at Oxford and at Zurich. A member of the Augustinian order, he knew the strictly Augustinian tradition of medieval thinkers such as Giles of Rome and Gregory of Rimini as well as the theology of Thomas Aquinas. He was also well trained in the biblical languages – indeed, both theologically and linguistically, Vermigli was probably the most highly trained of the Reformed thinkers of his generation. In his day, Vermigli was known as a significant biblical commentator whose mastery of the biblical languages was second to none – and, by way of the efforts of Robert Masson, who compiled a full system of theology out of Vermigli's many writings, as a major dogmatician.

Andreas Hyperius (1511–64), the least-known of this group of thinkers, studied theology at Tournai and Paris. From the pen of Hyperius we have the most concerted attempt of any Reformed thinker of his generation to establish a methodological basis for Reformed theology: we have, first, a full *Methodus* or body of Christian doctrines, in which Hyperius not only provides a synopsis of the major doctrinal topics but also indicates how they ought to be organized. In addition, he wrote treatises on the method of theological study and the 'practice' of preaching. He also wrote an influential catechism and several biblical commentaries.

CONFESSIONAL ORTHODOXY AND SCHOLASTICISM

Historical overview

The historical trajectory of 'Calvinist' orthodoxy after the time of Calvin can be divided into roughly three eras: early orthodoxy, from the mid-sixteenth century to the time of the Synod of Dort (1618–19) and its aftermath; high orthodoxy, from c. 1620/40 to the end of the seventeenth century; and late orthodoxy, from the end of the seventeenth century well into the eighteenth. And, of course, forms of Calvinism or Reformed theology remain into the present, represented by various Reformed and Presbyterian denominations. The present essay traces primarily the late sixteenth-century development, with a few comments concerning significant issues in the early seventeenth century. Our focus here is on the development of Reformed thought from the time of Calvin, Bullinger, and other mid-sixteenth-century codifiers of the Reformed faith to the end of the era of early orthodoxy – thus, from c. 1565 to c. 1620/40. Given the nature of the theological efforts of Calvin and his contemporaries, the Calvinist or Reformed tradition had, around 1565, a well-defined doctrinal codification that took the form of a series of national or regional confessions and catechisms, several major gatherings of Christian doctrine into systems or compendia (in fact, one from each of the five above-noted codifiers), and a burgeoning exegetical tradition that had already commented on the entire Bible several times over.

The confessions and catechisms by themselves provided an indication of the shape and direction of later Reformed thought. There was what can only be called a burst of confessional activity among the Reformed that began toward the middle of the sixteenth century. In the *Consensus Tigurinus* (1549) the Calvinian Reformed line of Geneva and the Zwinglian or Bullingerian line of Zurich came to terms on the doctrine of the Lord's supper by finding a confessional vehicle in which the Genevan sense of Christ's spiritual presence and of the identification of sacraments as means of grace could be presented at the same time as the Zurich representational or memorialistic view with its understanding of sacraments as ordinances and not means. The document is, in fact, a model for the unity and diversity of the Reformed faith – it does not isolate a single eucharistic definition as orthodoxy but instead allows a particular spectrum of views.

This breadth also appears in the group of confessional documents that defined the international Reformed faith in the subsequent decades: the Gallican Confession (1559), the Scots Confession (1560), the Belgic Confession (1561); the Thirty-nine Articles of the Church of England (1563), the Heidelberg Catechism (1563), and the Second Helvetic Confession (1566). The result of this mid-sixteenth-century confessional codification was a trajectory of theological development very different from that of Lutheranism: whereas the Reformed, between the time of the *Consensus Tigurinus* and the Second Helvetic Confession, established a confessional foundation for their churches and theology, the Lutherans were engaged in bitter internecine struggle over Christology, the eucharistic presence, the relationship of faith and works, the character of original sin, and the relationship of human willing to divine grace in the work of salvation – prior to the resolution of the controversies in the Formula of Concord (1579). Prior to achieving their confessional codification, the Lutherans engaged in a debate for more than twenty years over whether salvation was in fact accomplished by grace alone or by synergism, the interrelationship of human willing and divine grace. By way of contrast, the Reformed, on the basis of an achieved confessional codification, took less than six months to identify and excise the problem of synergism at the Synod of Dort.

During this era of confessional stabilization and the rise of orthodoxy, Reformed or Calvinist thought did undergo a remarkable development. In German Reformed lands, following the publication of the Heidelberg Catechism, writers such as Zacharias Ursinus (1534–83), Caspar Olevianus (1536–87), Petrus Boquinus (d. 1582), and Jerome Zanchi (1516–90) produced a massive doctrinal contribution to the Reformed faith. Ursinus, the primary author of the Heidelberg Catechism, developed in lectures an extended exposition of the catechism and a series of 'scholastic exercises' in theology that formed the basic pattern of theological education in his era. Olevianus wrote the first major Reformed treatise on the covenant between God and human beings and a lengthy exposition of faith based on the Apostles' Creed. Boquinus wrote a theological system stressing the concepts of the communion of the faithful and covenant. Zanchi produced an important personal confession of faith in which he commented on all major doctrinal points and also developed a vast, albeit fragmentary, system of doctrine noteworthy for its grasp of the older theological tradition, particularly that of the Middle Ages, and for its appropriation for Reformed theology of the body of principles and distinctions used by the medieval doctors. These Heidelberg theologians also wrote a vast series of treatises in defence of Reformed positions against Lutherans and Roman Catholics and they testified to their sense of continuity with the preceding generation by constructing compendia of Calvin's *Institutes*: in this latter genre, we have contributions from both Olevianus and Zanchi.

In Switzerland, particularly in Geneva, there were also significant developments. On the one hand, Calvin's chosen successor, Theodore Beza (1519–1605), continued to supervise the work of the academy in turning out Reformed theologians and pastors for work in the churches and schools, particularly of France and the Netherlands, and to defend the developing Reformed tradition on such issues as Christology, predestination, and the Lord's supper. Although he wrote no theological system, Beza did produce a series of significant shorter instructional works – two confessions of faith, a catechism, and a 'book of Christian questions and answers' in catechetical format. Beza also superintended the gathering of the Harmony of the Reformed Confessions (1580) in response to the Lutheran Formula of Concord. Certainly, Beza's most important contribution was his *Annotations on the New Testament*, in which he evidenced his mastery of humanistic philological techniques and his ability to offer a biblically grounded basis for Reformed teaching. It was during the time of Beza's supervision of the Academy of Geneva that it produced such eminent Reformed teachers of the late sixteenth and early seventeenth centuries as Lambert Daneau (1530–95), Francis Junius (1545–1602), and Johann Polyander (1568–1646) and, in addition, that brilliant defector from the Reformed faith, Jacobus Arminius (1559–1609).

In this era, the French and Dutch Reformed also developed, and did so under the pressure of intense persecution at the hands of Roman Catholics. In addition to the framing of the French Reformed faith by the Gallican Confession, the third quarter of the sixteenth century saw the development of a distinct French Reformed style that would be exported to other

Reformed centres, notably to England, in the latter part of the century: specifically, the rhetorical and logical or dialectical models of Petrus Ramus (c. 1515–72), much debated in their time, had a vast impact on the structuring of Reformed theology in the early orthodox era. Ramus argued for the replacement of Aristotelian categories of predication with topics elicited from the materials of argument, at least in the organization and exposition of the major academic disciplines, including theology. This approach itself was not at all revolutionary: the use of a topical or place logic had been effectively advocated in the fifteenth century by Rudolf Agricola, and the Agricolan pattern had been developed by Melanchthon and, arguably, adopted by Calvin as well. Ramus' importance stems instead from the pointedness of his advocacy of the topical method and, above all, from his connection of the topical model with a method of division of the topic into subtopics, all organized into the form of charts utilizing 'French brackets' as a visual tool.

The massive impact of this approach is seen in Reformed tracts, treatises, theological systems, and commentaries of the late sixteenth and early seventeenth centuries. In brief, Ramus offered his age an approach to organization and, indeed, architectonics, that proved eminently useful in the construction of well-argued systems of theology and in the production of clearly organized biblical commentaries. In the latter case, as evidenced in the works of Johannes Piscator (1546–1625) and Jean Diodati (1576–1649), the diagrams could be effectively conjoined with the rhetorical analysis of text. Ramus' influence, however, must be fairly strictly limited to method: older scholarship has claimed an association between the advocacy of Ramist logic and a non-predestinarian, *a posteriori*, salvation-historical and covenantal approach to theology. This claim, however, fails for lack of any solid historical documentation. There is, in the first place, a clear use of Ramist method by staunch predestinarians; in the second place, there is no ultimate separation in Reformed theology between covenantal and predestinarian thinking, and in the third place there is no clear association of Ramism with the foundations of Reformed covenant thought.

The Calvinism or Reformed theology of the British Isles developed along doctrinal lines quite similar to the continental development. The churchmen and theologians who returned from cities of refuge on the continent following the death of Queen Mary were strongly allied to the Reformed faith: they had developed theologically in such places as Geneva and Strasbourg and, unlike the theological Reformers of the Henrician era, had few ties to Wittenberg. Writers such as William Whittingham (c. 1524–79) and Thomas Gilby (d. 1585) were associated with the Geneva Bible, in which a Genevan Reformed set of marginal glosses was juxtaposed with a highly successful rendering of the text of scripture into English. Whittingham and Gilby are also associated with other translation efforts, such as the translation of Beza's short treatise on predestination, the *Tabula praedestinationis*, into English. Other returning churchmen, including John Jewel (1522–71) and Edmund Grindal (1519–83), returned to become Elizabeth's bishops and were instrumental in giving a Reformed tendency to the church of the Elizabethan Settlement.

In the last two decades of the sixteenth century, English Reformed theology was the dominant model in the universities, certainly at Cambridge, where Thomas Cartwright (1535–1603), William Whitaker (1548–95), and William Perkins (1558–1602) framed the doctrinal teaching of the university. Cartwright was the teacher of several generations of Puritan or Reformed thinkers, and Perkins stands as a major English codifier of such doctrines as predestination and covenant, as well as one of the major English proponents of the Ramist approach to organization and argument. Following 1590, English theology experienced a controversy that is of importance if only because it is a nearly perfect foreshadowing of the Arminian controversy in the Netherlands. Peter Baro (1534–99), who had been Lady Margaret professor of divinity at Cambridge since 1574, began to argue against a strictly forensic doctrine of justification by grace through faith alone and to propose a doctrine of election on the condition of human belief or, indeed, choice to believe. Conflict began immediately in the university. Whitaker, the Regius professor of divinity, opposed Baro directly, Perkins produced his treatise on predestination, *A Golden Chaine*, and Archbishop John Whitgift (c. 1530–1604) supervised the drafting of the Lambeth Articles (1595), in which a Reformed doctrine of grace and election was affirmed.

At the same time that the English were developing an early orthodox form of Reformed theology, a parallel development was under way in Scotland, with such writers as Robert Rollock (1555–99), Robert Howie (c. 1565–1645), John Sharp or Scharpius (c. 1572–1648), and John Cameron (1579–1625). All four demonstrate the international character of the Reformed movement: Rollock taught at St Andrews and Edinburgh, and his works, particularly his commentaries, were known on the continent and respected by, among others, Theodore Beza. Howie studied at Aberdeen, Rostock, Herborn, and Basel, and the greater part of his published works appeared at Basel. He taught at St Andrews and Aberdeen. Sharp taught both in France, at Die, and in Edinburgh – and Cameron was the moving force behind theological developments at the Academy of Saumur in the early seventeenth century. These thinkers are also of importance to the development of Reformed covenant theology.

Development of Reformed theology in the Netherlands was tied, in the latter half of the sixteenth century, to the dedicated work of French- and

Genevan-trained ministers and, following the founding of the University of Leiden (1575), to the efforts of Genevan-trained professors such as Daneau and Junius. The Belgic Confession, written by Guy (or Guido) de Brés (1522–67) on the model of the Gallican, was ratified by a series of synods in the Low Countries between 1566 and 1581 as the confessional standard of the Dutch Reformed churches. These synods also confirmed the use of the Heidelberg Catechism as the primary ground of religious instruction for the Dutch churches. These decisions set the stage for the theological conflict leading up to the Synod of Dort. As the seventeenth-century Arminian historian, Gerard Brandt, indicated, the term 'Reformed' meant two things in the late sixteenth-century Netherlands: either the general alteration of the churches from an unreformed Romanism to a Protestant faith purged of abuses, or the advocacy of a Calvinistic or Reformed confessional settlement. The former usage Brandt identified as more typical of the laity, the latter of the majority of the clergy. In this context, it was not unusual for individual Protestant clergy to object to certain elements of the confessionally Reformed faith, particularly to the doctrine of election or predestination. There were such protests between 1581 and 1600, at a time when the newly graduated and ordained Arminius was serving as a minister in Amsterdam.

When Arminius was appointed to the faculty of theology in Leiden (1602), there was some initial protest over his theology, but he had not yet published any writings and he was able to allay the fears of clergy and colleagues in a series of interviews and orations. Shortly after his appointment, however, his views on predestination, Christology, and the usefulness of late sixteenth-century Jesuit theology caused controversy, particularly with his colleagues Francis Gomar (1563–1641) and Lucas Trelcatius the Younger (1573–1607). From 1604 until the end of his life (1609) he was engaged in nearly constant controversy. At the centre of the debate were Arminius' views on predestination and the way in which the concept of divine foreknowledge that he had learned by reading the writings of the Jesuit theologian Luis de Molina shaped his conception of the relationship of divine grace to human choice. In brief, Arminius held that God elects to salvation, on the basis of his foreknowledge, all those who have come to belief. The human choice to believe precedes the divine choice to save individuals. Arminius was censured for this teaching and, in 1610, when his followers presented an admonition or *Remonstrance* to the Dutch Reformed church, their reaffirmation of his views precipitated the debate that led to the Synod of Dort.

The decisions or 'Canons' of Dort reaffirmed, against the Arminians, the basic Reformed or Calvinistic doctrines of the pervasive original sinfulness of human beings, the necessity of an entirely gracious divine election to salvation, the perseverance of the elect in their salvation by God's grace, and the limitation of the application of the all-sufficient satisfaction of Christ to the elect. Inasmuch as this was an international synod, with delegates from Switzerland, the German Reformed cities, and England, as well as the Dutch delegates in attendance, its decisions were broadly representative of the Reformed faith and a normative statement of these doctrinal points for the seventeenth century.

Some basic definitions

The development and institutionalization of the Reformed tradition can best be defined and the nature of its continuity with the Reformation understood when the two terms typically used to characterize it are properly understood: orthodoxy and scholasticism. In brief, 'orthodoxy' refers to the theological content of the Reformed tradition and 'scholasticism' to one of the methods used in its exposition. Orthodoxy simply means 'right' or 'correct teaching' and, in the case of the Reformed tradition, has been framed by such confessional documents as the Gallican Confession, the Belgic Confession, the Scots Confession, the Heidelberg Catechism, and (from the seventeenth century) the Canons of Dort and the Westminster Standards. 'Scholasticism', by contrast, refers to the academic and often highly technical method for the definition and elaboration of this theological orthodoxy – as distinct from other methods of exposition such as the catechetical, exegetical, and homiletical.

The distinction between method and content is important if only because of the lingering tendency of some writers to make the interrelated mistakes of, first, confusing scholasticism with a particular theological content – in the case of Reformed theology, a deductive predestinarianism at the source of every doctrinal point – and then of assuming that scholastic approaches to theology produced a doctrinal content at considerable variance with the theology of the Reformation. Examination of the documents of the era, however, demonstrates quite the opposite: the methodological vehicle of scholasticism carried Calvinist thought forward into the seventeenth century different in form but virtually the same in basic content as the thought of Calvin and his contemporaries. The differences between Reformed orthodox theology and the thought of any given Reformer, moreover, are best accounted for, not in terms of methodological change, but in terms of the inherent varieties of formulation in the Reformed tradition, the cultural and geographical diversity of the movement itself, and the numerous thinkers involved who offered different nuances at all points in the history of the Reformed churches. Thus, the differences between Calvin's theology and the thought of a late sixteenth-century Calvinist such as Perkins or Polanus are hardly more pronounced than the differences that can be observed in Calvin's own time between his thought and the thought of Musculus or Bullinger.

It is also important to recognize that the term 'scholastic', as understood in the sixteenth and seventeenth centuries, indicated an academic style and method and, therefore, cannot be applied as an exhaustive descriptor of any particular thinker. In other words, a Reformed or Calvinist thinker who used scholastic method in the classroom of a university would not use it in preaching or in catechizing the young. The confessions and catechisms of the Reformed written during the era of orthodoxy, therefore, share a doctrinal foundation with the scholastic theology of the era, but are not themselves to be considered as 'scholastic' documents.

Reformed orthodoxy, moreover, must be defined in terms of the limits set on theological speculation and development by the confessions of the Reformed churches and not, as some historians have done, in terms of particular preferred trajectories of thought, often defined entirely on the basis of their analysis of an individual founder of the faith, such as Calvin or Bullinger. This problematical practice has led to a rather narrow view of Reformed orthodoxy as excluding, for example, the federal theology of Johannes Cocceius and his followers, the variant teachings of the seventeenth-century theologians at the Academy of Saumur, and the modified or even diluted Cartesianism of a fairly large number of mid- and late seventeenth-century Reformed theologians. Despite the intense debate over each of these seventeenth-century developments, none of them falls, strictly speaking, outside of the bounds of Reformed or Calvinist orthodoxy as defined by the confessional documents of the sixteenth and seventeenth centuries.

THE THEOLOGICAL TRADITION

What we have already begun to describe in our identification of the roots and branches of the Reformed tradition and in our discussion of the successive generations of Reformed theologians and the rise of a scholastic orthodoxy is a single but variegated Reformed tradition, bounded by a series of fairly uniform confessional concerns but quite diverse in patterns of formulation – not two or more traditions, as is sometimes claimed.

The theological task

The success of the Reformation left Protestant forces in command of large geographical areas. With this ground gained, Protestantism was increasingly defined in religious matters by confessional documents and, from an institutional perspective, proved capable not only of surviving but also of developing. Such development, framed by confessional definition, in turn provided a context for the rise of educational issues somewhat different from those faced by the Reformers themselves. The Protestant universities were now pressed to formulate and teach theology in detail to generations of students and pastors who had been raised Protestant – and at the same time to identify Protestantism as not only *a* form but the *correct* form of Christianity over against the claims of Rome.

From an educational or pedagogical perspective, the era of early ortho-doxy was, for the Reformed churches, an era in which theologians had to concern themselves with methods of education, specifically with the her-itage of logic and rhetoric, the practice of exegesis, and the proper identifica-tion and arrangement of theological *loci* or topics for the sake of teaching. Increasingly, the Reformed universities and, given the nature of the aca-demic curriculum, the large-scale theological systems, were modelled on scholastic disputations. At the same time, the logical tools of the early Ref-ormation, notably the Agricolan place logic as modified by Melanchthon, and the later method known as Ramism, were used by Reformed thinkers to give form and structure to their theology. The formal and methodolog-ical result of this development was a Reformed scholasticism, a theology academic in its method, structured around the traditional method of dispu-tation and definition, but altered from the medieval versions of scholastic method by its training in late Renaissance logic and rhetoric.

Some definition is necessary here: the place logic of Agricola and Melanchthon emphasized the examination of the text of a document in order to identify the topics or central issues presented there. This approach led directly to a pattern of biblical interpretation and theological formu-lation that related the exegesis of the text of scripture directly to the task of eliciting standard topics or 'places', *loci communes*, from scripture and then using these topics as the core of theology. This approach is found early on in the Reformation in Melanchthon's *Loci communes* (1521; final edi-tion, 1560) and is evident also in Calvin's *Institutes* (1539; final edition, 1559). It is also a significant methodological link between the Reformation and later Protestant orthodoxy, given the tendency of late sixteenth- and seventeenth-century Reformed thinkers to continue the *locus* method both in their biblical exegesis and in their theological systems.

As is the case with much of the theological development that took place in the sixteenth century, the detailed presentation of rules for theological formulation – whether on the larger scale of methods for the whole of a theological system or on the smaller scale of definitions of theology as a discipline and finely grained arguments concerning the relationship of biblical interpretation to doctrinal formulation – the rise of Reformed orthodoxy meant the explicit statement of norms and issues that had often been left unstated or barely sketched out by the Reformers. In true Renaissance fashion, the Reformers did produce a variety of treatises on theological pedagogy, indicating how theology ought to be studied. Melanchthon and Bullinger are noteworthy for their essays.

Scripture and exegetical issues

One of the erroneous contrasts often made between the theology of the Reformers and that of their orthodox and scholastic successors presents the theology of the Reformation as a biblical and exegetical theology and that of the Reformed orthodox as a highly dogmatic and rational theology, largely negligent of exegetical issues. It is important to remove this fiction explicitly and entirely. Like the Reformers, the Protestant orthodox held scripture to be the Word of God, and understood the relationship between God as the primary author of the whole and the prophets and apostles as the human authors of each part on the analogy of 'dictation'. This identification of scripture as the authoritative Word was the basis for the Reformers' insistence that scripture alone is the final norm for theology and of the Reformed orthodox identification of scripture as the 'cognitive foundation' or *principium cognoscendi* of theology, in contrast to the fallible, albeit useful, standard of the church's tradition and the standards of contemporary teachers, councils, or philosophical argument.

We can certainly speak of a development of the Reformed doctrine of scripture from the Reformation into the era of orthodoxy: the later theologians, honed by debate with Roman Catholics, offer detailed discussions of the clarity and sufficiency of the text. Specifically, they argued that, although all texts in scripture are not equally clear, yet the truth that is necessary to salvation is clearly and sufficiently given, and that the difficult portions of text can be interpreted by properly trained clergy in the light of the clear statements found in other places and on the basis of an understanding of the original languages. It is possible to identify, in other words, the development of a fairly refined doctrine of scripture in the late sixteenth century – but it is quite incorrect to claim that the later writers depart from the basic teaching of the Reformation. It is certainly incorrect to assert that the Reformers understood scripture as anything other than the infallible, inspired Word of God and the sole foundation for Christian teaching – or to assert that the later orthodox developed a mechanical form of the doctrine of scripture that was insensitive to the power of the preached Word.

144 *Richard A. Muller*

Predestination and covenant

It is one of the more curious errors of interpretation of the Reformed tradition to speak of 'Calvin's doctrine of predestination' as if it were his own peculiar formulation, and something new grafted on to an earlier, less predestinarian movement. Whereas it is true that several different formulations of the doctrine are to be found in the Reformed tradition, all three of the basic forms have the same basic implication: some members of the human race are eternally known by God as those who will be saved by grace through faith, and the others are justly damned for their sins. Thus, from the beginnings of the Reformation, we can discern a double predestinarianism, a language of divine election and reprobation similar to Calvin's, in Bucer and probably in Zwingli. Calvin quite clearly taught both election and reprobation of human beings, considered eternally by God as created and fallen – what would come to be called the 'infralapsarian' view. While Bullinger could define the doctrine as a double decree (as he did in his *Decades*), he could also, as in the Second Helvetic Confession (a work largely his), argue for a single predestination consisting only in God's election of some, leaving the remainder of humanity to its own devices and, as a result, to its damnation (another form of infralapsarianism). Rather than prompting us to use the confession to argue for a deep rift between Calvin and Bullinger, the difference between the confession and the *Decades* ought to alert us to the differing needs of personal formulation (as in the *Decades*) and public or corporate statement (as in the confession).

In the work of Calvin's associate and successor, Theodore Beza, primarily for the purpose of defining predestination in such a way as to exclude all divine foreknowledge of human merit or demerit, we encounter a tendency to argue for double predestination, election and reprobation, as defined in the mind of God prior to the will to create – the so-called 'supralapsarian' view. Beza's motive in arguing in this fashion was to exclude all possibility of understanding human merit as a ground of the divine choice of some for salvation. Still, Beza's approach appealed to only a minority of the Reformed thinkers of the orthodox era, notably William Perkins, Francis Gomar, and Johannes Maccovius (1578–1644), while the infralapsarian model was ensconced as the confessional norm in the Canons of Dort. The Reformed orthodox doctrine of predestination differs from the doctrine found in Calvin and his contemporaries only in its form of presentation and precision of definition; in the era of orthodoxy, it received closely defined scholastic elaboration, and debates arose between proponents of the infra- and supralapsarian definitions – the substance of the doctrine, however, was unchanged. In other words, the basic premise of the doctrine, whether formulated as a single or double decree or in infra- or supralapsarian terms, is that salvation rests on the free and sovereign election of God, and damnation results from human sin.

A similar issue arises in the development of the Reformed doctrine of the covenant: the doctrine was formulated differently by theologians of the generation of Calvin and Bullinger – with Bullinger providing the more significant doctrinal statement in various treatises, and Calvin offering primarily exegetical and homiletical statements. In addition, the trajectory of the development of the doctrine between the time of Calvin and the era of orthodoxy remains somewhat unclear. Both Calvin and Bullinger wrote at length of the covenant of grace – Bullinger in several treatises and in his commentaries, and Calvin in both commentaries and sermons, although not in his *Institutes*. Although there are some minor differences in formulation, both Calvin and Bullinger proposed a thoroughly gracious covenant given unilaterally by God as the basis of salvation, and both used bilateral language in describing human responsibility in covenant with God. The Reformed doctrine of covenant is, therefore, neither opposed to nor in tension with the Reformed doctrine of predestination, which also declares a grace unilaterally bestowed by God and assumes human responsibility and obedience under and enabled by grace.

Following 1560, both Musculus and Ursinus proposed, albeit very briefly, a concept of a covenant in creation that had certain affinities with medieval conceptions of creation as an order established and maintained by God. This concept, together with a view of unfallen human nature as capable of understanding God's law, was developed by such thinkers as Olevianus, Fenner, Perkins, Gomar, Rollock, and John Ball (1585–1640). It was developed into an elaborate doctrine of two covenants, the covenant of works or nature and the covenant of grace, with the covenant of grace following out a historical pattern of several Old Testament administrations followed by its fulfilment or complete revelation in the New Testament. This model became increasingly important in the Reformed theology of the seventeenth century, as exemplified in the works of Johannes Cocceius (1603–69), Franz Burman (1632–79), and Herman Witsius (1636–1708).

It is clear that the early orthodox Reformed thinkers do not oblige the excessively neat categories of those modern historians who have claimed 'tensions' in Reformed theology between a covenantal and a predestinarian model or between bilateral and unilateral definitions of covenant. Indeed, such early synthesizers of covenantal theology as Fenner, Rollock, and Perkins held to clearly enunciated doctrines of predestination and often were able to fold both unilateral and bilateral definitions of covenant into their theologies. By way of example, Perkins taught a doctrine of full, double predestination and a unilaterally bestowed covenant of grace, at the same

time (and without either apparent contradiction or internal tension) arguing for a bilateral character of covenant once bestowed, according to which
human beings were called on to act responsibly before God.

Christology and atonement

Reformed teaching concerning the person of Christ was, from its beginnings, fundamentally orthodox and formulated in the context of the great
ecumenical creeds, particularly the Chalcedonian Formula. Still, there are at
least two highly significant features of the Reformed approach that distinguish it from other approaches to the person of Christ, particularly that of
the Lutherans. From its beginnings, Reformed Christology focused on the
issue of the integrity of the divinity and humanity of Christ in his person,
teaching what is technically called a *communicatio idiomatum in concreto*
or 'communication of proper qualities in the concrete'. Reformed thinkers
such as Zwingli, Bucer, Calvin, and Bullinger were intent on affirming the
fullness of Christ's divinity and the genuineness of his humanity, and consistently refused to allow a flow of divine attributes from the divine to the
human. Thus, all of the attributes of each of the natures belong to the concrete 'person' of the incarnate Word – the person of Christ is omniscient
and omnipotent, according to the divine nature; finite and subject to death,
according to the human nature.

The doctrinal point has a series of very specific applications, all of
which remain typical of Reformed theology into the era of orthodoxy: the
Reformed insist that, in his ascension to heaven, Christ remained fully
human, concluding that his humanity could not, therefore, be present bodily
in the Lord's supper. This teaching was posed not only against the Roman
Catholic doctrine of transubstantiation (which claims that the eucharistic
elements are transformed into Christ's body and blood) but also against the
Lutheran understanding of a bodily presence of Christ with the bread and
wine, by reason of the ubiquity of Christ's resurrected humanity. From the
Reformed perspective, to claim that a human nature has the attribute of
being everywhere constitutes a denial of humanity, which can be in only
one place.

The other central emphasis of the Reformed Christology, one that it
took directly from Calvin, is its understanding of Christ as mediator in
terms of his threefold office as prophet, priest, and king – namely, as the
revealer and fulfilment of God's promise, as the sacrifice for sin, and as the
ruler of God's kingdom. Calvin did not invent the concept, but he gave it a
prominence in Reformed thought that continued into the era of orthodoxy.
Whereas Calvin had used the threefold office primarily to describe distinct
functions of Christ's work, later Reformed theology developed the doctrine

historically as well, indicating that, although each office was eternal and had been revealed in the mediatorial work of the Word throughout history, the prophetic office was most prominent in the revelatory work of the Word in the history of revelation, the priestly office in the sacrificial life and death of Christ, and the kingly office in the final reign of God. The significance of the doctrine is certainly to be found in the way in which it roots the understanding of Christ's person in his historical work and in its stress on the breadth of Christ's work, not only in his atoning death but also in his revelatory mission and in his rule and headship over the people of God. This last issue relates directly to the covenantal emphasis of Reformed orthodoxy.

Reformed theology also presented, both in the Reformation and in the era of orthodoxy, a doctrine of the mediatorial work of Christ that paralleled the Reformed emphases on salvation by grace alone and on divine election. Whereas Calvin, Bullinger, and others of their generation did not themselves make a major issue of the limitation of Christ's atoning work to the elect alone, later Reformed thinkers elaborated the point, particularly because of the controversies in which they became involved. There has been some scholarly disagreement on this point – and sometimes a doctrinal wedge is driven between 'Calvin' and the 'Calvinists', as if Calvin taught a 'universal atonement' and later Reformed writers taught a 'limited atonement'. Yet, when the terms and definitions are rightly sorted out, there is significant continuity in the Reformed tradition on this point.

The terms 'universal' and 'limited atonement' do not represent the sixteenth- and seventeenth-century Reformed view – or, for that matter, the view of its opponents. The issue was not over 'atonement', but over the 'satisfaction' made by Christ for sin – and the debate was never over whether or not Christ's satisfaction was limited: all held it to be utterly sufficient to pay the price for all sin, and all held it to be effective or efficient only for those who were saved. The question concerned the identity of those saved and, therefore, the ground of the limitation – God's will or human choice. Thus, both Calvin and Bullinger taught the sufficiency of Christ's work of satisfaction for all sin as well as the universal preaching of the gospel and, at the same time, recognized the efficacy of Christ's work for the faithful alone – and both taught that faith is the gift of God, made available to the elect only. The Reformed orthodox did teach the doctrine more clearly. In response to Arminius, they brought the traditional formula of sufficiency for all sin and efficiency for the elect alone to the forefront of their definition, where Calvin and Bullinger hardly mentioned it at all. The orthodox also more clearly connected the doctrine of election to the language of the limitation of the efficacy of Christ's death. This solution is presented in the Canons of Dort in concise formulas.

As the seventeenth century progressed, Reformed theologians such as John Davenant in England and Moses Amyraut in France offered a concept of 'hypothetical universalism', according to which the efficacy of Christ's death is hypothetically available to all who believe. In its time, this view was considered problematic by many of the Reformed orthodox, given that it conceived of an unrealized (indeed, an intentionally unrealized) will in God. Still, inasmuch as the doctrine never claimed to broaden the efficacy of Christ's death on the assumption that non-elect individuals might actually believe, it can hardly be identified as an actual alternative to the more typical Reformed teaching of the limitation, by the will of God, of the efficacy of Christ's death to the elect. If there is a difference between 'Calvin' and the 'Calvinists' (or between Bullinger or Musculus and the Reformed orthodox) on this point it is simply that in the case of the Reformers, one must make a little effort to 'connect the dots', whereas the Reformed orthodox made sure, against various doctrinal adversaries, that the picture was presented in full.

CONTINUITY AND DISCONTINUITY IN THE DEVELOPMENT OF 'CALVINISM'

By way of conclusion, we should take explicit notice of the issue of the development of Reformed theology and the related issue of the continuity and discontinuity between the thought of the reformers and later Reformed theology. The framing of these issues is important: if, for example, we had taken as an initial premise that Calvin was the sole significant founder of the Reformed faith and that 'Calvinism' was the best descriptor of this theological tradition, there would have been an almost immediate temptation to compare late sixteenth- and seventeenth-century writers with Calvin on fairly refined points of doctrine and then, on the basis of noted differences, to declare a substantive discontinuity. When the issues are framed by a broad, confessional definition of the Reformed tradition, with Calvin as one of its major early codifiers, an entirely different picture emerges – one which, moreover, is far more respectful of the historical materials. There are, certainly, differences in nuance and detail between the theology of Calvin and the theologies of later Calvinistic or Reformed thinkers, but there are equivalent differences in nuance and detail both between the teachings of Calvin and the views of his contemporaries and among various later Reformed writers. These differences, moreover, are not typically such as would press any of the many and various Reformed writers of the sixteenth and seventeenth centuries beyond the confessional boundaries of Reformed theology. There is, in other words, a broadly defined doctrinal continuity in the developing Reformed tradition, a doctrinal continuity that, moreover, can be traced through the methodological transformations of that theological tradition from an early sixteenth-century religious protest, drawn out in concert with debates between humanist and scholastic pedagogy to later sixteenth- and seventeenth-century forms in which the humanist pedagogy has influenced the academy and produced, not a humanist, antischolastic theology, but a humanistically retooled late Renaissance scholasticism.

12 The theology of Thomas Cranmer

PETER NEWMAN BROOKS

If historians have generally regarded Thomas Cranmer as the most complex character among the churchmen of the sixteenth-century Reformation in England, his theological legacy, particularly when finely tuned, is none too difficult to determine. For, somewhat akin to Beethoven's masterly *Eroica* symphony, there is a heroic quality about the life and work of the diligent scholar Henry VIII chose to be archbishop of Canterbury. Modern scholarship may spurn such a judgement, no doubt deeming it 'old hat', *simpliste*, even partisan and divisive. Nevertheless, there remains an extraordinary dimension to the martyred Tudor primate.

It is tempting to take the parallel further and embrace all four movements of the *Eroica*. Just as Beethoven opened up a new symphonic scene, Cranmer's involvement with Henry and Cromwell in their spirited break with Rome over the king's 'divorce' surely provided a dramatic start (*allegro con brio*) to a Cambridge don's career at the Tudor court. With the mass as the focal point and purpose of priestly ministry, any second stage of development in the direction of church reform also demanded slow, even dignified (*larghetto*!) consideration, particularly when the royal creed continued to cleave to Catholicism (papal recognition only excepted). And although it would be inappropriate to liken work on the *Book of Common Prayer* that followed to the light, playful passage of the *scherzo*, the Protestant convictions of a young and eager Edward VI at least gave Cranmer new freedom to experiment. As for the finale, what could be more frustrating than the quickening pace (*allegro molto*) of court faction, of the accession of Mary the Catholic, Roman renewal, and Protestant pastoral vision unfulfilled?

Of supreme significance for any Tudor succession, Henry's 'privy matter' has long been central to academic debate. Ably analysed by a full spectrum of scholars from Elton to Scarisbrick, the so-called 'divorce' also provides essential background to the implementation of royal supremacy and the profound consequences such constitutional change had for the two English provinces of the medieval Western church. In such a context of *haute politique*, Cranmer's role was invidious. Albeit raised by Henry to be primate of all England and confirmed by the necessary papal bulls, he had been dealt a hand with few aces. For Cranmer came to Canterbury to do the royal bidding to beg 'to procede to the examination, fynall determynation, and judgement in the . . . grete cause touching Your Highness'.

In short, the new archbishop was obliged not merely to promote a royal argument and in effect to dispense with a papal dispensation that had allowed Henry to marry Katerina, widow of his elder brother Arthur, but must also satisfy himself that biblical backing existed for the case. To any priest, this posed a real crisis of conscience, and few scholars have shown any sympathy for the foggy isolation that besieged Cranmer. Wolsey's inability to bring the canon lawyers to heel had failed the royal cause. Accordingly, the shrewd insights of Cromwell and Henry combined to call a new tune, brilliantly abandoning canon for statute law and the establishment of royal supremacy over the church. Loyal to both his sovereign and the now exalted vice-gerent and vicar-general in spirituals (for Thomas Cromwell had effectively become a kind of Gilbertian 'Lord High Executioner'), the primate duly accepted what most historians recognize as revolutionary change in matters constitutional. For Elton this had been achieved by 'omnicompetence of statute'. Yet for the primate, such a problem of conflicting authorities needed justification from, and recourse to, the highest Christian authority, Cranmer finding his own ultimate reassurance in holy scripture. Nor was this merely the biblical backing of the Old Testament, namely the reconciliation of conflicting texts in Leviticus 18 and 20 and Deuteronomy 25 used to deny the validity of the king's first marriage – but a full commitment to royal as distinct from papal authority in full accord with the medieval struggle and traditional stance of *regnum versus sacerdotium*.

Behind crowded political events and constitutional change, Cranmer was conditioned by theological understanding to find reassurance in the Pauline doctrine expressed in Luther's defence of temporal government in *Von weltlicher Oberkeit* ('On secular authority', 1523). For a Cambridge don whose traditional scholastic training had already been challenged by the heady atmosphere of the 'new' *humanist* 'divinity', this projected him into something of a mid-life crisis. He had yet to come to terms with the essential 'law versus gospel' core of Luther's message. Rather was he drawn in the early 1530s to the way Pastor Osiander of Nuremberg favoured a Tudor cause the Wittenberg reformer had himself rejected. After all, Cranmer's ambassadorial role was precisely to secure support for Henry against Pope Clement VII, and he was able to back royal authority for good apostolic reasons of obedience to the godly prince (Romans 12). Increasingly scripture was becoming central to his thought, and Pauline notions of obedience provided the pivotal planks for a ministry that gave Cranmer the necessary confidence to ride even Tudor court faction in developing his ministry as a reformer. As he busied himself in the set task of gaining allies for Henry's campaign, he had grasped the role of the prince in the divine economy. And when the pope had to be repudiated before any kind of change could appear on his pastoral agenda, the rejection of canon law was of fundamental importance. Those who deem this to be capitulation to the crown and betrayal of the Catholic faith should note Patrick Collinson's judgement that Cranmer, rather than succumbing to the king, manipulated Henry's capriciousness to further the cause of a reformed Church of England.

In the mid-1530s the archbishop thus urged acceptance of the royal supremacy. But he did so with ever-increasing conviction that such sovereignty reflected a divine order confirmed by the apostolic counsel of holy scripture. A letter of February 1535 clearly indicated that the laws of papal government not only 'suppressed Christ' but also 'set up the bishop of [Rome] as a God of this world'. Concentrated courses of sermons were delivered at St Paul's Cross, where, among others, Cranmer denounced the pope as Antichrist. And the primate made no bones about reaching that conclusion from 'scripture . . . [and] divers expositions of holy saints and doctors', drawing *catena* from a wealth of material from his own canon-law commonplaces in the process. When reporting his progress to Henry the following year, Cranmer spelt out the principal points of sermons he had himself 'preached against the erroneous doctrine' not of a pope but of a demoted 'bishop of Rome' whose usurped power he declared to be 'contrary of God's Word'. If the ancient imperial see deserved any reverence as *sancta sedes Romana*, such was but 'holiness in name' and could in no way justify papal 'glory and pomp . . . covetousness . . . unchaste liveing, and the maintenance of all vices'. It was, in short, an outspoken Cranmer who informed his prince that he 'spake against the bishop of Rome his laws', denouncing many of them as 'contrary to God's laws' and accordingly 'not to be esteemed so highly' as the pope 'would have them'.

In parallel with resolving the problem of the canon law and papal sovereignty over the Western church in favour of *public* obedience to a royal supremacy that he had conceived in scriptural terms, the *private* Cranmer had also begun to explore the nature of Christian commitment expounded by Luther and the Wittenberg party line. Free from the straitjacket of scholasticism – although such training was to keep him in the mould of its systematic skills when engaged in the great debate over the eucharist – Cranmer's search for theological truth incurred a twofold debt. First and foremost, a new grasp of the way of salvation owed much to

Luther's 'rediscovery' of the gospel; and secondly, his whole approach to biblical understanding followed Erasmian philology as the latest fashion in learning.

Although Cranmer is best known for revising and refining a doctrine of the eucharist, setting it out in language congregations could grasp in 'a tongue understood of the people', the 'new divinity' challenging traditional Roman teaching gave prior consideration to penance before turning to the mass. Taking his lead from the present writer's pioneering work in Cranmer's massive commonplace books, Ashley Null has analysed Cranmer's fascination with both the early fathers and significant medieval theologians such as Bede, Peter Lombard, Hugh of St Victor, Aquinas, and Bernard. He seems convinced that, just like Luther some years before, Cranmer in the 1530s began to perceive the apostolic message of Paul. This Cranmer did no longer in scholastic terms but rather within the precise parameters that bounded Luther's dramatic 'rediscovery' of *justificatio sola fide*. Just as Renaissance artists and writers saw perfection in a classical past, so sixteenth-century reformers went beyond even Augustine to embrace a New Testament emphasis they found in Pauline doctrine. This was the apostle's insistence that humanity must remain estranged from the creator God and altogether sinful until, *in faith*, individuals claimed the saving work of Christ for themselves to secure the imputed righteousness which alone made them acceptable in the beloved. If the donnish Dr Cranmer was an unlikely subject for any 'Damascus-road experience', roving ambassadorial duties in 1532 certainly brought Nuremberg within range and provided every opportunity for him not merely to flirt with, but seriously to study, the new 'Martinism'. That he was impressed is clear from his readiness to marry into the Osiander family, for the good Lutheran pastor could in no way have presided over such a solemn ceremony for his wife's niece Margarete if he had not already welcomed the bridegroom as a believer in the household of faith.

The whole affair may suggest the reckless witness of the newly converted. If so, Cranmer's readiness publicly to parade in the ranks of reformers convinced of the truth of Martin Luther's great gospel obsession – namely that, for salvation, simple faith has priority over good works – received a singular setback. For when the aged Warham died, Henry VIII summoned the archdeacon of Taunton home to serve him as archbishop of Canterbury! In such circumstances, caution had to cloud Cranmer's new theological vision, discretion *de temps en temps* proving wiser for the wider cause than any stance of a Mr Valiant-for-Truth. Nevertheless, despite his respect for the king's own conservative commitment to the Catholic creed of Christendom – papal claims alone excepted – the new primate readily challenged a number of annotations Henry made to the *Institution of a Christian Man* (1537), a key formulary setting out the doctrine of his newly established church. Three of Cranmer's sentences indicate a kinship with Lutheran theology, and did so in striking economy of language:

> Works only which follow our justification, do please God; forsomuch as they proceed from an heart endued with pure faith and love for God. But the works which we do before our justification, be not allowed and accepted before God, although they appear never so good and glorious in the sight of man. For after our justification only begin we to work as the law of God requireth.

This is not, however, to suggest that the peaks and troughs of Henry's reign ever gave Cranmer and his small group of reformers an easy ride. If the high point of their achievement came with the publication of the 'Great Bible' (April 1539), to which in the following year the archbishop contributed his exuberant preface, the nadir was surely the act of six articles, brazen buttress of 'the old religion' in the matter of penance and the mass, shortly followed by Cromwell's fall from power and execution in 1540. Nevertheless, public reversal in no way prevented the primate's private research, and, while Henry lived, Cranmer not only rode the court faction but devoted himself to biblical, and particularly to patristic, study. Plans for promoting preaching – both reviving that sorely neglected ministry, and securing an acceptable overall standard by the preparation of approved homilies – fell foul of the Canterbury Convocation in 1542. No small wonder when that same body was even divided over preserving the 'Great Bible' without major revision! Undaunted, however, Cranmer kept abreast of continental theology. He was attracted to Luther's biblical views on the sacrament of the altar, if only for the Wittenberg reformer's firm and uncompromising acceptance of Christ's institution (in Latin, *Hoc est corpus meum*), and resolute refusal to dilute such biblical categories after the fashion of the Swiss.

Passing reference has already been made to *florilegia* focused on penance. But among the British Library's Reformation treasures stand some fifty folios from a commonplace section that Cranmer and his chaplain-secretaries devoted to the eucharist. Many such gleanings were harvested to afford extra strength to a 'real presence' understanding of that sacrament. In addition to patristic material, there are citations from the controversy that raged between Luther and the Swiss in the great Marburg debate (1529), citations which make clear Cranmer's familiarity with, and support for, Luther's stand on the unadulterated, plain sense of the New Testament record. Eucharistic quotations from the *Dialogus* (1530) are listed, and in much the same order, to indicate profound respect for the reformed scholarship that gave every consideration to the other side of the argument in what had become a *cause célèbre*. Above all, the commonplace evidence reveals a truly conscientious dimension in a Cranmer who, unlike the Athenians of old, refused in theology to embrace 'some new thing' without good cause. Not that secretarial notes, archiepiscopal *marginalia*, and a selection of his own writings on kindred subjects – all of them interrelated and focused on fundamental issues of the 'new divinity' – command respect as a theology. Compared with the analyses of Calvin's definitive *Institutio*, and even with Luther's more occasional writings, Thomas Cranmer's contribution is slim.

Cranmer's strength is to be found elsewhere, and his contribution to reformation is best remembered for the liturgical skills that powered an essentially pastoral theology. Having witnessed new forms of worship for himself when travelling on embassy in Europe, he was encouraged by such samplings in serious liturgical study and personal experiment. Ratcliff made much of private compositions still extant, which he dated to the early 1540s; and if David Selwyn has noted the liturgical section of the primate's library to be 'mainly of medieval origin', his parallel judgement that much of the collection 'may have suffered the fate of Cranmer's Protestant books' has also found acceptance. So when making a speech at the coronation (February 1547) to uphold a youthful Edward VI as 'God's Vice-gerent and Christ's vicar within [his] own dominions', Cranmer had already done much to ensure that 'God [was] truly worshipped, and idolatry destroyed'.

By July, Protector Somerset had used the council to set forth, by royal prerogative, a *Book of Homilies* in which Cranmer wrote of 'Salvation', 'Faith' and 'Good Works' in language so Lutheran and opposed to traditional orthodoxies (approved in a formulary of 1543, the *King's Book*) that it roused the ire of none other than Stephen Gardiner. The bishop of Winchester had an important point to make, and fully appreciated that acceptance of 'justification by only faith' had the gravest implications for the sacramental doctrine of the Western church. Adamant that 'only faith' was a 'sophism', he accorded it no place in a properly Catholic creed. He therefore warned his archbishop to abandon Luther's heresy. Gardiner was not only clear that 'the eucharist . . . cannot stand with that doctrine', but also convinced that such matters 'are so joined and interdependent that whoever had admitted the doctrine of *only faith* in justification is compelled to reject the sacrament of the eucharist in the way we profess it'. When Parliament assembled that autumn (1547), the sacrament was safeguarded from any who might choose to defame or revile it. And the following spring, a royal proclamation permitting reception 'under both kinds, that is to say, of bread and wine' prefaced

'The Order of the Communion' to afford the Latin – 'without the varying of any other rite or ceremony in the Mass' – an English inset of confession, absolution, and some 'comfortable words' from scripture before the priest administered the consecrated elements to his people.

If caution certainly characterized this little 'Order', as with Cranmer's English Litany of 1544, the shadows are as important as the light. Starting at Easter (1 April) 1548, liturgical reform began to transform the priestly rite of sacrifice into a communion of the people, and to do so in dignified, but everyday, language. All had to be done piecemeal, for any comprehensive service book needed most careful compilation and had to secure widespread approval before being introduced to the dioceses and parishes of the Tudor state. As it was, this interim rite found Cranmer indebted to work Martin Bucer had drafted for use in both Strasbourg and Cologne. But news spread fast, the Frankfurt Book Fair even securing copies of the 'Order' in the very month it was first published! Reformation Europe had been alerted, and Cranmer's revolution was underway.

Ahead lay frustration and fulfilment. Although Cranmer's reforming vision did not fail him, times were when his nerve almost gave way. Radical change came with the publication of a *Book of Common Prayer* in 1549; but when chairing the Windsor Commission that preceded it, with solemn sessions for assembling and debating the drafts of various services and their appended rubrical instructions to the clergy there proposed, the primate was made aware of mounting opposition to the project he so greatly prized. Nothing seemed straightforward, and to prepare everything possible for the acceptance of this first Prayer Book, key sectors of both church and state had to be squared. For example, any formal gathering of a convocation dominated by senior traditionalist clergy was bound to prove troublesome and to delay the religious settlement urgently sought by Protector Somerset's regime. Then too, there could be ridicule in the House of Commons if any measure imposing new church services found knights of the shire and burgess members ignorant and unprepared. So stealth tactics were used, and specially convened gatherings were used to inform first the bishops, then a select band of university theologians, and ultimately the majesty of the whole Upper House.

This is no place to set out the fascinating details leading to the imposition of the liturgy by Act of Uniformity in 1549. With the official publication of the *Book of Common Prayer*, however, the kingdom was legally bound to comply with changes in worship which, if they retained much traditional structure from liturgies of the 'old religion', Cranmer's spiritual skill had augmented with a range of prayers at least sympathetic to the new doctrines of reformation. And above all, the archbishop's committee had condensed into a single service book – apart from the *Ordinal*, which did not appear until much later in the year – no fewer than five quite distinct medieval components. Henceforth missal, breviary, pontifical, sacerdotal (manual), and processional were made available to clergy and people as *Common Prayer*. Traditional complexity had been exchanged for a single service book of both altar and handy size. Catchpenny printers had much to gain from the change, but almost as if pastoral concern regulated prices as well as prayers, the Whitchurch and Grafton editions sold from an affordable 'II shyllynges' to 'in past or bords not aboue the pryce of thre shyllynges and eyght pens'.

Of equal importance to his reforming agenda was Cranmer's 'sound and comfortable doctrine' of the eucharist. The particular focus of years of scriptural and patristic study was his 1549 service of 'holy communion'. Although, just as Luther did in his Formula of 1523, he admitted it to be 'commonly called the mass', there was no escaping real determination to remove notions of propitiatory sacrifice in a service designed to dwell on Christ's own sacrifice, on the 'sacrifice of praise and thanksgiving', and on the offering by those present of their 'souls and bodies, to be a reasonable, holy and lively sacrifice'.

Despite a full measure of personal satisfaction – for Cranmer held his service book to be one that 'sette forth a very godly ordre agreable to all good people' – both priestly and popular protest followed in the so-called 'prayer book riots'. From Devon and Cornwall came demands that the Privy Council reject the very idea of more frequent communion and permit the retention of sacramentals such as 'holy bread and holy water', oblations for the living and the dead, as well as prayers for the departed. The primate's response was swift and to the point. He scorned such ignorance and ridiculed the misguided theology of those priests who misled their people as 'wicked and false guides'. Had he not prefaced his Prayer Book with pastoral principles he intended for the good of the church? For explanatory instructions on ceremonies had been appended, and these clearly set out 'why some be abolished and some retained'. Cranmer's own words best outline the argument:

> Of such ceremonies as be used in the church, and have had their
> beginning by the institution of man: some at the first use were of
> godly intent and purpose devised, and yet at length turned to vanity
> and superstition: some entered . . . by undiscreet devotion, and such a
> zeal as was without knowledge; and . . . because they have much
> blinded the people, and obscured the glory of God, are worthy to be
> cut away, and clean rejected. Others there be, which although they
> have been devised by man, yet it is thought good to reserve them still,
> as well for a decent order in the church . . . as because they pertain to
> edification.

The primate evidently by no means regarded the language of compromise as the language of defeat. He preferred to stand by sanity as the middle ground, and in this sense his preface early gave expression to *via media* – for many the abiding theological characteristic of English reformation.

That he was not one to promote dull Catholic uniformity in the revision of old rites is confirmed by the way his revision of public worship managed to express Reformation theology: 'For we think it convenient that every country should use such ceremonies, as they shall think best to the setting forth of God's honour and glory.' As for the popes, they and their ceremonies were 'adversaries to Christ, and . . . rightly called Antichrist'. Nor was such condemnation intended as mere polemic, and the primate penned a pastoral judgement to note that

> Christ ordained his bread, and his wine, and his water, to our great comfort, to instruct us and teach us what things we have only by him. But Antichrist on the other side hath set up his superstitions, under the name of holiness, to none other intent, but as the devil seeketh all means to draw us from Christ, so doth Antichrist advance his holy superstitions, to the intent that we should take him in the stead of Christ, and believe that we have by him such things as we have only by Christ; that is to say, spiritual food, remission of our sins, and salvation.

After clever attacks from the conservative Gardiner, and the radical John Hooper (that 'English Zwingli'!), Dudley's new regime dictated a religious policy of extremism. This presented Cranmer with a window of opportunity and enabled him in 1552 to update his 'godly book' in a way that, if it did not 'improve' or 'vary from' his original *Book of Common Prayer*, at least brought out a liturgy altogether free from ambiguity. In this undertaking, the archbishop was indirectly assisted by the invited critique of the distinguished Strasbourg reformer Martin Bucer. Exiled by the Augsburg Interim of 1548, and welcomed to Lambeth and to Cambridge, Bucer became the university's first Regius professor of divinity. By far the most important part of his *Censura* dealt with holy communion. Clear that Reformation principles can 'never sufficiently execrate' the mass and its surrounding superstitions, Bucer undoubtedly helped Cranmer to avoid any of the former confusion that could be used to 'twist' the prayer of consecration 'into a means for maintaining and confirming the infinitely wicked and blasphemous dogma of transubstantiation of the bread and wine into the body and blood of Christ'.

The best Reformation liturgies were composed to care for all who sought to worship in spirit and in truth; and, if somewhat daunted by Bucer's seniority in the Protestant cause, Cranmer had nothing to fear. In a 'Preface to the Reader' of his *Defence of the True and Catholic Doctrine of the Supper of the Lord* (1550), the archbishop had gone to great lengths and justified his understanding from scripture and the fathers of the primitive church. He had urged rigorous uprooting of the weeds hitherto choking the Lord's vineyard, if only because, 'unpulled up', he realized they must in time return fertile ground to wilderness. So when from a wide experience Bucer made his point, Cranmer responded by removing, in 1552, much misleading ambiguity. The very word 'mass' disappeared from the title of a service now termed an 'Order for the Administration of the Lord's supper'. No longer did 'the priest' stand 'humbly afore the midst of the Altar' but rather 'at the north side of the Table'. Unlike its predecessor of 1549, too, the new service no longer rehearsed the *Gloria*, but used the Ten Commandments as a prelude to readings of scripture in set passages for the epistle and the gospel of the day. After the Nicene Creed and the sermon (the rubric directing a sermon at this point in the service is the only such instruction in the book and indicative of the insistence in Reformation theology that Word and sacrament go together), the prayer for the church, confession and absolution all precede the *Sursum corda*, an introit to the canon of great antiquity. Next came the so-called 'prayer of humble access', its new position, with that of the prayer for the church, being clearly opposed to notions of propitiatory sacrifice or adoration of bread and wine so feared by Bucer.

In short, by redistributing the various components of the old canon, Cranmer had skilfully weeded out the deeply rooted sacrificial emphasis of the medieval mass, even to the total avoidance of the very word 'consecration'. For the prayer that followed simply recited the scriptural record of Christ's institution of his Last Supper. How appropriate therefore that striking reference to the new service in the *Greyfriars' Chronicle*, namely that '. . . on Allhallow day beganne the boke of the new servis of bred and wyne in Powlles'.

In the end it was, of course, Edward's untimely death that halted the quickening Protestant pace of reformation in England. Moreover, by signing the 'device' designed to alter the succession in favour of a Dudley dynasty, Cranmer had effectively signed his own death warrant. But terrible times of tribulation in the Tower of London and Oxford's town gaol, Bocardo, only served to deepen his obsession with a practical, pastoral theology of penance and the eucharist. Such scriptural understanding as he gained, Cranmer used to promote the Word for the worship of God in the cure of souls.

If ambiguity had at times obscured the cause, extraordinary fortitude in a finale when every recantation was itself recanted demands recognition and even reverence. For here was an evangelical theologian, a Cambridge man of the sixteenth-century Reformation, who strove hard and long to achieve doctrinal change. A period figure perhaps, but one whose efforts for genuine reform of the English church were recognized by his university with a statue above the door of the old Selwyn Divinity School. Built in 'an English style of the 16th century; the material red brick and stone' (*Instructions* approved by a syndicate of 1875), it is ironic that the building should have been ranged in front of the College of St John the Evangelist, founded by a charter obtained from Henry VIII by John Fisher in 1511.

13 The theology of the English reformers

CARL R. TRUEMAN

While it was not until the advent of the works of William Perkins in the late sixteenth century that England produced a theologian of truly international stature, the earlier phases of the English Reformation witness to the work of a number of talented individuals who were able to draw upon that of their continental counterparts and take advantage of the developments in university education in order to articulate distinctively Protestant theologies within the English context. Thus, while the theological contribution of the English reformers was in no way as significant as their innovations in, say, liturgical practice, it nevertheless stood in positive relation to continental movements and defined the kinds of debate that were to shape English church life until the end of the seventeenth century.

ORIGINS

The wider field of the intellectual history of the Reformation has, over recent decades, preoccupied itself with tracing dogmatic and exegetical trajectories back into the theological world of the Middle Ages. Study of the English Reformation over the same period has, however, been to a large extent the preserve of social and political historians with little interest in theology. Their work has tended not to take English Reformation theology seriously in terms of its place within the ongoing Western tradition of thought. In addition, the slight and occasional nature of many of the theological productions of the English Reformation, combined with little hard evidence (for instance, in the form of citations) regarding relations to late medieval thought, has made such study almost impossible to raise above the level of educated guesswork.

The state of historical evidence prevents the establishment of definite and precise intellectual connections between Lollardy and leading English Reformation theologians. We are, however, on much safer ground with respect to the role of contemporary intellectual currents in the various debates. That humanism had made an impact on Cambridge in the second decade of the sixteenth century is beyond dispute, and the establishment of a discussion group later nicknamed 'little Germany' at the White Horse Inn in that town, with future Lutheran Robert Barnes as its guiding light, indicates the existence of a movement within the university that was at least very interested in Reformation theology, even if the involvement of Stephen Gardiner in such meetings indicates that not all were setting out on the path to reformation.

When Wolsey founded Cardinal's College (later Christ Church) at Oxford and took over the brightest and the best from Cambridge to give the institution some intellectual backbone, the plan backfired spectacularly, and led to mass imprisonment in the college's fish cellar of those involved in the reading of books that were considered forbidden. The list of books indicates that the young fellows were reading, among others, works by Huss, Wycliffe, Bucer, Oecolampadius, Zwingli, and Luther. As with the White Horse Inn in Cambridge, these indicate that there was a deep interest amongst young intellectuals in the currents of theological thought then gaining ground on the continent. Then, as English Protestants in the 1520s began to produce their own theological works, it became clear that the works of continental theology to which they had been exposed were more than just sources of inspiration: the dependence of individuals such as Tyndale and Frith upon continental originals as the textual basis of some of their most significant writings indicates the level of literary debt that was owed by the English to the continental Reformation.

That the intellectual ferment of the Reformation made its first inroads in England at Oxford and Cambridge was hardly surprising, given their status as university towns; and, indeed, they continued to be the focal points of continental influence on English theology, principally through the presence of Martin Bucer at Cambridge and Peter Martyr Vermigli at Oxford as professors of divinity during the reign of Edward VI. Precise questions of individual influence on particular points are difficult to establish with certainty, though it would seem that both men served to strengthen the hand of the moderately reformed Edwardian establishment against both the Catholic conservatives and the more radical reformed parties that looked to Zurich (such as John Hooper) and Geneva (such as Bartholomew Traheron) respectively. This is certainly the case with Bucer's involvement in the English scene.

While specific points of influence on particular individuals may often be hard to pinpoint, it is nonetheless clear that continental thought had a decisive impact upon English thought at this time in terms of its general shape and emphases. The issues of justification by faith, sacramental theology, and, later on, predestination reflect concerns that were typical of the continental debates of the time, although, with the notable exception of Robert Barnes, a specifically Lutheran view of the eucharist had few high-profile defenders in England at this time. Times of exile, under Henry VIII and then, most significantly, under Mary, ensured that many English theologians had first-hand experience of the Reformation on the continent; and, during those periods when religious policy in England appeared to be flowing in favour of Protestantism, these exiles returned, thus importing continental debates and ideas to the arguments surrounding the shape and purpose of the English church. Indeed, as regards the theology of the early English Reformation it is often hard not to see it, in relation to the continent, as a footnote to the main theological text or merely as variations on an already established theme.

THE SHAPE OF ENGLISH REFORMATION THEOLOGY

Given the fact that the basic contours of English Reformation theology were largely set by debates on the continent, it is not surprising to find that justification by faith played a significant role in the 1520s and '30s. In this context, the most significant writings were undoubtedly those of William Tyndale, both because of their clarity and, more importantly, because of their relation to his larger work of biblical translation and commitment to making the Bible comprehensible to the layperson. Tyndale adopted the language of Pauline discourse as picked up by Luther, with its emphasis upon the basic categories of law and gospel, faith and works, in order both to articulate his understanding of salvation and to provide the reader of scripture with the basic interpretative categories necessary for understanding it.

Nevertheless, in Tyndale's writings, emphases different from those of Luther can be discerned right from the very start. In his first published theological tract, the preface to the abortive 1525 translation of the New Testament, Tyndale uses Lutheran language in a way that is subtly different from that of Luther himself. For example:

When Christ is this wise preached, and the promises rehearsed Y then the hearts of them which are elect are chosen and begin to wax soft . . . For when the evangelion is preached, the spirit of God entereth into them which God hath ordained and appointed unto eternal life, and openeth their inward eyes, and worketh belief in them. When the woeful consciences taste how sweet a thing the bitter death of Christ is, how merciful and loving God is through Christ's purchasing and merits, they begin to love again and to consent to the law of God, how that it is good, and ought to be so, and that God is righteous which made it.

The language is very close to that of Luther; indeed, the textual basis of the preface as a whole is Luther's own preface to his 1522 edition of the German New Testament; but the emphases are different. The positive language with regard to the law and the attention paid to the transformative work of the Holy Spirit both indicate that what we have in Tyndale is not straight Lutheranism but a modification of Lutheran theology in the context of a subtly different understanding of the Christian life, one where bondage to and freedom from sin are more important than guilt and remission; and where the work of the Spirit and the love he elicits are given a higher profile than the work of Christ and the faith of the believer.

Later in his writings this bears fruit in the language of double justification and in the increasing importance of covenant in his understanding of both the Christian life and the framework within which the Bible is to be understood. To take the former first:

> And when Paul saith, 'faith only justifieth'; and James, that 'a man is justified by works and not by faith only'; there is a great difference between Paul's *only* and James's *only*. For Paul's *only* is to be understood, that faith justifieth in the heart and before God without help from works, yea, and ere I can work; for I must receive life through faith to work with, ere I can work. But James's *only* is this wise to be understood; that faith doth not so justify, that nothing justifieth save faith; for deeds do justify also. But faith justifieth in the heart and before God; and the deeds before the world only, and maketh the other seen.

While it has been argued that such language represents a basic deviation from his earlier Lutheranism to a more works-centred approach, it is clear from assessing his work as a whole that there was no pristine early Lutheran phase and that the language here is shaped by the exegetical exigencies of explaining the teaching of the letter of James within a Protestant framework. Tyndale's sentiments are consistent with a broadly Protestant understanding of justification set within an anti-Pelagian framework for understanding grace. In this, his approach is typical of the time and finds corollaries in the work of his contemporaries, John Frith and Robert Barnes.

The second fruit of Tyndale's concern for giving a more practical twist to Luther's doctrine of justification emerged in his understanding of covenant. This fulfilled a neat dual role in his theology: it provided the layperson with a simple framework for unlocking the message of the Bible; and it allowed the Christian life to be expressed in a manner that explicitly bound together both the divine initiative and the human response as two sides of the soteriological coin. While the concept developed over the whole period of his active writing career, from 1525 to 1536, it reached its full development in the preface to his 1534 edition of the New Testament:

> The right way, yea, and the only way to understand the scripture unto salvation, is that we earnestly and above all things search for the profession of our baptism, or covenants between us and God. The general covenant, wherein all other are comprehended and included, is this: If we meek ourselves to God, to keep all his laws, after the example of Christ, then God hath bound himself unto us, to keep and make good all the mercies promised in Christ throughout the scripture.

Taken at face value, such a statement would appear to be a long way from the kind of theology being nurtured at Wittenberg; set within the familial context that Tyndale chooses to apply, however, the gap does not seem to be quite so great. Works done do not merit justification but flow from a prior conviction of justification and of the love of God, who rewards them as a father rewards his own children for trifles. The issue for Tyndale is ultimately one of how the necessity for obedience within the Christian life is to be articulated.

Tyndale's theology is a microcosm of the intellectual theological life in the England of his day, which consisted essentially of an eclectic appropriation of the results of continental theological debates within an educational and political context that was shaped by the rising humanism of the English universities and the exigencies of the king's plans to reform church and state. As such, it reflected a pattern that was to continue throughout the reigns of Edward and Mary, when Protestant theologians found themselves at first a rising force and then a persecuted minority. The intellectual agenda of the continent, however, continued to play a powerful part, as the debates about election and predestination demonstrate.

ELECTION AND PREDESTINATION

Medieval England produced two predestinarian theologians of European stature and influence: Thomas Bradwardine (c. 1295–1349) and John Wycliffe. Despite this pedigree, concern with predestination was not a central distinctive of the theology of the early English Reformation. Indeed, to the extent that Lollard theology can be reconstructed, it would appear to have been generally Pelagian in hue and thus ironically the very antithesis of Wycliffe's own thought on this matter. While it is quite clear that reformers such as Tyndale, Frith, and Barnes operated within an anti-Pelagian soteriological framework, there is no sign that this functioned in general as anything other than the necessary implication of their anthropology. Questions concerning the origins of evil, the justice of God, and whether predestination is to salvation only or essentially double are not raised in their writings, where the accent is rather upon the moral impotence of humanity and the consequent necessity of the unilateral gracious action of God in salvation. Having said this, the presence of the traditional distinction between God's hidden will and his revealed will is present in Barnes' *Supplication*, in such a form as to indicate both his sensitivity to the exegetical and theological issues raised by an anti-Pelagian anthropology, and his dependence upon Luther's 1525 work *On the Bondage of the Will* as a theological and textual source. Nevertheless, the doctrine of predestination does not occupy the same place in Barnes' thought of the 1530s, either theologically or rhetorically, that it plays in Luther's thought during the mid-1520s.

Under Edward and then under Mary, there were two significant exceptions to this comparative lack of interest in predestination that we find in the Henrician reformers. The first was the long-running debate that took place between the former Genevan exile, Bartholomew Traheron, and the former Zurich exile and future bishop, John Hooper. The only evidence we have for the controversy is to be found in a number of letters sent by John ab Ulmis, Traheron, and Hooper to Bullinger. While it is difficult to state in detail what Hooper's positive view of predestination is, since he is much clearer about what he rejects than about what he affirms, it would seem that his position is not far removed from that of Melanchthon, whom he appears to use as a textual source for his arguments at significant points. Whether he is a synergist is a moot point, since he never explicitly declares himself to be so, but the tendency in his thought is clearly in such a direction, driven by a desire neither to posit any twofoldness to God's will nor to lessen the moral imperatives of the Christian life. Traheron's explicit commitment to the position of Calvin would seem almost certainly to have been the source of tension. It is not insignificant that the debate took place between two exiles, and the constant recourse to Zurich for advice indicates that what was taking place here was not so much a domestic squabble as a local manifestation of tensions within the wider movement of the Reformation in Europe. These tensions were heightened by the return of exiles to England at a time when the direction of theological policy was, to an extent, in a state of flux; at such a point in time, the importing of debates from abroad was both inevitable and guaranteed to generate controversy of precisely this kind. That the debate appears to have been so localized and not to have precipitated any great change of direction within the theological policy of the English Reformation as a whole indicates the extent to which detailed discussion of the doctrine of predestination was not a leitmotif of the English settlement.

While the Edwardian articles were anti-Pelagian and contained a moderate but definite statement on predestination, that the doctrine was not a major point of concern for members of the hierarchy is evident from the second predestinarian debate. It has been pointed out that predestination was 'a basic and central assumption' for Cranmer, as for the evangelicals as a whole (Hooper being the obvious exception), and it would certainly be a travesty of truth to try to drive a wedge between England and the continent on this point. Nevertheless, Hooper's position did not mean that he was excluded from the hierarchy in the way that his view of vestments had threatened to do; and during the Marian regime the reaction of Nicholas Ridley to the second major predestinarian debate is instructive.

This debate took place in the King's Bench Prison, where both parties found themselves incarcerated; and it involved, on the side of the mainstream Reformation, John Bradford, and on the side of the radicals, Henry Hart. Hart was leader of the so-called free-will men, a group of separatists whose popular piety was essentially Pelagian in its attitude to anthropology and predestination. The initial point at issue had been Hart's disapproval of Bradford and friends because they played gambling games in order to pass the time. This appears to have upset Hart's sensibilities, advocate of a very strict lifestyle that he was. As with Augustine and Pelagius, however, the debate soon moved beyond the practicalities of the Christian life to the conceptual framework within which these practicalities were to be understood. While Hart's contributions to the debate do not survive, we have three relevant pieces from Bradford: *A Treatise on Election and Free Will*; *A Brief Sum of Election*; and *A Defence of Election*.

Bradford's arguments place an overriding emphasis upon the will of God as the ultimate and unfathomable cause of salvation. Thus, he declares:

> There is neither virtue nor vice to be considered according to any outward action, nor according to the will and wisdom of man; but according to the will of God. Whatsoever is conformable thereto, the same is virtue, and the action that springeth thereof is laudable and good.

This leads Bradford to a position which, while explicitly single predestinarian, yet has a strong tendency towards the double position. Hence, while he rejects (as he must) the notion that God is the cause of evil, he does at times infer predestination from the very being of God in a manner that would seem to demand the double position. In addition, he makes a distinction between first (unrevealed) and second (revealed) causes that precludes speculation about the origin of reprobation while yet leaving the question tantalizingly unresolved.

The theological importance of the doctrine to Bradford is obvious from the way in which it is so intimately connected to his doctrine of God; nevertheless, the origins of the actual dispute in the practicalities of the Christian life also indicate the profoundly pastoral nature of election as Bradford understood it: it is that which undergirds God's saving action and thus provides an objective (and therefore entirely secure) basis for assurance. This is Bradford's own primary concern in the matter, a concern made all the more important by his belief that assurance is the key issue separating the Reformation theologians from their Catholic counterparts.

Given Bradford's own concern for this matter, one of the most interesting points in the debate is the response of Nicholas Ridley to Bradford's request for theological assistance in the controversy. Ridley responded with a treatise that is now lost but which he describes in the following terms:

> I have in Latin drawn out the places of the scriptures, and upon the same have noted what I can for the time. Sir, in those matters I am so fearful, that I dare not speak further, yea, almost none otherwise than the very text doth, as it were, lead me by the hand.

The comment is interesting. There can be no doubt that Ridley, as one of the theological architects of the Edwardian Reformation, stood within the broad Augustinian anti-Pelagian tradition on predestination, but he is here far more cautious than one might have expected. The most plausible explanation would seem to be that this was not an issue over which the leading reformers in England wished to precipitate trouble, especially given the fact that the cause was at this point in serious trouble, a view supported by the ease with which even an outspoken individual such as Hooper, opposed as he was to decretal predestinarianism, was assimilated into the establishment and felt able to subscribe to the theological articles of the Edwardian settlement. Bradford, like Hooper and Traheron, is thus something of an exception to the general rule in his interest in this doctrine. Whether this interest derives from personal reflection upon the necessary framework for assurance or from the influence of his close friend, Martin Bucer, or from some combination of the two, is now impossible to establish. What is clear, however, is that tensions within the establishment on the issue of predestination may have been controlled and contained within early English Protestantism, but they were nonetheless present below the surface and did not originate in the disputes associated with the much later impact of Dutch Arminianism and the policies of James I and Charles I.

THE CHURCH

Ecclesiology occupied perhaps the lion's share of the reformers' activity once England broke with papal supremacy and, even more so, when Edward VI succeeded to the throne. Broadly speaking, the church settlement was politically Erastian, with the king at the head not just of state but also of church. Structurally, it was episcopalian: the old medieval framework of dioceses and parishes, along with many of the incumbents, simply could not have been abolished by the reformers even if they had wished to do so, which they emphatically did not. Sacramentally and liturgically, its theology was defined by the two Edwardian books of *Common Prayer* (1549 and 1552). It was this last point that was to prove most problematic during the reign of Edward VI and was, indeed, not only to create disastrous tensions within the English church but also to contribute to fomenting war between England and Scotland in the seventeenth century. Not until the Act of Toleration in 1689, when some limited freedom was allowed for those who wished to opt out of the state church and its liturgical practices, did the problems created for English society by the *Book of Common Prayer* begin to subside.

While the debates were thus to rumble on for some 140 years, the basic lines of dispute emerged very early on in the book's life. The first edition, of 1549, was in general a very moderate document, designed to move the English church in a firmly Protestant direction while yet, for political reasons, trying to alienate as few as possible of those politicians and churchmen sympathetic to the old religion. The document thus found an unfortunate (from the Protestant perspective) ally in the Catholic bishop Stephen Gardiner, who, though confined to the Tower, produced a work arguing, among other things, that the book was compatible with Catholic belief in the real presence in the eucharist. This was undoubtedly a deliberate attempt to unsettle the Protestant cause, for Gardiner had no sympathy at all with the real aims of the book. Nevertheless, the fact that he was able to write as he did to unsettle Cranmer reflects the careful and diplomatic nature of the language of the first book.

The real problem with the book turned out to be its retention of key aspects of Catholic ceremonial aesthetics and procedures and its use of certain elements of pre-Reformation medieval theology. While the latter – for example, prayers for the church in heaven – were edited out of the second edition in 1552, the former were in large part retained, and so the problems

170 Carl R. Trueman

which first emerged in the clash between Hooper and his supporters on one side, and Cranmer and Ridley on the other, were to continue for the rest of the century and on into the seventeenth.

The issue with Hooper surrounded the retention of the mention of saints in the oath of supremacy and the need for ministers to wear a surplice. The matter came to a dramatic head in his subsequent confrontation with Cranmer concerning the details of his consecration as bishop of Gloucester, which included no surplice and no oath to the saints. The latter was eliminated by the young Edward VI himself, who struck the clause out with his own pen once it had been brought to his attention. On the former point, however, Cranmer and Ridley stood firm, and Hooper eventually submitted to wearing the surplice at his consecration, though only after a spell in prison.

The dispute is theologically interesting for two reasons. First, it was at heart a struggle over who ran the Church of England. The ecclesiological point at issue was the authority of the government-appointed bishops, and Cranmer's victory was necessary if the kind of episcopalian settlement envisaged by church leaders and government officials was to become a reality. Indeed, this is how Cranmer and Ridley played the whole controversy: while Hooper focused on the abuses contained within the ceremony, they focused on the issue of who was in control of the church. While the goal of a more thorough reformation of church practice was undoubtedly the aim of both sides, Cranmer and Ridley were determined that this should be achieved in a manner that respected episcopal hierarchy and was thus orchestrated from the top down. The victory of Cranmer was, therefore, a crucial precedent that influenced the whole future of the Anglican church.

Secondly, the debate revealed the existence within England of a Protestantism that wished to move far more quickly to a thorough reformation than did Cranmer, and for this reason: that its basic understanding of what did and did not constitute obedient worship was radically different from that of the archbishop. For Hooper and those like him, what was not specifically demanded in worship by an explicit command of the Word of God was therefore illegitimate and constituted an act of idolatry. This notion, which came to known as the 'regulative principle' of worship, was to be the foundation of much of later Puritan thinking concerning Anglican reform, and a source of seemingly endless argument in the late sixteenth and seventeenth centuries.

In Edwardian England, the most vociferous exponent of the regulative principle was the Scottish reformer, John Knox. At a sermon preached at Newcastle in April 1550, Knox presented his case in the form of two syllogisms:

> That all worshipping, honouring, or service of God invented by the brain of man in the religion of God, without his own express commandment, is idolatry. The mass is invented by the brain of man without any commandment of God. Therefore it is idolatry.
>
> All honouring or service of God, whereunto is added a wicked opinion, is abomination. Unto the mass is added a wicked opinion. Therefore it is abomination.

The two syllogisms, relentless in their logic, allow no room for a halfway or a staged reformation, depending, as such things would, upon a category of *adiaphora*, or things indifferent, in order to prevent themselves from being categorized as idolatrous or abominable. The logic of Knox's position is such that anything the church does is either good and proper (in that it is explicitly enjoined by scripture) or blasphemous (in that is not so enjoined). Reformation for Knox is something that allows only for the categories of black and white: for him there are no grey areas, for any act is either obligatory or idolatry. The mass, with its ornate ceremonialism, its commitment to the real presence of Christ's humanity on the altar, and its attendant notion of sacrifice, was not something found in the scriptures; to Knox's Reformed mind, therefore, it was not simply unnecessary and inexpedient, but positive blasphemy, and thus not to be tolerated. Here we have in a nutshell the basis for much of the Puritan discontent with the Anglican settlement: for the next century and a half, the radicals within the Anglican church who wished to see a more thorough reformation saw no need to develop their arguments beyond the logic and underlying hermeneutic of Knox's syllogisms.

While these syllogisms capture the mindset of the radicals within the Anglican church, they also had a more immediate impact upon the theology of the English Reformation. When the Prayer Book revisions were completed and the 1552 edition had gone to press, it came to Knox's attention that the requirement had been retained for kneeling at communion when receiving the elements. The Scotsman raised an objection to this in a sermon preached before the king, and there followed an immediate suspension of the printing. Then, after some frantic discussion and debate, the printing was completed but with the insertion of the so-called 'black rubric' into the text. (in the first run, it was actually a slip of paper inserted into the completed book.) The rubric declared that, although kneeling was being retained in the communion service, this did not in any way imply worship of the elements, and thus of any real presence:

> For as concerning the sacramental bread and wine, they remain still in their very natural substances, and therefore may not be adored, for that were Idolatry to be abhorred of all faithful Christians. And as concerning the natural body and blood of our Saviour Christ, they are in heaven and not here. For it is against the truth of Christ's true natural body, to be in more places than in one at one time.

This terse statement, containing such an impeccably Reformed argument against the physical presence of Christ's humanity in the sacrament, was the most clear rejection of the doctrine in the second Prayer Book. Further, while the outcome was scarcely a victory for the hard-line Reformed party (after all, it was but a small compromise by Cranmer, for kneeling remained obligatory, albeit with its underlying purpose clarified), it was also Knox's single most significant contribution to the English Reformation and, while removed from later editions (but restored in 1662), bears eloquent testimony both to the ineradicably Protestant intention behind the English Prayer Book and to the existence of an influential body of opinion within the Edwardian church that was ill at ease with the Cranmerian pace of reform.

CONCLUSION

In terms of creative and sophisticated theology, the English Reformation was not in the same league as other continental centres of Protestantism at the time. England produced no Luther or Calvin, and not even a Zwingli. Nevertheless, the English Reformation as it progressed under Edward and suffered severe setbacks under Mary, was clearly played out against the wider intellectual context of the European Reformation: key debates on justification, election, and ecclesiology are all related to events and ideas on the continent, where, of course, many of the English Reformers had spent time in exile and where their visions of reform had been forged. In addition, many of the debates in the English Reformation, while perhaps relatively small-scale compared to continental parallels, did exhibit characteristics that were to come to the fore in subsequent years under Elizabeth, James, and Charles, when English theology did finally emerge as a significant player on the European intellectual stage.

Indeed, in the clash between Traheron and Hooper, and Bradford and Hart, we witness in microcosm the debates that were to tear the church apart under the Stuarts, where debates over predestination were to become factionalized, with Puritans opposing Laudians, and where the rejection

of Reformed understandings of predestination was to carry with it conno-
tations of pro-French political sympathies and pro-Catholic ecclesiastical
commitments. Such issues are far in the future from the perspective of the
1540s and '50s, but it is clear that this is not an issue that emerges only after
the rise of continental Arminianism and English Laudianism; it is a point
of tension from the Reformation's very inception.

More important (though not, as the struggle became factionalized, unre-
lated) is the battle over precisely what the face of the English church should
look like. This, in essence, is precisely the issue that led Hooper to clash with
Ridley, and Knox to clash with Cranmer. The political necessity of Cranmer's
'softly, softly' approach to ceremonies and ecclesiology was inevitably going
to upset the more radical elements within the church. Given the nature of
the English settlement, this was to be an issue for a further century and a
half. The vestiarian controversies of Elizabeth's reign, the terrible Covenant-
ing Wars in Scotland, and the bloodbath of the English Civil War, were all
to a greater or lesser extent linked to the issue of how far the English Reformation should extend both theologically and, in the case of the covenanters,
geographically as well. As with predestination, however, while the scale of
later debates might have been greater, and the stakes very much higher, the
principles at issue were already being fought over within the corridors of
church and secular power in the middle years of the sixteenth century.

14 The Scottish Reformation: theology and theologians

DAVID F. WRIGHT

To the best of my memory, no monograph has ever been devoted to 'The Theology (or Theologians) of the Scottish Reformation'. The name most likely to spring to mind as theological animator of the movement is that of John Knox, yet, among the several roles he played in it, historians have not cast him characteristically as a theologian. James S. McEwen's selective account is judiciously entitled *The Faith of John Knox*, and even Richard G. Kyle, the author of *The Mind of John Knox*, which is the nearest we have to a comprehensive exposition of his thought, had to grant that 'as a theologian Knox developed no dramatically fresh interpretations, nor will he ever be accorded the status of a first-rate thinker of the Protestant Reformation'.

Such a verdict would not have worried Knox himself, as is clear from his introduction to the only sermon he ever committed to print, indeed the only exposition of any portion of scripture thus preserved from over two decades of 'al my studye and travayle within the Scriptures of God'.

> That I did not in writ communicat my judgement upon the Scriptures, I have ever thought and yet thinke my selfe to have most just reason. For considering my selfe rather cald of my God to instruct the ignorant, comfort the sorrowfull, confirme the weake, and rebuke the proud, by tong and livelye voyce in these most corrupt dayes, than to compose bokes for the age to come, seeing that so much is written (and that by men of most singular condition), and yet so little well observed; I decreed to containe my selfe within the bondes of that vocation, wherunto I founde my selfe especially called.

God had revealed to him, Knox believed, 'secretes unknowne to the worlde', and as a consequence, 'he made my tong a trumpet, to forwarne realms and nations, yea, certaine great personages, of translations and changes, when no such thinges were feared, nor yet was appearing, a portion whereof cannot the world denie (be it never so blind) to be fulfilled'.

What this meant for Knox's writings, which occupy six volumes in David Laing's mid-nineteenth-century edition, was not so much that they

174

would not be theological as that their theological temper would be variously prophetic, pastoral, polemical, controversial and practical rather than dogmatic, systematic, or expository. This is true even of Knox's treatise on predestination, by far his longest work on a theological topic but one that is 'far from being . . . systematic, and perhaps not even internally consistent'.

A similar evaluation must be made of the best-known doctrinal production of the Scottish Reformation, the Scots Confession, approved by Parliament in 1560. Knox was one of the compilers of this confession, which has in the modern period enjoyed widespread appreciation, not least by comparison with the other confession that has dominated the Scottish Reformed tradition, the Westminster Confession of 1647. The Scots Confession, not least in the arrangement of its articles, betrays the haste with which it was drafted. Its distinctive flavour was well captured by Edward Irving:

> The Scottish Confession was the banner of the church, in all her wrestlings and conflicts, the Westminster Confession but as the camp-colours which she hath used during her days of peace; the one for battle, the other for fair appearance and good order . . . [The former] is written in a most honest straight-forward manly style, without compliment or flattery, without affectation of logical precision, or learned accuracy, as if it came fresh from the heart of laborious workmen, all the day long busy with the preaching of the truth, and sitting down at night to embody the heads of what they continually taught. There is a freshness of life about it.

T. F. Torrance has rightly drawn attention to the inclusion on the title page of the first printing of the confession in 1561 of Matthew 24:14, 'And this glaid tydinges of the kingdom shalbe preached throught the hole world for a witness to all nations and then shall the end cum': 'This is quite startling', says Torrance, for, in contrast to every other confessional statement issued during the Reformation, it gives primary importance to the missionary calling of the Church.

More must be said about the Scots Confession later in this essay. For the moment it illustrates the characteristically kerygmatic and pastoral tone that, through Knox, informed Scottish Reformation theology. It also brings to our notice another feature of this Reformation's theological endeavours – their corporate or even ecclesial nature. In a movement on which no single master reformer stamped his dominant genius, the determinative theological standards were team efforts, such as the Scots Confession and the *First Book of Discipline* (1560). The service book which ordered the Reformed worship – and much else – of the kirk was likewise the work of a group of Scottish and English exiles at Frankfurt in 1555, whence it was adopted by the English-speaking congregation in Geneva, which counted Knox among its pastors. After his return to Scotland, the church's General Assembly ordained its use in 1562, and it was printed that year in Edinburgh, as *The Forme of Prayers and Ministration of the Sacraments*. It is misleadingly referred to as 'John Knox's Liturgy', for, unlike Thomas Cranmer's *Book of Common Prayer*, it was not largely the creation of a single draughtsman. There are good grounds for viewing the theological expressions of the Scottish Reformation as transcripts of a communal theological enterprise.

The continental origins of *The Forme of Prayers* points to a third mark of theology in the Reformation in Scotland, namely, its largely dependent or derived character. The relatively late date of its decisive Reformation Parliament in July and August 1560 reflected and facilitated the Reformed kirk's reliance on more original achievements elsewhere, in England and on the continent. From its second Scottish printing in 1564/5 (as earlier in editions issued in Geneva in 1556 and 1561), *The Forme of Prayers* had bound with it an English translation of Calvin's French Genevan catechism published in early 1542. It retained this place through numerous subsequent editions of what gradually became known as the *Book of Common Order*. The first catechism of Scottish origin to be widely used in Scotland was *A Shorte Summe of the Whole Catechism* by John Craig, published in Edinburgh in 1581.

Although the Scots Confession was the doctrinal *chef d'œuvre* of Knox and his colleagues, it was not the only Reformation confession to enjoy some currency in Scotland. The First Helvetic Confession was drawn up in 1536 by a group of Swiss and South German theologians led by Heinrich Bullinger and Martin Bucer in an effort to advance Protestant consensus on the Lord's supper. The Latin and German texts were not published until 1581 and 1828 respectively, but an English translation was issued in London probably in 1548 and clearly attributed to George Wishart, the Scottish reformer who had been burnt as a heretic in St Andrews in March 1546. It was entitled *The Confescion of the Fayth of the Sweserlädes*. Although in this edition Wishart's rendering has presumably been anglicized, his work of translation attests not only his links with Swiss Reformed centres, but also his conviction of its usefulness for Protestant stirrings in his homeland. Further research should clarify much that remains unclear about Wishart's translation.

In 1566 the General Assembly of the Scottish church gave its approval to the Second Helvetic Confession compiled by Bullinger that same year, reserving its position only on the confession's commendation of the major festivals of the Christian year. However, the influence of this confession probably remained limited. Although the General Assembly instructed the publication of a translation made by Robert Pont (1524–1606), no trace of it has been found. The assembly's spokesmen reported its endorsement of the confession's doctrine in fulsome terms, but in reality its pervasive Catholic spirit and patristic sympathies would not have had a wide appeal in Scotland.

In addition to the Geneva Catechism, editions of *The Forme of Prayers* from 1562 until well into the next century included as the first or second item a short confession of faith that had been used by the English congregation in Geneva. It was based in part on the confession by Valérand Poullain used in Frankfurt. It appeared in the 1556 Geneva printing of *The Forme of Prayers*. Little attention has been paid to this confession of faith, which is ordered according to the clauses of the Apostles' Creed, with an extended treatment of the 'one holy Church'. Here one encounters a visible church identifiable by, not two, but three marks. The inclusion of ecclesiastical discipline is noteworthy in a confession apparently produced in Geneva, where Calvin, for all his zeal for church discipline, pointedly declined to erect it into a mark of the true church. The author may more likely be William Whittingham than John Knox, although the elevation of discipline would be welcome in Reformed Scotland. The confession's brevity, together with its terseness and clarity, must have made it unusually accessible to believers in the Reformed kirk.

It is characteristic of service books in the early Reformed tradition to be heavily didactic in function. In addition to the provision for the reading and expounding of the scripture, lengthy exhortations and wordy prayers fulfilled a teaching function. *The Forme of Prayers* of the early 1560s in Scotland contained, as we have seen, both the Geneva Catechism and the confession of faith of the English congregation in Geneva. According to the title page of the 1562 edition it also included 'the confession of faith whiche all they make that are received into the universitie of Geneva'. This had in fact been printed in a Genevan version of *The Forme of Prayers* of 1561, and also in a 1566 edition (printed in Geneva for a Rouen publisher), but it was omitted from the Edinburgh 1562 text, and was not listed among the contents. This little-noticed confession has been identified as one of the sources of the Scots Confession. The compilers of *The Forme of Prayers* (1561) declared it to be useful beyond the Academy of Geneva as 'verye profitable for all Townes, Parishes, and Congregations, to discerne the true Christians from Anabaptistes, Libertines, Arrians, Papistes, and other Heretikes'. Written throughout in the first person singular, it evinces predictable Genevan features, such as its realistic theology of baptism and the Lord's supper – in both, 'God giveth us in dede and accomplisheth trully that whiche is there figured . . . I joyne with the signes the possession and the use of that which is there presented', while omitting others, for example discipline and pre-destination or election. The first-person format and some other elements, including its polemics against papists and heretics ancient and modern, give this confession a sprightly vigour.

Another area in which Scottish dependence on the fruits of reform else-where was evident lay in the use of vernacular translations of the Bible. As far as is known, no Scottish reformer displayed any interest in a transla-tion into Scots. The English versions, which had appeared in a steady stream since William Tyndale's 1526 New Testament (which had found its way into Scotland by early 1527), would suffice. Some adaptation to Scots might take place between the printed text and pronunciation. Nevertheless, from their own day to the present, the reformers, and particularly Knox, have been berated for their neglect of the Scots tongue. Alexander Alesius (or Alanus, 1500–65), a native of Edinburgh and graduate of St Andrews, who spent most of his reforming career in Germany and England, conducted a vigor-ous literary campaign in defence of vernacular scriptures during 1533–4, but he wrote in Latin from the continent.

The English translation produced by Protestant exiles in Geneva (New Testament 1557, complete Bible 1560), which became known as the Geneva Bible, was the obvious candidate for official adoption in newly Reformed Scotland. A reprint of the second edition of 1562 was the first Bible to be published in Scotland, by Alexander Arbuthnot in Edinburgh in 1579 (known from Arbuthnot's late assistant as the Bassendyne Bible). Long after the appearance of King James' so-called 'Authorized' Version of 1611, the Geneva Bible continued in use in Scotland for varying periods in different places. John Knox almost certainly had no part in the translation, although he cited some Old Testament verses according to the 1560 text a couple of years in advance of its publication. His use prior to this time had been eclectic, not even excluding the influence of the Vulgate's Latin, nor did he switch to sole reliance on the Geneva Bible once it was available. Neverthe-less, the mind of pious church-people in Reformation Scotland was shaped by the unambiguously Protestant, and often pointedly Reformed (rather than strictly Calvinist), flavour of the Geneva Bible's extensive annotations and other readers' aids. This reminds us that the scriptures in the com-mon tongue were received throughout the Reformed churches in a complex context of authorized interpretation.

The phrase 'scripture alone' appears far less often in Reformation writ-ings than is popularly supposed. It stands in reality for 'scripture supreme' – over all other human and ecclesiastical authorities. The phrase is absent from the Scots Confession, where we find, however, two occurrences of

'the plain Word of God' (arts. 18, 20). This characteristically Knoxian note –
other favourite epithets are 'manifest' and especially 'express' – exemplifies the greater rigour with which the scriptural criterion was applied in
Scotland than in other theatres of the Reformation. (It should be said in
passing that the records of the Scottish Reformation afford no support for
the fond notion of some modern scholars that the reformers in general dif-
ferentiated between the written scriptures and some distillate or essence
thereof alone called 'the Word of God'. The Scots Confession puts the issue
beyond doubt, by its use of expressions such as 'the written Word of God'
[art. 18] and by its unvarying reference to the Bible's text.) Knox enunciated
more than once what in later Scottish church history would be known as
the 'regulative principle'.

> No honoring knaweth God, nor will accept, without it have the express
> commandement of his awn Word to be done in all poyntis.

> All wirshipping, honoring, or service of God inventit be the braine of
> man, in the religion of God, without his own express commandement,
> is Idolatrie.

Both quotations come from Knox's address before the assembly of the north
delivered at Newcastle in 1550, edited by Laing as *A Vindication of the Doctrine that the Sacrifice of the mass is Idolatry*. When the fathers of the Reform
demurred, as we have noted, at a clause in the Second Helvetic Confession
on the celebration of Christmas, Easter, the ascension, and Pentecost, the
ground cited was that 'we dare not religiously celebrate any other feast-day
than what the divine oracles have prescribed'. There was, it seems, little
or no room for *adiaphora*, 'things indifferent' on which belief and practice
might acceptably vary in face of the silence of scripture, at least in the early
years of the Scottish Reformation.

The role of the Bible in the reform of the Scottish church requires some
mention of the prominence given to the Old Testament and to the Psalms
in particular. Both were typical of early Reformed Protestantism, by comparison with Lutheran and Anglican varieties. The reasons for this lie in
differing correlations of law and gospel with the two testaments, in the
Reformed emphasis on the 'third use' of Old Testament law (as a blueprint
for the ordering of personal and communal life in the Christian era) and,
in a tighter doctrine of scripture as God's Word uniformly throughout, as
well as in the kind of personal identification with the vocation of prophetic
watchman already observed in Knox. Several of the major reformers discerned in the vicissitudes of the psalmist a pattern poignantly relevant to
their own experiences. Thus in *The First Blast of the Trumpet against the*

Monstrous Regiment of Women (1558), Knox justifies the magistrate's duty to punish not only crimes such as theft and murder but also 'suche vices as openly impugne the glorie of God, as idolatrie, blasphemie, and manifest heresie' by citing the exemplary actions of kings Hezekiah, Jehoshaphat, and Josiah. On a very different note, the Scots Confession's fifth article, preceding those on the incarnation and work of Christ, is entitled 'Of the Continuance, Increase, and Preservation of the Kirk'. It deals with God's special care for 'his Kirk in all ages fra *Adam*', prior to the coming of Christ. A more centrally focused article 'Of the Kirk' comes later, at a more predictable place, between human imperfection and the immortality of the soul (art. 16), to be followed shortly by another on the 'notes' of the true kirk (art. 18).

The pervasive Old Testament ethos of much of Scottish Reformed worship and piety no doubt owes much to the privileged place held by the psalter. The inspiration was again of Genevan origin. The England congregation in that city had fifty-one metrical psalms in its first *Forme of Prayers* in 1556. By the 1561 edition the total had risen to eighty-seven, and to the full 150 by the second Scottish edition, of 1564. (For some reason the first, in 1562, lacked psalms altogther.) The prominence of the psalms in this service book led to editions with titles such as *The CL. Psalmes of David in English metre. With the Forme of Prayers* ... (1575) and then omitting mention of *The Forme of Prayers* altogether (1587ff.). The singing of metrical psalms in Scotland after 1560 owed something to late medieval practice and more to English Protestant versions and usage, just as the English *Book of Common Prayer* was used in Scotland until *The Forme of Prayers* took over. Psalmody, to the exclusion of the singing of hymns of human composition and without instrumental accompaniment, would dominate Scottish Presbyterian worship until the nineteenth century. If, in Reformation Scotland, sung psalms were not quite the battle songs of the persecuted Huguenots in France, they reinforced a sense of identification with the Davidic people of God in the Old Testament.

This is an appropriate juncture to say something about Scots Gaelic in relation to the Reformation. 'By 1500 Gaelic would have been spoken mainly in areas to the north of the "Highland Line", but also in Kyle and Carrick, and in Galloway.' Protestantism would be slow to reach some areas in the northwest, but in parts of the southwest, especially Kyle, Lollardy had prepared its way. John Carswell's translation-cum-adaptation of *The Forme of Prayers, Foirm na n-Urrnuidheadh*, was the first Gaelic printed book to be published in Scotland or Ireland. It appeared in Edinburgh in 1567. Carswell was superintendent of Argyll and bishop of the Isles, and it was to local church polity that he adjusted parts of the book. It kept the confession of the English congregation in Geneva, but replaced Calvin's catechism with a much shorter catechism, still based on Calvin but Carswell's own work. (Calvin's Latin Catechism of the Genevan Church of 1545 would be published in Gaelic c. 1630.) No psalms were included, and indeed a Gaelic psalter and progress towards a Gaelic Bible were still a century off. Carswell's *Foirm* contained one unique item, 'The manner of blessing a ship on going to sea'. This earliest Protestant venture into Gaelic was a milestone no less in the development of language and culture than in religion. It betrays no sense of a distinctively 'Celtic' theology that welcomed or resisted Protestant dress.

The Scottish Reformation settlement of 1560 and the immediately succeeding years is often given a misleading impression of having sprung already full-grown, without ancestry, like Melchizedek – and from Geneva. Study of the evangelical movement in Scotland in the preceding decades gives the lie at least to the mono-Genevan account of religious reform. Yet the fruits of that movement in the mid-1550s cannot be easily specified in concrete terms. As Martin Dotterweich summarizes in his recent thesis on 'The Emergence of Evangelical Theology in Scotland in 1550', by that date 'Luther's teaching on salvation, combined with the reading of the Bible, had become for some Scots the centre of Christian life'. Yet it also has to be said that

> The history of evangelicalism before 1500 cannot be a history of 'great men'. The most notable individuals, [Patrick] Hamilton and [George] Wishart, had a combined presence in the country of no more than ten years. Those who produced evangelical treatises for their homeland, with the exception of Alesius, published no more than a single work each. The great majority of Scotland's evangelicals maintained a quiet and unobtrusive existence.

This interpretation discerns major continuity between evangelical and Protestant in justification by faith alone – the core Lutheran gospel of the free grace of Christ. This had led to criticism or denial of traditional beliefs and practices such as purgatory and the intercession of the saints, but without abandonment of the institutional church, at least as dispenser of the sacraments. Persistence in proscribed study of the Bible in English fostered, perhaps in combination with Lollard antisacerdotalism, secretive conventicling. But the decisive advance would come, according to Dotterweich, in ecclesiology, in which the critical focus fell on the rejection of the mass as idolatrous and the first Protestant observances of the Lord's supper. Knox's teaching and initiative to this end capped the broadbrush preaching of Wishart on churches true and false.

A summary must suffice of the leading persons and episodes in pre-1560 Scottish evangelicalism. Regions of southwest Scotland, and especially Kyle (Ayrshire), harboured pockets of Lollardy from at least the late fifteenth century. Knox's *History of the Reformation in Scotland* records the trial in 1494 of 'the Lollards of Kyle'. The charges against them reflect, to judge by extensive English documentation, a cluster of typically Lollard attitudes, which foreshadowed Protestantism in holding to the priesthood of all believers and clerical marriage, in rejecting images and relics, prayer to Mary, and transubstantiation, and in sharp criticism of indulgences and extensively of the papacy. But neither justification by faith nor the right to common-language Bible reading was alleged against them. Both, however, were unambiguously attested in the same area a generation or so later in a Scots version of a Wycliffe New Testament attributed to Murdoch Nisbet of Hardhill, Loudon, in Ayrshire. This translation itself cannot be dated more precisely than the late fifteenth or early sixteenth century, but it was later provided with a prologue to the New Testament and a preface to Romans, both of which ultimately derive largely from Luther, and with extensive marginal notes and references. Dotterweich has shown that all of these additions were taken from an English New Testament of Miles Coverdale of 1537–8. No hard evidence exists of the wider influence of Nisbet's manuscript (discovered only in 1893), but analysis of both its text and its various supplements reveals an evangelical with Lollard roots still evident (he omitted Coverdale's note qualifying Jesus' prohibition of swearing) who has adopted a massive corpus of Protestant doctrine, mostly of a Lutheran colour, on justification by faith, predestination, the authority of Scripture, law and gospel, the theology of the cross, faith and works, even the motif of *simul iustus et peccator*.

Nisbet's New Testament has attracted close interest from students of the Scots language, sometimes as forlorn evidence of what might have happened to produce a Bible in Scots. But on this score his manuscript had no future, based as it was on a Wycliffite version translated from the Vulgate. Dotterweich's discovery of Nisbet's source in Coverdale's New Testament, firmly dated in 1537–8, itself provokes surmises and questions. At that advanced date as far as English Bibles were concerned (by 1537 two full versions were circulating in England with royal permission), why bother with a Wycliffite version in manuscript? One answer must focus interest afresh on the Scots tongue. In the absence of another Scots translation, at least here was a relatively recent one whose deficiencies could to some extent be covered by prefatory and marginal interpretation. This in turn underlines Nisbet's commitment (if the new dating after 1537–8 allows Nisbet to be both translator and supplementer) to communicate to his neighbours in

Ayrshire a full-blooded Lutheran gospel. Such a diet surely bred a generation of dissenters, for the present assembling only in lay Bible study groups, fit to be recruited to sterner service by later preachers with wider perspectives.

Ports on the east coast of Scotland provided probably the earliest entrée to Lutheran treatises and copies of Tyndale's New Testament. Some imbibed the new gospel at first hand, while studying or otherwise sojourning abroad. St Andrews nurtured a nest of dissenters, of whom the best-known is Patrick Hamilton, whose burning for heresy there in early 1528 made him the proto-martyr of the Scottish Reformation. While in Germany, Hamilton had writ-ten a set of commonplaces later translated into English and first published in the early 1530s as *Dyvers Frutful Gatheringes of Scrypture concernyng Faith and Workes* but popularly known as *Patrick's Places*. They set forth in short phrases and simple logical statements a patently Lutheran understanding of law and gospel, faith and works, and justification by faith alone. No reader could mistake the sharp challenge of Hamilton's message. His *Places* circu-lated widely, not least because of the impact made by Hamilton's burning in 1528. Knox's *History* depicts far-flung questioning aroused by news of his fate and lively stirrings of evangelical thought in the university itself. Beyond doubt, Alexander Alesius was one whose encounters with Hamilton alive and dying set him on the path to Protestantism. Two other St Andrews graduates who later addressed Protestant treatises to Scotland from the con-tinent may well have been contemporaries of Hamilton's in the university. John Gau's *The Richt Vay to the Kingdom of Hevine*, published in Malmö in 1533, was 'the first substantial Lutheran treatise to be published in Scots'. It consists largely of a translation of a Danish work of the same title which in turn was based on treatises by the Augsburg reformer Urbanus Rhegius and Luther himself. As a handbook for evangelical discipleship, *The Richt Vay* expounds the standard catechetical bases of the Decalogue, Apostles' Creed, Lord's Prayer and *Magnificat*. Although not concerned with the reform of the church as such – its focus is more personal and domestic – it propounds a more thoroughgoing application of Lutheran theology than any earlier work of Scottish origin. Apart from justification by faith and its corollaries, *The Richt Vay* highlights vernacular Bible reading and ventures into the contrast between a true church and a false.

Gau ends his work with a commendation of the martyrdom of Patrick Hamilton, which had been witnessed by John Johnsone, little-known author of a treatise published in Antwerp or Malmö in 1536 entitled *An Confortable Exhortation: of oure Mooste Holy Christen Faith and her Frutes*, addressed to his fellow Scots from abroad. Its teaching is both heavily biblical in quoted content and firmly Lutheran in flavour, much along the lines of Gau. Little can be asserted with confidence of the influence of either Gau or

Johnsone. Knox mentions neither, but the group of St Andrews Lutherans whose focal centre was Patrick Hamilton demonstrated again the truth of Tertullian's dictum that 'the blood of the martyrs was the seed' – in that case, of evangelical theology.

In the 1530s and '40s incipient Protestant faith continued to spread and strengthen in Scotland, not least through reading of the New Testament, which was briefly authorized in 1543. For the most part, however, charges of heresy pursued those apprehended in possession of the scriptures in the vernacular or espousing Lutheran opinions. Leadership by reforming ministers or scholars was largely lacking, but members of the nobility and gentry were more forthcoming. Indeed, in these decades it was some of the latter who purveyed the best evangelical theology of the day in Scotland. Sir John Borthwick, who moved in court circles, was accused of heresy in 1540 and condemned in his absence after fleeing to England. The charges included a drastic critique of the papacy and indulgences, ownership of an English New Testament and books by Erasmus, Melanchthon, and Oecolampadius, and espousing the 'English heresies'. Borthwick was patently an overt evangelical. By the time he wrote extended replies to the allegations, before 1559, his 'theological beliefs can be identified confidently as Reformed'. His condemnation was annulled in 1562.

Also active at the court of James V was the lawyer Henry Balnaves, who had probably been at St Andrews during Hamilton's burning. His long-standing Protestant sympathies issued in his openly joining the 'castilians' in St Andrews after the assassination of Cardinal David Beaton in 1546. When the castle was captured by the French in the next year, Balnaves was imprisoned in Rouen, where in 1548 he composed a solid treatise on justification. He managed to get it conveyed to Knox when the latter's galley put in at the port. Knox revised it, adding chapter divisions, marginal notes, and a summary. Although it was then got into Scotland, it was lost until rediscovered in 1584, when it was published in Edinburgh as *The Confession of Faith, Conteining How the Troubled Man Should Seeke Refuge at his God.* It is generally known as Balnaves' *Treatise on Justification.* Its dependence on Luther's *Lectures on Galatians* (1535) is considerable, and 'in imagery, argumentation, and language, Balnaves never strays far from Luther'. The work was intended for instruction of lay folk, which probably explains its repetitiousness and very extensive quotation of Scripture. Nevertheless, it still stands as the weightiest exposition of Protestant theology produced by a Scot so far. Yet it was not a manifesto for reform, which this phase of markedly Lutheran evangelicalism in Scotland failed to produce.

The propagation of Protestant doctrine in Scotland had reached its most radical and provocative in the preaching tours of George Wishart through

Fife, Angus, Ayrshire, and the Lothians during 1544–5. Wishart's burning at the stake as a heretic in 1546 in St Andrews in turn precipitated the murder of Beaton. Note has already been taken of Wishart's translation of the First Helvetic Confession (1536), published after his death in 1548. This imported a decidedly Reformed strain of Protestant theology, evident in its advocacy of iconoclasm, insistence on church discipline, its firmer formulation of the authority of scripture, presaging Knox's regulative criterion, and its sacramental teaching mediating between Lutheran and Zwinglian emphases.

Wishart left no other written works. Knox records little of the content of his preaching, but does report that he expounded Paul's letter to the Romans, so fertile a source for evangelical doctrine throughout the Reformation. The account of Wishart's trial, however, which Knox incorporated into his *History* from Foxe's *Actes and Monuments*, throws much light on Wishart's radicalizing Protestantism. The text suggests that on some issues, such as the scripture principle and the sacraments, Wishart stood somewhat to the left of the First Helvetic Confession, implying an influence more Zwinglian than anything else. His replies to the charges repeatedly claimed that he had taught only what was in scripture and nothing beyond. Auricular confession had no biblical justification. The church, and God himself, were found wherever there was true preaching of God's Word and lawful use of the sacraments. This pointed to a drastic simplification of worship.

The import of Wishart's doctrine soon manifested itself in his former attendant and bodyguard, John Knox. Having joined the castilians in St Andrews and been pressurized into preaching his first sermon, on Daniel 7:24–5, Knox uttered so defiantly Protestant a proclamation that some commented, 'Others sned [lop] the branches of the Papistry, but he strikes at the root, to destroy the whole', and others, 'Master George Wishart spake never so plainly, and yet he was burnt: even so will he be.' Instead, Knox had to defend himself against nine charges drawn from his preaching. Already he insisted repeatedly that unless 'God in expressed words has commanded' ceremonies, they neither proceed from faith nor please God, but are sin. He cited the divine prohibition in Deuteronomy 4:2 against adding to or diminishing from what the Lord had commanded.

Knox escaped the fate of Wishart but spent most of the next dozen years outside Scotland, in England and in various places in France, Germany (Frankfurt) and Switzerland, especially Geneva. A number of his writings of this period were addressed to non-Scottish readerships, at least explicitly. His most substantial theological work, his defence of predestination (published in Geneva in 1560 but written a couple of years earlier), refuted an English Anabaptist critique – and probably also deliberately lined the author up in hearty agreement with Calvin. Even *The First Blast of the Trumpet* (1558), arguing that female rule defied both natural and divine law, had Queen Mary Tudor of England centrally in its sights – and backfired on Knox when she was soon succeeded by reform-friendly Elizabeth. But this polemical treatise, like other writings of pastoral counsel directed to the faithful in England, would be invaluable grist for the mill of reform in Scotland, as too his *Vindication of the Doctrine that the Sacrifice of the mass is Idolatry*, an address at Newcastle in 1550.

Two works in particular illustrate the course of the evangelical movement in Scotland in his absence. *A Most Wholsome Counsell how to Behave Ourselves in the Myddes of thys Wycked Generation touching the Daily Exercise of Gods Most Holy and Sacred Worde* (1556) exhorted Scots believers to study of the Scriptures and family worship in house churches or 'privy kirks'. *The Appellation of John Knoxe . . .* (1558) appealed against the sentence of excommunication passed in his absence by 'the false bishoppes and clergie of Scotland', but over their heads to the nobles and to the common people (here backed up by his open letter *To his Beloved Brethren the Communaltie of Scotland bound with The Appellation*), urging them to take the advancement of church reform into their own hands. His arguments draw heavily on Old Testament models. The book exemplifies the political theology that persuaded Knox of the lawfulness, and even obligation, of removing impious and tyrannical rulers. Such doctrine justified the role of the 'lords of the congregation' who first compacted together in late 1557 to promote thoroughgoing reform of the Scottish church.

Between the late 1540s and the Reformation settlement of the early 1560s, little written theology serving the Reformation cause appeared in Scotland, or elsewhere for Scotland, except for Knox's publications. Closely allied to Knox in Frankfurt and Geneva was Christopher Goodman (1519– 1603), formerly professor at Oxford. He joined Knox in Scotland in 1559 and was minister at Ayr and then St Andrews until 1565, when he left for England never to return. In addition to contributing to *The Forme of Prayers*, the Geneva Bible and the metrical psalms, he published in Geneva in 1558 *How Superior Powers Oght to be Obeyd of their Subjects: and wherin they may lawfully be disobeyed*. This presentation of the case for the rightful overthrow of tyrannical and ungodly rulers went beyond even Knox in its decisive radicalism. Goodman's influence on the early Reformed kirk extended also to the notion of the covenanted nation.

Knox's works continued to be predominant in the years from 1560 on. This may be illustrated by briefly noting the meagre literary contribution of the five other Johns who are credited, with Knox, with the drafting of both the Scots Confession and the *First Book of Discipline*. John Winram published only a vernacular catechism in 1546, the first to circulate in Scotland. No copy has survived, and at that stage in his career we may surmise that it reflected a moderate reformism soon to be overtaken by events. In addition to being a member of the drafting committee, Winram, with William Maitland of Lethington, advised Parliament on the draft confession. This review softened the asperity of some expressions and judgements, and, more significantly, dropped a section sanctioning the right of resistance to civil rulers. John Willock's theological temper has been characterized by Duncan Shaw as more stringently Zurich-tending, through contacts with Bullinger and others of the stricter Reformed such as John Laski. Shaw provisionally attributes the moderate article on election in the confession to Willock, along with a couple of other statements, but apart from a few letters Willock left nothing in writing. Nothing more survives from John Row, minister of Perth from 1560 to 80, a noted linguist and one of the drafters of the *Second Book of Discipline* (1578) also. John Douglas may have contributed the paragraphs on reform of the universities to the *First Book of Discipline* from his long years as provost of St Mary's College and rector of the university, St Andrews. The only writing bearing his name is the letter from leaders of the Reformation notifying Beza of their approval of the Second Helvetic Confession. Finally, John Spottiswoode, superintendent of Lothian and father of the church historian of the same name, bequeathed no written legacy.

In these circumstances, whatever may be recalled about the education and overseas experience of the other five, it is understandable why the Scots Confession has so often been depicted as Knox's Confession. A corrective assertion is likely to remain vacuous until contributions by other Johns can be specified. Ian Hazlett's important analysis of the diverse sources of the confession must be complemented by an attempt to relate them to one or other of the Johannine draftsmen, or, more pertinently, to one of the other five.

Even if one moves beyond such co-operative documents as the confession and the *First Book of Discipline*, two or three decades pass before works of Reformed Protestant theology appear in any numbers. John Craig, noted earlier as author of a widely used Calvinian Catechism in 1581, was also involved in the compilation of the *Second Book of Discipline* and drew up the so-called King's or Negative Confession of 1581. His 'Form of Examination before the Communion' of 1590–2 became standard usage as a short catechism in congregation, home and school. Craig was a prominent figure in the kirk and a theologian of quality, although he misrepresented his master Calvin in teaching that in the supper Christ's 'natural' body was received.

Contemporary and associated with Craig in the *Second Book of Discipline* and other endeavours was Robert Pont (1524–1606), a versatile writer with calendrical calculations a special interest. He translated the Second Helvetic Confession, versified several psalms in metre (as Craig too had done), wrote a preface to Bassendyne's Bible, and in 1573 published at St Andrews a short Latin catechism in verse for those to be admitted to the Lord's supper, one of several such Latin compositions used in Scottish schools in this period. Patrick Adamson (1537–92), an opponent of the Presbyterianism embodied in the *Second Book of Discipline*, and so often of Craig and Pont, likewise produced in 1573 in verse a Latin version of the English translation of Calvin's (French) Genevan Catechism (as printed with the 1564 *Forme of Prayers*). A gifted linguist and productive writer, but mostly of occasional pieces, Adamson lived an embattled existence as Archbishop of St Andrews in defiance of the General Assembly (1575–92). John Davidson (c. 1549–1604), generally identified from the scene of his last ministry, Prestonpans, near Edinburgh, was active far and wide in the Reformed cause. His literary prowess lay chiefly in verse, with poems in praise of Knox and in lament over his death. Late in life he wrote *Some Helpes for Young Schollers in Christianity* (1602), a catechism and his major prose publication, which continued to be quoted long after his death. Davidson's sureness of touch is visible in his subtly bipartite definition of faith: 'a hearty assurance of forgiveness or a hearty receiving of Christ'. The tale of catechisms is not complete without mention of the Heidelberg Catechism, published in Edinburgh in Latin in 1591 and first in English there in 1615. Often known as the Palatine Catechism, it enjoyed wide acceptance in Scotland.

But among the generation after Knox pride of theological place should probably belong to Robert Bruce (c. 1554–1631), who was minister of Edinburgh (St Giles) from 1587 until banished in 1600. There he preached series of memorable sermons, of which the most celebrated are his *Sermons upon the Sacrament of the Lords Supper*, published in Scots in 1590/1, and then in English translation at London in 1614. The latest edition was in 1958 by T. F. Torrance, who commends especially Bruce's grasp of the doctrine of union with Christ. Bruce has been frequently quoted for asserting that the sacrament was appointed,

> not that you may get any new thing, but that you may get the same thing better than you had it in the Word . . . that we may get a better hold of Christ than we got in the simple Word, that we may possess Christ in our hearts and minds more fully and largely than we did before, by the simple Word.

These sermons combine solid Reformed theology, partly undergirded by the fathers, with a rich devotional spirituality. They reflect, however, a profound understanding of the Lord's supper not easily reconciled with the infrequency of observance characteristic of most Scottish Presbyterianism.

This survey of the later sixteenth century has been thin on biblical exposition. Here too, as library lists record, dependence on continental commentaries was the norm. The chief architect of the *Second Book of Discipline*, Andrew Melville (1545–1622), was on any measure an outstanding scholar. His Latin lectures on Romans are extant in a student's copy made in 1601 from Melville's own text, but they were not published until 1850 and remain untranslated. Melville lectured on the Pauline letters after becoming principal of St Mary's College, St Andrews, in 1580. His Romans was appended in 1850 to the much longer commentary on the same letter by Charles Ferme (1566–1617), compiled in Latin during his ministry at Fraserburgh in the latter decades of his life, published in 1651 and newly translated into English in the mid-nineteenth century. Melville spoke for all his contemporaries in holding that in universities the scriptures were to be studied in the original languages. He argued this in his unappealingly titled S*cholastica diatriba de rebus divinis* ('Scholastic diatribe concerning divine matters') (Edinburgh, 1599). By the end of the century we are certainly into the post-Reformation era. It is indubitably to this later period that we should assign the numerous biblical commentaries, sermons, and theological treatises of Robert Rollock (c. 1555–99), first principal of Edinburgh University and promoter of covenant theology. The commentary by the inventive mathematician John Napier (1550–1617), *A Plaine Discouery of the whole Revelation of Saint John* (Edinburgh, 1593), merits a mention because it attests his indebtedness to Christopher Goodman's sermons on the book at St Andrews in around 1564–5.

In the early years after 1560 Knox was the most prolific of Reformation theological writers, but he was not alone. John Erskine (1509–90), laird of Dun (Montrose), was one of the most theologically astute of the lords of the congregation in the late 1550s. He had welcomed George Wishart in 1543 and was brought decisively over to the reform by Knox in 1555. After 1560 he was recognized as a preacher and as superintendent of Angus. From a group of small treatises Erskine wrote from 1559 on, Frank Bardgett has made a case for his importance as a theologian of grace with a central grasp of union with Christ, close to Knox in his view of God's providential intervention in history and in eschatology, but more skilled than any – and certainly than Knox – 'in blending political realities with Reformed theology'. At times a theological writer of unusual eloquence for sixteenth-century Scotland, he is interpreted by Bardgett as essentially in tune with the First Helvetic

Confession but more accommodating in his political theology. One wonders why he was not recruited as the seventh John.

Among other theologically able writers of Knox's generation was David Fergusson (c. 1525–98), minister of Dunfermline. In *Ane Answer to ane Epistle written by Renat Benedict* (1563), he defended the portrayal of the mass as idolatry, taking his stand on the Scots Confession and scripture. He also argued that Reformation doctrine, far from being novel, was that of the early church. He published a sermon on Malachi 3 (1572) and collected Scottish proverbs (1589; not published until 1641). The latter reflected his reputation for joviality. For knowledge of the early church fathers few in Scotland in his day could compare with George Hay (c. 1530–88), minister in Aberdeenshire and then at Eddleston, south of Edinburgh. He supported Knox's stand in refusing Queen Mary's right to have mass, and in 1563 published a learned *Confutation of the Abbote of Crosralguels Masse*. Abbot Quintin Kennedy had declined a public disputation. This rare book has been as rarely studied.

A survey of Scottish Reformation theology throws up few theologians of note, indeed only one, to judge by standard introductions. The Scots Confession, its most celebrated product, is more generally appreciated. Karl Barth's Gifford Lectures of 1937–8 at Aberdeen on *The Knowledge of God and the Service of God* were 'a theological paraphrase and elucidation of the [Scots Confession] as it speaks today and as we today by a careful objective examination of its content can hear it speak'. His references to this 'good confession' are mostly sympathetic. Would that he had not called it 'the confession of John Knox'.

All analysis of the confession, until a critical edition is forthcoming, must start from Ian Hazlett's groundbreaking article of 1987. Elsewhere, in a brilliant brief cameo of the Scottish Reformation, he calls it 'broadly "Catholic and Reformed" in theology, with a Calvinist but not explicitly predestinarian flavour'. The general character of the confession, noted near the beginning of this essay, deserves to be highlighted. 'Its essential spirit is that of a manifesto, a zealous proclamation, a prophetic call to action . . . [It is a] striking blend of evangelical activism with dogmatic apologetics.' Its preface casts it as a testimony to 'the doctrine which we profess', subject to correction from God's holy Word if deviation therefrom can be shown. It also sets it in the context of the conflict with Satan for the souls of the human race. Satan's 'filthy synagogues' (art. 18) are spoken of as 'the Romanists, the Roman Church' (arts. 21, 22), but never is the pope, papacy or papists mentioned by name. Nevertheless, the polemical thrust against 'the horrible harlot, the false Kirk' (and also the Anabaptists) is clear enough (art. 18). Attempts to discern a plausible structure in the confession, such as a Catholic non-controversial section (art. 1–10) and a second section dealing with the controverted issues of the age (11–25), are only partially successful. What can be said without challenge is that the confession sets forth the full credal convictions of its compilers rather than focusing solely on disputed doctrines, but in so doing it couches traditional dogmas (for instance, of the Trinity, Christology, the fall) in the language and emphases of Reformed theology. So the 'wonderful union between the Godhead and the humanity of Christ Jesus' is said to have arisen 'from the eternal and immutable decree of God from which all our salvation springs and depends' (art. 7).

It is widely acknowledged that the chief theological inspiration of the confession is Calvin and that Knox is the main channel of that influence. Hence its distinctives are often identified by comparison with Calvin's theology. They include the absence of double predestination (to which Knox's massive defence of the doctrine clearly subscribes), along with a diffuse division between elect and reprobate (art. 8, headed 'Of Election', is mostly about the rationale for Christ's incarnation and crucifixion); a stronger stress on regeneration (art. 3 already, 12) than on justification (only art. 10, citing Romans 4:25); a stern rejection of the notion that sacraments are only 'naked and bare signs' (art. 21) – a much-quoted statement apparently directed at quasi-Zwinglian ideas, and thoroughly Calvinian at base; discipline as a third mark of the church (arts. 18, 25), which undeniably goes beyond Calvin but has, as we have seen, Genevan roots; the duty of rulers to protect true and eradicate false religion, and of obedience to rulers, so long as they 'vigilantly fulfil their office' (art. 24). Debate has persisted on the confession's teaching on this last topic, partly because of the uncertain implications of this qualification, partly because earlier, in article 14, the repression of tyranny is included among good works.

The confession will continue to tax its interpreters, not least because it deals with several topics in more than one place, incorporates different organizing principles for the heads of doctrine – creed, history of salvation and *ordo salutis* all contribute – and is pervasively informed by biblical rather than systematic-theological concerns. The speed of its composition must be borne in mind at all times, which may mean that its sources are distant and not immediate. The unknown extent of revisions required by Parliament is another factor possibly bearing on its incoherence. Yet undeniably it is an attractively militant, evangelistic (even if the word 'gospel' does not reappear after the title page) and pastoral confession, from which users may be justified in deriving varying theological emphases – since no doubt the six Johns brought nothing less to it.

For the theology of Knox himself, the student has a number of good-quality guides available, even though we still await what might become a classic on the subject. The contours of Knox's theology have been emerging at several points throughout this essay. He was not a theologians' theologian: 'Knox was never a systematic thinker and left no coherent body of theology or political theory. The six substantial volumes of his collected works read more like sermons pursued by other means than academic tracts or treatises.'

Foremost among his dominant convictions was the sovereign authority of the Word and will of God. His thinking and writing were saturated with the Bible, such that at times whole paragraphs consist almost entirely of biblical quotations and allusions. The Word of God was wielded as a weapon by God's prophet, which required that true doctrine and divine vocation have the ascendancy over considerations of policy and prudence. Knox's God intervened in power in human affairs, for weal and for woe. Calamity and tribulation were not the lot of the ungodly alone, and unalloyed prosperity often presaged the more resounding downfall of the reprobate. God was a very busy actor in Knox's *History of the Reformation*, now raising up, now throwing down, granting victory, punishing the idolatry of a wicked queen, visiting his displeasure on the earth with flood or deep freeze, multiplying the number of believers, directing the fire of troops with deadly accuracy.

Such a faith in an ever-active almighty God encompassed the prophet's conviction that he was admitted to the secret counsels of the Deity. Knox was not alone among the Scottish Reformers in professing prophetic powers; Wishart, Craig, Row, Davidson, and Fergusson, all mentioned in this essay, shared Knox's prophetic sensibility. It served to bolster his remarkable, flint-hard tenacity and certainty. And this cluster of beliefs, about divine intervention in present history, the power of the divine Word and the overriding summons to prophesy and proclaim, both fed on and fed that identification with the story and people of the Old Testament that is so marked a feature of Knox's writings.

The overall aim can be described as a godly commonwealth – a covenanted nation – ruled by a godly monarch, who promotes the true church and punishes the false, not at his or her own whim but according to the guidance of God's ordained ministers. Knox championed the autonomy of the church, and was no doubt thankful that the exercise of discipline free of civil control was granted in Scotland more readily than in most centres of the Reformation Europe-wide. This was just as well, since his theology made it an indispensable mark of the church.

Concentration on some of the more obtrusive or distinctive traits in Knox's beliefs may obscure the common ground he shared with the great majority of the magisterial Reformers. To the fore must be the gospel of the free grace granted by Jesus Christ alone and received by faith alone. The six Johns can have had not the slightest difficulty in agreeing on the sumptuous terms in which this rediscovered core message of Protestantism is expressed, and repeated, in the Scots Confession. The bearer of this good news might seem barely compatible with the fearsome trumpeter of God before princes. Like Samuel Rutherford later, Knox was a man made up of extremes. His gentler pastoral teaching may be sampled in Henry Sefton's useful compilation. On his death-bed, Knox had his wife read to him the biblical passage 'where I cast my first anchor'. It was John 17. By working through this Johannine discourse, James McEwen has suggestively shown how many elements in Knox's theology may find a centre in one biblical locus, pointing to a theology as much Johannine as it is Pauline.

15 An introduction to Anabaptist theology

WERNER O. PACKULL

Modern scholarship identified a variety of reform movements within what continues to be called *the* Reformation. Besides the major distinction between Protestant and Catholic, or geographical distinctions (such as the English Reformation), one encounters socio-political designations, such as the princely, the city or communal reformation. Of course, the older, more purely theological distinctions between a Lutheran and Reformed (Calvinist) Reformation have lived on as well. The notion of a 'Radical Reformation' entered the historiography with George Williams' encyclopedic work by that title in 1962. His basic distinction between 'magisterial' and 'radical' reformers has shaped the nomenclature to the present. 'Magisterial' designates those reformers who received support from or collaborated with temporal authorities, be they civic or princely. The radicals, by choice or default, received no such support. Williams' third edition (1992) used both theological and social categories to designate radicals. Thus evangelical rationalists, antitrinitarians, Anabaptists, spiritualists, as well as rebellious peasants, appear under the rubric of radical reformation. Given the topological sweep of his work from Spain to Poland, its erudition and generous spirit, Williams' work remains a classic.

Williams' daunting work is also an impossible act to follow. This essay will be more restricted, focused primarily on the Anabaptists, who make up the core of studies on the radical reformation. But even this shrinkage of focus faces the challenge of diversity. The uninitiated may well despair as to the variety of crusading, pacifist, evangelical, antitrinitarian, sabbatarian, communistic, apocalyptic, mystic-spiritualistic and biblically literalistic Anabaptists. Any attempt at distilling theological essence from such manifest variety seems at best a hazardous undertaking.

The preliminaries call for a generic overview of the major Anabaptist groupings to be subjected to this theological investigation: the Swiss Brethren, the Hutterites, the Melchiorite-Münsterites, and the Mennonites. This would, of course, not be a proper investigation of Anabaptists without another qualifier, namely that two of the theologically most sophisticated and, in this paper, most quoted leaders, Balthasar Hübmaier and Pilgram Marpeck, do not easily fit into any of the camps described below.

A GENERIC OVERVIEW

Swiss Brethren

The Swiss Brethren have the honour of having been the firstborn Anabaptists and the carriers of the birthmark of the Zwinglian reformation: a spiritual-commemorative view of the Lord's supper. It was Huldrych Zwingli's calculated co-operation with the magistrates of Zurich that led to a parting of ways with his erstwhile supporters, who insisted on a stringent and speedy application of *sola scriptura* to all church reforms. The radicals were exercised about a number of issues as the reformation of Zurich unfolded, beginning with justification by faith, clerical celibacy, use of images, prohibition regarding the eating of meat during Lent, and, above all, the nature of the eucharist. The city council's hesitation to ban the mass and proceed with a reformed ceremony of the Lord's supper raised the ire of the radicals. New issues arose when Zurich's council used religious reforms to expand its authority over its rural dependencies by appropriating the church tax and usurping the right to appoint the clergy in the villages.

As early as mid-June 1523, Conrad Grebel, a future Anabaptist leader, registered his sympathy for the rural communities that sought to reform the tithe. When Zwingli sided with Zurich's governing interests, the political-religious issues became galvanized into opposition against him. Curiously, the first refusals of child baptism were registered in the villages of Witikon and Zollikon, whose preachers were at odds with Zurich's council. Rejection of child baptism and the introduction of adult baptism became the defining issue between Zwingli and his former supporters. A disputation on the subject on 17 January 1525 in Zurich set the stage for the final break. Unconvinced by Zwingli's equation of circumcision with baptism and other paedobaptist arguments, Grebel, Felix Mantz, Georg Blaurock and others proceeded with adult baptism, most probably on 21 January 1525.

Once set in motion, the Anabaptist movement spread rapidly through a sympathetic network of reform-minded radicals. Preachers such as Simon Stumpf at Höngg, Johannes Brötli at Zollikon and Wilhelm Reublin at Witikon had prepared the way. Reublin won Balthasar Hübmaier, the reformer of Waldshut, the theologian *par excellence* of early Anabaptism, for the cause. While Hübmaier's attempts to establish a magisterial form of Anabaptism in Waldshut and later in Nicolsburg failed, and his political ethic was rejected by most, his literary apologies for adult baptism proved highly influential. Implicated in the peasant rebellion and the establishment of Anabaptism in Hapsburg territories, Hübmaier became one of the notable early Anabaptist martyrs (1528).

With the onset of persecution and suppression, Anabaptists became a hunted minority, a reality that found expression in the Schleitheim Articles (1527). Besides believers' baptism and a memorial form of the Lord's supper, the seven articles in this early Swiss Anabaptist document enshrined separation from the world, a call for strict discipline, and congregational elections of leaders, and refusal as true Christians to use the sword or to give an oath. Comprehensive theological statements these seven boundary or identity markers were not. A congregational order, originating at about the same time, called for frequent celebrations of the Lord's supper, the voluntary sharing of spiritual and material resources, and the establishment of the congregation as the hermeneutic community, in which the scriptures were to be read and interpreted. This church order migrated east, where it was adapted by Pilgram Marpeck's circle and the Hutterites.

Hutterites

The Hutterites were by no means the only Anabaptist community located in Moravia. Persecuted Anabaptists from Switzerland, the Rhineland, the Palatinate, Hesse, Schwabia, Franconia, Austria, and the Tyrol fled to Moravia, where powerful nobles permitted them to settle on their estates. Consequently, numerous Anabaptist refugee communities formed in Moravia, including the Brethren at Austerlitz, the Gabrielites, Philipites, Hutterites, and other dissenters. Of the various groups, the Hutterites became the most numerous; their codices, dating from the sixteenth century on, contain a rich deposit of Anabaptist works, featuring some forty different authors. They also kept an impressive Chronicle and produced through their leader, Peter Riedemann, the most substantial early Anabaptist 'Confession' (1542).

Melchiorites and Münsterites

Melchior Hoffman was one of those extraordinary figures to stumble across the Reformation stage. A furrier by trade, Hoffman made his first appearance (1524) as a Lutheran in Livonia. Implicated in iconoclastic riots that left several dead or wounded, and monasteries and churches in the city of Dorpat plundered and gutted, Hoffman was forced off the Lutheran stage. His subsequent way-stations included Stockholm, Lübeck, the court of the king of Denmark, Flensburg, Frisia, and Strasbourg, to mention only the more important places of his ministry. On a visit to Strasbourg in 1529–30 Hoffman made contact with Anabaptism and subsequently introduced his own brand in East Frisia, baptizing his first converts in Emden. When his first converts were executed in the Netherlands, a shocked Hoffman suspended baptisms and returned to Strasbourg, a city he believed would play a pivotal role in the restoration of true Christendom. So certain was he regarding this matter that he challenged the authorities to intern him, claiming that within six months cataclysmic events would transform Strasbourg into the new Jerusalem and bring about his release. His prophecies failed; Hoffman spent the rest of his life in prison.

While Hoffman languished in Strasbourg's dungeon, the movement initiated by him spread through East Frisia, Westphalia, and the Netherlands. Jan Matthijs, a baker from Haarlem, resumed the baptisms suspended by Hoffman. Emissaries of Matthijs introduced Anabaptism to the city of Münster, and with the help of the city's reformer, Bernd Rothmann, and local notables converted to the cause, he turned Münster into an Anabaptist stronghold. The events that followed are probably the best-known but least-understood in Anabaptist history. The salacious elements – polygamy, communism, the theatrical goings-on at the 'royal court' of Jan van Leiden (a journeyman tailor and would-be actor, who succeeded Matthijs after the latter's suicidal sally against the besieging forces) – entered the magisterial historiography of the Reformation and popular perceptions as representative of Anabaptism as a whole. But Jan's restitution of the Davidic kingdom, complete with a harem of sixteen concubines and Matthijs' beautiful widow as royal queen, remains difficult to reconcile with sober, moral Anabaptist practices elsewhere. Obviously, desperate circumstances in the besieged city were partly to blame for the aberrations.

Emaciated by starvation and betrayed by defectors, Jan van Leiden's kingdom came to a horrible end in late June 1535. The murderous slaughter of its survivors by blood-mad mercenaries and the stench of rotting bodies tend to be less well remembered than Münster Anabaptist excesses. Bernd Krechting, Bernard Knipperdolling and Jan van Leiden, the most notable prisoners taken alive, were put on public display and subjected to a most cruel death. The final act of this bloody drama took place in front of the cathedral and in full view of a large crowd gathered to see the three prisoners torn apart bit by bit with red-hot tongs. The bishop, reinstated by mercenaries, enjoyed a special armchair view.

Post-Münster Melchiorites fragmented into a number of factions. A small, marauding band of highwaymen under the leadership of Jan van Batenburg, who was executed in 1538, did not outlive their leader by long. Before his execution, Batenburg maliciously implicated some of the peaceful Melchiorites, among them David Joris. Joris emerged temporarily as a mediator between various Melchiorite factions, guiding some of the surviving pro-Münsterites into more peaceful channels. His own metamorphosis into a spiritualist-inspirationist helped to mute the apocalyptic theme of vengeance present among the Melchiorites, while his rejection of outer ceremonies, including baptism, permitted his followers to survive as Nicodemites. Given to dreams and visions, Joris proved a most prolific writer, bequeathing hundreds of incoherent 'formless writings' to his followers. But neither volume nor content of these writings seemed suited to sustain a visible community. Their metaphorical language, which has mystified modern scholars, leaves unexplained the numerous reprints of Joris' writings into the next century. His own household community in Basel, where he had taken shelter under an assumed name, dissolved with his death.

Mennonites

Far more coherent and community-building proved the teachings of the former priest, Menno Simons, who joined the Anabaptists after the Münster debacle in 1536. Co-opted into the leadership, Menno made it his mission to gather, nurture and lead the scattered post-Münster flock. His relationship to the Melchiorites continues to stir controversy. Abraham Friesen has sought to deny any connection, claiming that Menno rejected Melchiorite teachings on biblical grounds. But the historical evidence runs counter to such claims. True, Menno joined a group sobered by the events in Münster. But Obbe Philips, who probably baptized Menno and certainly promoted his leadership, had himself been won for Anabaptism by emissaries of Jan Matthijs. Later, riddled by doubt as to the genuineness of his baptism, Obbe dropped out of the movement altogether. Menno remained and, along with Dirk Philips, Obbe's brother, denounced both Münsterite violence and Jorist Nicodemism, insisting instead on the establishment of visible, disciplined, separated congregations. By the second half of the sixteenth century, the 'Mennonites' dominated in the north, having spread from Holland and Frisia to Schleswig Holstein, and established settlements in the Vistula delta.

ANABAPTIST THEOLOGY

Any attempt at constructing a comprehensive Anabaptist theology runs the risk of imposing foreign structure and foreign criteria on Anabaptist thoughts. Robert Friedmann held that Anabaptists produced no explicit theology, but through the study of the scriptures nurtured an 'existential' faith. Walter Klaassen made a similar point, suggesting that Anabaptists had little use for 'idea-ism', placing the emphasis instead on discipleship, faith lived. In other words, Anabaptists were more concerned with orthopraxis than orthodoxy. Nevertheless, attempts have been made to identify a theological core. Friedmann himself suggested a 'kingdom theology' as the defining principle informing the implicit theology of the Anabaptists. He then proceeded to elucidate its implications under traditional theological categories. I am inclined to follow his example, using slightly different or altered headings: scripture and its interpretation; God and creation; anthropology; Christology and soteriology; ecclesiology; political theology; eschatology; and Anabaptist and spiritualist relations.

Scripture and its interpretation
The problematic sola scriptura

Agreement exists that Anabaptists adopted the Reformation principle of *sola scriptura*. But were Anabaptists, as Friedmann put it, 'simply students of the Scriptures'? True, Anabaptists searched the scriptures and insisted on the strict application of the *sola scriptura* principle for all matters of faith and conduct. But what exactly did this mean, apart from quoting the Bible against tradition perceived to have been corrupted by extrabiblical teachings and practices? Balthasar Hübmaier and early Swiss Anabaptist leaders interpreted Matthew 15:13: 'All plants which the Heavenly Father has not planted should be uprooted', as meaning that everything not explicitly commanded in the scriptures needed to be uprooted. Indeed, on the basis of this principle, some Anabaptists initially rejected music and singing. It was assumed that the scriptures were 'bright and clear' and in no need of glosses; that is, interpretation. Yet, in the light of disagreements as to the meaning of biblical texts, qualifiers were added: only those endowed with spiritual discernment could penetrate the true meaning of the scriptures. Not surprisingly, these qualifications did not automatically lead to unanimity. On the contrary, they stirred controversy and promoted different emphases and orientations.

From its inception, Anabaptism was New Testament in orientation, with a preference for the teachings of Jesus, such as the Sermon on the Mount. Besides the synoptics, the letters of James and Peter were, according to Friedmann, favoured by Anabaptists in keeping with a *Nachfolge*, discipleship emphasis. This emphasis allegedly contrasted with the Pauline-Augustinian orientation of the magisterial reformers, an orientation focused on the redemptive work of Christ. But these generalizations need qualification.

Hermeneutical questions

As noted earlier, Anabaptist church orders implied a congregationalism based on the priesthood of all believers that functioned as the 'hermeneutic community'. It was assumed that discernment by consensus would arrive at the proper meaning of the scriptures. It was further argued that, by abandoning an egalitarian, church-centred hermeneutic, the major reformers shifted the locus to scriptural texts and hence to theological experts. But the actual workings of the hermeneutic community within Anabaptism seems also to have varied from group to group and to have fallen short of the ideal, due to early charismatic and later institutionalized leadership. Besides, group dynamics favoured literates when it came to reading and interpreting the scriptures. Nevertheless, when compared with the magisterial reformers, who made the interpretation of the scriptures a monopoly of the educated elite, Anabaptists did empower the laity to participate in the interpretation of the scriptures. Swiss Brethren perhaps came closest in practice to the ideal of congregational hermeneutics, but they came under criticism from other Anabaptists, such as Pilgram Marpeck, for refusing to let their shepherds lead and for allowing the sheep to chastise the shepherds. In contrast, Hutterites developed a strong leadership structure with special privileges for the 'elders' who guided the hermeneutical task. And even the Swiss Brethren developed hermeneutical aids in the form of concordances to facilitate biblical guidance and to proof-text their convictions and practices. Such institutionalization of biblical discernment could not help but predetermine the hermeneutical task and dampen 'dialogue at the bar of the Word of God' (Yoder). Thus the 'living epistemology of early Reformation congregationalism' was at best a first-generation phenomenon leading to the formation of a tradition of interpretation that provided a future reference point for generations to come. But this does not mean that the hermeneutical task had fossilized or become unnecessary; it continued because of challenges from within and without.

Arnold Snyder recently revived Walter Klaassen's paradigmatic use of letter and spirit to make further distinctions within Anabaptist biblicism. Accordingly, Grebel, Sattler, Hübmaier, Riedemann, and Menno belong to the more literalist camp, while proponents of the inner Word, such as Hans Denck, Hans Hut, and Leonhard Schiemer, belong into a more spiritualist and/or apocalyptic camp. In this schemata, Pilgram Marpeck and his circle are assigned a mediating role. Snyder's research suggests that in the last quarter of the sixteenth century some Swiss Brethren, under a 'Marpeckian' influence, tempered their literalist tendencies and embraced the sophisticated tools of 'figurative exegesis', especially as applied to the Old Testament.

But the challenge for this development had come, in part at least, from without. Evidence indicates that the disputations between representatives of the Reformed faith and Anabaptists influenced the latter to reconsider the relationship between Old and New Testament. Continuing to hold to an ethical Christocentricism as the superior revelation of the New Testament, Anabaptists were prepared not only to examine discontinuities but also continuities between the testaments. Marpeck and his circle, stimulated by controversy with spiritualists, delivered the most serious early Anabaptist attempt at relating Old and New Testament through a progressive salvation history, focused on God's progressive revelation, a concept of fundamental exegetical importance (Yoder). Accordingly, Christ's incarnation and redeeming work ushered in not only a higher revelation but also a new and higher covenant of God's relation to humankind. Marpeck's sense of the newness in Christ, therefore, seemed so strong that he accepted not only two testaments but also postulated two covenants, a novelty Lutherans and Reformed did not share.

Menno Simons, faced with the same task, granted a two-fold meaning to the Old Testament: a literal meaning for the people under the Law and Old Testament and a spiritual meaning for those under the New Testament. And while Menno showed little interest in allegorical interpretation, he was fond of traditional typological interpretations as they related to Christ. Thus Melchizedek, Samson and David could all be interpreted as types of Christ.

But this brief summary does not exhaust all the hermeneutic issues; given Anabaptist diversity, many questions remain. Finally, it must be noted that Anabaptists had never been absolute *sola scriptura* purists; they accepted the Apostles' Creed, the *Didache* (*Doctrine of the Twelve Apostles*) and the Nicene Creed as authentic expressions of apostolic, biblical teachings. They of course also brought their sixteenth-century context to bear on the interpretations of sacred texts.

God and creation

Arguments from silence are never entirely persuasive, but since the reformers who debated the Anabaptists did not accuse them of antitrinitarianism, it may be assumed that they were accepted as orthodox on this issue; the exception being a small group of Italian and Polish non-trinitarians (Socinians), some of whom also engaged in adult baptism. As a rule, Anabaptists did not dwell on what seemed to them highly abstract or speculative issues with little or seemingly no direct practical application to *Nachfolge*; they pleaded not only ignorance but manifested reticence and lack of interest. Presumably the former grew out of the experience of having become entangled in arguments with professional theologians more highly educated than most Anabaptists. But even though Anabaptists made it clear that it was more important to obey God than to speculate about the nature of the Godhead, they also meant to be trinitarians. At the Frankenthal Disputation (1571) the Reformed acknowledged Anabaptist orthodoxy in regard to the

Trinity, and, in an elaboration of their views written shortly thereafter, the Swiss Anabaptists confessed one God and three distinct persons, and that the Holy Spirit, common to the three, proceeds from the Father and the Son, being dispensed into believing hearts by the Son. The Father had created all things through the Son and could be known only through the Son, while the essential oneness of the three was also indicative of the oneness of believers with Christ and one another in the church.

Among early Anabaptists it was Peter Riedemann, a shoemaker turned Hutterite missionary, who gave the subject of God and creation repeated attention. He had been questioned on this and other topics by Lutheran theologians upon his imprisonment in Marburg in 1540. Using primarily the Genesis account and the Apostles' Creed, Riedemann described God the Father as the creator and source of all life, who has being in himself and has neither beginning nor end. Elsewhere Riedemann confessed one God, creator of the universe, who fills heaven and earth with his divine glory, omnipotent, omnipresent, unchanging. About the second person in the Trinity, Riedemann confessed that the Son as the Word was with God in the beginning and present in the creation process. Emphasizing the oneness of the Son and the Father, he held that at the incarnation the Word, that is, God himself, took on human nature, and that in Christ the divine and human natures joined in a hypostatic union.

He confessed further that the Holy Spirit proceeded from the Father and the Son, yet remained for ever in both Father and Son. And while he held that God the Father, Son, and Holy Spirit are of one substance and essence, 'three names' but one, it would be amiss to interpret the apparent monotheistic thrust as intentionally unorthodox, for Riedemann clearly recognized the division of labour in the Godhead – the Father's in creation, the Son's in salvation, and the Spirit's in building the post-Pentecost church. It is true that in using the analogy of fire, heat, and light to illustrate the possibility of three in one – 'where one of them is, there are all three, but whoever lacks one, lacks all three' – Riedemann may not have satisfied the scholastics of his day, but he was, after all, not a trained theologian. Neither was Marpeck, who wrote: 'the Son of Man cannot be without the Father and the Spirit, nor can the Spirit and the Father be without the Son of Man. Consequently, the external essence (reality) of the Son is one in essence (reality) and works in the Father and the Spirit.' Many more examples could be provided that the major Anabaptist groups considered themselves orthodox trinitarians.

Before leaving the subject of the Trinity, it seems noteworthy that Riedemann made a unique attempt to use inner trinitarian relations to argue for community of goods. Just as Father, Son, and Holy Spirit were one and shared each other's properties, so the true followers of Christ should be one and share all spiritual and temporal gifts. Riedmann saw this mandate revealed in the creation order. He noted that God had created nothing for mere private, individual use but everything for mutual benefit. Disobedience and the fall had destroyed the original, beneficial order. Idolatrous, selfish love for temporal things led to private property and, in turn, to a preoccupation with material possessions. Spiritual matters were neglected; the Creator forgotten. By turning to the worship of created, material things, humankind abandoned the divinely ordained order. But some reminders remained: the sun by day, the course of the heavens by night, the air breathed, all witnessing that the original purpose of the created order had been originally intended for the benefit of all. He clinched his argument with the observation that at death all temporal possessions were left behind. Riedemann concluded that private possessions were evidence of the fallen order which Christ had come to restore. True followers of Christ would voluntarily forsake private property and hold all things in common for the benefit of one another and the whole congregation of God.

Anthropology

The previous discussion has already touched on Anabaptist views of the fall and its implication for creation. The intention in this section is to focus on the understanding of the consequences of the fall and the nature of evil. As noted, Anabaptists seemed less influenced by neo-Augustinianism; they favoured forms of voluntarism but without their late medieval, sacramental underpinnings, because they considered the latter instrumental for the corruption of the church. On first thought, it may seem paradoxical that the Anabaptists, who accepted the fall of humankind and postulated the total corruption of the church, should hold to forms of voluntarism both in terms of soteriology and ecclesiology. Or are these corollaries? Indeed, Anabaptists suggested a correlation between an overemphasis on the consequences of original sin, the forensic understanding of justification and the moral apathy evident among the population that had involuntarily become Lutheran or Reformed. Anabaptist voluntarism was therefore not simply a matter of late medieval neo-Pelagianism surviving subconsciously in the minds of Anabaptists, but a conscious reaction to inconsistencies perceived to exist in the magisterial camp between the proclamation of the gospel and the lack of moral improvement. The more sophisticated Anabaptist leaders consciously aimed at correcting the flawed theology of the main reformers by embracing a theology that would hold divine initiative and human responses in creative tension.

True, early Swiss Anabaptists spent little or no time contemplating the nature or significance of original sin. The topic appears to have been a non-issue between them and Zwingli; indeed, oblique references to the subject suggest they shared Zwingli's view that original sin amounted to an inherent tendency toward evil, an illness, and that its consequences were mortality. It was during the controversy over baptism that the Brethren developed the notion that children remained innocent until they sinned deliberately. This view has led to charges that Anabaptists held an extrabiblical view that endowed children before accountability with a supralapsarian nature and after accountability with the infralapsarian nature of Adam (Tanneberger). Seen from this perspective, Anabaptist anthropology is faulted not only as inconsistent but also as superficial in its understanding of original sin and the profound nature of evil. It is further alleged that Anabaptist voluntarism as a whole runs the risk of a false optimism and, even more seriously, depreciates Christ's atonement.

But these criticisms assume and misapply Lutheran standards of orthodoxy. Why should Anabaptists begin with Luther's crushing sense of sin and his tortured personal search for a righteous and merciful God? Surely, Lutherans today admit that Luther's anthropology was not Paul's and that a more inclusive biblical anthropology shifts assumptions towards forms of voluntarism. Anabaptists rejected both irresistible sin and its corollary, irresistible grace, and were more interested in appropriating the benefits of Christ's redeeming work than in theological-logical correctness concerning the nature of sin and evil. And while it is true that ordinary Anabaptists tended to identify sin simply with disobedience to Christ's commands and New Testament norms, it must also be said that they did not blame original sin for their failings.

Not surprisingly, the most sophisticated Anabaptist statement on anthropology came from Hübmaier's pen. Hübmaier distinguished three constituents of the human being: body, soul and spirit. In the prelapsarian state these three functioned harmoniously in accordance with divine intentions, but the original act of disobedience corrupted body and soul. As a consequence, the body was destined to perish, and the soul, now badly damaged, was unable to distinguish between good and evil and hence no longer able to will the good. But the spirit remained a point of contact between the human and the divine spirit (Reimer). Through the redemptive work of the 'second Adam', the soul was restored to its proper function and relationship with the spirit. Together, spirit and restored soul could will the good. Thus responsibility to choose the good had been restored through Christ's redeeming work and the effects of original sin had been partly mitigated, although the wages of sin remained death.

Clearly, Hübmaier's view did not deprive God of salvific initiative through Christ but premised the ability to respond positively on the initiative in Christ. There is no belittling of the work of Christ here. He died for all, and through his efficacious sacrifice the spirit is freed to illuminate the soul so that all can once more distinguish between good and evil, as well as will the good. Thus the promise had come true with regard to original sin that 'the son should not bear the iniquities of the father' (Ezekiel 18:20).

But how influential was Hübmaier's sophisticated attempt at embracing both divine initiative and human responsibility? Presumably only a few of the better educated leaders would have understood his nuanced qualifications, which David Steinmetz appropriately labelled 'semi-Augustinian' and Torsten Bergsten described as *reformatorisch*. No doubt, unschooled artisans hauled before the bar of theologically trained inquisitors articulated a less qualified voluntarism.

Although one can find variations of intensity with which Anabaptists defended or advocated voluntarism, one can speak of a consensus on this matter, whether one consults Marpeck, Menno, Riedemann, Denck, or others. The reasons for this consensus are not difficult to find. Anabaptists had come at the conclusion that the theology of the major reformers was flawed and that it undermined human accountability. Hence Anabaptist theology was weighted toward a voluntarism made possible through Christ's redeeming work. Charges of innate perfectionism as a result of a faulty view of sin, repeatedly levelled against Anabaptists, find no basis in fact. Indeed, discipline prescribed in Anabaptist congregational orders prepared for the opposite: sins need to be confessed, repented of, disciplined, and forgiven. Hutterite school orders assumed the need for strong discipline on the premise that 'the human heart is bent toward evil from its youth on'. Here too one encounters the orientation toward the practical, the real-life application rather than abstract theory.

Christology and soteriology
The debate about true faith
Anabaptists generally accepted justification by faith, crudely directed against an assumed Catholic works righteousness, but they added that saving faith must manifest itself in discipleship and good works. They joined the chorus of criticism that those claiming to be justified by faith alone produced no visible fruits – indeed, that they denied the need to. Such a faith could not be a true faith, but was, according to the letter of James, dead. Consequently a number of first-generation Anabaptists – Denck, Hut, Schiemer and others – joined the debate begun by Müntzer with Luther about the nature of true saving faith. Luther emphasized the instrumentality of the Word of God, God's saving promise, found in the scriptures, present in

the sacraments and in the proclamation of the gospel, heard, believed and trusted. The righteousness appropriated in justification by faith was, for Luther, the righteousness of Christ *extra nos*. Müntzer disagreed with Luther on how true faith was born. He accused Luther of preaching a 'sweet Christ' and neglecting the 'bitter Christ'. Saving faith, according to Müntzer, was born through an inner cross-experience, a dying with Christ to self and sin and a rising to new life with him. True faith born in this cathartic experience bore fruit by transforming the inner person and his or her outer behaviour. As noted, Anabaptists joined the criticism that Reformation preaching had brought no moral improvement in the life of its adherents. The Lutheran view of justification as forensic, an alien righteousness, bestowed *extra nos*, *gratis propter Christum*, seemed to them like cheap, powerless grace that left lives untransformed. The primary issue from the Anabaptists' perspective was therefore not justification by faith but the nature of true faith and the nature of justification. A justification that changed mere status and not the person seemed a make-believe justification. True believers confessed Christ come into the flesh, their flesh, the Christ *in me*. And justification was understood as being made righteous or pious (*fromm*). God's saving grace through Christ was regenerational when appropriated by true faith. Such a faith manifested itself by obedience to Christ in discipleship or *Nachfolge*.

Christ's redeeming work

Anabaptist Christology and soteriology came together in the emphasis on the Christ in me. One can call Anabaptist Christology applied Christology with little concern for abstract doctrinal discussions about the union of the two natures in Christ. Anabaptists were interested in the consequences of Christ's reconciling work, its transformational power and effect in changed lives, in its empowerment to follow the example of Christ. Present reality rather than a mere historical event was of significance. It does not follow, therefore, that Anabaptists neglected or sought to minimize the work of Christ. If anything, they sought to honour and expand its effect and significance for everyday life.

When Anabaptists spoke or wrote about Christ's redeeming work, they used all three traditional theories interchangeably without specific differentiation or elaboration. Thus one encounters the ransom theory combined with the 'Christ the victor' theme. Accordingly, Christ defeated the powers of evil and set the prisoners free. But one also finds the atonement, satisfaction theory, that Christ's sacrifice atoned or made propitiation for the sins of humankind and appeased the just and righteous wrath of God. And, as noted, Anabaptists repeatedly emphasized following Christ's example, becoming conformed to and like-minded with him, the *imitatio* or moral-ethical view.

Hübmaier, who stressed the priority of grace and faith in salvation while seeking to guard against iron-clad determinism, based on either the fall or predestination, wrote that Christ had come to make sinners righteous and whole. He thanked God for the 'rosa red blood', spilled by the Son, and defined saving faith in an almost Lutheran sense as the gift of the one who comes in it, Christ. Indeed, Hübmaier seemed to imply a one-time forensic wiping away of guilt and sin, while seeking to combine it with a continuing regeneration, revitalizing the fallen will (Tanneberger).

The two Anabaptist lay theologians, Marpeck and Riedemann, clearly reveal a Lutheran influence on their soteriology. Marpeck accepted the instrumentality of the preached Word in giving birth to justifying faith. His colleague, Leupold Scharnschlager, wrote: 'I teach the righteousness before God which come through faith in Jesus Christ to all and upon all who truly believe. And we are made righteous (*fromm*) without any merit of our own, only by his grace through the salvation of Christ.' Indeed, Scharnschlager repeated Luther's formula of justification 'by faith alone'. These views led Harold Bender to argue that on justification Marpeck and his circle stood 'halfway' between the Swiss Brethren and the Lutherans. Friedmann was therefore simply wrong when he claimed that soteriology was of little or no concern to Anabaptists and that it entered Anabaptist consciousness only in tension with Protestantism. It would be more accurate to note that Anabaptist soteriology was syncretic. Marpeck embraced the *solus Christus* and *sola gratia* of the Reformation, emphasizing the redemptive work of Christ. But unlike Luther, who emphasized the deliverance and freedom that came with justification by faith, Marpeck placed the emphasis on being transformed from being dead *in* sin to being dead *to* sin.

Many more examples could be cited. Riedemann, for example, wrote of Christ as 'our righteousness and goodness' and as having no righteousness apart from the one that Christ works in us. The point is that Anabaptist soteriology did not reject justification by faith but emphasized that true faith and true justification are ultimately regenerational.

Melchiorite Christology

As already noted, Anabaptist Christology had a variety of faces. Marpeck distinguished between the two natures of Christ but considered both present in revelation and salvation. Anabaptists generally accepted the Apostolic and Nicene Creeds and hence considered themselves orthodox, not only on the Trinity but also in matters of Christology. But they did not accept the

Lutheran notion of the ubiquity of Christ, stressing instead the presence of the resurrected Christ at the right hand of God.

A unique Christology entered Anabaptism in the north through a misunderstanding between Melchior Hoffman and Caspar Schwenckfeld. Emphasizing the progressive divinization of Christ's human nature, Schwenckfeld held that the glorified, clarified, and ascended Christ had become wholly divinized. Hoffman, who, according to Schwenckfeld, had misunderstood him, projected the divinization process backwards to Christ's immaculate conception and argued that Christ had brought his heavenly flesh from heaven, so that at the incarnation he took nothing from Mary. Indeed, Mary's function was limited to that of an incubator. This 'Melchiorite' Christology of the heavenly flesh, accepted by Hoffman's converts, took on a life of its own in Münster and found its way through Dirk Philips and Menno Simons into northern Anabaptism and to the Mennonites. It has served historians well in tracing Hoffman's influence and identifying him as the link responsible for bridging southern and northern Anabaptism. But what role did the heavenly-flesh Christology play in Mennonite thinking? Sjouke Voolstra has shown that the celestial-flesh Christology had implications, above all, for Menno's view of the church. As one longing to be conformed to Christ, seeking to be one with him, united with him in one body as the true church, the pure bride of Christ, Menno placed the emphasis on the purity of the church and its members. The sanctified life of the church and its members constituted the 'visible proof' of Christ's presence in his congregation, a congregation of true penitents. Contrary to accusations of docetism and monophysitism made by his opponents, Menno's main point was the need for purity in the church, a possibility because of the spiritual presence of Christ in his people and the congregation (Voolstra). But the church needed to be vigilant as to its purity, hence the discipline, the ban.

Ecclesiology
Restoration of the pristine church
The last topic has already introduced ecclesiology and it seems proper to commence with Anabaptist notions of the fall of the church. In an ecumenical age, the tendency is to overlook the nasty polemics of a bygone era. But like it or not, the Anabaptists were citizens of a polemical age. At the Bern Colloquium (1538), Swiss Brethren representatives outdid the Reformed in rejecting the papal church as utterly corrupt. The Reformed were willing to grant that through the ages God had kept an undefiled faithful few, even in the Church of Rome, but the Anabaptist representatives refused to accept such a view. They insisted that the papal church and everyone in it was fallen; indeed, that the papal church was the Babylonian whore.

A variety of reasons were cited for its fall and utter corruption. Following Müntzer, some Anabaptists suggested a fall immediately after the apostles, when temporal concerns took precedence over spiritual matters and the distinctions between laity and clergy appeared. This anticlerical view of the fall was supplemented with a rereading of the Constantinian turning point. The privileges granted to Christians by Constantine proved to be not the church's victory but its doom. Under Pope Sylvester (314–35) the church had entered an unholy alliance with the secular power of that day. Others saw a final corruption of the church with the canonization of paedobaptism under Pope Nicholas II (1058–61). All agreed that in the sixteenth century the papal church was in league with Antichrist, beyond renewal or reform. It was therefore necessary to rebuild or restore the church on apostolic foundations.

Unlike Luther, whose starting point had been personal salvation, the search for a merciful God, Anabaptists searched for the true, pure church. Ecclesiological concerns, therefore, assumed a most important role in Anabaptism's beginnings and its subsequent evolution. Friedmann suggested that, at the core, Anabaptist ecclesiology was informed by Jesus' teachings about the kingdom of God. Rather than assign the kingdom a futuristic status, Anabaptists sought to make it a present reality in their life and communities. The kingdom was to be made visible in the church, restored to its pristine apostolic purity. True followers of Christ gathered in closely knit, disciplined communities in which the rule and command of Christ prevailed. Spiritual warfare existed between the kingdom of darkness and the kingdom of God, whose members consequently suffered persecution. Entry into the kingdom of God came upon confession of faith, baptism, and voluntary submission to its discipline. Earliest congregational orders called for the sharing of spiritual and temporal gifts. Hutterites made community of goods a sign of the true church; other Anabaptists settled for mutual aid.

All rejected the hierarchical, sacramental, sacerdotal aspects of the Roman Church, holding that the powers of the keys were vested in the congregation of Christ's true followers. Despite severest persecution, or because of it, Anabaptists insisted that the true church needed to be visible, hence the exodus to Moravia, where life in community proved possible – although, even there, periodic persecution added to the long list of martyrs. Indeed, persecution came to be seen as a sign of the true church, an extension of Christ's suffering in his members and theirs with him. The emphasis on maintaining the fellowship meant that discipleship and following Christ was not an individualistic affair; it involved life in community. United with Christ their head, as the members of his body, brothers and sisters mutually assisted each other spiritually and in temporal matters. In the true church, pilgrim's progress was not made alone.

As noted, restoration of the true church to its pristine purity meant a return to its New Testament manifestations. For Hutterites, this meant the Jerusalem model and the abolition of all private property. For Marpeck and his group of urbanites, the experiment with community of goods had ceased with the Jerusalem church and was therefore not binding. In contrast, the ordinances of the church – baptism, the Lord's supper, the ban – could not be compromised. They extended Christ's presence into the community of the faithful. Through it, Christ's work of transforming and conforming members of his body into his own image continued. For Christ dwelt not in buildings of stone and wood but in 'living temples', the regenerate members of his body.

Church ordinances
Baptism

As noted, the Reformation brought a re-examination of all teachings and church practices; nothing escaped scrutiny and re-evaluation. Future Anabaptists were in the vanguard of this great inquest, as five sacraments were discarded, the eucharist was reinterpreted, and the validity of paedobaptism was questioned. Among the early critics of paedobaptism was Müntzer, who advocated postponement until children reached the canonical age of accountability, seven. Andreas Carlstadt and Jacob Strauss, whose writings were read by the future Anabaptists in Zurich, also questioned paedobaptism. But the decision for adult baptism came from former supporters of Zwingli – Grebel, Mantz, Blaurock, and others – whose search of the scriptures for the meaning of baptism led them to conclude that it was for adults only. The most salient argument came from a literal reading of the syntax of the Great Commission: teach, believe, baptize (Matthew 28:19; Mark 16:16). This baptismal order had been commanded by Christ himself and no child baptisms had been recorded in the New Testament. Armed with this evidence, the extrabiblical arguments of the defenders of paedobaptism, such as the argument for a sleeping faith in the child, or faith by proxy of parents or godparents, had to give way. Paedobaptism was unmasked not only as lacking a scriptural foundation but also as perpetuating the evils of creating involuntary Christians, removing personal responsibility, and making a mockery of the true meaning of baptism. Rites that used salt and chrism to exorcise demons from innocent children fostered superstitions and offended sensibilities. In their debate with paedobaptists, the Anabaptists developed a theology of the child to argue against such malpractices. Zwingli himself may have stimulated this development when he suggested that children belonged to the kingdom of God as long as they remained innocent, and that the sign of belonging, baptism, should not be denied them. Early Swiss Anabaptists subsequently argued that, before reaching the age of responsibility, children were the beneficiaries of Christ's saving work, a view criticized as extrabiblical (Tanneberger). At least the universal application of the benefits of Christ's atoning work for all children left none of the children in limbo. But this view of universal benefits was not consistently shared by all Anabaptists. Menno appeared to limit the benefits to children with believing, regenerate parents only.

All Anabaptists rejected a sacramental, *ex opere operato* understanding of baptism; all, in one form or other, distinguished between an inner and outer baptism and ascribed salvivic power only to the inner. Nevertheless, the outer retained an important ecclesiological function as a rite of passage into the community of the faithful.

Studies of individual Anabaptists and the rationale they gave for adult baptism reveal considerable variations. Hübmaier, who considered the subject in seven of his works, provided the most persuasive arguments. Beginning with a demolition of Zwingli's identification of Old Testament circumcision with New Testament baptism, he proceeded to argue that baptism constituted a covenant of a clear conscience with God, witnessed to by Father, Son, and Holy Spirit. When combined with references to an inner washing and the circumcision of the heart, baptism came to designate the process of redemption. Since Hübmaier insisted that God's Word and Spirit co-operated in creating saving faith, the prerequisite for regeneration, his views cannot simply be dismissed as neo-Pelagian, because ultimately God's action preceded human response.

In Hübmaier's thinking, ecclesiology and baptismal theology were inextricably interwoven. Entrance into the church came through baptism upon confession of faith. In this sense, not in the traditional sacramental sense, baptism meant an entry into the salvivic community in which Christ's sanctifying work continued among like-minded brothers and sisters. Thus water baptism as an outer witness to an inner process amounted to more than an individualistic confession of faith; it meant a commitment to community, submission to the rule of Christ.

Finally, attention needs to be drawn to the only baptismal liturgy from the pen of an Anabaptist theologian, Hübmaier. It included admonition to self-examination, the Lord's Prayer and the Apostles' Creed. The congregation was to kneel and join in a prayer for the candidate; the baptizer then laid his hands on the neophyte, used the trinitarian formula, poured water on his head, and welcomed him into the Christian community. The ceremony concluded with, 'God be with you and your spirit. Amen.'

Presumably Hübmaier intended this ceremony for Nicolsburg, where he also wanted the church bells rung for the traditional times of prayer. What is not clear is whether he was able to implement these ceremonial practices before his arrest or whether other Anabaptists followed his example. What is clear is that his attempts at establishing a magisterial Anabaptism in Nicolsburg failed.

The Lord's supper

The eucharist, at the heart of medieval worship, became a major bone of contention not only between Catholics and the reformers, but also within the Reformation camp. Early Swiss Anabaptists absorbed a Zwinglian view and accordingly rejected the bodily presence of Christ. Drawing on the Apostles' Creed, Anabaptists argued that the glorified Christ resided at the right hand of the Father until his return in judgement. As Anabaptism spread, arguments became more sophisticated and nuanced. Oswald Glaidt held to an 'eating in faith', but refused to elaborate because the controversy about the eucharist created too many divisions. He urged that the emphasis be placed on gratitude and thanksgiving for the risen Christ, who interceded on behalf of his people at the right hand of the Father. Jörg Zaunring, a proto-Hutterite who was less reticent, used the subject to polemicize against old and 'new papists', the Lutherans, whom he also numbered among the 'eaters of idols'. Zaunring distinguished three meanings of Christ's body: his mortal body; the clarified post-resurrection body; and Christ's body as the church. He argued that the words 'This is my body' could not refer to Christ's mortal body, because he was seated at the table with his disciples at the time when he spoke them. Moreover, John 6:63 stated clearly that flesh profits nothing. Neither could the words refer to Christ's resurrected body, because the first martyr of the church, Stephen, testified to Christ's presence in heaven. It followed that at the last supper Jesus referred to his body as the church, his true followers, who, in breaking bread and drinking from the cup, remembered that he had purchased them with his blood. It should be evident that it was an attempt at a purely biblical view of the Lord's supper; philosophical arguments had no credence with Anabaptists. The memorial celebration, which could allow for a spiritual presence, was focused on Christ's work on the cross and solicited from the participants a confession of solidarity with Christ in his suffering. Zaunring gave this ceremony a radical, anticlerical thrust: it ruled out monks, nuns, priests, bishops, cardinals, the pope, benefices, mass, processions, and all academic hats and caps. He went on to denounce debauchery, drunkenness, adultery, and blasphemy, sins he claimed were widespread among those who 'ate the idols daily'. In short, the mass was condemned as at the root of false religion and lack of public morality.

In contrast, members of Christ's true body shared the mind of Christ, and suffered with and for him. No altar, monstrance, or special vessels were needed for the memorial meal; the focus was on oneness with Christ and with one another, an emphasis that found expression in Anabaptist fondness for the analogy of grapes crushed to make wine and grains ground to make bread, a parable found in Hutterite and Mennonite sources. From a more traditional perspective, the memorial celebration shifted the focus from the one celebrated to the celebrants. Rejecting the objectification of Christ's presence, Anabaptists emphasized faith and remembering. But it involved more than remembering a historical event; it meant a celebration of Christ's continuing work in the lives of his people. Anabaptist eucharistic thought has consequently been described as pneumatologic rather than Christological (Rempel). But differences of emphases existed between the various groups. The Gabrielites, who, according to Hutterites, treated the bread and wine as spiritual food, allegedly turned the Lord's supper into a 'false outward show' by having a ceremonial cup carried about in 'papist fashion', with a cloth wrapped around it as if it were sacred.

Little is known about the frequency of the celebration or of the ceremonial ritual involved. The oldest church order implied celebrations at every gathering, several times a week. But this view could not have survived long. Eventually the celebration became restricted to twice or three times a year.

The ban

Repeated reference has been made to discipline. Anabaptists considered discipline a sign of the true church, the ban, a church ordinance commanded by Christ. Grebel alluded to the need for the ban as early as his letter to Müntzer (1524). Other Reformed leaders, such as Oecolampadius and Dominicus Zili, favoured its introduction, but Zwingli rejected it. Hübmaier, as in other matters, provided the most articulate argument for its need, while the Schleitheim Articles prescribed it as a necessary element to keep the church undefiled. Scriptural support was found in Matthew 16:19 and 18:15–17. In these texts, Christ granted to the church the keys of the kingdom, and with them authority to loose or to bind, to remit or to retain sins. Christ also prescribed a three-stage process of dealing with open sinners in the church: private admonition; admonition before one or two witnesses; and an open admonition and hearing before the congregation. Thus, according to the 'rule of Christ', the congregation wielded the authority to judge the affair, although in practice the pronouncement of judgement and the application of the ban were delegated to the appointed leaders. The ban could consist of the lesser discipline of exclusion from the Lord's supper until amends had been made, or of the ultimate punishment of excommunication. In the case of the latter, the unrepentant was turned over to the devil, and further communications with him or her were forbidden. Every member of the community was expected to guard zealously the purity of the church. Open sins needed to be dealt with openly. If the offender proved truly penitent in heart and conduct, he or she would be reaccepted.

Differences in degree of severity with which the ban was applied appeared between the southern and northern Anabaptists. At issue was the practice of shunning, introduced among Menno's followers in the north. Under the strictures of shunning, marital relations were suspended; neither food and drink nor table nor marriage bed could be shared. Swiss and south German Anabaptists refused to endorse marital avoidance, and the practice was eventually discontinued in the north as well, but not before it had become a key issue among the Swiss and led to a parting of ways with the followers of Jacob Amann, whose followers, the Old Order Amish, continue the practice to this day.

Footwashing

At this point attention needs to be drawn to footwashing, a ceremony closely associated with the Lord's supper in some Anabaptist groups. The beginnings of this practice remain obscure. Biblical precedent was found in Christ's action of washing the disciples' feet before the last supper. Like shunning, footwashing appears to have originated in the north, although Hübmaier may have performed a ceremony of this nature in Waldshut in 1525. If so, he did not develop a theological rationale for it in his writings. None of the early Swiss sources make mention of it; neither do Hutterite sources. Sebastian Franck's *Chronicle* of 1531 seems to contain the earliest reference to the practice, while supporting evidence comes from a little-known group of Anabaptists in Halberstadt, Thuringia, under the date 1535. Marpeck's *Verantwortung* refers to the practice, and the oldest Anabaptist song book, the *Ausbund* of 1564, contains a hymn for its observance. Dirk Philips' *Enchiridion* of the same year provides further details, and conservative groups, such as the Old Order Amish, continue the practice into the present, with an emphasis on its symbolic meaning of humility, expressed in service to others.

Political theology

A unique contribution in a violent age was Anabaptist pacifism, or, more accurately, non-resistance (*Gewaltlosigkeit*). In contrast to modern pacifism, which has taken on forms of non-violent action strategies aimed at political-social ends, non-resistance as understood by Anabaptists means literally accepting powerlessness and abstaining from any use of force or coercion, even in self-defence. For Anabaptists, non-resistance was not a calculated survival strategy but a principle for Christian life and conduct; an assumed non-political kingdom ethic revealed by Christ. The scriptural mandate was taken from Matthew 5:39, 'resist not evil'. True, the non-resistance ethic was not immaculately conceived by Word and Spirit. It was born by trial and error, between hope and despair, under persecution that denied Anabaptist legitimacy and left them powerless. Not all Anabaptists responded with uncompromising separation from the world and with non-resistance. The original articulators of this response were Grebel, Mantz, and a former Benedictine prior, Michael Sattler, who left his stamp on the Schleitheim Articles. These articles made it clear that coercion and the use of the sword had no place in the 'perfection of Christ', that is, the true church. And while they granted secular authorities a providential role in curbing evil in the 'sub-Christian' society, they could not participate in the coercive structures and means necessary to control evil in the world. Consequently, Anabaptists refused to bear arms, to give the oath, or to bring litigation before courts of law. Followers of Christ, they argued, could not hold offices of responsibility in the world, and, *vice versa*, a magistrate could not be a member of the true church. For Christians found their ultimate object lesson in the cross of Christ which taught to forgive, to repay evil with love, to love enemies, to pray for persecutors, to go the extra mile. Non-resistance, therefore, had implications for every aspect of Christian life. It meant deference to others, not seeking one's own advancement. In short, the ethic of non-resistance dictated a behaviour foreign and foolish to the world. It was the way of love and suffering, revealed and exemplified by the life and death of Christ.

The definitive study of Anabaptist political ethics by James Stayer meticulously documents variations existing within Anabaptism. He categorized Grebel, Sattler, Mantz, and in a milder form, Denck, as holding to a radical 'separatist non-resistance' point of view. But he noted that the first-generation scenario was complicated by the fact that a number of early leaders – Reublin, Brötli, and Hans Krüsi – found themselves on the side of rebellious peasants, at odds with and actively resisting the authorities. Nevertheless, by the second generation the Swiss Brethren uniformly accepted the Schleitheim Articles.

The same cannot be said of Hübmaier, who defended the legitimacy of the use of the sword by the authorities and rejected the stark dualism of the Schleitheim Articles. Besides emphasizing the providential nature and necessary role of legitimate government, ordained by God to defend the innocent and punish the evildoers, Hübmaier believed magistrates could be true Christians and should defend true religion. But, as noted, his 'real politics' failed to procure a defender of the Anabaptist faith.

Hut and Hoffman, both 'apocalyptic zealots' (Stayer), retained an ambivalent political ethics. Hut, who had supported Müntzer and the peasants' cause, expected God to use the Turks in punishing Christendom; in the meantime, Anabaptists were to wait patiently and suffer persecution. Stayer used the appropriate methaphor of the 'sheathed sword'to describe Hut's interim ethics. Hoffman, by contrast, evolved towards genuine non-resistance, while the movement launched by him in the north took on features of an apocalyptic crusade against the 'godless', only to collapse with Münster. Under the sobering effects of that collapse, it was possible for Dirk Philips and Menno to redirect and reorganize some of the surviving Münsterites and remaining Melchiorites into peaceful channels. Like the Swiss and the Hutterites, Menno upheld Jesus' life and death as the example to follow. Vengeance was to be left to God, and all violence eschewed. Participation in war and capital punishment was rejected. Yet Menno seemed to allow for the possibility of godly Christian rulers and originally even called on rulers to wield authority on behalf of true religion. But during the later part of his life, Menno moved towards uncompromising non-resistance, and second-generation Mennonites adopted the Schleitheim position (Stayer). Only the Waterlanders retained a more moderate point of view.

In the Anabaptist communities of Moravia, non-resistance won out against Hübmaier's 'realism'. Riedemann provided a statement as clear and separatist as the Schleitheim Articles on behalf of the Hutterites. Marpeck, whose urbane moderation has made him a favourite among Mennonite and free-church scholars, but whose influence on his own contemporaries is still being disentangled, certainly insisted on the separation of church and state. Yet he showed greater latitude and less enthusiasm for legalistic injunctions than did the Swiss Brethren or the Mennonites.

The diversity in early Anabaptist political theology, as first outlined by Stayer, has been acknowledged by Mennonite scholars (Snyder). And even though non-resistance joined baptism in the master narrative of Anabaptist history and Mennonitism only in the seventeenth century, thanks to the influence of martyrologies, it has become the dominant theme of that narrative, nurturing Mennonite identity and offering a prophetic voice.

Without question, Anabaptist political theology should raise more than eyebrows among the descendants of the persecutors whose theologies under the banner of orthodoxy or just-war theories called for the suppression of 'heretics' or served the governing powers to drum up support and provide the chaplains for war, while the Christian witness for peace languished.

Eschatology

Studies of Anabaptist eschatology remind us how near the last judgement seemed to many during the social-political convulsions accompanying the Reformation. Anabaptists had their share of end-time prophets. Hut and Hoffman gave adult baptism an apocalyptic meaning: the sign of Thau, the sealing of the end-time elect. Hoffman, the author of a commentary on Daniel 12 and a hefty volume on the mysteries hidden and revealed in the Apocalypse, was steeped in apocalyptic texts. He discerned that the Reformation ushered in the end of time. Convinced that he was living in the sixth period of church history, during which the events of the sixth trumpet, the sixth vial, and the sixth seal would unfold, Hoffman sought and found confirmation for the developments of his own day in the Apocalypse. He believed that the corruption of the church, which had set in during its third period with the distinction between laity and clergy, the veneration of saints, the perversion of the Lord's supper, and the practice of paedobaptism, would be reversed. In this scheme of things, the letter addressed to the church of Philadelphia held special significance: it promised that the end-time church would receive the 'key of David', the key to understanding the apocalyptic visions. Having fallen out with the Lutherans, Hoffman came to see the true end-time church in the persecuted Anabaptists. His supporters, in turn, saw in him the second Elijah, sent by God to unmask the Babylonian whore and seal the divinely appointed quota of 144,000 end-time elect. Hoffman's end-time scenario included the restoration of the spiritual Jerusalem and the conversion of the Jews. The search was on for the second witness or Enoch to reveal the second coming. It is worth noting that Hoffman's apocalyptic brand of Anabaptism was neither clearly separatist nor clearly non-resistant, and that he looked to the free imperial city of Strasbourg and later to the episcopal city of Münster to advance the apocalyptic calendar. A latecomer to Anabaptism, Hoffman meshed his apocalyptic vision with adult baptism, a memorial view of the Lord's supper, an emphasis on the transformational nature of true faith, and an insistence that the scriptures could be understood only by the spiritually illuminated.

Anabaptist and spiritualist relations

The relationship between Anabaptists and spiritualists is not without its problems. Boundaries between spiritualists and Anabaptists tended to be more porous than typologies separating the two permit. At times, the two are found in one and the same person, such as Denck, an Anabaptist who placed the emphasis on the inner word. Even more problematic is the case of David Joris, who evolved toward an elusive inspirationalism, complete with dreams and visions. Spiritualist tendencies also made inroads among the Dutch Mennonites or the Doopgesinnte Waterlanders, whose evolution took a different direction than that of the Frisians influenced by Menno and Dirk Philips. Similar developments toward spiritualism were evident in Moravia under the leadership of Gabriel Ascherham. Indeed, a number of individual Anabaptists shifted into the spiritualist camp, among them Christian Entfelder, Johann Bünderlin, and Jacob Kautz.

Apart from individualism, it is indeed difficult to find a common denominator among the spiritualists. Theologically, they played down the significance of all outer elements, emphasizing the importance of the inner, divine, spiritual presence or the role of the Spirit. This did not prevent them from supporting their antimaterialist spirituality with biblical arguments, such as 1 Corinthians 3:6: 'the written code kills, but the Spirit gives life'; or their preferred eucharistic text in John 6:63: 'It is the spirit that gives life, the flesh is of no avail.' Heuristically, they emphasized the illumination of the text or of the reader as more important than the letter of the text. This much some Anabaptists would have conceded, but they parted with the spiritualists when these declared externals, including all church ordinances and the visible church itself, *adiaphora*. Generally, spiritualists played down historical aspects of the faith. They looked upon the divisions in Christendom over externals as scandalous. Only one of the sixteenth-century spiritualists, the 'spiritualist pietist' Caspar Schwenckfeld, sought to establish conventicles of like-minded lovers of God, and only he left behind a visible community named after him.

It can be argued that spiritualists followed the trajectory of one of the major late medieval religious trends, the antimaterialist one, which found its popular, pietist expression in the *devotia moderna*. Influenced strongly by Neoplatonic realism, the spiritualists took antimaterialist spirituality to its logical conclusion. Thus the spiritual communion advocated by Schwenckfeld seemed devoid of any external mediation. Essentially he shared with Denck the emphasis on the inner word, applied not to metaphysical speculations but to the nurture of inward spirituality. Schwenckfeld and his circle of friends suspended both baptism and the Lord's supper because of their divisiveness. Only the inner, primordial spiritual word could produce true faith. Inner, spiritual baptism did not need any outer ritual. It was more important to feast on the spiritual heavenly manna, Christ, than to quarrel over the nature of his presence in the elements or the external form of ceremonies. Yet Schwenckfeld was a true student of the scriptures.

Spiritualism could serve a variety of functions and join in a host of alliances not limited to Anabaptism or the Radical Reformation. Its favourite expression appears to have been Nicodemism, a privatization of religious beliefs and practices, permitting escape from discrimination and persecution. But this assessment is not entirely fair to those genuinely appalled by the divisive polemic vendettas fought out publicly over religious matters, or to those who longed for true spiritual renewal and fought for toleration. It was from their ranks that the clearest and most persuasive voices were heard against intolerance, persecution, and suppression.

CONCLUSION

Any assignment of this nature calls for selectivity. In seeking to ferret out an Anabaptist theology I was naturally drawn to those writers who provided the most substantive statements. The most serious flaw that comes with such selectivity, of picking and choosing and splicing together, is that it may create a melting-pot theology. I have sought to avoid this wherever possible by pointing to variety. I also remain apprehensive about this exercise in failing to provide a sense of the ethos in which Anabaptists composed their thoughts. Anabaptists did not have the benefits of research libraries; they wrote while on the run, at times with a price on their head, or in prison awaiting execution. And how can one communicate the muffled, haunting voices of the thousands of martyrs? Perhaps my failings can be forgiven because I have unapologetically tried to present a sympathetic view of these defamed and reviled sixteenth-century seekers of the kingdom of God. I am cognizant of the fact that some of my Mennonite colleagues would prove more critical of their ancestors than I as a Lutheran have chosen to be. This pertains particularly to some of the less attractive aspects of Anabaptism, the noted perfectionist tendencies, the disciplinary use of shunning, and the ban, which created divisions and extremes.

16 Catholic theologians of the Reformation period before Trent

DAVID BAGCHI

It would be a mistake to suppose that all theologians who remained loyal to Rome during the first three decades of the Reformation were exclusively engaged in polemical activity against the 'new' gospel. For many academic theologians, perhaps for most, business would have gone on much as usual. But at the very least, especially for those in lands most affected, the religious upheavals altered fundamentally the *context* in which their theology was done. At the same time, their ranks were swelled considerably by those without academic appointments. Bishops, chaplains, members of religious orders lacking university connections – even kings, dukes, and lesser laypeople – all took up the pen in defence of traditional religion. For Catholics as much as for Protestants, theology became too important to be left to the divines.

The widely differing backgrounds of the Catholic controversialists alert us to the fact that their theological approaches differed as widely, and it is not surprising that the clamour of voices that would make themselves heard in the debates at Trent (Thomist and Dominican, Scotist and Franciscan, Augustinianist and Augustinian, to name but the loudest) could also be heard in earlier decades. It is no longer possible for us to speak of 'pre-Tridentine Catholic theology' in the singular, as Lämmer could in the middle of the nineteenth century; rather, we have to deal with a number of theologies and their exponents. Nor can we any longer attribute this variety to mere 'lack of clarity' (*Unklarheit*) as to what was the Catholic faith, as was done in the middle of the twentieth century (notably by Jedin and Lortz). All these theologies were equally rooted in the tradition, and to judge them proleptically by later Tridentine formulations is to embrace a Whig view of history no longer in vogue.

Such variety does not lessen the importance of these theologies. Rather, it makes them an even more fascinating object of study in their own right, and provides an even more valuable perspective for the study of 'Reformation theology' in the narrower sense of Protestant theology. For the purpose of surveying this vast body of literature, we shall need to consider first the historical context of the corpus before looking at the salient theological features and suggesting areas for future research.

CONTEXT

Attempts have been made to characterize different phases of Catholic anti-Reformation theology before Trent. Usually this has involved identifying a shift from an earlier period in which polemic, directed at the enemy, predominated, to a later one distinguished by the use of propaganda, for the consumption of other Catholics (so Jedin, Dolan, Chrisman); but none of these attempts has commanded general agreement. Although such generalizations are always hazardous, it seems to me more helpful to think in terms of not one but two shifts of emphasis, and therefore of three rather than two phases of Catholic theological writing, before Trent. The first was indeed characterized chiefly by its use of polemic, and the third chiefly by propaganda. But between these phases came a period of ten years or more in which the predominant context for Catholic theology – and German Catholic theology in particular – was imperial policy.

The polemical phase, 1518–c. 1530

This phase begins of course with the first public salvoes against Luther's ninety-five theses against indulgences. These came initially from those most closely involved in the case: Johann Tetzel, the indulgences preacher who was the immediate cause of Luther's protest against the practice, but who was also papal inquisitor for the region; Tetzel's mentor, Konrad Koch ('Wimpina'), professor at the university of Frankfurt-on-Oder; and Sylvester Prierias, the papal courtier charged with the preliminary investigation of suspected heresy. Tetzel and Prierias may have found it difficult to distinguish due process from personal vendetta, but both were clever enough to recast Luther's attack on indulgences as an attack on papal authority. To this extent they anticipated the tactic of their more energetic colleague, Johann Maier von Eck. Eck was a formidable theological street fighter who cornered Luther at the Leipzig Disputation (1519) on this very point. Thereafter, he took upon himself not only the detailed refutation of Luther's theology but also its condemnation, by agitating for, and then promulgating in Germany, the bull *Exsurge Domine*.

Anti-Lutheran polemic dominated the scene until 1525, after which further targets presented themselves with the south German and Swiss reformations. The carnage of the Peasants' War was mercilessly and somewhat inconsistently exploited by Catholic writers. It enabled them to criticize Luther both for being too revolutionary (the rebellion confirmed that seditious tendencies had always been latent in his message) and for being too reactionary, in that he first supported the peasants' demands and then turned against them for backing their demands with force.

The high-water mark of Catholic polemical theology came with the presentation of the *Confutation* to Charles V at the Diet of Augsburg. It was a moderate attack on a moderate Protestant confession, and was the first and last time that German Catholic theologians were able to concert their efforts on a single target. Though now forgotten, and indeed dwarfed by the historical significance of the Confession it purported to refute, the *Confutation* is a succinct defence of (recent) tradition, while being almost completely free of gratuitous invective.

The political phase, c. 1530–1541

Both the diets of Augsburg (1530) and Nuremberg (1532) represent the beginning of a *Realpolitik*. Whatever the findings of the polemical theologians, the Protestant territories were now too strong for the emperor to crush by force, particularly given the Turkish threat. The fact of a divided German church had to be accepted, at least until the papacy could countenance a general council, and in the meantime theologians had a role in reducing conflict and preparing the doctrinal groundwork for a council. And so in the late 1530s and early 1540s, a series of religious colloquies was held. Catholic theologians who had flourished in the earlier, polemical, phase regarded these exercises as pointless, and did their best to obstruct them; but others emerged who, while firm in their own faith, sought genuinely to find common ground with Protestants. The hard-liners tended to be those who emphasized ecclesiology as the chief bone of contention between the two sides, men such as Eck and Albert Pighi (author of the 1538 *Defence of the Ecclesiastical Hierarchy*). The moderates tended to be those who emphasized areas of more immediate relevance to the Christian life, and who recognized that the reformers had identified real problems. Johann Gropper and Gaspar, Cardinal Contarini, who are to be included in this camp, were both supporters of the theory of double justification, and both found themselves in trouble with the Roman authorities because of it.

The propaganda phase, 1541–1545

In 1541, the Colloquy of Regensburg (or Ratisbon) ended in failure. This marked the end of the pre-Tridentine colloquies, and it also arguably marked a shift in papal policy, from reform and reconciliation (exemplified by the curia's frank internal report, the *Consilium de emendanda ecclesiae*) to confrontation and repression (exemplified by the establishment of the inquisition in Rome). The long-awaited general council was at last in sight, and until it met little could be achieved by Catholic theologians

by a continuation either of polemic against or of dialogue with their opponents. This is reflected in the nature of Catholic theological literature, which
finally moves wholeheartedly to the task of propaganda for home consumption. The late 1530s had already seen the publication of catechisms by the
ex-Lutheran Georg Witzel (1535) and the Dominican Johann Dietenberger
(1537). These were now joined by Friedrich Nausea's *Catholic Catechism*
(1543). In addition to the catechisms were the sermon collections, published
to edify and inform the preaching of Catholic clergy in contested territories.
Eck was ahead of this particular game, having published his postils throughout the 1530s. But the 1540s saw the publication and republication of several
more sermon sequences, most importantly Bishop Johann Faber's (1541),
Nausea's (1542), and Johannes Hoffmeister's (1547). The tone of Catholic
theological publication was now set for the remainder of the sixteenth century, with the majority of publications aimed at consumption by fellow
Catholics (notably the catechisms of Peter Canisius and of Trent itself), and
only a small amount of weighty polemic against Protestants (for instance
by Robert Bellarmine).

ISSUES

In the following section, I shall deal with the theological topics by
their perceived ranking according to contemporary Catholic sources. The
'top nine' controverted issues in Germany in the late 1530s, according to
a survey undertaken by the conciliar nuncio Peter van der Vorst, were as
follows:

1. papal supremacy
2. the cult of the saints
3. auricular confession
4. purgatory
5. the mass
6. communion in both kinds
7. the veneration of images
8. the administration of baptism in Latin
9. monastic vows and clerical celibacy

However reliable van der Vorst was as a guide to the priorities of ordinary
Catholics, most Catholic controversialists would have agreed with something like this order of priorities.

Ecclesiology

Van der Vorst's list identifies issues of church government as the principal Catholic concern. Out-and-out papal absolutism did have its defenders

among the sixteenth-century Catholic controversial theologians, though perhaps not so many as might be supposed. Hard-liners such as Prierias and Pighi, and arguably Cochlaeus and Eck, denied that a pope could ever be heretical, and elevated papal teaching, alongside scripture and tradition, to be a third source of revelation. Ambrosius Catharinus, the Italian Dominican and a maverick in many respects, supported the notion of papal infallibility and denied to councils any authority independent of the pope. The majority of Catholic theologians did not, however, go this far.

Humanists in particular tended to support the idea of consensus. Thomas More, despite giving his life for papal supremacy over the English church, was not a papalist; in France, Josse Clichtove combined a strongly hierarchical view of the church with the idea that the pope is subject to church law (that is, to conciliar decrees) in a way that has been described by a modern commentator as contradictory. Even Cajetan, the scourge of conciliarists such as Jacques Almain, cannot readily be seen as a defender of papal absolutism from his showing in the Reformation debate. Significantly, he relates Christ's promise to Peter about the power of the keys (Matthew 16) to Matthew 18 and John 20, where the same power is given equally to all the disciples. Cajetan concludes that Peter received the power of the keys, not in his own right, but *in persona ecclesiae* or *in persona apostolorum*, as a representative of all the apostles rather than as a leader set apart from them.

Cajetan is credited with having helped to sink conciliarism, the belief that the church should be governed by councils rather than by the papacy. Certainly, after the bull *Pastor aeternus gregem* (1516), which outlawed the belief, one would not expect to find full-blooded conciliarism among the public defenders of Rome; but among most of those defenders who were also members of the Franciscan order, which had a history of friction with the holy see, one does find a certain coolness when it comes to their defences of papal power. Thomas Murner, for example, seemed to find it more congenial to write against Luther on subjects other than the papacy. His perfunctory treatment in *Von dem Papsttum das ist von der höchsten Obrigkeit des Glaubens* ('Of the papacy, that is, of the highest authority of the faith') has rightly been described as 'the driest and stodgiest of all Murner's anti-Lutheran polemic'. His heart was evidently not in it. The Franciscan provincial Kaspar Schatzgeyer did not deal with the issue of papal primacy in any of his writings. His silence on this point is especially odd in view of his otherwise comprehensive engagement with Luther's arguments. Alveldt, another friar minor, did tackle this issue head on, in his *Super apostolica sede* ('On the apostolic see'; 1520). But even here, it has been argued that his defence of the papacy was a strange one, because it makes the pope head of a church which is primarily the company of all faithful people, not the hierarchy.

Catholic theologians before Trent identified ecclesiology – not that they used that word, of course – as a, or perhaps the, key point at issue very early on in the Reformation debate. It soon became clear that the standard early sixteenth-century arguments for papal primacy would not work: it was little use employing anti-conciliarist arguments against people who believed that councils could err and had erred as much as popes. The early evangelical appeal to secular authority in ecclesiastical matters obliged Catholic writers to reach back to earlier controversies, notably those connected with William of Occam, the fourteenth-century Franciscan who had promoted the power of the emperor over that of the pope. Appeals to Peter's two swords (Luke 22:38 – traditionally a proof-text for Petrine authority over both church and state), and even to the long-discredited 'Donation of Constantine', abounded.

Scripture and tradition

All Catholic writers of the period rejected the Protestant attempt to elevate scripture over tradition as a theological authority. Indeed, the idea that one might be played off against the other was incomprehensible to them, since both derived from the same divine source, and both were inspired by the Holy Spirit: there was no idea of a tradition independent of scripture or opposed to it. The tactics they adopted in defending this point of view, however, varied. Some Catholics (notably the English defenders – King Henry VIII, More, John Fisher, Edward Powell) took a principled stand on their right to regard tradition as a legitimate source, and cited it freely, alongside scriptural evidence, in refutation of Protestant teaching; others tried to beat Protestants at their own game by using scripture exclusively. Schatzgeyer, the most impressive of the first wave of continental controversialists, stands out in this respect. His writings were scrupulously fair, and leave one with the strong impression that he was using the dispute, in good medieval fashion, to attain to a deeper understanding of the truth – to turn heat into light. Moreover, his exclusive appeal to scripture goes beyond the routine parade of proof-texts to what, in a later century, would be called a 'biblical theology'. Schatzgeyer has been charged, both in his own day and in ours, with developing a Catholic *sola scriptura* principle, and regarding the Bible as its own interpreter. But his writings suggest that he held to the established belief in the consensus of scripture and tradition, and that he differed from his contemporaries only in being a peculiarly sensitive exponent of it.

Sacraments

The majority of the controversial issues contained in van der Vorst's list related in some way to the mass or the sacraments; this emphasis is reflected in Catholic polemical publishing in the decades before Trent, in which about one-third of all titles published were concerned mainly or wholly with sacramental theology or practice. This is unsurprising, given the importance of the rites-of-passage sacraments (baptism, confirmation, matrimony, extreme unction) for ordinary folk, and given the centrality of the eucharist and the closely related sacrament of confession to the life of all Christians. The sacrifice of the mass – not itself a sacrament but even more important to Catholics than the sacrament of the eucharist – and ordination were in a category apart: each was a precondition of the other, and both were preconditions of all the other sacraments.

As Peter Lombard, three centuries before, had restricted the number of sacred things that can legitimately be designated sacraments to seven, so Protestants considered only the sacraments of the gospel (those explicitly enjoined by Christ, baptism and the eucharist) as real sacraments. Many Catholic writers appealed to the *Ecclesiastical Hierarchy*, attributed to Dionysius the Areopagite (Acts 17:34), for a very early testimony to the existence of seven sacraments. It is surprising that so many leading humanists did so (Cochlaeus, Eck, Faber, and Fisher among them), since the antiquity of Pseudo-Dionysius had already been challenged by Valla and Erasmus; in polemical terms, certainly, more was to be gained by defenders of the curial church from using the Pseudo-Dionysian corpus, and its theological defence of both earthly and heavenly hierarchies, than from abandoning it.

Of the dominical sacraments, baptism was not on the whole a controverted point between Catholics and mainstream Protestants: it is significant that its appearance in van der Vorst's list, in second to last place, is due to differences over baptismal liturgy, not baptismal theology. The theology of the eucharist was a different matter, and the Catholic agenda was set early on by Luther's *Babylonian Captivity of the Church* (1520). Luther had identified three ways in which the eucharist had been 'taken captive' by the new Roman Babylon: the withholding of the consecrated wine from laypeople; the doctrine of transubstantiation, namely that the underlying 'substance' (though not the outward appearance, or 'accidents') of the consecrated bread and wine was exchanged for the substance of Christ's flesh and blood; and, above all, the belief that the consecrated elements were offered by the priest to God the Father as a 'sacrifice' of the Son, and that this 'sacrifice of the mass' was variously comparable with, equal to, or better than the sacrifice on the cross.

Most Catholic writers recognized that the reservation of the chalice from the laity was a practice that could not readily be proved from scripture or the practice of the church, at least before the twelfth century. The doctrine of concomitance (that one who consumed only the body of Christ received as much grace as one who consumed both the body and the blood) was a clarification of existing practice rather than a theological justification for it, and the church had always tolerated exceptions to the rule, most notably the concession of the chalice to the entire kingdom of Bohemia. There was, then, nothing in either allowing or disallowing laypeople the chalice that concerned any fundamental of the Christian faith. Predictably, some conservative theologians saw it as an issue of authority rather than of reason, and it was the layman King Henry VIII who put this most bluntly: he did not know why the church had withdrawn the chalice from him, but he did know that it was for his own good. At the other extreme, the so-called eirenic theologians such as Georg Witzel regarded the lay chalice purely as a matter of church order, not as something fundamental to the faith, and saw in it the opportunity to make a minor concession that could bring disaffected laity back to Rome. An interesting position was that taken by Cochlaeus, who, in his anti-Luther polemic in the 1520s, made communion in one kind the article by which the church stood or fell, but who in the 1530s and '40s applauded the concession of the chalice for the same reasons as did Witzel.

Luther's insistence that the mass be seen as a testament or benefit, something that God does for us rather than a sacrifice we offer to God, was based on a false dichotomy, so far as his Catholic opponents were concerned; and the same argument on the lips of other evangelicals met the same response. Cochlaeus was among the first to point out that the Protestant conception of the mass was too narrow. It is a two-way process, not one in which believers passively receive a benefit or hear the reading of a will, but one in which they actively celebrate, by praying, singing, processing, bell-ringing, censing, kneeling, standing, offering, distributing, communicating, blessing – all ultimately in obedience to Christ's command to '*Do* this . . .' The benefits to the participants, the merits of the mass, vary according to their disposition; but it is interesting that the forgiveness of sins is not one of them, according to Cochlaeus' reckoning. For Protestants, the declaration of the forgiveness of sins would become and remain the most important role of the eucharist, and would earn the particular censure of the Tridentine fathers, despite dissenting voices such as that of Nausea.

There was far less consensus among Catholic theologians when it came to defining the nature of the relationship between the sacrifice of the mass and the sacrifice of the cross. As Iserloh has shown, some (such as Eck) saw it as a repetition, a fresh oblation, while others (such as Cajetan) regarded it, in Thomist terms, as an unbloody re-presentation of the once-for-all sacrifice on Calvary. Johann Mensing took the Thomist view to its logical conclusion by attributing to Calvary a past as well as a future efficacy. He regarded the various sacrifices of the Old Testament, even those not associated with Melchizedek (who provided the type for Christ's priesthood, according to the letter to the Hebrews), as pre-presentations of Calvary. Such a diversity of understanding of what is arguably the focus of Catholic life is explained by Iserloh by the absence of any dogmatic definition of the subject until Trent. Indeed, the sacrifice of the mass is the principal evidence in the case for the existence of a widespread *Unklarheit*, a lack of theological clarity on the eve of the Reformation that allowed Protestant errors to grow unchecked until they were too firmly rooted to be eradicated.

The *Unklarheit* theory is an attractive one with a strong explanatory power; but arguably it rests too much on the view that historical events happen inevitably. In this case, it is assumed that the 'correct' answer, which Trent was bound to endorse, was the Thomist one. But before Trent it was by no means obvious that the Thomist solution would win widespread acceptance. The weakness of the *Unklarheit* approach is perhaps shown by the related case of transubstantiation. So far as dogmatic definitions were concerned, this was an open-and-shut case: the Fourth Lateran Council had endorsed the doctrine. According to the *Unklarheit* theory, this should have meant that there would have been a united front among Catholics against its detractors. But Schatzgeyer refused to use the term 'transubstantiation', presumably because it dated only from the thirteenth century and could not be regarded as traditional, and rejected it as an attempt to explain the real presence – a mystery of the faith – in scientific terms. Schatzgeyer's position was indistinguishable from Luther's.

Salvation, grace, and free will

As with the sacrifice of the mass, there had been no recent dogmatic definition on the doctrine of justification in spite of the fact that the late Middle Ages had seen a proliferation of theological activity on the subject. Luther's understanding of justification by grace through faith alone was agreed to be quite orthodox in one respect (the case of children below the age of discretion who cannot perform morally good works), and several Catholic writers publicly agreed that there was a sense in which faith belonged to justification proper in a way that works did not (so Clichtove, Dietenberger, and Schatzgeyer). Eck and Jakob Latomus joined in affirming that Luther was correct in his statements about justification and faith, provided that they were not designed to dissuade simple folk from doing good works. Fatefully, however, the positions of the two sides were not as close as they might have seemed, and the fault was very largely Luther's own. His understanding of faith was a rich and multi-faceted one that had grown through his deep academic and personal engagement with the question over several years. 'Faith' for Luther was an entity that included complex affective and fiduciary emotions lacking in the traditional understanding of *fides* as simply one – and not the greatest – of the three theological virtues of faith, hope, and love. It was therefore as a human virtue rather than a divine gift that Luther's Catholic opponents interpreted it, and this explains why they understood *sola fide* as implying exclusive reliance on a human mental faculty, pretty much the polar opposite of what Luther intended to convey. (Catholics were not alone in this; recent studies have emphasized the extent to which 'justification by faith alone' was adapted and ameliorated by later Protestants, who assumed that the affective dimension – what earlier theologians had termed *fides caritate formata*, 'faith formed by love' – was missing from this bare formulation.)

The position of Catholic polemicists before Trent cannot, however, be attributed entirely to a tragic verbal misunderstanding. All agreed that the operation of divine grace did not preclude human moral responsibility, either in the preliminary or initial stages of the *ordo salutis*, or in persevering to the end. A pastoral and a religious consideration were never far from their minds. Most Catholic writers on this topic, including Erasmus and Eck, saw themselves as treading a middle course between Manichaeism and Pelagius, between a fatalism leading to moral licence on the one side, and a denial of divine grace on the other. Protestants were on the side of licence, as was proved by the German Peasants' War (so Cochlaeus and others), and by the moral turpitude prevalent in their territories (so Witzel and others). The religious consideration was the humility that should properly accompany thoughts about one's eternal destiny. Protestants, it was argued, seemed to presume dangerously upon God's mercy; the safer course, as well as the more humble, was to see the soul as a *viator*, a pilgrim *en route* to the holy city, who could never be entirely sure of reaching the final destination until safely within its walls.

Saints, images, and other aids

Because we cannot be sure of our final salvation until the end, it would be foolish, as well as impious, to ignore the help made available to the Christian by the communion of saints. Catholic defenders of indulgences typically commended the treasury of merits in this way as a type of celestial insurance policy. Both the invocation and the veneration of the saints were defended on these grounds too. Protestants had objected to the cult, and (particularly in south Germany and Switzerland) to the associated use of images, on the grounds that at best it got in the way of the Christian's relationship with God, and at worst it became a substitute for worship of God. Catholic responses were all very similar, though different in quality. Schatzgeyer based a thoughtful and original defence on the Bible and the creeds. Christianity, he wrote, is all about *Einigkeiten*, 'unities' or, better, 'relationships': the manifold *Einigkeiten* bind together the persons of the

Trinity, they bind the believers to the Trinity as a whole and to individual persons of it, and they bind believers to one another in the body of Christ. Moreover, Jesus, who was fully human as well as fully divine, was naturally bound to his human mother, Mary, and, as we are bound to him, so is she to us. These bonds are not dissolved by death. It is therefore entirely natural and appropriate, and in full accord with scripture, that the saints in heaven in general, and our holy mother in particular, should pray for us and we to them. Attempts to find a biblical basis for the cult of the saints from proof-texts were less fortunate, and the normally impressive Clichtove was on stronger ground in appealing to church custom.

POSSIBLE DIRECTIONS FOR FUTURE RESEARCH

Not surprisingly, most research on pre-Tridentine Catholic theologians of the sixteenth century has been carried out by Roman Catholic scholars, particularly through the series *Reformationsgeschichtliche Studien und Texte* (1906–), *Corpus Catholicorum: Werke katholischer Schriftsteller im Zeitalter der Glaubensspaltung* (1919–), and *Katholisches Leben und Kämpfen* (changed to '*und Kirchenreform*' in 1966) *im Zeitalter der Glaubensspaltung* (1926–), all founded by the Gorres-Gesellschaft and published in the German Catholic heartland of Bavaria. It would, however, be a mistake to suppose that Roman Catholic scholarship on this topic has enjoyed a unified approach. Erwin Iserloh's motivation was to demonstrate that the Catholic case in the sixteenth century by no means went unheard, and that men like Eck, however rebarbatively and indeed badly, did a necessary job in representing it. Iserloh himself, however, was working in an expressly ecumenical context, carrying the mantle of Lortz by attempting to understand the Reformation by, for instance, an appreciation of the religious power of Luther – something that Catholic scholars (most notably Jared Wicks in our own day) are often much better at explaining than Protestants. A different approach is that represented by Remigius Bäumer, who has been concerned with emphasizing the value of what the Catholic controversialists achieved for Roman Catholic self-definition, and who has been notably uninterested in the ecumenical motivation of Lortz and Iserloh: Bäumer's heroes are the hard-line Catholics who were hostile, or at least unenthusiastic, towards sixteenth-century efforts at rapprochement.

In recent years, Protestant scholars have turned their attention to the Catholic controversialists, often to great effect. (One thinks here especially of Mark U. Edwards Jr's important work on Catholic publishing.) As the labours of the *Corpus Catholicorum* editors and others continue to make more and more texts available to scholars worldwide, and as familiar texts finally receive definitive editions (Henry VIII's *Defence of the Seven Sacraments* was not properly edited until the 1990s), the writings of Catholic theologians will continue to be an important growth area in Reformation studies as a whole. To conclude this survey, I set out what may well be particularly fruitful areas for further research and reflection.

Intellectual influences
An important step will be to shed more light on the intellectual background of individual writers and their motivation in opposing the Reformation publicly. Monique Samuel-Scheyder's study of Cochlaeus's early humanism provides one model of how this might be done.

Catholic reform
Many Catholic controversialists were also severe critics of church abuses. Erasmus is deservedly the most famous; but most were interested in the church's reform and spiritual renewal, and yet this did not lead them to challenge the church's teaching. On the contrary, Clichtove's concern to improve the behaviour and standing of priests inspired him to a more highly clericalist ecclesiology than was usual at the time. At the very least, we need to consider revising the language we use in order to avoid the implicit contrast between Protestant 'reformers' and Catholic 'conservatives'.

The search for the origins of the Catholic/Protestant divide
Until relatively recently, it was assumed that early Protestant theology was coterminous with the doctrine of justification. Scholarship over the last twenty years or so has tended to marginalize its importance, and Catholic controversialist studies have mostly borne this out: for whatever reason, justification was not a topic that attracted specific refutations in the numbers that other topics (the papacy, the mass) did. It may therefore be time to revisit the question, posed by Hubert Jedin, whether the 'flashpoint' of the Reformation was ecclesiology rather than soteriology.

Sounding the depth of the Catholic/Protestant divide
It is incumbent on historians not to be unhistorical. But historical theology will always ask itself if there is any contribution it can make to the concerns of the church of the present day. At a time of encouraging ecumenical progress, there are still hard questions to be asked about the possibility of essential, structural differences between Protestantism and Catholicism (such as Daphne Hampson has recently argued), and the writings of the sixteenth-century controversialists is an obvious starting point for such an enquiry. Questions such as these become more, not less, important at a time

of a widely noised 'crisis' in Protestantism and after a long papal reign which has seen a growing split between a conservative papacy and liberal Catholics in North America and Europe.

Historical biography

Given the importance of this area of study for the two questions mentioned above, it is hardly surprising that the early Catholic literary response to the Reformation has not always been dealt with according to the best traditions of historical impartiality. Some of the pen-portraits of controversialists published in the *KLK* series as recently as the 1980s, for example, still smack of hagiography. The important task of lifting these figures out of obscurity has been achieved, and earlier calumnies against them have been expunged. Now is the time for a mature and critical reflection on their strengths and weaknesses; but it is important that they be evaluated in their own terms, not by comparison with Aquinas or with Trent on one hand, or with the reformers on the other.

17 The Council of Trent

DAVID C. STEINMETZ

The general councils of the medieval Catholic Church were instruments for crisis management. This was particularly true in the early fifteenth century, when the church was divided by two, and then three, rival claimants to the papal throne. Unlike chapter meetings and episcopal visitations, councils were not a routine part of the church's self-governance. When the Council of Trent finally convened in 1545, it was only the nineteenth general council in the long history of the Catholic Church.

The crises that provoked councils might be internal to the Catholic Church, such as the rise of the Joachite heresy, or stimulated by external pressures such as the Turkish invasion of Europe. They might touch on matters of the church's doctrine or of its practice. Early councils articulated the dogmas of the Trinity and the two natures of Christ. Later councils decided on the place of icons in Christian worship, defined the doctrine of transubstantiation, and ended the scandal of a divided church.

Popes were often reluctant to take the risks inherent in the convocation of a general council. They were painfully aware that the Council of Constance had deposed three competing popes and installed a fourth. By the time of Luther, however, it was generally conceded, even by theologians who were jealous defenders of papal power, that under certain circumstances the convocation of a general council might be the church's only recourse to resolve a crisis that had proved impossible to resolve in any other way.

When Pope Paul III convened the Council of Trent in 1545, he did so in response to a crisis that had become unmanageable. Some elements in the crisis were old and had troubled the church for years. Critics, both Catholic and Protestant, repeated an ancient litany of abuses that still waited for reform, abuses such as the non-residency of bishops, the lax enforcement of clerical celibacy, and the promotion of unqualified or under-age candidates to high ecclesiastical office. Other elements in the crisis were in fact new. In the 1520s Luther, Zwingli, and Bucer offered a wide-ranging critique of traditional Catholic theology that challenged the teaching authority of the Catholic Church at its core. There was no way for the Catholic

233

Church to ignore that theological challenge indefinitely or to fail to respond to it.

The theological critique started as an intra-Catholic debate. All of the Protestant reformers had been baptized in the Catholic Church and many of them, such as the archbishop of Canterbury, Thomas Cranmer, and the former general of the Capuchin order, Bernardino Ochino, had risen to important leadership positions in it. Even Luther had been a professor on a Catholic theological faculty and a district vicar in the Augustinian order. But by the time of the opening of the council, Luther had been excommunicated for more than twenty years and the Reformation had taken root in large sections of northern Europe. Had the Protestants evolved during this time into permanent outsiders, as Cardinal Carafa argued, or were they still Catholic sheep who had temporarily gone astray? The answer was not clear.

What was clear was that the Protestant critique of Catholic doctrine was not a blanket rejection of the long theological tradition they both shared. Except for a few dissenters at the margins of the movement, Protestants affirmed with Catholics the ancient dogmas of the Trinity and the two natures of Christ. When Luther stated at the beginning of the Schmalkaldic Articles that he had no quarrel with traditional Christian teaching concerning the Trinity and the two natures of Christ, he was speaking for a broad consensus of Protestant reformers that included prominent non-Lutherans such as Zwingli, Bucer, Calvin, and Cranmer.

The Protestant critique focused on other issues. It challenged Catholic views on such questions as the authority of scripture and tradition, the proper understanding of the justification of the sinner, the nature of the church and its ministry, and the theology of the sacraments, especially the sacraments of penance and the eucharist.

The council met first in 1545 in Trent in northern Italy. Because of Trent's strategic location between the centres of imperial and papal power, it was a site acceptable to both. For political reasons the council was moved in 1547 to Bologna, a location that proved utterly unacceptable to Emperor Charles V. Fourteen bishops loyal to the emperor resisted the proposed change and remained in Trent. Faced with the implacable opposition of the imperial party to the change of venue, Paul III suspended the council on 13 September 1547.

When Paul III died on 10 November 1549, he was succeeded on the papal throne by Cardinal Del Monte, who took the name Julius III. Julius III had been the first papal legate to the Council of Trent and was determined to reconvene it. He reassembled the council in Trent in 1551. During its second period the council dealt with a number of important issues, including the sacraments of penance, eucharist, and extreme unction. Unfortunately, the political situation in northern Italy deteriorated before the council could complete its business. When Maurice of Saxony attacked his former ally, the Emperor Charles V, he placed the city of Trent in danger. Reluctantly the pope suspended the council on 23 April 1552, fully intending to reconvene it within two years. But for a variety of reasons the council remained suspended and did not meet again for a decade.

Cardinal Cervini, like Julius III a former papal legate to Trent, was elected as Pope Marcellus II but died within a month of his election. Cardinal Carafa, who had long thought that the hope of reconciliation with the Protestants was a dangerous illusion, replaced Marcellus as Pope Paul IV. Paul was committed to a vigorous programme of reform but was no longer interested in reconvening a general council.

In 1559 Pius IV was elected pope. Unlike Paul IV, Pius had not abandoned his desire to see the suspended council finish its reforming work. He vowed, against influential opponents who preferred an entirely new council in an entirely new location, to reconvene the long-suspended council in its original location. In a bull published in 1560 the pope announced his intention to reassemble the council in Trent at Easter, 1561. In fact the council did not meet until 18 January 1562.

Many of the figures prominent in the first sessions of Trent were now dead. They had been replaced by a new generation of leaders, among them the cardinal archbishop of Milan, Charles Borromeo, the president of the council, Ercole Gonzaga, and the papal legate, Stanislaus Hosius. Under their leadership the council energetically tackled the unfinished agenda begun in 1545, reaffirming the work of the earlier sessions and issuing a long series of new decrees and canons dealing with both institutional and theological reform. When the council adjourned on 4 December 1563, its decrees were submitted to Pope Pius IV, who confirmed them on 26 January 1564.

The Council of Trent was as important for its institutional as for its theological reforms – perhaps, in some cases, even more important. But institutional reforms, however far-reaching, lie outside the scope of this book, which is concerned solely with theological issues This chapter will examine how the Catholic Church at Trent met the theological challenge of its Protestant critics. In particular, it will ask how Trent defined Catholic teaching on four bitterly disputed issues; namely, the authority of scripture and tradition, the doctrine of justification by faith, the nature of the church and its ministry, and the theology of the sacraments.

SCRIPTURE AND TRADITION

The Council of Trent addressed the theme of scripture and tradition in its fourth session, held on 8 April 1546. In a decree on the canonical scriptures, the council made four important points. While it had no quarrel with Luther and other Protestants over the canon of the New Testament, it disagreed with them over the canon of the Old. Protestants rejected as apocryphal later books in the medieval canon such as Sirach and Judith. While they readily agreed that many of the so-called apocryphal books could be read with profit (Luther for his part was fond of quoting Sirach 2:1), they refused to regard them as divinely inspired texts binding on faith and order.

The Council of Trent reaffirmed the larger medieval canon as the normative standard for the life and teaching of the Catholic Church. The council recognized that there were important theological texts in the later apocryphal literature that lent additional support to the Catholic doctrine of purgatory. Rejection of these books by the council would therefore have come at an unacceptable theological price.

The second decision made by the council is somewhat more surprising. The council declared that the Latin Vulgate translation of the Bible should be the authoritative edition of the Bible for Catholic teaching. Not all Catholics welcomed this decree. Catholic humanist scholars had long argued that one should study texts in their original languages. Original texts were to always be preferred to translations, however brilliant. Anyone who wanted to understand Aristotle and did not know Greek (as Thomas Aquinas and Duns Scotus did not) operated at an insuperable disadvantage, since translations are by their very nature interpretations of the texts they translate. Erasmus insisted that a knowledge of Greek was essential for any serious study of the New Testament and mercilessly criticized the failings of the Latin Vulgate translation. The Protestants, on the whole, accepted the humanist arguments and insisted that Christian ministers should be instructed in the three theological languages, Hebrew, Greek, and Latin.

Switching from the Latin Vulgate to the Greek and Hebrew texts that underlay them was not without its problems. The primary problem was the extent to which such a move destabilized the text. The *Annotations* by Erasmus on the New Testament had already demonstrated that the Greek text, properly understood on its own terms, might call into question theologically sensitive material in the venerable Latin translation. Quite naturally, the Protestants were not alarmed by the destabilizing potential of the Greek and Hebrew texts, since they were themselves destabilizers, engaged in a programmatic critique of traditional Catholic teaching on a wide range of subjects. But many of the bishops at Trent were less sanguine.

Catholic critics of the humanists could point to the undeniable fact that the Catholic Church had never relied on the Hebrew text of the Old Testament for its teaching or its liturgy. There were, of course, competent Christian Hebraists in the Middle Ages, such as Nicholas of Lyra and Paul of

Burgos, who made rabbinic scholarship accessible in Latin translation for Christian readers. But Hebrew had never been in common use in Christian circles.

The church had first relied on the Greek New Testament and on a Greek translation of the Old Testament called the Septuagint. With the decline of Greek as a daily language in the western Roman Empire, Latin-speaking Christians shifted gradually to Latin translations of the Bible and finally to a translation by Jerome. By 1545 the Catholic Church had relied on Jerome's Latin text for over a millennium. It was the Latin Bible that shaped Catholic teaching, liturgy, devotion, and practice. Some Catholic theologians even argued that the Latin Bible was as superior to the original Greek and Hebrew texts as a finished piece of furniture is superior to the raw materials from which it was crafted. When Erasmus grumbled that there were problems with the Latin text, he was asked whether there were any problems with the Greek text (which, of course, there were, as Erasmus knew only too well). In the end the Council of Trent opted for the stable Latin text.

Trent's third decision was its careful delineation of the relationship of scripture and unwritten apostolic traditions. The council was not interested, in its final decree, in defining the place of post-apostolic traditions or in wasting time over apostolic customs that had fallen out of use. The fathers at Trent were, on the whole, surprised by the Protestant tendency to cite the Bible against church tradition. The authority of the church's teaching rested on revelation. That revelation was found partly in the Bible and partly in the apostolic traditions that had been handed down from generation to generation. In spite of attempts to shift the discussion of the council to the larger subject of ecclesiastical tradition in general, including conciliar decisions and papal decrees, the council focused in its decree on the more limited issue of unwritten apostolic traditions.

Catholic theologians knew, of course, that not every Catholic teaching could be found explicitly in scripture. The issue had been raised in the early church. St Augustine in the late fourth and early fifth centuries had used the practice of infant baptism, for which no unambiguous texts in the New Testament could be found, as an example of the complementary relationship of written scripture and oral tradition. Everyone knew by word of mouth that infant baptism had been established by the apostles. Therefore, in the silence of scripture, the church must follow its ancient traditions, secure in the knowledge that scripture and tradition ultimately coinhere.

The reformers had no place in their theology for unwritten apostolic traditions, but that did not mean they had no place for ancient tradition, whatever their overheated rhetoric might sometimes have suggested. Indeed, they claimed on more than one occasion to be more traditional than their

Catholic opponents, who had in their view succumbed to non-traditional innovations in theology and practice introduced in the Middle Ages. Protestants regularly argued that they were 'more ancient than thou' on the issues that mattered most, and certainly more Augustinian than their Catholic opponents on the crucial issues of sin, grace, and free will.

To demonstrate their theological continuity with ancient teaching, Protestants issued anthologies of quotations from the fathers of the early church. They were convinced that these anthologies supported their views concerning issues such as the nature of the eucharist and justification by faith. What Protestants did not accept was the notion that there was an unwritten source for the church's knowledge of God's self-revelation outside the written source of holy scripture, There was no source co-equal to scripture in its authority for faith. Ecclesiastical tradition undoubtedly played, for them, an important role as a guide to the proper interpretation of scripture. But tradition was not and could never be, for them, a source co-equal with it. If examples of infant baptism could not be found in the New Testament (and the texts generally cited were clearly ambiguous and non-compelling), the practice must nevertheless be justified and justifiable on the basis of exegetical arguments.

The Council of Trent decided that the self-revelation of God to the church was not restricted to the Bible alone. The written Word of God was, of course, authoritative for Catholic teaching. But some teachings were not found in the explicit written teaching of the Bible. They were contained in the oral traditions preserved by the faithful since the earliest days of the church's life. To describe the dual nature of God's self-revelation the council used the words *partim-partim*, 'partly-partly'. Explicit Catholic teaching is found partly in scripture and partly in the church's tradition.

The two sources, written and unwritten, were commended by Trent to the Catholic faithful as co-equal in authority. They were co-equal because they came ultimately from the same ancient source, either directly from the mouth of Jesus or indirectly from the apostles, who were inspired by the Holy Spirit. The importance of this claim for Catholic theology is impossible to exaggerate. Unlike their Protestant counterparts, Catholics were not unduly troubled by the silences of scripture. Tradition spoke when and where scripture was silent. Both written scripture and unwritten tradition were bearers of God's ancient self-revelation to the Catholic Church. Catholics should therefore accord tradition the same affection and reverence that they accorded holy scripture.

The last point made by Trent was to warn against the private interpretation of the Bible. By private interpretation the council fathers had in mind any interpretation, whether by individuals or groups, that clashed with the received teaching of the Catholic Church. This ban applied to all heretical interpretations, whether published or unpublished. The right to judge 'the true sense and interpretation of the holy scriptures' belongs to the Catholic Church alone. Transgressors should be brought up on charges before their bishops, denounced before church courts, and punished with the pains appropriate for such heretical violations.

JUSTIFICATION

Medieval Catholic theologians did not, as a general rule, organize their discussions of the forgiveness of sins under the heading of justification by faith, even though the word 'justification' is Pauline and was in use in Catholic theological discourse. The term was pushed into the centre of sixteenth-century theological discourse by Luther. Generally speaking, medieval theologians preferred to discuss the forgiveness of sins under the broader heading of grace.

Students of theology at Erfurt, where Luther had studied, were introduced to a dizzying array of Latin terms for grace: *gratia creata*, *gratia increata*, *gratia praeveniens*, *gratia subsequens*, *gratia operans*, *gratia cooperans*, *gratia gratis dans*, *gratia gratis data*, and *gratia gratum faciens*, each term specifying some important aspect of grace inadequately represented by other terms. While all of the terms were important, the crucial term for grace as the justifying activity of God was *gratia gratum faciens*, the grace that makes sinners pleasing to God. The term is crucial because it makes clear that justification in Catholic theology is a process in which sinners are slowly transformed by divine grace into saints. The focus remains throughout on a real transformation by grace and not merely on an act of forgiveness, though both are important. To be forgiven by God is to be initiated into a life-transforming change that is not complete until believers, having been made perfect as their Father in heaven in perfect, experience in heaven the beatific vision of God.

Protestants generally drew a distinction between justification as the action of God in forgiving sinners and sanctification as the action of God in transforming forgiven sinners into saints. Justification, for them, was not only an act by which God forgives sins and no longer imputes the guilt of them to believers. After all, Catholic theologians could readily accept forgiveness and non-imputation as constitutive elements of justification. It was also the act by which God imputes to believers the righteousness of Christ.

In other words, Protestant Christians believed they could stand confidently before God, not because they had actually been transformed by grace into real saints (though they agreed with Catholics they were in a process of gradual transformation), but because they had been reckoned righteous on the grounds of the righteousness of someone else; namely, on the grounds of the righteousness of Christ. Here Catholics and Protestants parted company. The imputation of the righteousness of Christ was no part of traditional Catholic teaching.

Still, they did agree that the justified life was also a sanctified life. Although Protestants no longer regarded Christians as just on the ground of their actual transformation, they nevertheless insisted that an actual transformation was the inevitable fruit of living faith. Even Luther, who argued on numerous occasions that good works were the spontaneous response of faith to God's mercy, nevertheless spent a good deal of time attending to moral instruction. Protestants drew out the implications of the Ten Commandments and the Sermon on the Mount for the life of faith. Commentators on Paul did not stop with his theological ideas, rich as they undoubtedly were, but probed his ethical teaching as well.

Protestants confessed with Catholics that the Christian life was a life of virtue. They never doubted that was so, though they differed in their assessment of virtue's role. They did not see virtue, even infused virtue, as the basis, in whole or in part, of the sinner's justification by God. Justification for them was grounded entirely in the imputed righteousness of Christ. Good works were the fruit of justification, not its partial cause or even its *causa sine qua non*. The later hymn of Augustus Montague Toplady (1740–78) summarized the central conviction of the early Protestants about the grounds of justification: 'Nothing in my hand I bring, simply to thy cross I cling.'

Trent considered in its deliberations a compromise formula on justification that had been drawn up in 1541 as part of the Catholic–Protestant Colloquy at Regensburg. The formula was called the doctrine of double justice. It had been proposed to the colloquy as Article 5 of the so-called Regensburg Book by the Roman Catholic theologian, Johann Gropper, later the archbishop of Cologne, and Martin Bucer, the leading reformer in Strasbourg. The article was debated, passed, and defended by the papal legate, Gaspar, Cardinal Contarini. But it was rejected by both Martin Luther and the Vatican and so came to nothing.

Girolamo, Cardinal Seripando, the general of the Augustinian order, revived the ideas from Regensburg and incorporated them in an early proposal to the council. Double justice combined the Catholic stress on a real transformation of sinners with the Protestant idea of the imputation of the righteousness of Christ. Much of the doctrine sounds like traditional Catholic teaching. Grace is given to sinners through the ordinary means of grace and slowly transforms them into real saints. Because of the power of concupiscence in this life, however, sinners are retarded in their growth and unable to meet the demanding standards of God's righteous judgement in the hour of their death. Christ's righteousness is therefore imputed to sinners as a supplement that will make up the deficit between their own inherent righteousness and the claims of God's final judgement. The righteousness that satisfies God is partly the result of a gracious transformation (a more or less Catholic notion) and partly the result of a supplementary imputation of Christ's righteousness (a more or less Protestant notion).

The council rejected the compromise proposal on multiple grounds. It offered a Lutheran view of the power of concupiscence, undercut the role of purgatory, and proposed a view of imputation for which the fathers at Trent could find no biblical authorization. What the council embraced was the moderate Augustinianism that had marked the main currents in medieval theology. The bishops at Trent were not interested in mediating the differences between the various theological schools. As much as possible, they aimed for a broad consensus and declined to define theological positions too closely.

From the standpoint of ordinary believers the justified life starts with the sacrament of baptism. Baptism washes away the guilt and punishment of sin and inserts the newly baptized child into a state of grace. Concupiscence remains in the soul, not as sinful in itself, but as a 'tinder of sin', an inclination to sin that must and can be resisted with the help of grace. Sinners are just to the extent that they have been transformed by grace, a long process that is not finished until they finally are admitted to the presence of God and become in their own turn saints. There is no place in this scheme for imputed righteousness of any kind. Trent's doctrine of justification is a doctrine of real transformation by divine grace.

THE NATURE OF THE CHURCH AND ITS MINISTRY

Luther had rejected the notion that the Catholic hierarchical priesthood was essential to the life of the church. The right to preach and preside at the eucharist had been given in baptism to all Christians. But for the sake of good order in the church, the right to perform these tasks publicly was conferred by the laity on the pastor. The pastor should in his turn have been 'rightly called' to the work, both by God and by the church, and have a vocation that could be discerned by the laity and clergy who examined him. In the place of the Catholic hierarchy of bishops, priests, and deacons Luther substituted a single ministry of Word and sacraments. The practical governance of the church was shared by governmental and ecclesiastical officials, who assumed mutual responsibility for the education of pastors and the well-being of local parishes.

Reformed churches also displaced the threefold order of bishops, priests, and deacons, and substituted a fourfold ministry of pastors, teachers, elders, and deacons. Teachers were responsible to teach the young, and deacons (who were lay officers and not clergy) managed the care of the poor and socially disadvantaged. Pastors were responsible to preach, preside at the sacraments, and oversee the pastoral care of the parish. Responsibility for the spiritual life of the local congregation was shared by the pastor with lay elders.

Anglicans maintained the threefold order of bishops, priests, and deacons, but merged the traditional structure with a theology that did not always well support it. In the course of the sixteenth century, tensions between supporters of the traditional structure and its radical critics led to the formation of the Puritan party in the Church of England and the eventual secession of some dissenters into the English Presbyterian, Congregationalist, and Baptist churches. If not all Anglicans could agree with Catholics that bishops belonged to the *esse* of the church – that is, that the church could not exist for long without them – they were at least convinced against the dissenters that bishops belonged to the *bene esse* of the church – that is, that the church was clearly better off for having them.

Trent, however, did not waffle on this question. It reaffirmed the necessity for the church's life of the hierarchical priesthood of the Catholic Church. Although it affirmed seven orders, the three most important were bishops, priests, and deacons. Deacons are members of an intermediate order with limited responsibilities. In due course they will be ordained as priests. Priests preside at the sacraments, especially at penance and the eucharist, and so mediate the grace of Christ to the faithful in their local congregations. Bishops are essential because they have the power to ordain new priests and so assure the laity that they will have the sacramental resources to assist them in the life of faith. Without bishops, no priests; without priests, no sacraments; without sacraments, no church. The logic, so far as Trent was concerned, was compelling.

Trent also reaffirmed the traditional teaching that ordination, like baptism, confers an indelible character on the new priest. A priest could cease to use his sacramental power or have it suppressed by ecclesiastical authorities, but he could never under any circumstances lose it. Even a defrocked and disgraced priest is still a priest. Once a priest, always a priest. Unlike Luther, Trent taught that priesthood is not merely a vocation like any other and priests are not laity on special assignment. Ordination effects an ontological change in the one ordained. No layperson, however gifted and pious, can confect a valid eucharist, but any priest, however limited and unworthy, can.

THEOLOGY OF THE SACRAMENTS

Trent followed medieval tradition by listing seven sacraments: baptism, confirmation, penance, eucharist, ordination, matrimony, and extreme unction. But the heart of the sacramental ministry of the priest is the daily celebration of the eucharist. In the eucharist Christ is really present; in the other sacraments Christ's power is present. While all of the sacraments – especially baptism, penance, and eucharist – are extremely important, the fact of Christ's real presence makes the eucharist especially important to the Catholic faithful.

There were sacraments in the Old Testament, too, but the sacraments of the old law, such as circumcision and Passover, were effective on the basis of the pious disposition of the participants (*ex opere operantis*). The sacraments of the New Testament are more powerful because they are effective on the basis of the proper performance of the rite (*ex opere operato*). When a validly ordained priest, using the elements of bread and wine and water and the correct words of institution, offers the sacrifice of the mass, intending by his action what the Catholic Church intends, the bread and wine are unfailingly transubstantiated by God into the true body and blood of Christ. The presence of Christ does not depend on the holiness of the priest or the piety of the lay recipients. Recipients will receive the body and blood of Christ if they are in a state of grace; that is, not in a state of mortal or serious sin. The objective reality of Christ's presence is never dependent on the spiritual zeal of priest and people, but on the unfailing reliability of the sacrament itself.

Trent repeated the decision of the Fourth Lateran Council in 1215 to describe the real presence of Christ in the eucharist by using the term 'transubstantiation'. This word rests on a philosophical distinction between substance (what a thing really is) and accidents (how a thing appears to our senses). When priests consecrate the elements of bread and wine, the accidents of the bread and wine remain unchanged. The bread still looks, smells, and tastes like bread. Consecrated bread is indistinguishable from unconsecrated bread. But the substance of the bread and wine has been transformed by God into the substance of the body and blood of Christ.

Furthermore, the celebration of the eucharist is a sacrifice in which the body and blood of Christ are re-presented in unbloody form to God the Father to renew for the local congregation the gracious benefits of the sacrifice of Christ on the cross. The priest does not re-sacrifice Christ, since the crucifixion on Calvary was a once-for-all, non-repeatable event. In that sense Trent regarded re-sacrifice as an impossibility. What the priest does is to re-offer in the present the unique sacrifice made in the past. The mass is therefore properly called a sacrifice, since it is something offered to God to obtain a benefit obtainable in no other way.

Against Protestants of whatever stripe, the Council of Trent insisted that the eucharist was a sacrifice offered to God and not merely a benefit offered to the church, that the real presence of Christ should be explained by using the indispensable term 'transubstantiation', that the whole Christ, body and blood, was present equally in the cup and in the consecrated host, that the sacrament was effective *ex opere operato* and not merely *ex opere operantis*, and that the communion of the people was not essential to a valid eucharist. In the end it did not matter to Trent whether one affirmed with Luther the presence of Christ 'in, with, and under' the elements or confessed with Calvin a 'spiritual real presence'. By rejecting the notion of sacrifice and the mystery of transubstantiation, the Protestants had effectively set themselves outside the ancient Catholic consensus. While Luther's teaching was undoubtedly better and closer to the truth than the mere memorialism of the radical Protestants, it was no less heretical.

The decisions of Trent met with mixed response among Catholics, who were, on the whole, far more receptive to the doctrinal decisions of Trent than to its attempts at moral and institutional reform. For their part Protestants were unfailingly critical. The most extensive Protestant response to the Council of Trent was undoubtedly the *Examen Concilii Tridentini*, published in 1565 by the Lutheran theologian, Martin Chemnitz. But the honour of being the first Protestant theologian to respond to Trent seems to belong to John Calvin, who in 1547 published a modest treatise, *Acta Synodi Tridentini cum Antidoto*. Unlike Chemnitz, who dealt with the canons and decrees of Trent from its first sessions in 1545 through to its last in 1563, Calvin commented only on the earliest sessions of Trent from 1545 to 1547. But they were important sessions at which decisions were rendered on such issues as scripture, apostolic tradition, original sin, justification, and the sacraments in general.

It is clear from Calvin's response to Trent that he was unfamiliar with the actual debates at Trent, which, after all, were not published during his lifetime, and was therefore limited in his analysis to the text of the decrees themselves. But it is difficult to believe that a knowledge of the variety of positions argued at Trent would have made any difference to Calvin. What mattered to him was not how the debates proceeded, but how they finally ended. His response to Trent's decree on scripture can be taken as a representative example.

The canon of scripture

Calvin conceded that there was some ambiguity in the early church about which books should and should not be included in the church's canon. The Council of Carthage and even St Augustine listed the books cited by Trent as canonical. Against such authorities, however, Calvin repeated the opinion of Rufinus and Jerome that the so-called apocryphal books should be regarded as ecclesiastical rather than canonical. As ecclesiastical books they might properly be read to the people but could not be used to establish doctrine.

In Calvin's view Trent needed a canonical Apocrypha in order to establish some very doubtful doctrines. 'Out of the second of the Maccabees', he wrote, 'they will prove Purgatory and the worship of saints; out of Tobit satisfactions, exorcisms, and what not.' Calvin did not suggest that the books were worthless and ought not to be read by the faithful, but only that they could not be cited as the foundation of Christian doctrine.

The primacy of the Latin Vulgate

The decision of Trent to favour the Vulgate translation over the original Greek and Hebrew texts left Calvin breathless with disbelief. The humanist principle that an original text was always to be preferred to a translation seemed to Calvin unarguable. Worse yet, the Latin text of the Vulgate was in his view (and in the view of Erasmus and other humanists) riddled with errors and mistranslations.

Calvin was only too happy to catalogue some of the more egregious errors. Where Psalm 2 says in the Hebrew, 'kiss the son', the Vulgate translates 'lay hold of discipline'. Where Psalm 132 promises that God will bless the food of his people, the Latin text instead reads 'his widow blessing, I will bless', thus reading *vidum* for *cibum*. When David complains in Psalm 32 that his sap was turning into the drought of summer, the Vulgate substitutes, 'I am turned in my sorrow until the thorn is fixed.' While Calvin was willing to admit in some cases that the Vulgate was faithfully following a bad translation of Hebrew in the Greek Septuagint, the Greek precedent did not excuse the Catholic Church from its responsibility to abandon the Vulgate for the more reliable Hebrew text that underlay it. When God spoke to the prophets and apostles, he did not speak Latin.

Calvin did not address the question whether there were difficulties in the Greek and Hebrew texts as well as in the Latin Vulgate, or entertain the argument that the Vulgate with all its problems might nevertheless prove to be more reliable than the Greek and Hebrew manuscripts the church currently had in its possession. No one, after all, owned the original autographs of the Bible. And there was always the possibility, however

246 David C. Steinmetz

remote, that the Greek text of the Old Testament offered sixteenth-century Jews and Christians the translation of a more ancient Hebrew text than the Hebrew text they currently used – in which case Calvin's critique of the Vulgate's adoption of readings from the Septuagint would prove moot.

Calvin simply accepted the humanist arguments against translations without debate or reservation. The church must establish its teaching on the basis of the 'original' Greek and Hebrew texts. The priority of original texts over translations was for him a theological first principle, grounded, so far as one can determine, in arguments based on reason alone.

Written scripture and unwritten apostolic traditions

Calvin had already dealt with some of these questions in his *Reply to Sadoleto*. He protested at that time that many of the doctrines and practices the Catholic Church put forward as apostolic traditions were in fact innovations and novelties introduced into Catholic life and thought during the Middle Ages. Such doctrines and practices did not have roots in patristic tradition and could therefore not be apostolic. Indeed, the leadership of the Catholic Church was in Calvin's view so out of touch with ancient Christian tradition that it labelled the recovery of ancient tradition by the Protestant reformers as the dissemination of novelties.

In the *Institutes* Calvin argued that scripture contains everything 'necessary and useful' for the church to know. While tradition had an important role to play for Calvin as commentary on the sacred text of scripture, it could never itself take the place of scripture or be regarded as of equal authority. In the *Antidote* the problem that seemed to worry Calvin about the so-called unwritten traditions was the prospect that the Catholic Church would justify later doctrinal innovations and departures from ancient Christian tradition by claiming that such later innovations belonged in fact to unwritten apostolic traditions, which the Catholic Church had preserved and was alone competent to judge. By what norms such judgements were to be rendered was left unspecified.

Rejection of private interpretation

The problem of unwritten traditions was coupled in Calvin's mind with the claim of the Catholic Church to have the sole right to interpret scripture correctly. It is important to read Calvin's words in their proper historical context. He was, after all, not a seventeenth-century Protestant divine, born in the Reformed Church and formed by the Heidelberg Catechism and the Second Helvetic Confession. His attack on the Catholic Church was not a conventional theological polemic, written by a lifelong Protestant, who had never seen a mass, much less presided at one. Calvin was, after all, a cradle

Catholic, whose conversion to the Protestant cause was the deliberate and considered act of a young adult.

When Calvin therefore catalogued what he regarded as incredible biblical interpretations proposed by the Catholic Church, he was doing more than complaining about bad exegesis, which, like the poor, the church has always with it. Consistently bad exegesis was a sign to Calvin that Catholic claims to universal teaching authority were unfounded. Apostolic succession ought to be marked by apostolic success (or at least not marked by exegetical disaster). If the Reformation could fairly be described as, at least in part, a loss of confidence in the teaching authority of the Catholic Church, then Calvin's remarks could be seen as a first-hand expression of that loss of confidence. The loss he described was the loss he suffered.

In the end, the opposition of Protestant reformers such as Calvin to the decrees of Trent only served to underscore how important the Council of Trent was for the consolidation of Catholic teaching. For two generations Protestants had challenged Catholic theology in sermons, pamphlets, commentaries, confessions, theological treatises, and catechisms. Now at last Catholics had a clear and authoritative statement on all the disputed questions of the day. There was no longer any excuse for Catholics to stammer or retreat in confusion when witnessing to their faith. Trent had weighed the arguments of the Protestants on scripture and tradition, justification, eucharist, priesthood, and the nature of the church, and found them wanting. By doing so, it made clear that in its view a deep and unbridgeable gap had opened in the sixteenth century between the teaching of the Roman Catholic Church and the dissenting doctrines of the Protestant reformers. Reconciliation with Protestants would no longer be possible except on the basis of Trent's restatement of Catholic teaching. Unable to find a way to heal the breach in Western Christendom between Protestant and Catholic, Trent finalized the split.

Conclusion: directions of further research

DAVID C. STEINMETZ AND DAVID BAGCHI

What next?

Or, to frame the question somewhat more precisely, what problems in historical theology are likely to engage students of the Reformation in the twenty-first century? The short answer, of course, is that historians will continue to be fascinated by many of the same problems that fascinated their predecessors in the twentieth. There will always be fresh generations of scholars who will be captivated by the theology of the great figures of the sixteenth century – whether Luther or Calvin or Teresa of Avila – and who will devote their careers to resolving unresolved issues in the interpretation of their thought.

At the same time, it is very unlikely that newer research will retain the focus of older scholarship. Luther scholarship may be taken as a case in point. Luther scholars in the early twentieth century spent incredible energy examining his theological development prior to 1520. They attempted with varying degrees of success to identify the exact moment in Luther's early development in which he had the sudden theological insight that he later claimed had set him on the road to Reformation. Not surprisingly, more recent scholarship has shifted its focus. Historians now ask who Luther was at every stage of his life and how he was received, not merely by his admirers, but also by his detractors.

One can note similar shifts in the study of the theology of John Calvin. Calvin scholars are no longer satisfied to rely solely on Calvin's *Institutes of the Christian Religion* as the definitive statement of his theology, important as that work undoubtedly may be. They now read the full range of his writings – catechetical, polemical, 'exegetical, and theological – including his sermons and letters. When they do study the *Institutes*, as they inevitably must, they are aware of the complex interconnections between that work and his other writings'.

The canon of important texts for Calvin studies has gradually grown in size. Historians have prepared – and are still preparing – new critical editions of Calvin's French sermons, long available only in manuscript.

They have edited the records of the Company of Pastors and the Genevan Consistory, two important institutions in which Calvin was for many years the leading figure. Texts such as the consistory records help Calvin scholars to place theological issues in their proper social context.

For example, when Calvin and his associates made infant baptism a public ceremony performed before a local congregation rather than a private ceremony limited to a small circle of family and friends, they were putting into practice what was for them an important theological principle. They were also inadvertently (as consistory records reveal) setting the stage for the public embarrassment of a prominent Genevan family in which the paternity of a child was in dispute.

Similarly, the Calvinist reform of infant baptism served as a point at which the Calvinist redefinition of sanctity might become in fact an unwelcome interference in long family tradition. As a matter of principle Calvin no longer wanted to have children named after medieval saints such as Claude and Claire, but only after biblical saints such as Abraham and Esther. If a father named Claude wanted to name his firstborn son Claude as well, he could no longer readily do so under the new regime. He could, of course, slip away to a French village outside the territory under the control of Geneva and have his son baptized as Claude by an agreeable Catholic priest, who saw nothing wrong with the practice of naming children after medieval saints. Even though the Protestant pastors in Geneva might complain, they would nevertheless recognize Catholic baptisms as valid, even if children were given unauthorized names.

Sermons also give historians access – an admittedly one-sided access, to be sure, but a genuine access nonetheless – to theological life at the parish level. The pastoral problem faced by the Protestant reformers at the parish level was not the problem faced by the early Christian missionaries to northern and central Europe. The first missionaries converted the various Germanic tribes from the worship of deities such as Odin and Freya to the worship of the Christian God. But conversion from paganism was not the order of the day in sixteenth-century Europe. Even if the population of Europe was a good deal less Christian than it should be, it was no longer pagan in any meaningful sense of the term. In the sixteenth century the Christian religion was universally presupposed by most Europeans, even when it was not universally followed. The Christian God and the Christian religion were accepted as the way things were.

The problem from the standpoint of the Protestant reformers was not that Europeans had not been formed as Christians but that they had been formed incorrectly. The model of Christianity they had been taught by the Catholic Church was defective, both in its teaching and in its practices. The project that absorbed the energy of the reformers was the re-education and re-formation of a population that had been incorrectly formed in Christianity.

Catechetical literature and sermons give us some insight into how Protestant clergy understood their task and set about to implement it. For example, on Marian holidays, Protestant parsons explained why they were no longer celebrating the particular Marian feast day, what the Catholic Church had, in their view, erroneously taught about Mary, and what was the correct (namely, Lutheran or Reformed or Anglican) view of her place in the scheme of things. Similarly, funeral sermons offered Protestant clergy an opportunity to praise the life of virtue and to underscore the difference between the sanctity valued by the Catholic Church and the sanctity recommended by a Protestant reading of the Bible. On occasion, Protestant theologians were even able to explain difficult points of doctrine more clearly in their popular preaching than in their formal theological writings.

Fortunately, large collections of sermons have survived from the sixteenth century. Some, such as the sermons of Cyriakus Spangenberg on Romans, were published by the author himself. Others were commemorative volumes, often compiled by sons who, like their fathers, were Lutheran or Reformed pastors. The sons compiled the sermons, not only as an act of filial piety, but also as a contribution to the spiritual life of a new generation of readers denied the privilege of hearing the sermons when first delivered. Historians have only begun to mine these sermons as important sources for understanding Reformation theology, though sermons have already proved indispensable for defining Lutheran attitudes towards the Virgin Mary and Calvinist views of Christian sanctity.

One of the most promising areas of theological research has been the renewed interest in the history of biblical interpretation in the sixteenth century. In a way, it is surprising that Reformation historians have been relatively slow to develop the full range of resources this field provides. After all, the sixteenth century was a golden age of biblical studies. It was the period in which scholars issued an unprecedented number of new critical editions of the Bible, from the Complutensian Polyglot prepared by the Catholic faculty at the University of Alcalá to the Greek New Testament of Erasmus. Luther, who was not the first to translate the Bible into German, was certainly the most successful. His success was mirrored by the success of William Tyndale, a large portion of whose translation into English survives in the Authorized (King James) Version of the Bible.

But the Bible was not merely translated and read. It was interpreted. And the number of exegetical lectures and commentaries published in the sixteenth century stands in sharp contract to the much smaller number of surviving commentaries from the century preceding. While university professors of theology in the fifteenth century lectured on the Bible as part of their normal duties, only Denys the Carthusian left a large body of exegetical material for the later church to read, mark, and ponder.

By contrast, the sixteenth century published more commentators on the Bible than any busy pastor could easily read. Melanchthon alone wrote five commentaries on Romans, though only three of them were authorized by him for publication. While Luther's lectures on Romans were not published during his lifetime, other Lutheran commentators were quick to fill the gap – commentators such as Brenz, Bugenhagen, Cornerus, Cruciger, Dietrich, Hemmingsen, Hesshusen, Hunnius, Knoepken, Lossius, Major, Mylius, Osiander, Sarcerius, Selnecker, Spangenberg, Strigel, Weinrich, and Wigand. Their efforts to interpret Paul's letter to the Romans were duplicated by Catholics such as Dominic Soto and Ambrosius Catherinus Politus, radicals such as Bernardino Ochino and Fausto Sozzini, and Reformed theologians such as Heinrich Bullinger and John Calvin. While the fifteenth century left a rich deposit of important commentaries on the *Sentences* of Peter Lombard from diverse figures including John Huss, John Capreolus, and Gabriel Biel, the sixteenth century left an extraordinary number of biblical commentaries.

The earliest treatments of commentary literature in the twentieth century, such as those of Vogelsang and Ebeling, tended to focus on hermeneutics; that is, on the principles used by various commentators in their interpretation of the biblical text. Historians argued, for example, that Luther in his very early *Dictata super Psalterium* (1513–15) focused on the tropological sense of the Psalms, which he combined with a literal-prophetic reading that made Christ the subject of virtually every psalm. Later scholarship focused more intently on the exegesis itself.

After all, sixteenth-century theologians wrote very few treatises on hermeneutics. Their passion was exegesis. Indeed, the interpretation of the Bible was so important to them that they filled their bookshelves with multiple editions of new commentaries, even commentaries by interpreters with whom they differed theologically. Historians who make no attempt to understand the exegesis of these commentaries will never fully understand the mindset of the theologians who wrote them. Furthermore, by comparing the exegesis of, say, the Sermon on the Mount by multiple interpreters from diverse perspectives, historians can see in sharp relief the theological similarities and differences among interpreters in an age that drew no sharp line between biblical interpretation and constructive theology.

The Bible was not the only text at stake in the sixteenth century. The Reformation was almost as much an argument about the meaning of the early Christian fathers – especially St Augustine – as it was about the Bible. It was important for both Protestants and Catholics, but especially for Protestants, to demonstrate that their teaching concerning justification and the sacraments was not an unheard-of innovation, but rather the recovery of a neglected and poorly understood past. Protestants and Catholics wanted to be able to claim that their views were more ancient than the views of their opponents, more in harmony with the teaching of the ancient, undivided church. Even when Protestants were arguing among themselves and no Catholics were listening to their conversation, they still appealed to the teaching of the ancient church for support of their views. Lutherans such as Hesshusen quoted Augustine against Calvin to support the Lutheran understanding of the real presence of Christ in the eucharist, only to discover that Calvin had favourite quotations of his own from Augustine. When, after Calvin's death, the Lutheran theologian Giles Hunnius appealed to the early church to subvert the influence of John Calvin in Saxony by attacking what he regarded as the Arian tendencies in Calvin's Christology, he was answered in kind by the Reformed theologian, David Pareus.

Not that the use of the fathers always led to disagreements. Historians who study the use of the fathers in the sixteenth century can also uncover broad agreements over the meaning of certain ancient Christian texts. For example, young Augustine thought that the deeply conflicted person in Romans 7 was Paul himself under the law. 'O wretched man that I am!' describes the predicament of pious Jews, like Paul, who attempt to gain righteousness by keeping the Torah. Older Augustine was convinced that Romans 7 points to a conflict experienced by Christians, who live under grace (and only by Christians). Surprisingly, the majority of Catholics and Protestants did not differ in their interpretation of this text. They were in overwhelming agreement that the reading of Romans 7 by the older Augustine was the correct one. Paul was writing of life under grace rather than under law.

The new interest in the use of the early Christian writers by Catholics and Protestants in the sixteenth century complements, but does not supplant, an older interest in the influence of medieval theology on Reformation thought. From Ritter and Vignaux to Oberman and Grane, Reformation historians explored the impact medieval theology continued to exert, even among figures who had announced that they had made a sharp break with medieval ways of doing theology. Early interest centred on Luther, especially the young Luther, and his relationship to the Occamist theological and philosophical tradition in which he had been trained. But the scope of the enquiry rapidly broadened as historians examined the influence of medieval thought on other figures from Bucer and Hübmaier to Calvin and Zwingli.

Sometimes the enquiry has been framed too narrowly, as though Luther the Augustinian friar, Zwingli the secular priest, and Bucer the Dominican friar were raised as Protestants and only stumbled across medieval theology in the course of their academic studies. They were themselves late medieval Catholics, whose minds had been formed by the scholastic, mystical, and ascetic theology that formed their teachers and friends. The first generation of Protestant clergy did not learn about Catholic sacramental theology by reading Protestant denunciations of the mass and penance, but by presiding at mass and hearing confessions. Their new Reformation theology grew out of a medieval matrix, which the reformers sometimes reaffirmed, sometimes modified, and sometimes abandoned.

Historians are probably at the end of an era that posed grand theses about the influence of medieval thought on the Reformation. It no longer seems adequate to argue that the disagreement at Marburg between Luther and Zwingli was a clash between the *via moderna* and the *via antiqua* or to regard Luther's early theology as an adaptation of the school theology of the Augustinian order, in which John Staupitz played a crucial role as the mediator of the theology of Gregory of Rimini. Historians are now satisfied to answer more modest questions and to examine the influence of Johannes Duns Scotus or Bernard of Clairvaux on Zwingli and Calvin without projecting the results of that enquiry on to too large a canvas.

One of the areas of enquiry long out of favour has been the transition from the loosely organized and polemical theology of the first generation of reformers to the tightly organized and scholastic theology of their successors. Variously described as a return to method, a return to Aristotle, or a return to scholasticism, the movement in late sixteenth- and early seventeenth-century theology known as the beginning of Protestant orthodoxy has been an unpopular subject, except among historians and theologians whose own theological positions are similarly orthodox. More liberal interpreters, who dislike on theological grounds what they regard as 'dry scholasticism', have regarded the development of Protestant scholasticism as a fall from grace, as a lapse into rigid modes of thought, or even as a betrayal of the Reformation itself.

Such negative views are difficult to sustain on purely historical grounds. In spite of the complaints of the Renaissance humanists, medieval scholasticism was a lively intellectual movement. It engaged the energies of many of the finest minds in the history of Christian theology, from Anselm of Canterbury and Peter Abelard to Thomas Aquinas and William of Occam. There is no *a priori* reason for an impartial observer to suspect that Protestant scholasticism was any less lively or intellectually challenging. Nor was it a betrayal of the Reformation, once its admittedly different mode of discourse is understood. On the whole, it would be more accurate to see Protestant scholasticism as a natural development of the catechetical task of the Reformation. Just as catechisms provided orderly but elementary expositions of the Christian faith for Protestant congregations, so scholastic manuals of theology provided advanced instruction for Protestant leaders. The earliest Reformation writings stressed the points of doctrine that were in dispute with Rome. Later writings attempted to offer a more coherent vision of the whole, including doctrines not at issue in the Reformation. One can see evidence of this development in the earlier and later editions of Melanchthon's *Loci Communes* and Calvin's *Institutes*. Viewed from this perspective, the shift to scholastic method seems to be a logical next step and a natural development from what had gone before.

There were also ecumenical reasons for the use of scholastic method. Protestantism was, and remained, a minority movement in a religious world dominated by a renewed and revitalized Catholicism. Catholic theology had never abandoned scholastic method or its long-standing attempt to write theologies that offered a comprehensive Christian vision of reality. If Protestants did not offer a comprehensive and coherent vision of Christian theology to enquiring minds, Catholics would. Furthermore, Catholic theologians such as Cardinal Bellarmine read Protestant theology carefully and subjected it to rigorous critical analysis. The Protestant scholastics were equipped by their training to respond in kind.

Not that scholastic method had ever completely disappeared from Protestant thought. One can argue that the *Loci Communes* of Melanchthon and the *Institutes* of John Calvin were in some important senses 'scholastic' as ordered discussions of theological doctrines resting on scripture, tradition, and even (if minimally) philosophy. Melanchthon never lost his interest in Aristotle, and Luther cheerfully presided at theological disputations throughout his later years. Furthermore, the medieval scholastic model of verse-by-verse exposition of the Bible became in its own way the model for Protestant sermons.

But there were differences from medieval scholasticism as well as similarities. Catholic scholastics abandoned lectures on the *Sentences* of Peter Lombard in favour of lectures on the leading theologians of the various orders. Dominicans and Jesuits heard lectures on the theology of Thomas Aquinas, and Franciscans on Duns Scotus. For their part, Protestant scholastics paid attention to Greek and Hebrew philology to a degree that would have astonished medieval theologians. Such similarities and differences between medieval and early modern scholasticism need further study, even if some promising first steps have been taken. Undoubtedly, fresh explorations will have implications for the larger question of 'confessionalization' in early modern Europe.

Like Protestant scholasticism, some formerly neglected subjects are now receiving the attention they deserve. The Radical Reformation was rescued from the endangered-species list in the middle of the twentieth century. Books, articles, translations, and critical editions of the writings of Anabaptists, spiritualists, and antitrinitarian theologians are now readily available, though more attention has been paid to Anabaptists than to radical figures such as Bernardino Ochino or Fausto Sozzini.

The participation of women in the theological disputes of the sixteenth century has captured the imagination of some historians. While, for a variety of cultural reasons, early modern women did not leave a large body of theological writings, they did leave some. Historians are now aware of figures such as Anne Askew, Marie Dentière, Argula von Grumbach, and Katherina Schütz Zell, who offer direct evidence of how the Reformation was understood and appropriated by women.

Historians have made important strides in the study of the Catholic Reformation. Since Hubert Jedin wrote his monumental history of the Council of Trent, historians have explored such topics as the early Catholic controversialists and the origin of the Jesuits. But there is still a good deal to be done on Catholic theology in the first half of the sixteenth century, especially in the response of Catholic biblical interpreters to the stimulus and challenge of Protestant exegesis. Thomas Cardinal Cajetan devoted his last years to the writing of biblical commentaries, including a commentary on the much disputed letter of St Paul to the Romans. His commentary on Romans, however, was not alone. Other Catholic commentators on Romans included Jean Arboreus, Benedict Arias Montanus, John Colet, Gaspar Contarini, Desiderius Erasmus, Jean de Gagney, Marino Grimani, Claude Guilliaud, Jacques Lefèvre d'Etaples, Ambrosius Catherinus Politus, Jacopo Sadoleto, Alfonso Salmeron, Girolamo Seripando, Dominic Soto, and Francisco de Toledo. While the exegetical works of Erasmus, Lefèvre, and Colet on Romans are well known, the same cannot be said of the rest. On the whole, the rich collection of Catholic contributions to biblical interpretation in the sixteenth century remains undervalued and largely unexamined.

Which brings us back to the question with which we began: what next? – only this time as a question directed more specifically to you as a student of Reformation theology. The Conclusion has suggested some lines of research that you might continue or broaden, ranging from a fresh examination of the social context of theological enquiry in the sixteenth century to a reassessment of the role of Protestant scholasticism. Some of you may write new studies on biblical interpretation (including Catholic biblical interpretation), on the deployment of patristic authorities in theological discourse, on the medieval context of Reformation thought, or on the role of women as active participants in theological disputes. Others will mine new sources, such as consistory records and volumes of collected sermons, or read old sources with new eyes. Inevitably, still other historians will discover new questions to ask and fresh lines of enquiry to pursue. The most important thing for beginning students to remember is that suggestions for further research (like the suggestions in this brief chapter) are only suggestions and that historical enquiry flourishes best when it is restricted least. Good historians have the courage to go wherever their curiosity leads them and to study whatever captures their imagination. It has never been otherwise.

Select bibliography

The late medieval background

Hagen, Kenneth, ed. *Augustine, the Harvest, and Theology (1300–1650)*. Leiden: E. J. Brill, 1990.

Oberman, Heiko A. *The Dawn of the Reformation: Essays in Late Medieval and Early Reformation Thought*. Grand Rapids, MI: Eerdmans, 1992.

Oberman, Heiko A. *The Harvest of Medieval Theology: Gabriel Biel and Late Medieval Nominalism*. Grand Rapids, MI: Eerdmans, 1967.

Oberman, Heiko, and Frank A. James III, eds. *Via Augustini: Augustine in the Later Middle Ages, Renaissance and Reformation*. Leiden: E. J. Brill, 1991.

Janz, Denis R. *Luther on Thomas Aquinas: The Angelic Doctor in the Thought of the Reformer*. Stuttgart: Franz Steiner Verlag, 1989.

Janz, Denis R. *Luther and Late Medieval Thomism: A Study in Theological Anthropology*. Waterloo, Canada: Wilfrid Laurier University Press, 1983.

Lollardy

Arnold, T., ed. *Select English Works of John Wyclif*. 3 vols. Oxford: Clarendon Press, 1869–71.

Aston, Margaret. *Faith and Fire: Popular and Unpopular Religion, 1350–1600*. London: Hambledon Press, 1993.

Aston, Margaret. *Lollards and Reformers: Images and Literacy in Late Medieval Religion*. London: Hambledon Press, 1984.

Biller, Peter, and Barrie Dobson, eds. *The Medieval Church: Universities, Heresy, and the Religious Life: Essays in Honour of Gordon Leff*, in Studies in Church History, Subsidia 11. Woodbridge: The Ecclesiastical History Society in association with The Boydell Press, 1999.

Catto, Jeremy. 'Wyclif and Wycliffism at Oxford 1356–1430', in *The History of the University of Oxford*, II: *Late Medieval Oxford*. Jeremy Catto and Ralph Evans, eds. Oxford: Clarendon Press, 1992, pp. 175–261.

Deanesly, Margaret. *The Lollard Bible and other Medieval Biblical Versions*. Cambridge: Cambridge University Press, 1920.

Hudson, Anne. *Lollards and their Books*. London: Hambledon Press, 1985.

Hudson, Anne. *The Premature Reformation: Wycliffite Texts and Lollard History*. Oxford: Clarendon Press, 1988.

Hudson, Anne, ed. *Selections from English Wycliffite Writings*. Cambridge: Cambridge University Press, 1978.

Hudson, Anne, and Pamela Gradon, eds. *English Wycliffite Sermons.* 5 vols. Oxford: Clarendon Press, 1983–96.
Kenny, Anthony. *Wyclif.* Oxford: Oxford University Press, 1985.
Kenny, Anthony, ed. *Wyclif in his Times.* Oxford: Clarendon Press, 1986.
Lambert, M. D. *Medieval Heresy: Popular Movements from Bogomil to Hus.* London: Edward Arnold, 1977.
Leff, G. *Heresy in the Later Middle Ages.* 2 vols. Manchester: Manchester University Press, 1967.
McFarlane, K. B. *John Wycliffe and the Beginnings of English Nonconformity.* London: English Universities Press, 1952.
Matthew, F. D., ed. *The English Works of Wyclif hitherto unprinted.* London: Early English Text Society, original series 74, 1880; revised edition 1902.
Pitard, Derrick, ed. 'Bibliographies for Lollard studies' (electronic bibliography sponsored by the Lollard Society at <http://home.att.net/~lollard/bibhome.html>).
Scase, Wendy. '"Heu! quanta desolatio Angliae praestatur": A Wycliffite Libel and the Naming of Heretics, Oxford 1382', in *Lollard Influences: Dissent and Reform in Late Medieval England*, Jill Havens, Derrick Pitard and Fiona Somerset, eds. Woodbridge: Boydell & Brewer, 2003, pp. 19–36.
Scase, Wendy. *Piers Plowman and the New Anticlericalism.* Cambridge: Cambridge University Press, 1988.
Scase, Wendy. *Reginald Pecock. Authors of the Middle Ages*, III, 8. Aldershot: Ashgate, 1996.
Swanson, Robert. *Church and Society in Late Medieval England.* Oxford: Basil Blackwell, 1989.
Thomson, John A. F. *The Later Lollards 1414–1520.* London: Oxford University Press, 1965.
Thomson, Williel R. *The Latin Writings of John Wyclyf.* Toronto: Pontifical Institute of Medieval Studies, 1983.
Watson, Nicholas. 'Conceptions of the Word: the mother tongue and the incarnation of God', in *New Medieval Literatures*, I. Wendy Scase, Rita Copeland and David Lawton, eds. Oxford: Clarendon Press, 1997, pp. 85–124.
Wilks, Michael. *Wyclif: Political Ideas and Practice: Papers by Michael Wilks*, selected and introduced by Anne Hudson. Oxford: Oxbow Books, 2000.
Workman, H. B. *John Wyclif.* 2 vols. Oxford: Clarendon Press, 1926.
John Wyclif, *Wyclif's Latin Works*, 36 vols. London: Wyclif Society, 1882–1922.

Hussitism

Bartoš, František. *Počátky české Bible.* Prague: Kalich, 1941.
Bartoš, František, ed. *Orationes, quibus Nicolaus de Pelhřimov, Taboritarum episcopus, et Ulricus de Znojmo, Orphanorum sacerdos, articulos de peccatis publicis puniendis et libertate verbi dei in Concilio Basiliensi anno 1433 ineunte defendebunt.* Tábor: Nákladem Jihočeské Společnosti, 1935.
Clifton-Everest, John M. 'The eucharist in the Czech and German prayers of Milíč z Kroměříž', in *Bohemia* 23 (1981), pp. 1–15.
Fudge, Thomas A. '"Ansellus dei"and the Bethlehem chapel in Prague', in *Communio Viatorum* 35, no. 2 (1993), pp. 127–61.

Fudge, Thomas A. 'Hussite infant communion', in *Lutheran Quarterly* 10, no. 2 (1996), pp. 179–94.

Fudge, Thomas A. 'Luther and the "Hussite" catechism of 1522', in *Confessional Identity in East-Central Europe*. Graeme Murdock and Maria Crăciun, eds. Aldershot: Ashgate, 2002.

Fudge, Thomas A. *The Magnificent Ride: The First Reformation in Hussite Bohemia*. Aldershot: Ashgate, 1998.

Fudge, Thomas A. '"Neither mine nor thine": Communist experiments in Hussite Bohemia', in *Canadian Journal of History* 33 (April 1998), pp. 25–47.

Fudge, Thomas A. 'The night of antichrist: popular culture, judgment and revolution in fifteenth-century Bohemia', in *Communio Viatorum* 37, no. 1 (1995), pp. 33–45.

Heymann, Frederick G. 'The national assembly of Čáslav', in *Medievalia et Humanistica* 8 (1954), pp. 32–55.

Holeton, David R. *La communion des tout-petits enfants: Étude de mouvement eucharistique en Bohême vers la fin du moyen-âge*. Rome: CLV Edizioni liturgiche, 1989.

Holeton, David R., and Zdeněk V. David, eds. *The Bohemian Reformation and Religious Practice*. 3 vols. Prague: Academy of Sciences of the Czech Republic, 1996–2000.

Huss, Jan. *Magistri Johannis Hus: Tractatus de ecclesia*. S. Harrison Thomson, ed. Cambridge: W. Heffer & Sons; Boulder: University of Colorado Press, 1956.

Huss, Jan. 'On simony,' in *Advocates of Reform*. Matthew Spinka, ed. Philadelphia: The Westminster Press, 1953, pp. 196–278.

Kaminsky, Howard. *A History of the Hussite Revolution*. Los Angeles: University of California Press, 1967.

Kaminsky, Howard, ed. 'Peter Chelčický: treatises on Christianity and the social order', in *Studies in Medieval and Renaissance History* 1 (1964), pp. 105–79.

Macek, Josef. *Ktož jsú boží bojovníci: Čtení o Táboře v husitském revolučním hnutí*. Prague: Melantrich, 1951.

Molnár, Amedeo. 'Eschatologická naděje česk', in *Od reformace k zítřku*. Prague: Kalich, 1956, pp. 11–101.

Morée, Peter C. A. *Preaching in Fourteenth-Century Bohemia*. Heršpice: EMAN, 1999.

Palacký, František, ed. *Documenta Mag. Joannis Hus vitam, doctrinam, causam in constantiensi concilio actam et controversias de religione in Bohemia annis 1403–1418 motas illustrantia*. Prague: Friedrich Tempsky, 1869.

Patchovsky, Alexander, and František Šmahel, eds. *Eschatologie und Hussitismus*. Prague: Historický ústav, 1996.

Říčan, Rudolf. *The History of the Unity of Brethren*. C. Daniel Crews, trans. Bethlehem, PA: The Moravian Church in America, 1992.

Werner, Ernst. *Jan Hus: Welt und Umwelt eines Prager Frühreformators*. Weimar: Verlag Hermann Böhlaus Nachfolger, 1991.

Erasmus
Sources

J. Leclerc, ed. *Desiderii Erasmi Opera Omnia*. Leiden, 1703–6.

Opera Omnia Des. Erasmi Roterodami. Amsterdam, 1982.

The Collected Works of Erasmus. Toronto, 1988.

Studies

Augustijn, Cornelius, *Erasmus: His Life, Works, and Influence.* J. C. Grayson, trans. Toronto: University of Toronto Press, 1991.

Backus, I. 'Erasmus and the Spirituality of the Early Church', in *Erasmus' Vision of the Church*, Hilmar M. Pabel, ed. Kirksville, MO: Sixteenth Century Journal Publishers, Inc., 1995, pp. 95–114.

Bentley, Jerry H. *Humanists and Holy Writ: New Testament Scholarship in the Renaissance.* Princeton, NJ: Princeton University Press, 1983.

Chantraine, George. 'L'Apologia ad Latomum: deux conceptions de la théologie', in *Scrinium Erasmianum*, II. J. Coppens, ed. Leiden: E. J. Brill, 1969, 51–75.

Farge, James. 'Erasmus, the University of Paris, and the profession of theology', *Erasmus of Rotterdam Yearbook* 19 (1999), pp. 18–46.

Grendler, Paul F. 'How to get a degree in fifteen days: Erasmus' doctorate of theology from the University of Turin', *Erasmus of Rotterdam Yearbook* 18 (1998), pp. 40–69.

Hoffmann, Manfred. *Rhetoric and Theology: The Hermeneutic of Erasmus.* Toronto: University of Toronto Press, 1994.

Kohls, Ernst-Wilhelm. *Die Theologie des Erasmus.* Basel: Helbing & Lichtenhahn/ Friedrich Reinhart Verlag, 1966.

Mansfield, Bruce. *Interpretations of Erasmus c. 1750–1920: Man on His Own.* Toronto: University of Toronto Press, 1992.

Mansfield, Bruce. *Phoenix of His Age: Interpretations of Erasmus c. 1550–1750.* Toronto: University of Toronto Press, 1979.

Oberman, Heiko A. *Forerunners of the Reformation: The Shape of Late Medieval Thought.* New York: Holt, Rinehart & Winston, 1966.

Olin, John C. 'Erasmus and the Church Fathers', *Six Essays on Erasmus.* New York: Fordham University Press, 1979, pp. 33–48.

O'Rourke Boyle, Marjorie. *Erasmus on Language and Method in Theology.* Toronto: University of Toronto Press, 1977.

O'Rourke Boyle, Marjorie. *Rhetoric and Reform: Erasmus' Civil Dispute with Luther.* Cambridge, MA: Harvard University Press, 1983.

Payne, John B. *Erasmus: His Theology of the Sacraments.* Richmond, OH: M. E. Bratcher, 1970.

Rummel, Erika. *The Confessionalization of Humanism in Reformation Germany.* New York: Oxford University Press, 2000.

Rummel, Erika. *Erasmus and his Catholic Critics*, 2 vols. Nieuwkoop: De Graaf, 1989.

Rummel, Erika. *Erasmus' Annotations on the New Testament: From Philologist to Theologian.* Toronto: University of Toronto Press, 1986.

Trinkaus, Charles E. *The Scope of Renaissance Humanism.* Ann Arbor, MI: University of Michigan Press, 1983.

Luther

Althaus, Paul. *The Ethics of Martin Luther.* Philadelphia, PA: Fortress Press, 1972.

Althaus, Paul. *The Theology of Martin Luther.* Philadelphia, PA: Fortress Press, 1966.

Asendorf, Ulrich. *Die Theologie Martin Luthers nach seinen Predigten.* Göttingen: Vandenhoeck & Ruprecht, 1988.

Asendorf, Ulrich. *Lectura in biblia: Luther Genesisvorlesung 1535–1545.* Göttingen: Vandenhoeck & Ruprecht, 1998.

Bayer, Oswald. *Promissio: Geschichte der reformatorischen Wende in Luthers Theologie*. Göttingen: Vandenhoeck & Ruprecht, 1971.

Baylor, Michael. *Action and Person: Conscience in Late Scholasticism and the Young Luther*. Leiden: E. J. Brill, 1977.

Bizer, Ernst. *Fides ex auditu: eine Untersuchung über die Entdeckung der Gerechtigkeit Gottes durch Martin Luther*, 3rd edn. Neukirchen-Vluyn: Neukirchener Verlag, 1966.

Bornkamm, Karin. *Christus – König und Priester: Das Amt Christi bei Luther im Verhältnis zur Vor- und Nachgeschichte*. Tübingen: Mohr Siebeck, 1998.

Braaten, Carl E., and Robert W. Jenson, eds. *Union with Christ: The New Finnish Interpretation of Luther*. Grand Rapids; MI, and Cambridge: Eerdmans, 1998.

Brecht, Martin. *Martin Luther*. 3 vols. Philadelphia, PA, and Minneapolis, MN: Fortress Press, 1985–93.

Cranz, F. Edward. *An Essay on the Development of Luther's Thought on Justice, Law, and Society*. Gerald Christianson and Thomas M. Izbicki, eds. Mifflintown, PA: Sigler Press, 1998.

Ebeling, Gerhard. *Luther: An Introduction to His Thought*. Philadelphia, PA: Fortress Press, 1970.

Ebeling, Gerhard. *Lutherstudien*, I. Tübingen: Mohr Siebeck, 1971.

Edwards, Mark U., Jr. *Luther and the False Brethren*. Stanford, CA: Stanford University Press, 1975.

Edwards, Mark U., Jr. *Luther's Last Battles: Polemics and Politics, 1531–46*. Ithaca, NY, and London: Cornell University Press, 1983.

Forde, Gerhard O. *On Being a Theologian of the Cross: Reflections on Luther's Heidelberg Disputation, 1518*. Grand Rapids, MI: Eerdmans, 1997.

Grane, Leif. *Martinus Noster: Luther in the German Reform Movement 1518–1521*. Mainz: Philipp von Zabern, 1994.

Grane, Leif. *Modus loquendi theologicus: Luthers Kampf um die Erneuerung der Theologie (1515–1518)*. Leiden: E. J. Brill, 1975.

Gritsch, Eric C. *Martin – God's Court Jester: Luther in Retrospect*. Philadelphia, PA: Fortress Press, 1983.

Hagen, Kenneth. *Luther's Approach to Scripture as Seen in His 'Commentaries' on Galatians, 1519–1538*. Tübingen: Mohr Siebeck, 1993.

Hagen, Kenneth. *A Theology of Testament in the Young Luther: The Lectures on Hebrews*. Leiden: E. J. Brill, 1974.

Helmer, Christine. *The Trinity and Martin Luther: A Study on the Relationship between Genre, Language and the Trinity in Luther's Works (1523–1546)*. Mainz: Philipp von Zabern, 1999.

Hendrix, Scott. *Ecclesia in Via*. Leiden: E. J. Brill, 1974.

Hendrix, Scott. *Luther and the Papacy*. Philadelphia, PA: Fortress Press, 1981.

Hendrix, Scott. 'Luthers Theologie,' in *Evangelisches Kirchenlexikon*, III. 5 vols. Göttingen: Vandenhoeck & Ruprecht, 1986–97, pp. 211–20.

Hermann, Rudolf. *Luthers Theologie*. Horst Beintker, ed. Göttingen: Vandenhoeck & Ruprecht, 1967.

Hoffman, Bengt. *Luther and the Mystics*. Minneapolis, MN: Augsburg, 1976.

Holl, Karl. *Gesammelte Aufsätze zur Kirchengeschichte*, I: *Luther*. 7th edn. Tübingen: Mohr Siebeck, 1948.

Junghans, Helmar. 'The center of the theology of Martin Luther', in Gerald S. Krispin and Jon D. Vieker, eds., *And Every Tongue Confess: Essays in Honor of Norman Nagel*. Chelsea, MI: BookCrafters, 1990, pp. 179–94.

Junghans, Helmar. *Der junge Luther und die Humanisten*, Weimar: Hermann Böhlaus Nachfolger, 1984.

Junghans, Helmar, ed. *Leben und Werk Martin Luthers von 1526 bis 1546*. 2 vols. Berlin: Evangelische Verlagsanstalt, 1983.

Kittelson, James M. 'Luther the theologian', in *Reformation Europe: A Guide to Research*, II. St Louis: Center for Reformation Research, 1992, pp. 21–46.

Kolb, Robert. *Martin Luther as Prophet, Teacher, and Hero: Images of the Reformer, 1520–1620*. Grand Rapids, MI: Baker, 1999.

Köstlin, Julius. *The Theology of Luther in its Historical Development and Inner Harmony*. Charles E. Hay, trans. 2 vols. Philadelphia, PA: Lutheran Publication Society, 1897.

Lienhard, Marc. *Luther Witness to Jesus Christ: Stages and Themes of the Reformer's Christology*. Minneapolis, MN: Augsburg, 1982.

Link, Wilhelm. *Das Ringen Luthers um die Freiheit der Theologie von der Philosophie*. E. Wolf and M. Mezger, eds. Berlin: Evangelische Verlagsanstalt, 1954.

Loewenich, Walther von. *Luther's Theology of the Cross*. Minneapolis, MN: Augsburg, 1976.

Lohse, Bernhard. *Martin Luther: An Introduction to His Life and Work*. Philadelphia, PA: Fortress Press, 1980. 3rd revised German edn. Munich: C. H. Beck, 1997.

Lohse, Bernhard. *Martin Luther's Theology: Its Historical and Systematic Development*. Roy A. Harrisville, trans. Minneapolis, MN: Fortress Press, 1999.

McGrath, Alister. *Luther's Theology of the Cross: Martin Luther's Theological Breakthrough*. Oxford: Basil Blackwell, 1990.

Miller, Gregory J. 'Luther on the Turks and Islam', in *Lutheran Quarterly* 14 (2000): 79–97.

Mühlen, Karl-Heinz zur. *Nos extra nos: Luthers Theologie zwischen Mystik und Scholastik*. Tübingen: Mohr Siebeck, 1972.

Oberman, Heiko A. *The Dawn of the Reformation: Essays in Late Medieval and Early Reformation Thought*. Edinburgh: T. & T. Clark, 1986.

Oberman, Heiko A. *Luther: Man between God and the Devil*. Eileen Walliser-Schwarzbart, trans. New Haven, CT, and London: Yale, 1989.

Ozment, Steven. *Homo spiritualis*. Leiden: E. J. Brill, 1969.

Pesch, Otto Hermann. *Hinführung zu Luther*. Mainz: Matthias-Grünewald-Verlag, 1982.

Peura, Simo. *Mehr als ein Mensch? Die Vergöttlichung als Thema der Theologie Martin Luther von 1513 bis 1519*. Mainz: Philipp von Zabern, 1994.

Prenter, Regin. *Spiritus Creator: Luther's Concept of the Holy Spirit*. Philadelphia, PA: Muhlenberg, 1953.

Preus, J. Samuel. *From Shadow to Promise*. Cambridge, MA: Harvard University Press, 1969.

Russell, William R. *The Schmalkald Articles: Luther's Theological Testament*. Minneapolis, MN: Fortress Press, 1995.

Saarinen, Risto. *Gottes Wirken auf uns: Die transzendentale Deutung des Gegenwart-Christi-Motivs in der Lutherforschung*. Stuttgart: Franz Steiner, 1989.

Siggins, Ian D. K. *Martin Luther's Doctrine of Christ*. New Haven, CT, and London: Yale University Press, 1970.

Pt. 1

Last time we mentioned "sisters and brothers" we talked abc
or like enemies and opponents. Are they on our side or are tl

They should be on our team right?

Deep down I think we want our brothers and sisters to be our
And this is one of the most special things we can ever do.

*But this week and next week we're going to hear stories froi
siblings.*

Who knows what envy is? It's very close to jealousy, but

"Envy" tells us about what it's like to be tied up by comparir
or a friend.

Do you ever feel envious of others?

Let me give you an example of envy. Let's think of two siste
shopping for clothes if they came home with a report card
decent grades - but not all A's, so no new shoes for her, bi

Kayla would be upset and jealous that Abigail gets ne

But listen, what Kayla is most upset about is the that she
she's had up to hear with Miss perfect WHO IS always c
watching tv - always washing her plate after dinner and
almost cannot help compare herself to her sister.

"Why does Abigail always have to get it right," Kayla wor
too." she said to herself.

Joseph

- Have you ever tried into slavery?
- It would be extreme
- There's a story in the
- Its not just
- . Always has to god is

Steinmetz, David C. *Luther and Staupitz: An Essay in the Intellectual Origins of the Protestant Reformation.* Durham, NC: Duke, 1980.
Steinmetz, David C. *Luther in Context.* Bloomington, IN: Indiana University Press, 1986.
Trigg, Jonathan D. *Baptism in the Theology of Martin Luther.* Leiden: E. J. Brill, 1994.
Vercruysse, Joseph. 'Luther's theology of the cross at the time of the Heidelberg disputation', *Gregorianum* 57, no. 3 (1976), pp. 523–48.
Wallmann, Johannes. 'The reception of Luther's writings on the Jews from the Reformation to the end of the 19th century', *Lutheran Quarterly* 1 (1987), pp. 72–97.
Watson, Philip S. *Let God be God: An Interpretation of the Theology of Martin Luther.* Philadelphia, PA: Fortress Press, 1947.
Weier, Reinhold. *Das Theologieverständnis Martin Luthers.* Paderborn: Bonifacius-Verlag, 1976.
Wengert, Timothy J. *Law and Gospel: Philip Melanchthon's debate with John Agricola of Eisleben over Poenitentia.* Grand Rapids, MI: Baker Book House; Carlisle: Paternoster Press, 1997.
Wicks, Jared. *Luther's Reform: Studies on Conversion and the Church.* Mainz: Philipp von Zabern, 1992.
Wicks, Jared. *Man Yearning for Grace: Luther's Early Spiritual Teaching.* Wiesbaden: Franz Steiner, 1969.

Melanchthon
Sources
A Melanchthon Reader. Ralph Keen, trans. New York: P. Lang, 1988.
Keen, Ralph, ed. *A Checklist of Melanchthon Imprints through 1560.* St Louis, MO: Center for Reformation Research, 1988.
Kusukawa, Sachiko, ed. *Melanchthon: Orations on Philosophy and Education.* Christine F. Salazar, trans. Cambridge: Cambridge University Press, 1999.

Studies
Fraenkel, Peter. *Testimonia Patrum: The Function of the Patristic Argument in the Theology of Philip Melanchthon.* Geneva: Droz, 1961.
Frank, Günter. *Die theologische Philosophie Philipp Melanchthons.* Leipzig: St Benno Buch und Zeitschriften Verlagsgesellschaft, 1995.
Keen, Ralph. *Divine and Human Authority in Reformation Thought: German Theologians on Political Order 1520–1555.* Bibliotheca humanistica et reformatorica 55. Nieuwkoop: De Graaf, 1997.
Kolb, Robert. *Nikolaus von Amsdorf (1483–1565): Popular Polemics in the Preservation of Luther's Legacy.* Nieuwkoop: De Graaf, 1978.
Kusukawa, Sachiko. *The Transformation of Natural Philosophy: The Case of Philip Melanchthon.* Cambridge: Cambridge University Press, 1995.
Kusukawa, Sachiko. *A Wittenberg University Library Catalogue of 1536.* Cambridge: LP Publications, 1995.
Maag, Karin (ed.), *Melanchthon in Europe: His Work and Influence beyond Wittenberg.* Grand Rapids: Baker Book House, 1999.
Maurer, Wilhelm. *Historical Commentary on the Augsburg Confession.* Philadelphia: Fortress Press, 1986.

Meerhoff, Kees. 'The Significance of Philip Melanchthon's Rhetoric in the Renaissance', in Peter Mack, ed., *Renaissance Rhetoric*. London and New York: Macmillan, 1994, pp. 46–62.

Meijering, E. P. *Melanchthon and Patristic Thought: The Doctrines of Christ and Grace, the Trinity, and the Creation.* Leiden: E. J. Brill, 1983.

Neusner, Wilhelm H. *Bibliographie der Confessio Augustana und Apologie, 1530–1580.* Bibliotheca humanistica et reformatorica 55. Nieuwkoop: De Graaf, 1997.

Quere, Ralph Walter. *Melanchthon's Christum cognoscere: Christ's Efficacious Presence in the Eucharistic Theology of Melanchthon.* Nieuwkoop: De Graaf, 1977.

Rosin, Robert. *Reformers, the Preacher, and Skepticism: Luther, Brenz, Melanchthon, and Ecclesiastes.* Veroffentlichungen des Instituts für Europäische Geschichte Mainz 171. Mainz: P. von Zabern, 1997.

Scheible, Heinz. *Melanchthon und die Reformation: Forschungsbeiträge.* G. May and R. Decot, eds. Mainz: Philipp von Zabern, 1996.

Scheible, Heinz, ed. *Der Theologe Melanchthon.* Sigmaringen: Thorbecke, 1999.

Schneider, John R. *Philip Melanchthon's Rhetorical Construal of Biblical Authority: Oratio Sacra.* Lewiston, NY, and Lampeter: Edwin Mellen Press, 1990.

Scribner, Robert W. *For the Sake of Simple Folk: Popular Propaganda for the German Reformation.* Oxford: Clarendon Press, 1994.

Wengert, Timothy J. *Human Freedom, Christian Righteousness: Philip Melanchthon's Exegetical Dispute with Erasmus of Rotterdam.* Oxford: Oxford University Press, 1998.

Wengert, Timothy J. *Law and Gospel: Philip Melanchthon's Debate with John Agricola of Eisleben over Poenitentia.* Carlisle: Paternoster; Grand Rapids, MI: Baker Book House, 1997.

Wengert, Timothy J. 'Philip Melanchthon's 1522 Annotations on Romans and the Lutheran origins of rhetorical criticism', in *Biblical Interpretation in the Era of the Reformation: Essays Presented to David Steinmetz in Honor of His Sixtieth Birthday.* R. A. Muller and J. L. Thompson, eds. Grand Rapids, MI, and Cambridge: Eerdmans, 1996, pp. 118–40.

Wengert, Timothy J. *Philip Melanchthon's Annotationes in Johannem in Relation to its Predecessors and Contemporaries.* Geneva: Droz, 1987.

Wengert, Timothy J., and M. Patrick Graham, eds. *Philip Melanchthon (1497–1560) and the Commentary.* Sheffield: Sheffield Academic Press, 1997.

Confessional Lutheranism

Bizer, Ernst. *Studien zur Geschichte des Abendmahlsstreits im 16. Jahrhundert.* Gütersloh, 1940.

Dingel, Irene. *Concordia controversa, Die öffentliche Diskussionen um das lutherische Konkordienwerk am Ende des 16. Jahrhunderts.* Gütersloh: Gütersloher Verlagshaus, 1996.

Dingel, Irene. 'Melanchthon und die Normierung des Bekenntnisses', in *Der Theologe Melanchthon.* Heinz Scheible, ed. Sigmaringen: Thorbecke, 1999, pp. 195–211.

Kolb, Robert. *Confessing the Faith: Reformers Define the Church, 1530–1580.* St Louis, MO: Concordia, 1991.

Kolb, Robert. *Luther's Heirs Define His Legacy: Studies on Lutheran Confessionalization.* Aldershot: Variorum, 1996.

Kolb, Robert, and Timothy J. Wengert, eds. *The Book of Concord: The Confessions of the Evangelical Lutheran Church.* Minneapolis, MN: Fortress Press, 2000.

Mahlmann, Theodor. *Das neue Dogma der lutherischen Christologie, Problem und Geschichte seiner Begründung.* Gütersloh: Gerd Mohn, 1969.

Richter, Matthias. *Gesetz und Heil: Eine Untersuchung zur Vorgeschichte und zum Verlauf des sogenannten Zweiten Antinomistischen Streits.* Göttingen: Vandenhoeck & Ruprecht, 1996.

Stupperich, Martin. *Osiander in Preussen, 1549–1552.* Berlin: de Gruyter, 1973.

Wengert, Timothy J. *Human Freedom, Christian Righteousness: Philip Melanchthon's Exegetical Dispute with Erasmus of Rotterdam.* Oxford and New York: Oxford University Press, 1998.

Wengert, Timothy J. *Law and Gospel: Philip Melanchthon's Debate with Johann Agricola of Eisleben over Poenitentia.* Grand Rapids, MI: Baker Book House; Carlisle: Paternoster Press, 1997.

Wenz Gunther. *Theologie der Bekenntnisschriften der evangelisch-lutherischen Kirche.* 2 vols. Berlin: de Gruyter, 1996–8.

Zwingli
Editions of Zwingli's works

The critical edition of Zwingli's works is:

Egli, Emil, et al. *Huldreich Zwinglis sämtliche Werke.* Berlin and Leipzig: C. A. Schwetschke, 1905–35; Zurich: Theologische Verlag, 1982– (chapter 8 above as *Z*). Some works are available only in an earlier edition, *Huldreich Zwinglis Werke.* Zurich, 1812–61. English translations of many of Zwingli's works are available.

Bromiley, G. W., ed. *Zwingli and Bullinger*, Library of Christian Classics, XXIV. London: SCM Press, 1953.

Hinke, William J., ed. *Zwingli: On Providence and Other Essays.* Durham, NC: Labyrinth Press, 1983, a re-edition of *The Latin Works of Huldreich Zwingli,* II. Philadelphia, PA: Heidelberg Press, 1912.

Jackson, Samuel M., ed. *Ulrich Zwingli: Early Writings.* Durham, NC: Labyrinth Press, 1986, a re-edition of *The Latin Works and the Correspondence of Huldreich Zwingli,* I, 1510–1522. New York: G. P. Putnam's Sons, 1912.

Jackson, Samuel M., ed. *Ulrich Zwingli: Selected Works.* Philadelphia, PA: University of Pennsylvania Press, 1972, a re-edition of *The Selected Works of Huldreich Zwingli.* Philadelphia, PA: University of Pennsylvania, 1901.

Jackson, Samuel M., and C. N. Heller, eds. *Zwingli: Commentary on True and False Religion.* Durham, NC: Labyrinth Press, 1981, a re-edition of Heller, C. N., ed. *The Latin Works of Huldreich Zwingli,* III. Philadelphia, PA: Heidelberg Press, 1929.

Selected Writings of Huldrych Zwingli, I: *In Defense of the Reformed Faith.* E. J. Furcha, ed. Allison Park, PA: Pickwick Publications, 1984.

Selected Writings of Huldrych Zwingli, II: *In Search of True Religion: Reformation, Pastoral and Eucharistic Writings.* Wayne H. Pipkin, ed. Allison Park, PA: Pickwick Publications, 1984.

Selected reading list

Gabler, Ulrich. *Huldrych Zwingli: His Life and Work.* Edinburgh: T. & T. Clark, 1987.

Locher, Gottfried W. *Zwingli's Thought: New Perspectives.* Leiden: E. J. Brill, 1981.

Stephens, W. P. *The Theology of Huldrych Zwingli.* Oxford: Clarendon Press, 1986.
Stephens, W. P. *Zwingli: An Introduction to His Thought.* Oxford: Clarendon Press, 1992.

Bucer
Selected reading list
Bibliographical

Backus, Irena, Pierre Fraenkel, and Pierre Lardet. *Martin Bucer, apocryphe et authentique: études de bibliographie et d'exegèse.* Cahiers de la Revue de Théologie et de Philosophie, VIII. Geneva, 1983.
De Kroon, Marijn, und Friedhelm Krüger, eds. *Bucer und seine Zeit: Forschungsbeiträge und Bibliographie,* Veröffentlichungen des Instituts für europäische Geschichte Mainz, LXXXII. Wiesbaden: Franz Steiner Verlag, 1976.
Stupperich, Robert, ed. *'Bibliographia Bucerana'* [original and secondary works], Schriften des Vereins für Reformationsgeschichte 58 (1952), pp. 37–96.
Wilhelmi, Thomas et al. eds. *Bucer-Bibliographie/Bibliographie Bucer.* Travaux de la Faculté de Théologie Protestante de Strasbourg, IX. Strasbourg: Association des Publications de Faculté de Théologie protestante, 1999.

Studies

Burnett, Amy Nelson. *The Yoke of Christ: Martin Bucer and Christian Discipline.* Sixteenth Century Essays & Studies, XXVI. Kirksville, MO: Northeast Missouri State University Press, 1994.
Courvoisier, Jacques. *La notion d'église chez Bucer dans son développement historique.* Études d'histoire et de philosophie religieuses publiées par la Faculté de théologie protestante de l'Université de Strasbourg, XXVIII. Paris: Librairie Félix Alcan, 1933.
De Kroon, Marijn. *Martin Bucer und Johannes Calvin: reformatorische Perspektive: Einleitung und Texte.* Göttingen: Vandenhoeck & Ruprecht, 1991.
De Kroon, Marijn. *Studien zu Martin Bucers Obrigkeitsverständnis: Evangelisches Ethos und politisches Engagement.* Gütersloh: Gütersloher Verlagshaus Gerd Mohn, 1984.
De Kroon, Marijn, et Marc Lienhard, eds. *Horizons européens de la Réforme en Alsace,* Société savante d'Alsace et des regions de l 'Est: Collection Grands Publications, XVII. Strasbourg: Librarie Istra, 1980.
Eells, Hastings. *Martin Bucer.* New Haven, CT: Yale University Press, 1931. Reprinted New York: Russell & Russell, 1971.
Greschat, Martin. *Martin Bucer: Ein Reformator und seine Zeit.* Munich: Verlag C. H. Beck, 1990.
Hammann, Gottfried. *Entre la secte et la cité: le projet d'eglise du reformateur Martin Bucer (1491–1551).* Histoire et Société, III. Geneva: Labor et Fides, 1984.
Hopf, Constantin. *Martin Bucer and the English Reformation.* Oxford: Blackwell, 1946.
Koch, Karl. *Studium pietatis: Martin Bucer als Ethiker.* Beiträge zur Geschichte der reformierten Kirche, XVII. Neukirchen-Vluyn: Neukirchener Verlag, 1962.
Krieger, Christian, and Marc Lienhard, eds. *Martin Bucer and Sixteenth Century Europe: actes du colloque de Strasbourg, 28–31 août 1991.* 2 vols. Studies in Medieval and Reformation Thought, LII–LIII. Leiden: E. J. Brill, 1993.

Krüger, Friedhelm. *Bucer und Erasmus: Eine Untersuchung zum Einfluss des Erasmus auf die Theologie Martin Bucers (bis zum Evangelien-Kommentar von 1530)*. Veröffentlichungen des Instituts für europäische Geschichte Mainz, LVII. Mainz: Franz Steiner Verlag, 1970.

Lang, August. *Der Evangelienkommentar Martin Butzers und die Grundzüge seiner Theologie*. Studien zur Geschichte der Theologie und der Kirche, II, 2. Leipzig, 1900. Reprinted Aalen: Scientia Verlag, 1972.

Müller, Johannes. *Martin Bucers Hermeneutik*. Quellen und Forschungen zur Reformationsgeschichte, XXXII. Gütersloh: Gütersloher Verlagshaus Gerd Mohn, 1965.

Neuser, Wilhelm. 'Selbständige Weiterbildung zwinglischer Theologie – Martin Bucer', in *Handbuch der Dogmen- und Theologiegeschichte*, II. Carl Andresen, ed. Gottingen: Vandenhoeck & Ruprecht, 1988, pp. 209–24.

Ritschl, Otto. *Dogmengeschichte des Protestantismus*, III. Gottingen, 1926, pp. 122–56.

Seeberg, Reinhold. *Lehrbuch der Dogmengeschichte*, IV, 2. 4th edn. Graz: Akademische Druck u. Verlaganstalt, 1954, pp. 551–7.

Selderhuis, H. J. *Marriage and Divorce in the Thought of Martin Bucer*. Kirksville, MO: Thomas Jefferson University Press at Truman State University, 1999.

Stephens, W. Peter. *The Holy Spirit in the Theology of Martin Bucer*. Cambridge: Cambridge University Press, 1970.

Strohl, Henri. *La pensée de la Réforme*. Manuels et Précis de Théologie, XXXII. Neuchâtel & Paris: Delachaux et Niestlé, 1951.

Van 't Spijker, Willem. *The Ecclesiastical Offices in the Thought of Martin Bucer*. Studies in Medieval and Reformation Thought, LVII. Leiden: E. J. Brill, 1996.

Wright, David F., trans. and ed. *Common Places of Martin Bucer*. The Courtenay Library of Reformation Classics, IV. Abingdon: Sutton Courtenay Press, 1972.

Wright, David F. ed. *Martin Bucer: Reforming Church and Community*. Cambridge: Cambridge University Press, 1994.

Calvin
Sources

Ioannis Calvini Opera Omnia, denuo recognita et adnotatione critica instructa notisque illustrate. W. H. Neuser et al., eds. Geneva: Librairie Droz, 1992–.

Ioannis Calvini Opera Quae Supersunt Omnia. 59 vols. Wilhelm Baum, Eduard Cunitz and Eduard Reuss, eds. *Corpus Reformatorum* XXIX–LXXXVII. Brunswick and Berlin, 1863–1900. (Abbreviated as *CO*.)

Ioannis Calvini Opera Selecta. 5 vols. Peter Barth and Wilhelm Niesel, eds. Munich. 1926–52. (Abbreviated as *OS*.)

Calvin, John. *Letters of John Calvin*. 4 vols. Jules Bonnet, ed. David Constable and Marcus Robert Gilchrist, trans. Philadelphia, 1858. Reprinted Grand Rapids, MI: Baker Book House, 1983, as vols. IV–VII of *Calvin's Selected Works*.

Calvin, John. *Supplementa Calviniana*, sermons inédits. Neukirchen-Vluyn Neukirchener Verlag, 1936–.

Calvin, John. *Institution of the Christian Religion (1536)*. Ford Lewis Battles, ed. and trans. Atlanta, 1975. Reprinted Grand Rapids, MI: Eerdmans, 1987.

Calvin, John. *Institutes of the Christian Religion*. John T. McNeill, ed. Library of Christian Classics XX–XXI, Philadelphia, PA: Westminster Press, 1960.

Calvin, John. *Tracts and Treatises in Defense of the Reformed Faith.* 3 vols. Henry
Beveridge, trans., with historical notes by T. F. Torrance. Grand Rapids, 1958.
Reprinted Grand Rapids, MI: Baker Book House, 1983, without the notes by
Torrance, as vols. I–III of *Calvin's Selected Works.*
Calvin's Commentaries. Trans. by the Calvin Translation Society in Edinburgh, 1844–
54. Reprinted in 22 vols. Grand Rapids, Baker Book House, 1984. See also the
new Rutherford House translation of the Old Testament commentaries.
Calvin's New Testament Commentaries. D. W. Torrance and T. F. Torrance, eds.
Edinburgh: St Andrew Press; Grand Rapids, MI: Eerdmans, 1959–72.

Secondary works

Balke, Willem. *Calvin and the Anabaptist Radicals.* William J. Heynen, trans. Grand
Rapids, MI: Eerdmans, 1981.
Barth, Karl. *The Theology of John Calvin.* Geoffrey W. Bromiley, trans. Grand Rapids,
MI: Eerdmans, 1995.
Bouwsma, William J. *John Calvin: A Sixteenth Century Portrait.* Oxford and New
York: Oxford University Press, 1988.
Cottret, Bernard. *Calvin: A Biography.* M. Wallace McDonald, trans. Grand Rapids,
MI: Eerdmans, 2000.
Ganoczy, Alexandre. *The Young Calvin.* David Foxgrover and Wade Provo, trans.
Philadelphia, PA: Westminster Press, 1987.
Kingdon, Robert M. *Adultery and Divorce in Calvin's Geneva.* Cambridge, MA:
Harvard University Press, 1995.
Lane, Anthony N. S. *John Calvin: Student of the Church Fathers.* Grand Rapids, MI:
Baker Book House, 1999.
McDonnell, Kilian. *John Calvin, the Church and the Eucharist.* Princeton, NJ: Prince-
ton University Press, 1967.
Monter, E. William. *Calvin's Geneva.* New York, 1967.
Muller, Richard A. *After Calvin.* New York: Oxford University Press, 2003.
Muller, Richard A. *The Unaccommodated Calvin.* New York: Oxford University Press,
1999.
Naphy, William G. *Calvin and the Consolidation of the Genevan Reformation.*
Manchester: Manchester University Press, 1997.
Niesel, Wilhelm. *The Theology of Calvin.* H. Knight, trans. Philadelphia, PA: West-
minster Press; London: Lutterworth Press, 1956.
Nijenhuis, Willem. *Calvinus Oecumenicus: Calvijn en de Eenheid der Kerk in het Licht
van zijn Briefwisseling.* The Hague: M. Nijhoff; 1959.
Nuovo, Victor L. 'Calvin's Theology: A Study of its Sources in Classical Antiquity'.
Unpublished PhD dissertation, Columbia University, 1964.
Oberman, Heiko A. *Initia Calvini: The Matrix of Calvin's Reformation.* Amsterdam:
Noord-Hollandsche, 1991.
Parker, T. H. L. *The Oracles of God: An Introduction to the Preaching of John
Calvin.* London, 1947. Revised edn, *Calvin's Preaching.* Edinburgh: T. & T. Clark,
1992.
Pettegree, Andrew W., Alastair Duke, and Gillian Lewis, eds. *Calvinism in Europe
1540–1620.* Cambridge: Cambridge University Press, 1994.
Pitkin, Barbara. *What Pure Eyes Can See.* New York: Oxford University Press, 1999

Prestwich, Menna, ed. *International Calvinism, 1541–1715*. Oxford: Oxford University Press, 1985.

Schreiner, Susan E. *The Theater of His Glory: Nature and the Natural Order in the Thought of John Calvin*. Studies in Historical Theology, III. Durham, NC: Labyrinth Press, 1990.

Schreiner, Susan E. *Where Shall Wisdom Be Found? Calvin's Exegesis of Job from Medieval and Modern Perspectives*. Chicago, IL: University of Chicago Press, 1994.

Steinmetz, David C. 'Calvin and the Irrepressible Spirit', in *Ex Auditu* 12 (1996), pp. 94–107.

Steinmetz, David C. 'Calvin as an Interpreter of Genesis', in *Calvinus Sincerioris Religionis Vindex: Calvin as the Protector of the Purer Religion*, Sixteenth Century Essays and Studies XXXVI. Wilhelm H. Neuser and Brian G. Armstrong, eds. Kirksville, MO: Sixteenth Century Journal Publishers, 1997, pp. 53–66. Also as 'Luther und Calvin am Jabbokufer', in *Evangelische Theologie* 57 (June 1997), pp. 522–36.

Steinmetz, David C. *Calvin in Context*. New York: Oxford University Press, 1995.

Steinmetz, David C. 'The Judaizing Calvin', in *Die Patristik in der Bibelexegese des 16. Jahrhunderts*. Wolfenbütteler Abhandlungen zur Renaissanceforschung. Wiesbaden: Otto Harrassowitz, 1999.

Steinmetz, David C. 'The Scholastic Calvin', in *Protestant Scholasticism*, Carl R. Trueman and R. Scott Clark, eds. Kingstown and Carlisle: Paternoster Publishing, 1999.

Thompson, John L. *John Calvin and the Daughters of Sarah: Women in Regular and Exceptional Roles in the Exegesis of Calvin, His Predecessors, and Contemporaries*. Geneva: Librairie Droz, 1992.

Wendel, François. *Calvin, Origins and Development of His Religious Thought*. Grand Rapids, MI: Baker Book House, 1950, 1963, 1997.

Calvinism after Calvin

Armstrong, Brian G. *Calvinism and the Amyraut Heresy: Protestant Scholasticism and Humanism in Seventeenth Century France*. Madison, WI: University of Wisconsin Press, 1969.

Asselt, Willem van. *The Covenant Theology of Johannes Cocceius*. Leiden: E. J. Brill, 2000.

Bangs, Carl. *Arminius: A Study in the Dutch Reformation*. Nashville, TN: Abingdon, 1971.

Bierma, Lyle D. *German Calvinism in the Confessional Age: The Covenant Theology of Caspar Olevian*. Durham, NC: Labyrinth Press and Grand Rapids, MI: Baker Book House, 1994.

Bray, John S. *Theodore Beza's Doctrine of Predestination*. Nieuwkoop: De Graaf, 1975.

De Gangi, Mariano. *Peter Martyr Vermigli, 1499–1562: Renaissance Man, Reformation Master*. Lanham, MD: University Press of America, 1993.

De Jong, Peter Y., ed. *Crisis in the Reformed Churches: Essays in Commemoration of the Great Synod of Dort, 1618–1619*. Grand Rapids, MI: Reformed Fellowship, 1968.

Harrison, A. W. *The Beginnings of Arminianism to the Synod of Dort*. London: University of London Press, 1926.

McKim, Donald M. *Ramism in William Perkins' Theology.* New York: Peter Lang, 1987.

McNeill, John T. *The History and Character of Calvinism.* New York: Oxford University Press, 1954.

Muller, Richard A. *God, Creation and Providence in the Thought of Jacob Arminius: Sources and Directions of Scholastic Protestantism in the Era of Early Orthodoxy.* Grand Rapids, MI: Baker Book House, 1991.

Muller, Richard A. *Post-Reformation Reformed Dogmatics.* Grand Rapids, MI: Baker Book House, 1989–.

Ong, Walter J. *Ramus: Method and the Decay of Dialogue.* Cambridge, MA: Harvard University Press, 1958.

Peterson, Robert A. *Calvin's Doctrine of the Atonement.* Phillipsburg, NJ: Presbyterian and Reformed Publishing Co., 1983.

Rainbow, Jonathan H. *The Will of God and the Cross: An Historical and Theological Study of John Calvin's Doctrine of Limited Redemption.* Allison Park, PA: Pickwick Publications, 1990.

Raitt, Jill. *The Eucharistic Theology of Theodore Beza: Development of the Reformed Doctrine.* Chambersburg, PA, 1972.

Trueman, Carl R., and R. Scott Clark, eds. *Protestant Scholasticism: Essays in Reassessment.* Carlisle: Paternoster Press, 1999.

Visser, Derk. *Zacharias Ursinus: The Reluctant Reformer, His Life and Times.* New York: United Church Press, 1983.

Cranmer
Sources

Cox, John E., ed. *Miscellaneous Writings and Letters of Thomas Cranmer.* Parker Society edn, II. Cambridge: Cambridge University Press, 1846.

Cox, John E., ed. *Writings and Disputations of Thomas Cranmer Relative to the Sacrament of the Lord's Supper.* Parker Society edn, I. Cambridge: Cambridge University Press, 1844.

Ketley, Joseph (ed.), *Liturgies of Edward VI.* Parker Society edn. Cambridge: Cambridge University Press, 1844.

Studies

Brooks, Peter Newman. *Cranmer in Context.* Cambridge: Lutterworth Press, 1989.

Brooks, Peter Newman. *Thomas Cranmer's Doctrine of the Eucharist.* London: Macmillan, 1992.

Collinson, Patrick 'Thomas Cranmer', in *The English Religious Tradition and the Genius of Anglicanism.* Geoffrey Rowell, ed. Oxford: Ikon, 1992.

MacCulloch, Diarmaid. *Thomas Cranmer: A Life.* New Haven, CT, and London: Yale University Press, 1996.

Null, Ashley. *Thomas Cranmer's Doctrine of Repentance.* Oxford: Oxford University Press, 2000.

Selwyn, David G. *The Library of Thomas Cranmer.* Oxford: The Oxford Bibliographical Society, 1996.

Selwyn, David, and Paul Ayris (eds.). *Thomas Cranmer: Churchman and Scholar* Woodbridge: Boydell & Brewer, 1993.

The English Reformers
General
Trueman, Carl. R. *Luther's Legacy*. Oxford: Oxford University Press, 1994.

Tyndale
Works, ed. Henry Walter. Parker Society, Cambridge: Cambridge University Press, 1848–50.
Daniell, David. *William Tyndale*. London: 1994.
Smeeton, Donald D. *Lollard Themes in the Theology of William Tyndale*. St Louis, MO: 1987.

Barnes
Clebsch, William A. *England's Earliest Protestants*. New Haven, CT: Yale University Press, 1964.
Hall, Basil. 'The early rise and gradual decline of Lutheranism in England (1520–1600)', in D. Baker, ed., *Reform and Reformation: England and the Continent (c. 1500–c. 1750)*. Oxford: Blackwell, 1979.
Trueman, Carl R. ' "The Saxons be sore on the affirmative": Robert Barnes on the Lord's supper', in W. P. Stephens, ed., *The Bible, the Reformation, and the Church*. Sheffield: Sheffield Academic Press, 1995, pp. 290–307.

Hooper
Carr, Samuel, ed. *Early Writings of John Hooper, DD*. Cambridge: Cambridge University Press, 1843.
Nevinson, C., ed. *Later Writings of John Hooper, DD*. Cambridge: Cambridge University Press, 1852.
Robinson, Hastings, ed. *Original Letters Relative to the English Reformation*. 2 vols. Cambridge: Cambridge University Press, 1846–7.
West, W. M. S. 'John Hooper and the Origins of Puritanism', in *Baptist Quarterly* 15 (1954), pp. 346–68; 16 (1995), pp. 22–46, 67–88.

Bradford
Works, ed. Aubrey Townsend. 2 vols. Parker Society, Cambridge: Cambridge University Press, 1848–53.
Hargrave, O. T. 'The freewillers in the English Reformation', in *Church History* 37 (1968), pp. 271–80.
Martin, J. W. 'English Protestant separatism at its beginnings: Henry Hart and the free will men', in *Sixteenth Century Journal* 7 (1976), pp. 655–74.
Penny, D. Andrew. *Freewill or Predestination: The Battle over Saving Grace in Mid-Tudor England*. Woodbridge: Boydell & Brewer for the Royal Historical Society, 1990.

Knox and Prayer Book revision
The Works of John Knox, ed. David Laing. Edinburgh: for the Bannatyne Society, 1846–64.
Kyle, Richard G. *Theology and Revolution in the Scottish Reformation*. Grand Rapids, MI: Baker Book House, 1980.

MacCulloch Diarmaid, *Thomas Cranmer: A Life*. New Haven, CT: Yale University Press, 1966, pp. 404–13.
Ridley, Jasper. *John Knox*. Oxford: Clarendon Press, 1968.

The Scottish Reformation
Bardgett, F. 'John Erskine of Dun: a theological reassessment', in *Scottish Journal of Theology* 43 (1990), pp. 59–85.
Cameron, James K., ed. *The First Book of Discipline*, Edinburgh: St Andrew Press, 1972.
Cameron, Nigel M. de S., David F. Wright et al., eds. *Dictionary of Scottish Church History and Theology*. Edinburgh: T. & T. Clark, 1993.
Dickinson, William Croft, ed. *John Knox's History of the Reformation in Scotland*. 2 vols. London, Edinburgh: Thomas Nelson, 1949.
Dotterweich, Martin Holt. 'The emergence of evangelical theology in Scotland to 1550'. Unpublished PhD thesis, University of Edinburgh, 2002.
Hazlett, W. Ian P. 'The Scots Confession 1560: context, complexion and critique', in *Archiv für Reformationsgeschichte* 78 (1987), pp. 287–320.
Henderson, G. D., ed. *The Scots Confession 1560*. Edinburgh: St Andrew Press, 1960.
Hewat, Kirkwood. *Makers of the Scottish Church at the Reformation*. Edinburgh: Macniven & Wallace, 1920.
Janton, Pierre. *John Knox (ca. 1513–1572): L'homme et l'œuvre*. Paris: Didier, 1967.
Kirk, James. *Patterns of Reform: Continuity and Change in the Reformation Kirk*. Edinburgh: T. & T. Clark, 1989.
Kyle, Richard G. *The Mind of John Knox*. Lawrence, KS: Coronado Press, 1984.
Laing, David, ed. *The Works of John Knox*. 6 vols. Edinburgh: Thomas George Stevenson, 1846–64.
McEwen, James S. *The Faith of John Knox*. London: Lutterworth Press, 1961.
Mason, Roger A., ed. *John Knox and the British Reformations*. St Andrews Studies in Reformation History. Aldershot: Ashgate, 1998.
Torrance, T. F. *Scottish Theology from John Knox to John McLeod Campbell*. Edinburgh: T. & T. Clark, 1996.
Torrance, T. F., trans. and ed. *The School of Faith: The Catechisms of the Reformed Church*. London: James Clarke, 1959.

Introduction to Anabaptist theology
'A Short Prospectus on Christ's Last Supper (Ain kurtze anzaigung des abentmals Christy)', in Lydia Müller, *Glaubenszeugnisse der Oberdeutscher Taufgesinnter*, I: *Quellen zur Geschichte der Täufer* 3. Leipzig: M. Heinius Nachfolger, 1938. New York: Johnson Reprint Corporation, 1971, pp. 143ff; also in *Episteln 1527–1797*, III. Elie, Manitoba: James Valley Book Center, pp. 510ff.
Armour, Rollin. *Anabaptist Baptism. A Representative Study*. Scottdale, PA: Herald Press, 1966.
Barret, Pierre, and Jean-Noel Gurgand. *Der König der Letzten Tage*. Michele Schönfeldt, trans. Herrsching: Manfred Pawlak Verlagsgesellschaft, 1987.
Baumann, Clarence. *The Spiritual Legacy of Hans Denck*. Leiden: E. J. Brill, 1991.
Bender, Harold. Baptism, *Mennonite Encyclopedia*. 5 vols. Scottdale, PA: Herald Press, 1956–. I pp. 224–28.

Bender, Harold. *Conrad Grebel c. 1498–1526. The Founder of the Swiss Brethren Sometimes Called Anabaptists.* Scottdale, PA: Herald Press, 1950.

Bender, Harold. 'Footwashing', *Mennonite Encyclopedia.* 5 vols. Scottdale, PA: Herald Press, 1956–. II pp. 347–51.

Bergsten, Torsten. *Balthasar Hubmaier: Anabaptist Theologian and Martyr.* W. R. Estep, Jr, ed. Valley Forge, PA: Judson Press, 1978.

Boyd, Stephen, B. *Pilgram Marpeck: His Life and Social Theology.* Durham, NC: Duke University Press, 1992.

Chronicle of the Hutterian Brethren, The, 1525–1665, I. Rifton, NY: Plough Publishing House, 1987.

Davis, Kenneth R. *Anabaptism and Asceticism. A Study in Intellectual Origins.* Scottdale, PA: Herald Press, 1974.

Deppermann, Klaus. *Melchior Hoffman: Soziale Unruhen und apokalyptische Visionen im Zeitalter der Reformation.* Göttingen: Vandenhoeck & Ruprecht, 1979.

Dyck, Cornelius J. 'The life of the Spirit in Anabaptist theology', in *Essays in Anabaptist Theology.* H. Wayne Pipkin, ed. Elkart, IN: Institute for Mennonite Studies, 1994, pp. 111–32.

Dyck, Cornelius J., William E. Keeney, and Alvin J. Beachy, eds. and trans. *The Writings of Dirk Philips.* Scottdale, PA: Herald Press, 1992.

Franck, Sebastian. *Zeytbuch und Geschichtbibel von Anbegyn bisz inn disz gegenwertig MD xxxj.jar.* Darmstadt: Wissenschaftlicher Verlag, 1969.

Friedmann, Robert. 'The doctrine of original sin as held by the Anabaptists of the sixteenth century', in *Essays in Anabaptist Theology.* H. Wayne Pipkin, ed. Elkart, IN: Institute for Mennonite Studies, 1994, pp. 147–56.

Friedmann, Robert. *The Theology of Anabaptism.* Scottdale, PA: Herald Press, 1973.

Friessen, Abraham. 'Present at the inception: Menno Simons and the beginning of Dutch Anabaptism', *Mennonite Quarterly Review* 72 (1998), pp. 351–88.

Goertz, Hans-Jürgen. *Konrad Grebel: Kritiker des frommen Scheins 1498–1526. Eine biographische Skizze.* Mennonitischer Geschichtsverein Bolanden. Hamburg: Kümpers Verlag, 1998.

Harder, Leland, ed. *The Sources of Swiss Anabaptism: The Grebel Letters and Related Documents.* Scottdale, PA: Herald Press, 1985.

Hillerbrand, Hans J., ed. *Radical Tendencies in the Reformation: Divergent Perspectives* in *Sixteenth Century Essays and Studies,* IX. Kirksville, MO: Sixteenth Century Journal Publishers, 1988.

Horsch, John, and Harold S. Bender. 'Biography', in *Menno Simon's Life and Writings: A Quadricentennial Tribute 1536–1936.* Scottdale, PA: Mennonite Publishing House, 1944.

Jelsma, Auke. *Frontiers of the Reformation: Dissidence and Orthodoxy in Sixteenth-Century Europe.* St Andrews Studies in Reformation History. Aldershot: Ashgate, 1998.

Klaassen, Walter. *Anabaptism in Outline.* Scottdale, PA: Herald Press, 1981.

Klaassen, Walter. *Anabaptism: Neither Catholic nor Protestant.* Waterloo, Ontario: Conrad Press, 1973.

Klaassen, Walter. *Living at the End of the Ages: Apocalyptic Expectation in the Radical Reformation.* New York: University Press of America, 1992.

Klassen, William, and Klaassen, Walter, eds. and trans. *The Writings of Pilgram Marpeck.* Scottdale, PA: Herald Press, 1978.

Krahn, Cornelius. 'Communion', *Mennonite Encyclopedia*. 5 vols. Scottdale, PA: Herald Press, 1956–. I, pp. 651–5.

Loewen, Howard J. *One Lord, One Church, One Hope, and One God. Mennonite Confessions of Faith*. Elkart, IN: Institute of Mennonite Studies, 1985.

McClandon, James William. 'Balthasar Hubmaier, Catholic Anabaptist'. *Mennonite Quarterly Review* 65 (1991), pp. 20ff.

Marpeck, Pilgram. *Clare verantwurtung ettlicher Artickel/ so jetzt durch jrrige geyster schrifftlich unnd mündtlich ausschweben*. [1531] (*A Clear Refutation*). English trans. in *The Writings of Pilgram Marpeck*. William Klasen and Walter Klaassen, eds. and trans. Scottdale, PA: Herald Press, 1978.

Neff, Christian. 'Ban', *Mennonite Encyclopedia*. 5 vols. Scottdale, PA: Herald Press, 1956–. I, pp. 219–23.

Packull, Werner O. 'Hoffman [Hofman], Melchior', *Mennonite Encyclopedia*. 5 vols. Scottdale, PA: Herald Press, 1956–. V, pp. 384–5.

Packull, Werner O. *Hutterite Beginnings: Communitarian Experiments during the Reformation*. Baltimore, MD: Johns Hopkins University Press, 1995.

Packull, Werner O. 'The origins of Swiss Anabaptism in the context of the reformation of the common man', *Journal for Mennonite Studies* 3 (1985), pp. 36–59.

Pipkin, Wayne H. 'The baptismal theology of Balthasar Hubmaier', *Mennonite Quarterly Review*, 65 (1991), pp. 34ff.

Pipkin, Wayne H., and John H. Yoder, eds. and trans. *Balthasar Hubmaier: Theologian of Anabaptism*. Scottdale, PA: Herald Press, 1989.

Reimer, A. James. 'The adequacy of a voluntaristic age', in *The Believers' Church: A Voluntary Church. Papers of the Twelfth Believers Church Conferenc*. William H. Brackney, ed. Kitchener, Ontario: Pandora Press, 1998, pp. 135–48.

Rempel, John D. *The Lord's Supper in Anabaptism: A Study in the Christology of Balthasar Hubmaier, Pilgram Marpeck and Dirk Philips*. Scottdale, PA: Herald Press, 1993.

Riedemann, Peter. *Peter Riedemann's Hutterite Confession of Faith* (a translation of his *Rechenschaft unserer Religion*). John J. Friesen, ed. Scottdale, PA: Herald Press, 1999.

Roth, John D. 'Community as Conversation: A New Model of Anabaptist Hermeneutics', in *Essays in Anabaptist Theology*. H. Wayne Pipkin, ed. Elkhart, IN: Institute of Mennonite Studies, 1994.

Snyder, Arnold. *Anabaptist History and Theology*. Kitchener, Ontario: Pandora Press, 1995.

Snyder, Arnold. *The Life and Thought of Michael Sattler*. Scottdale, PA: Herald Press, 1984.

Snyder, Arnold. 'The (not-so) simple confession of late sixteenth-century Anabaptists'. Part II: The Evolution of Separatist Anabaptism', *Mennonite Quarterly Review* 74 (2000), pp. 87ff.

Stayer, James M. *Anabaptists and the Sword*. Lawrence, KS: Coronado Press, 1972.

Stayer, James M. *The German Peasants' War and Anabaptist Community of Goods*. Montreal-Kingston: McGill-Queen's University Press, 1991.

Stayer, James M. 'The Radical Reformation', in *Handbook of European History 1400–1600: Late Middle Ages, Renaissance and Reformation*, II. Thomas A. Brady, Heiko A. Oberman and James D. Tracy, eds. Leiden: E. J. Brill, 1995.

Steinmetz, David C. 'Scholasticism and radical reform: nominalist motifs in the theology of Balthasar Hubmaier', *Mennonite Quarterly Review* 45 (1971), pp. 123–44.

Swartley, Willard, ed. *Essays on Biblical Interpretation: Anabaptist-Mennonite Perspectives*. Elkart, IN: Institute for Mennonite Studies, 1984.

Voolstra, Sjouke. *Menno Simons: His Image and Message*. Newton, KS: Mennonite Press, 1996.

Waite, Gary K. *David Joris and Dutch Anabaptism, 1524–1543*. Waterloo, Ontario: Wilfrid Laurier University Press, 1990.

Weingart, Richard E. 'The meaning of sin in the theology of Menno Simons', in *Essays in Anabaptist Theology*. H. Wayne Pipkin, ed. Elkart, IN: Institute for Mennonite Studies, 1994, pp. 157ff.

Wenger, J. C. *The Complete Writings of Menno Simons, c. 1496–1561*. Scottdale, PA: Herald Press, 1984.

Williams, George. *The Radical Reformation*. Kirksville, MO: Sixteenth-Century Journal Publishers, 1992.

Yoder, John H. 'The Believers' Church Conferences in historical perspective', *Mennonite Quarterly Review* 65 (1991), pp. 5–19.

Pre-Tridentine Catholic theology
Surveys and issues

Bagchi, David V. *Luther's Earliest Opponents: Catholic Controversialists, 1518–152*. Minneapolis, MN: Fortress Press, 1991.

Chrisman, Miriam U. 'From polemic to propaganda: the development of mass persuasion in the late sixteenth century', in *Archiv für Reformationsgeschichte* 73 (1982), pp. 175–95.

Dolan, Jay P. 'The Catholic literary opponents of Luther and the Reformation', in Erwin Iserloh, ed., *Reformation and Counter-Reformation*, History of the Church, V. London: Burns & Oates, 1980, pp. 191–207.

Edwards, Mark U., Jr, *Printing, Propaganda, and Martin Luther*. Berkeley, CA: California University Press, 1994, chapters 1, 3 and 7.

Pelikan, Jaroslav. 'Defenders of the faith' and 'The gospel and the Catholic Church', in *Reformation and Dogma of the Church, 1300–1600. The Christian Tradition: A History of the Development of Christian Doctrine*, IV. Chicago, IL: University of Chicago Press, 1984.

Translations

More, Sir Thomas. *Responsio ad Lutherum*, translated into English and furnished with much helpful apparatus in *The Complete Works of St Thomas More*, V. J. M. Headley, ed. New Haven, CT: Yale University Press, 1967.

Rummel, Erika, ed. *Scheming Papists and Lutheran Fools: Five Reformation Satires*. New York: Fordham University Press, 1993.

Studies of individual writers

Gogan, Brian. *The Common Corps of Christendom: Ecclesiological Themes in the Writings of Sir Thomas More*. Leiden: E. J. Brill, 1982.

Iserloh, Erwin, ed. *Katholische Theologen der Reformationszeit*, in Katholisches Leben und Kirchenreform, XLIV–XLVIII. Münster-Westfalen: Aschendorff, 1984–8.
McSorley, Harry J. *Luther: Right or Wrong?* Minneapolis, MN: Fortress Press, 1969.
O'Rourke Boyle, Marjorie. *Rhetoric and Reform: Erasmus's Civil Dispute with Luther.* Cambridge, MA: Harvard University Press, 1983.
Rex, Richard A. W. *The Theology of John Fisher.* Cambridge: Cambridge University Press, 1991.
Samuel-Scheyder, Monique. *Johannes Cochlaeus: Humaniste et adversaire de Luther.* Nancy: Presses Universitaires de Nancy, 1993.
Tavuzzi, Michael *Prierias: The Life and Works of Silvestro Mazzolini da Prierio, 1456–1527.* Durham, NC: Duke University Press, 1997.

The Council of Trent
Primary sources
Canons and Decrees of the Council of Trent. H. J. Schroeder, OP, ed. and trans. St Louis and London: B. Herder Book Co., 1950.
Concilium Tridentinum: Diariorum, actorum, epistularum, tractatuum nova collectio. 13 vols. in 18. Fribourg: Societas Goerresiana, 1901–85.
Calvin, John. 'Acta Synodi Tridentini cum Antidoto', in *Calvini Opera*, VII, pp. 365–506. Braunschweig: A. C. Schwetschke und Sohn, 1868.
Chemnitz, Martin. *Examen Concilii Tridentini.* Berlin: Gust. Schlawitz, 1861.

Secondary works
Jedin, Hubert. *A History of the Council of Trent.* Ernest Graf, trans. 2 vols. Cambridge, MA, and London: Thomas Nelson & Sons, 1957–61. Still the best history of the early sessions. For the complete history, see the German edition, *Geschichte des Konzils von Trient.* 4 vols. Freiburg i. Br.: Herder, 1949–75.
O'Malley, John W., SJ. *Trent and All That.* Cambridge, MA, and London: Harvard University Press, 2000. See the extensive bibliography appended to this careful historiographical study.

Index